S. WEIR MITCHELL, 1829–1914

S. WEIR MITCHELL, 1829–1914

PHILADELPHIA'S LITERARY PHYSICIAN

NANCY CERVETTI

THE PENNSYLVANIA STATE UNIVERSITY PRESS
UNIVERSITY PARK, PENNSYLVANIA

Library of Congress Cataloging-in-Publication Data

Cervetti, Nancy, 1947–
S. Weir Mitchell, 1829–1914 : Philadelphia's literary
physician / Nancy Cervetti.
p.   cm.—(Penn State series in the history of the book)
Includes bibliographical references and index.
Summary: "A biography of Philadelphia physician S. Weir
Mitchell. Examines his life and his interactions with many
prominent nineteenth-century Americans, including
Charlotte Perkins Gilman, Oliver Wendell Holmes, Jane
Addams, Winifred Howells, Edith Wharton, William Osler,
Mary Putnam Jacobi, Walt Whitman, and Andrew
Carnegie"—Provided by publisher.
ISBN 978-0-271-05403-2 (cloth : alk. paper)
I. Title.
II. Series: Penn State series in the history of the book.
[DNLM: 1. Mitchell, S. Weir (Silas Weir), 1829–1914.
2. Physicians—Philadelphia—Biography. 3. History,
19th Century—Philadelphia. 4. History, 20th Century—
Philadelphia. 5. Literature—history—Philadelphia.
6. Neurology—history—Philadelphia. WZ 100]
LC Classification not assigned
610.92—dc23
[B]
2012007105

The Pennsylvania State University Press is a member of the
Association of American University Presses.

It is the policy of The Pennsylvania State University Press to
use acid-free paper. Publications on uncoated stock satisfy
the minimum requirements of American National Standard
for Information Sciences—Permanence of Paper for Printed
Library Material, ANSI Z39.48–1992.

This book is printed on Nature's Natural,
which contains 50% post-consumer waste

For Lisa and Marianne

CONTENTS

ILLUSTRATIONS

ACKNOWLEDGMENTS

I am grateful to many people for their help and support during my years of research and writing about S. Weir Mitchell. My first thanks must go to Susan B. Case, former director of the Clendening History of Medicine Library in Kansas City. In 1994 she told me about a new collection of S. Weir Mitchell papers at the College of Physicians of Philadelphia and encouraged me to apply for a fellowship. Subsequent fellowships and travel grants from the Francis Clark Wood Institute for the History of Medicine at the College of Physicians have supported several summers of work in Philadelphia. I am most grateful for the support of the entire college staff, including Annie Brogan, Robert Hicks, Evi Numen, and Sofie Sereda. I particularly wish to thank Charles B. Greifenstein, now associate librarian and manuscripts librarian at the American Philosophical Society, for his willingness to answer my questions over the years and for his enthusiasm for Mitchell. I am grateful for a fellowship from the National Endowment for the Humanities and the Agency for Healthcare Research and Quality, which supported a year of extensive travel to gather and transcribe Mitchell's letters at numerous other archives. I am grateful to Professor Nancy Cott and the Radcliffe Institute for Advanced Study for the opportunity to attend a seminar on "Writing Past Lives: Biography as History" that focused on gender and biography. I thank my home institution, Avila University, for two yearlong sabbaticals. Special thanks also go to my Avila colleague Professor Robert Powell, herpetologist and field biologist, for his help with venomous snakes and German translations.

I am deeply indebted to Dr. David and Mrs. Rose Hausman for their kindness and hospitality in Philadelphia. The friendship and guidance of Professor Bernice Hausman at Virginia Tech has made this book possible. I also wish to thank Gregory Eiselein, professor of English at Kansas State University, and Marcia Meldrum, codirector of the Liebeskind History of Pain Collection at UCLA.

I gratefully acknowledge and thank the following librarians and institutions for their assistance and permission to quote materials in their possession: Lilla Vekerdy at the Bernard Becker Medical Library at Washington University, Rachel Ingold at the History of Medicine Collections at the Duke University Medical Center Library, Dawn McInnis at the Clendening Library at the University of Kansas Medical Center, Jessica Murphy and Frederic Burchsted at the Widener Library at Harvard University, Kathryn Hodson at the Special Collections Department of the University of Iowa Libraries in Iowa City, Heather Cole at the Houghton Library, Ellen M. Shea at the Schlesinger Library at the Radcliffe Institute, Jack Eckert at the Harvard Medical Library in the Francis A. Countway Library of Medicine, Megan Sniffin-Marinoff at the Harvard University Archives, Lee Spilberg at the Manuscripts and Archives Division of the New York Public Library, Pamela Miller at the Osler Library of the History of Medicine at McGill University, Nancy Shawcross at the Rare Books and Manuscript Library at the University of Pennsylvania, Hillary S. Kativa at the Historical Society of Pennsylvania, Eva Guggemos at the Beinecke Rare Book and Manuscript Library, R. Kenny Marone at the Harvey Cushing/John Hay Whitney Medical Library at Yale University, Roger Verdon at the Menninger Archives at the Menninger–Baylor College of Medicine, the Alderman Library at the University of Virginia, the Sterling Memorial Library at Yale University, and the Archie Dykes Library at the University of Kansas Medical Center. I thank the *Arizona Quarterly* and the *Journal of Medical Humanities* for their permission to reprint portions of chapters 3 and 4. Chapter 3 appeared as "S. Weir Mitchell and His Snakes: Unraveling the 'United Web and Woof of Popular and Scientific Beliefs'" in the *Journal of Medical Humanities* 28, no. 3 (2007): 119–33, appearing here by permission of Springer. Chapter 4 appeared as "From Civil War to Rest Cure" in the *Arizona Quarterly* 59, no. 3 (2003): 69–96, appearing here by permission of the Regents of the University of Arizona. I thank the College of Physicians of Philadelphia, the Historical Society of Pennsylvania, and the Rare Books and Manuscript Library at the University of Pennsylvania for their kind permission to reproduce illustrative material.

I am most grateful to Patrick Alexander, Patricia A Mitchell, and Stephanie Lang at Pennsylvania State University Press for their support and to Nicholas Taylor for his editorial guidance. I am also grateful to Sally Ebest, Tom Klammer, Roena Haynie, Sheelagh Manheim, and Faurrukh Hassan for their assistance. I dedicate the book to my daughters, Lisa and Marianne Williams, whose love and humorous insights have sustained me. Any faults and errors are my own.

A NOTE ON THE TEXT

Throughout the book, when I quote from correspondence and S. Weir Mitchell's autobiography, I follow the originals with a few exceptions. Whenever possible, Mitchell's spelling, capitalization, and punctuation have been retained, and I have avoided using the word *sic*. Rather than commas or periods, Mitchell frequently used dashes between phrases and between sentences. Omitting or replacing these dashes would significantly alter his voice and style. Therefore, most dashes have been retained. For the sake of clarity, I have replaced a few dashes at the end of sentences with periods or added a question mark. In a few instances, I have silently capitalized the first word of a sentence. I have eliminated the ampersand. Mitchell rarely underlined titles, and this practice has been retained. All original emphasis from quoted material has been retained, and no emphasis has been added anywhere in the book. I have italicized words originally underlined. For the sake of readability, I have sometimes grouped two or more citations into a single note. In understanding the relative value of sums of money, it is helpful to consult historical consumer price index conversion factors. For example, according to the consumer price index conversion factor of 0.036 for 1850, $1,000 then would be worth approximately $28,000 in 2010. See "Inflation Conversion Factors," retrieved January 3, 2012, from http://oregon state.edu/cla/polisci/sahr/sahr.

INTRODUCTION

Urbane, handsome, and smartly dressed, Silas Weir Mitchell attracted attention whenever he walked into a room. Tall and slender with a Van Dyke beard and blue eyes, he was impossible to ignore. With perfect assurance, it was his way to size up and immediately take command of a situation. He was a risk taker and experimenter, and apart from his father, he looked up to no living person. One of the striking aspects of Mitchell's story is the way he put aside the ennui of his childhood and the insecurity and recklessness of his youth to become a distinguished citizen of Philadelphia. He wrote that during his boyhood, all his family history was well-known to his father, "but he cared little for these matters and I, then, not at all. We were simply, as I take it, Scotch middle class, able folk and certainly of decent descent."[1] However, Weir Mitchell, as he preferred to be called, came to care a great deal about descent.

Due to his groundbreaking animal experimentation in the 1850s, Mitchell is recognized as one of the first physiologists in the United States. His research into the effects of rattlesnake venom set the stage for subsequent work in toxicology and immunology. His creation of the rest cure to treat hysteria and neurasthenia originated in his treatment of Civil War soldiers who suffered from burning pain and phantom limbs, the latter a term he coined. The war work won him an international reputation and the title of "Father of American Neurology." He wrote engaging and lucid prose and published myriad books and articles. In his fifties, after major achievements in physiology and neurology, he turned his attention to literature, writing short stories, novels, and poems. He also devoted substantial time to public service, especially as a member of the Board of Trustees at the University of Pennsylvania, a member of the Executive Committee of the Carnegie Institution, and a fellow of the College of Physicians of Philadelphia for fifty-eight years and its president for two nonconsecutive terms.

William Osler wrote that versatility was the striking feature of Mitchell's mind, and William W. Keen said that he was the most original, yeasty, and stimulating medical man he had ever met.[2] There can be no doubt regarding Mitchell's contributions, which make him a major figure in the history of medicine. His Renaissance range of interests provides a fascinating trip through the nineteenth century; his was a life in touch with the birth of physiology, the vivisection debates, Civil War medicine, the bizarre phenomena of hysteria, the birth of modern psychiatry, popular literature, and the privilege and indulgence of the Gilded Age. His correspondence provides an interior view of a generation that influenced social behavior and politics in the areas of medicine, education, literature, and philanthropy, and included friends like Oliver Wendell Holmes, William W. Hammond, William Osler, John Shaw Billings, William W. Keen, William Dean Howells, John Cadwalader, and Andrew Carnegie.

I first encountered Weir Mitchell while studying Virginia Woolf and Charlotte Perkins Gilman and their personal experiences with the rest cure. The first time I went to the College of Physicians of Philadelphia and examined the Mitchell Papers, I could see that while Mitchell admired writers like George Eliot and Edith Wharton and possessed a handful of female friends, overall he did not think highly of women. Instead, he used his charm, medical authority, and social prominence to confine them to caretaking. He was vehemently opposed to their education and careers, and unlike many of his contemporaries who felt the same way, he spoke openly about the "woman question." Even after he came to know women like Mary Putnam Jacobi and M. Carey Thomas and saw that women could succeed brilliantly as doctors, educators, and administrators, he remained adamant in his views. Mitchell intended to excel at whatever he did, and his war against women was no exception. His obstinacy hurt lives and interfered with his effectiveness as a physician, and it has cast a shadow over his contributions in experimental medicine and neurology.

A close look at Mitchell's education and the trajectory of his multifaceted career reveals the accomplishments and the prejudice against women as a jarring counterpoint that is rarely acknowledged. Depending on the discipline, scholars tend to ignore one or the other. In the humanities, scholars often focus on his relationship with Charlotte Perkins Gilman. Scholars in the history of medicine often disregard his problematic views regarding women. The tendency has been to lean to one side or the other, but the value of studying

Mitchell emerges in the mix. Mitchell's world is a microcosm illustrating how gender politics deformed the benevolent authority of medicine and sustained myth, idealization, and fantasy. While medicine made remarkable advances as a science and profession, it also became the most powerful weapon in the fierce nineteenth-century fight against women's rights outside the home. Mitchell's assumptions represent the attitudes of an age that attempted to bridle a force that was ultimately impossible to restrain.

There are many disturbing and fascinating elements of Mitchell's character. There is the uncanny way his extensive vivisection and war work with nerve injuries shaped his later treatment of women. There are his personal breakdowns and the use of outdoor exercise and camp life to restore his well-being and energy. There is his provocative personality and prejudice against women juxtaposed with deep and lasting homosocial bonds with exceptional men. And finally, there is his self-conscious attempt to construct a personal history while he lived it. He began as a scrappy kid in a middle-class family, a shy and insecure second son who disliked church and did poorly in school. Despite such a modest beginning and setbacks along the way, brick by brick he built a powerhouse of a life. He achieved wealth, status, and an international reputation, becoming a legendary figure for hagiographers and debunkers alike. Sometimes called a neurologist, literary physician, misogynist, poet, novelist, or aristocrat, it is difficult to pin him down. There is one activity, however, that permeates and unites these diverse identities, and that is Mitchell's writing.

The writing began early, when he was just a boy. In his home, bookshelves lined the dining room walls, and family bonds were formed and sustained in a space surrounded by hundreds of books. Reading aloud and debating at meals were daily experiences. Mitchell's father wrote and published verse and scientific literature, and Mitchell hoped that by reading and writing he might win his father's approval. Then he began to use the composing process to capture and clarify his ideas. He came to love the structural challenge of writing a good poem, and as he grew older, increasingly he realized the rhetorical power of language.

Mitchell often felt anxious and restless. He required a great deal of movement and activity, and so he would sail for Europe, go salmon fishing in Quebec, or go walking and riding across Mount Desert Island in Maine. Writing was the one activity that kept him anchored for a time. He enjoyed the sensual pleasure of pen, ink, and paper and was fussy about writing paraphernalia, often complaining about skimpy sheets and pale, anemic ink. He complained to his sister Elizabeth, "Bad letter writer I may be—doubtless am—, but I never did disgrace myself by employing such Lilliputian scraps of note paper as you use—Its a low way of saving money, I assure you." He told Amelia Gere Mason, "I hate the skimpy sheets you women seem to like. Why not write on the back of a post-stamp?" Bad paper and ink could even upset his ability to think: "If the ink be not black and—the paper smooth I am at once troubled as to what I am trying to record." In the quiet of a Sunday afternoon, he smoked a cigar and wrote gracious and leisurely letters. At other times, with his "unanswered" basket overflowing, he grumbled about how much he hated letter writing. Always, he sensed its public nature and possible importance. At the age of twenty-one he told his mother, "Number and keep my letters."[3] In his forties he developed a tremor and his handwriting began to slowly deteriorate.[4] In 1900, at the age of seventy-one, he wrote, "Oh! I want to write. . . . I am at my best, the brain gaining while the body is slowly adding vetoes to one's lessening joys. Blank the Body!" In 1909 he said, "The act of writing is becoming more and more difficult for me as the years go on and I more and more willingly resort to the hand of another." And in 1912, forced to dictate all his letters, he said, "For me to write now is not possible."[5]

More than anything else, Mitchell's writing acted as both canvass and mirror, and secured and sustained his success. He had a keen sense of life as a performance, and he continually pruned and edited his image. He burned letters and revised stories. And while other physicians stuck to medicine, Mitchell wrote about everything. He produced important scientific texts on snake venom, injuries to nerves, and mental illness. He told stories in the form of children's literature, case studies, and long narrative poems.[6] He populated historical romances with brave young men, villains, and women with small hands and feet—lovely women who, for him, had not lost their feminine charm. He was in constant demand as a public speaker and subsequently published many of his addresses. On a number of occasions he noted experimenting with various drugs. After reading an article about the use of mescal buttons by New Mexico Indians, for example, he requested an extract. After taking the hallucinogen, he wrote a paper about his experience that was presented to the American Neurological Society, published in the *British Medical Journal*, and cited as the first on the topic in scientific literature.[7] In terms of his life story, he wrote that he didn't "much like biographies except of men of action—I shall be apt to haunt anyone who 'biogs'—me." Even so, he often asked for the return of letters and selectively left materials for the person who "would be foolish enough in the future to write about me and wise enough to write of my friends."[8]

There are five previous biographies of Mitchell, by Anna Robeson Burr (1929), Ernest Earnest (1950), David Rein (1952), Richard D. Walter (1970), and Joseph P. Lovering (1971). The first biography is a hagiographic account marred by omissions, substantial and unacknowledged editing, and no documentation. Internally, Burr confuses sources, selects passages from various letters to present as a single letter, and edits excessively without notation.[9] Yet, in a kind of cascading effect, subsequent biographers and writers have relied heavily on Burr. Earnest depends on Burr, others depend on Burr or Earnest, and so it has gone on to the present. Even Richard Walter's fine medical biography relies on Burr to tell Mitchell's personal story.

I have tried to circumvent this chain reaction by gathering and depending on primary sources, an entire lifetime of writing that includes an abundance of correspondence, autobiographical writing, medical texts, addresses, novels, short stories, and poems. This abundance of personal, medical, and literary writing far exceeds anyone's attempt to control the story, however. And, rather than the great and arrogant nerve specialist, what emerges is an intimate impression of a shifting and problematic life that was aggressively engaged in numerous aspects of nineteenth-century culture and was wildly successful.

I

FAMILY MATTERS

For Weir Mitchell, a career in medicine was "the most entirely satisfactory of earthly pursuits" and the most honorable of all professions. He felt "ancestral pride in the splendor of its conquests, the courage and heroism of its myriad dead."[1] His great-grandparents in Scotland, John Mitchell and Agnes Tait, had eight children, and all five sons studied medicine. Mitchell felt especially proud that medicine had been in his family for three generations, and this was one of the reasons why he wanted his life's story to begin in Scotland. Venerating medicine's history and traditions, Mitchell spent a small fortune collecting old medical books and portraits of famous physicians. One of his most cherished gifts was a reproduction of William Harvey's Padua diploma, and it kept "noble company" in his study with Edward Jenner's inkstand.[2]

Born in 1766, Mitchell's grandfather Alexander was a "rosy blue-eyed man of great personal strength, rather reserved and with a certain gravity of manner."[3] He studied medicine at the University of Edinburgh and then immigrated to America. In Shepherdstown, Virginia, he met and married Elizabeth Kearsley. Also Scotch Presbyterian, her family had immigrated to America in 1717. Mitchell's father, John Kearsley, was born in Shepherdstown in 1793. Shortly after his birth, his mother became seriously ill and died four years later. Alexander remarried Ann Scott, and she gave birth to a son. When Alexander died in 1804, his brother in Scotland offered to take charge of John. At the age of eleven, Mitchell's father sailed for Leith.

At the ancient Academy of Ayr, John studied Greek, Latin, French, geography, bookkeeping, philosophy, and mathematics. He won silver medals and certificates for scholarly achievement, battled with the town boys, and roamed the Ayrshire countryside. At the age of seventeen, with a letter of introduction written by the academy's director, he left Ayr for the University of Edinburgh, where as a pleasant "strong handsome lad" and the only American, he became a social favorite. It was around this time that James Hogg taught Mitchell's father many of the quaint Scottish songs he would later sing to his family in America. Mitchell wrote that even as a much older man, his father "could recite the whole of 'Tam o' Shanter,' when of an evening his hot Scotch was brewed and we heard him recite or listened to him sing in his well-preserved tenor 'Burnie Boozle' or 'Ye Banks and Braes o' Bonnie Doon.' I remember that his singing of 'The Flowers of the Forest are a' Rede Awa' used to move some of us children to tears." When the poet Robert Burns died in 1796, John and his uncle's family mourned his death. Mitchell's great-grandfather was collector of excise at Dumfries, and Burns had been on his staff. Burns visited the Mitchell home and wrote the elder Mitchell several letters, including one in the form of a poem requesting money. Mitchell felt that the story of his Scottish ancestry was worth telling if only for this connection with Burns.[4]

In 1814, the year of Napoleon's abdication and the end of the War of 1812, John Mitchell returned to the United States only to discover that the British had destroyed his modest inheritance, including his father's books and silver. With the assistance of his mother's family in Virginia, he moved to Philadelphia and began to study medicine at the University of Pennsylvania and to work in the office of Dr. Nathaniel Chapman, a Virginian. During John's medical education and after his graduation in 1819, he made at least two lucrative trips to China as a ship's surgeon. On his first trip, he took along Samuel Johnson's *Lives of the Poets* and studied Milton and such cavalier and neoclassical poets as Waller, Cowley, Dryden, Addison, and Pope. He created a beautifully handwritten dictionary of quotations in three Chinese blank books, and in this way acquired an affectionate familiarity with British poetry of the seventeenth and eighteenth centuries.[5] After returning from the first voyage, John met Sarah Matilda Henry. Her father was an Irish Presbyterian and a wealthy manufacturer in Philadelphia. Since John possessed little except charm and good looks to recommend him, Alexander Henry opposed any talk of marriage and even went so far as to forbid the two from seeing each other or corresponding. But John and Matilda, as she was called, disobeyed her father and met secretly.

In a letter to Matilda written during the second China trip, John enclosed a list of books for her to read, cautioning that there "must be to the mind in the great ocean of life some guide to conduct the frail bark in which it resides, through its perilous voyage; and that it may not be left to the mercy of the tempest and the tide, some polar star, must be suspended on high, to direct in emergency." This "polar star" must originate in heaven and sacred scriptures, and John counseled, "Your course of reading therefore ought to commence with these oracles of God which have a decided claim to preeminence over every earthly production."[6] Despite such spirited advice to his fiancée, John did not read the Bible or attend church. He never discussed religion. He was a man who, according to his son, "at no time belonged to any church and was rather a liberal thinker for those days."[7] Self-sufficient and discerning, John was well equipped to determine his own course. But Matilda was different. Feeble and childish like other women, she needed external guidance and control as she voyaged through the great ocean of life. Weir Mitchell first learned this lesson about women from his father, growing up in a household where both parents accepted female inferiority and weakness without question. The conventional belief that a woman's life was a dangerous journey in a frail bark would later become a persistent theme in Mitchell's speaking and writing. In 1895, for example, when he addressed the first graduating class of women at Radcliffe, he concluded the address by saying, "I hope, my dear Dean, and you, ladies, that no wreck from these shores will be drifted into my dockyard. Sometimes I can refit the ruined craft. Alas! Sometimes I cannot."[8]

———

The red hair of John Mitchell's boyhood had turned a deep chestnut brown. He was six feet tall and well built, with striking Saxon blue eyes. While he was an attractive man with a charming and generous personality, he was quick to resent the least imputation on his honor and understood that there was only one way to settle a serious difficulty between gentlemen. Overall, he believed himself—with family from Scotland, relatives in Virginia who held fast to the Virginia code of honor, and success as a physician in Philadelphia—to be a fortunate man. Mitchell's younger sister Sarah, or Saidie as she was called, wrote that their father was a perfect gentleman and a man of rare accomplishments.[9]

After graduating from Jefferson Medical College in 1819, John Mitchell secured a position at the Philadelphia Medical Institute and gained a reputation as an effective chemistry lecturer and experimenter. He also attended meetings, gave addresses, published articles, and wrote poetry. In 1825, in an address to the Philadelphia Medical Society, he defended vivisection as a "noble resource against the tedium of inaction." He stated, "Let not your thirst for knowledge be repressed by the common *cant*.... Animals *do* suffer under the knife of the physiologist, but useful knowledge is promoted by their sufferings.... The lower animals were given to man for his *use*; and do we not use them more comformably to the will of the *Giver*, when we extract from them knowledge, than when, to gratify a low and pampered appetite, we crush millions of them at a mouthful?"[10] In 1833 he won an appointment as professor of chemistry at the Franklin Institute, where he was one of the first chemists in the United States to repeat the experiment of solidifying carbonic acid. In 1834, when he lectured on "the means of elevating the character of the working classes," he expressed the hope that the time was not far distant when high refinement and manual labor would be compatible. "Coarseness and vulgarity are disgusting, even to the vulgar," and there is no man however gross himself who is not pleased by the improved manners and literary attainments of his son. Addressing the women in the audience, he urged their improvement because of their role as mothers: "The character of the child is formed or deformed by the example and instruction of the mother.... How many Newtons have been withered in the bud—how many Franklins consigned to obscurity by the presence and the influence of a mother, who, herself totally ignorant of the value of knowledge, feels no disposition to encourage in her child, the love of science, or a taste for the arts!"[11] This stress on the importance of the mother in relation to the son was another prominent theme in nineteenth-century medical discourse. In early images of the uterus, fetal figures were always male, representing the commonplace notion that ideal pregnancies resulted in male births. As late as 1886 in his annual address, the president of the British Medical Association, Dr. Withers Moore, stated, "For bettering the breed of men, we need and claim to have the best *mothers of men*.... Can we exaggerate the importance to the future man of the quality of that mother-stuff?" Withers Moore felt that although Bacon's mother could not have produced the *Novum Organum*, "she—perhaps she alone— could and did produce Bacon."[12] As a means to an end, women must be trained and educated strictly for that end.

In 1839 John Mitchell was elected to the chair of the practice of medicine at Jefferson Medical College, and he held this position until his death. On at least two occasions he was awarded gifts for his service to the city of Philadelphia during epidemic outbreaks. He published widely in a number of medical journals on topics such as arsenic, chronic dysentery, acute and chronic rheumatism, epidemic fevers, medical ethics, and the diffusion of gases through membranes. He made significant contributions to the parasitic concept of infectious diseases, theorizing in his 1849 monograph *On the Cryptogamous Origin of Malarious and Epidemic Fevers* that an infectious agent caused such diseases. He used morphine in 1817, strychnine in 1818, and the active principle of cinchona bark (quinine) in 1821. He was a pioneer in the use of ether in childbirth and a type of suspension treatment for scoliosis.[13]

At that time, it was the custom in American medical schools for each class to appoint a committee to select and publish their favorite lectures. John Mitchell was a popular professor at Jefferson, and for this reason several of his lectures were selected for publication. He had a strong voice and candid style, and in one such lecture he criticized American medical journals, disturbed by "the recollection of the sad trash by which they are disfigured." He found them "very faulty in language, defective in structure, and utterly devoid of useful information." He was particularly disturbed by the ceaseless repetition of such meaningless phrases as "emulging the liver, bringing down the bile, evacuating the morbific agent, neutralizing the malaria, marsh exhalations, putrid emanations, nervous irritability, ideo and koino miasmata, septic evolutions, antiseptic defences."[14] With a direct and confident style, he did not shy away from harsh criticism of his colleagues and their methods. He was frequently chosen to deliver the commencement address (or the "Charge to the Graduates," as it was called). He was elected to the College of Physicians of Philadelphia and was a member of the American Medical Association, the Academy of Natural Science of Philadelphia, and the American Philosophical Society. He also served as grand master of the Grand Lodge of Pennsylvania.

When John Mitchell and Matilda Henry married on February 5, 1823, they set up house at 119 South Fifth Street. Their first three children were born there, Alexander Henry in 1823, Elizabeth Kearsley in 1825, and Silas Weir in 1829. Six more children followed: Sarah, Letitia, Walsh, John (who died in childhood), Chapman, and Edward. Matilda accepted as fact the secondary status and domestic role of all women, and raised her sons and daughters according to the traditional gender divisions found in religion and the law. Mitchell described his mother as a "simple instinctively maternal being."[15] His sister Saidie described her as a "gentle child-hearted person who cared for her boys most and to whom I rarely went with a child's joy or sorrow." Matilda, in her role as moral guide and disciplinarian, insisted that her children read three chapters of the Bible each day and five on Sunday, and taught them to interpret it literally. Once when

Saidie had done poorly with a lesson, Matilda quoted the last verse in Revelation, "which scared me into a more correct repeating of Scripture."[16] Weir recalled asking his mother about the Holy Ghost. Receiving no clear answer, he was convinced that the Holy Ghost was some form of actual ghost and lay awake at night dreading its appearance. Once, Matilda punished Weir for describing an imaginary gold carriage and a hen house. Grandfather Henry, who also talked a great deal about religion, said that he hoped to pass from this world into the next and be with Christ. But when he became ill, he was dreadfully alarmed that he would die. Mitchell puzzled over these contradictory attitudes.[17] Sometimes he stayed with his Aunt Henry on Germantown Road, where he could swim in the Wissahickon River above the Red Bridge. Like his mother and grandfather, his aunt was strictly Presbyterian and insisted that the children attend church twice on Sunday, say a text daily, and always remember early and late prayers. Mitchell noted the great length of Sunday service and how he once smuggled in a small volume of Frederick Marryat's novel *Mr. Midshipman Easy* to pass the time.

Looking back, he felt that his childhood "was a too sober life for an imaginative child and of it and its many repressions I carry away chiefly a memory of hated Sunday school and incomprehensible church, not of punishment physical, of passionate love for my mother, and of a sort of veneration for my father and, over and above all, of wearisome ennui which pursued me long." He disliked school as much as church and he devoured books to the neglect of lessons. With a "true book-love," he spent much of his time reading stories of travel and adventure like *Robinson Crusoe* and *The Arabian Nights*. He well remembered the time his mother destroyed the family copy of *The Arabian Nights* after deciding that "as long as it existed none of us would study and burned it before our eyes amid loud lamentations. It was for me an hour of pain. I did not know that ever again I could get that book." He was thrilled when his father took him in the gig to the old Fifth Street library, where he could check out any number of books. First he checked out Captain Cook's voyages, then a vast folio on Peru by the Spanish soldier–poet Garcilaso de la Vega, a book about the conquest of Mexico by Bernal Díaz del Castillo, and Southey's ponderous quarto on Brazil.[18] His sister Saidie remembered him best "as lying before any possible fire and reading impossible books."[19] He also enjoyed attending his father's chemistry lectures and visiting his private chemistry laboratory at the Philadelphia Medical Institute. He wrote that the laboratory was "like a fairy land and sometimes I was given chemicals to take home and then the joy with which I saw the beautiful colors of the precipitates I made I can never forget. Once or twice I succeeded in mildly blowing myself up."[20]

The house that Mitchell remembered best was located at 1100 Walnut Street. It was three stories high with back buildings, and servants to clean, cook, and serve the meals. The front room served as the parlor and also the waiting room, although most patients sent for their doctors. John Mitchell's medical office was in the back, where he kept a skeleton in the closet that the children called the "French lady." The noise of vehicles rarely disturbed the quiet neighborhood streets, and the residents were "plain, comfortable Philadelphia merchants, living moderately and in no way remarkable." Many neighbors were John's patients, and Mitchell recalled entering "the somber interiors of the houses, the black hair cloth covered furniture, the tasteless decorations and the simplicity of the lives passed in these homes." The city "was then clean and small, the country attainable by a short drive, and I can remember how often my father would drive out with two or three of us to the country and turn us out, of a hot July evening, to play by the roadside." On Saturdays the children had their weekly bath.[21]

With four brothers and many other boys in the neighborhood, there was no end to the pranks and mischief. The daily violence on the way to and from school was "hard and savage," involving fist and stone fights and bitter feuds with the high school boys. The Mitchell boys broke windows, threw decayed apples at passersby, shot the market people with long blowguns and peas, and tormented the pigs that strayed from the Irish shanties on the outskirts of town. In the summer months, they were often tempted to help themselves to the abundant melons and peaches growing along the Delaware and Jersey shores. While Mitchell was "by nature quiet and not apt to go in for rows and boyish mischief," he admired those who did and was but "too apt to follow a lead." Once, a stout Jersey man pursued the boys while they were carrying stolen watermelons under each arm and slipping down to their boat. Mitchell was the last in line. When the man caught up with him, Mitchell hurled a melon, which "broke on his head and effectually bowled him over. He was gory with the red core of the melon, as I saw him last. We beat a hasty retreat and shoved off just in time. I fancy we might have had the melons for the asking but then we should have lost the fun and the peril."[22]

Mitchell's younger brother Robert Walsh (or Walsh, as he was called) fought many battles and vendettas, about which their father appeared indifferent. But when John Mitchell heard that Weir had fought with a much bigger boy and the boy had tied one hand behind his back, John ordered Weir from the table, saying, "If, sir, you fight, and must fight, you must do it like a gentleman." Although Weir often characterized himself as quiet and shy, he also wrote that he was "always" nervous and excitable, "needing to have a sudden grip on myself in danger or when wrath arises." Like his brother Walsh, he had a short fuse, and hotheadedness and resentment emerge in many of the boyhood stories. Their mother may have wondered how with so much Bible reading and time in church these children could be so irascible and hot-tempered. By necessity the oldest Mitchell son was a different kind of boy. Alexander was disabled, and his room became the popular gathering spot for all the children after school and the place where the Christmas presents were kept. Weir frequently commented on the physical beauty of the men in his family, and he wrote that Alexander possessed a "singular personal beauty and so like the first Napoleon that the resemblance was often remarked upon." After Alexander died in 1839, Mitchell inherited his bedroom, his collection of coins, minerals, and autographs, and, somewhat reluctantly at the age of ten, his position as first son.[23]

As the Mitchell children grew, the physical fights evolved into intellectual battles, which delighted the older children and their father. John Mitchell valued both science and literature, and reading and discussing writers and poets were integral parts of family life. Mitchell wrote that around them at meals "were some two thousand books and often someone would quit the meal to find a book and triumphantly refute the adversary. Most of our talks were literary or of travel, history, etc. We used to attack my father's antique taste and slyly quote the new verse so as to trap him into admissions. I think while I was at college, I must have heard all of Akenside, Pope, and much of Dryden read aloud of evenings when the Scotch whiskey punch was brewed and songs followed, my father leading in his delightful tenor." One New Year's Eve, Mitchell read the poem "New Year" without mentioning Tennyson's name. When John expressed pleasure, the children were delighted that at last their father must admit of poets since Byron.[24]

John Mitchell had, according to his son, a southern disregard for expenditure, enjoying good food and company and often welcoming friends and colleagues into his home. During the Episcopal conventions in Philadelphia, several bishops stayed with the Mitchells, and Weir was admitted into the dining room during dessert. He remembered that the bishop of Tennessee "used tobacco and immensely annoyed my mother by regarding her polished steel grates as fit receptacles for the juice." He also remembered Bishop Meade, who belonged to an old Virginia family and whose father had been an aide to Washington. One evening, regarding his silver fork, Meade said to the black servant, "Here, boy, take this thing away and fetch me a real fork," and a two-pronged steel fork was brought from the kitchen. On another occasion, arriving with a broken trunk corded together and filled with ragged undergarments, Meade gave Matilda twelve dollars, instructing her to have the trunk repaired and purchase twelve pairs of socks, a dozen shirts, and other undergarments. Later in the day when he found a new trunk filled with new underclothes in his room, he said, "I suppose there was no change left over. Cities are expensive places."[25]

Other houseguests included John Mitchell's colleagues at Jefferson Medical College, men who would later become Mitchell's professors in medical school. There was Thomas Mütter, professor of surgery; Robley Dunglison, professor of the institutes of medicine and medical jurisprudence; Charles Meigs, professor of obstetrics and diseases of women and children; and Franklin Bache, professor of chemistry and Ben Franklin's grandson. Having inherited Franklin's "love of method," Bache carried to extremes his love of neatness. When he complained at a faculty meeting that the underside of the lower shelves in his laboratory were unpainted, the dean asked, "But who ever sees the under side of those shelves?" Bache replied, "I, sir, when I kneel to move apparatus," and the shelves were painted. Other friends included Oliver Wendell Holmes and Chief Justice John Bannister Gibson, as well as special visitors like Robert E. Lee, Jefferson Davis, Francis Scott Key, and Edgar Allan Poe. Mitchell remembered sitting on Key's knee and hearing him recite "The Star-Spangled Banner."[26] Once or twice a year, Poe would visit with a prospectus for a new literary journal, and John Mitchell would give him ten dollars. In Scotland John's grandfather had helped Robert Burns, and in a similar way he wanted to help Poe without offending his sensibilities. On one occasion after Poe left, John said, "That is a true poet, that is Mr. Edgar Poe." Weir wrote, "I entertained in those youthful days a form of boy worship for the creature called a poet, only known to me in books, and having seen one so near affected me strongly."[27]

Weir retained no pleasant memories of his various grammar schools; rather, he "loathed lessons and the paths of learning led through a vale of tears and fears." Once he was caught skipping school, and he had to go to bed at 4:00 p.m.

every day for a week with only bread and water. In school, physical punishment constituted the common method of disciplining boys, and his second teacher, "a red-headed cleric named Shaw," thrashed the boys at will "with simple brutalness." Then, around the age of thirteen at a school attended by around one hundred boys, Weir went under the "terrible rule" of the Reverend Samuel Crawford. John Mitchell had requested that his son be spared whippings; so, except for the stinging whack of the ruler on his hands, he escaped much of the brutality. Crawford "wore large spectacle glasses on a hawk-like nose and used to push one up on to his brow, forget it, put on a second, push that up when he needed far view, forget it, too, and then add a third and this was always a signal of gathering wrath." Over Crawford's desk and raised chair there were a number of rattans and several others called "Tobies," stored in a long tin case of water to preserve their pliancy. Armed with a Toby, Crawford "used to march about, sometimes on the floor and sometimes on top of the solid desks, distributing here and there a stout whack on the shoulders of the unlucky ones." He would say, "Now, sir, Toby has a good memory." When he acknowledged mistakes, he would say, "Well, that will do for the times when you deserved it and Toby forgot you. Ah, Toby knows the bad boys." Weir's only fond memories were of school friends like Charles and Henry Leland, Henry Wharton, the Meigs boys, and Toland, who in later years could recite whole cantos of Byron's "Childe Harold" and "Don Juan."[28]

At fifteen Mitchell entered the University of Pennsylvania to study chemistry, physics, moral philosophy, rhetoric, literature, algebra, geometry, and the classics. Still unable to concentrate on his studies, he later regretted the lost opportunity of these years. He remembered one professor of classics, the Reverend Dr. Wylie, "sometimes provost, known for us as Boss Wylie." The students went to his house on Bush Hill, where they were all examined together. Wylie was quite deaf and very nervous, and the students "unblushingly assisted one another and, if in trouble, had been told that to cross one leg over another and wag the upper leg" would drive the gentleman wild. "Stop that," he would say, in the ripest brogue. "But I can't, sir, I am nervous." Dr. Wylie would say, "Oh— well, that will do," and move on to the next student. Mitchell remembered another professor, Henry R. Reed, as a fine scholar of rhetoric and literature. But rather than learning, Mitchell's set was busy with billiards and drinking, "and I missed much I could have had from Reed." Although the studies were interesting, Reed "was so gentle that we took great liberties and were really a shameless set of reprobates." One day Reed asked the students to write about when and by whom Rome was taken. A boy sitting between Mitchell and Toland was absolutely ignorant and asked for their help. Winking and smirking, they alternately gave him slips of paper. A few days later Reed read the student's paper before the class, which included the information that Henry VII had conquered Rome on his way to the Twelfth Crusade and Julius Caesar had stormed it in the ninth century. Mitchell was suspended for two weeks and whipped by the student. There were other incidents of trouble and suspension, and in one fight Mitchell's nose was broken. He wrote, "I often wonder what saved me. Partly it was that all strong drinks were unpleasant to me and that all the men I refer to had far more money than I. Always I have had an ingrained dislike of debt and a certain modesty which then was as distinct as that of a girl. It saved me much. Also, my fondness for books gave me resources wanting to some, not to all, of these men."[29]

Around the age of sixteen, Mitchell began to spit blood, and although there was no other sign of lung disease, his father advised more time outdoors and more physical activity. As a result, along with a couple of friends, Mitchell was allowed to invest in a boat, which they kept at the South Street wharf on the Schuylkill River. For four years, rarely a weekday passed without a pull, a sail, or a game of cricket, and through these open-air activities Mitchell began what would become a deep and lifelong attachment to outdoor life. By this time, he "had written horrible verse and some as wretched tales. I knew little Greek and some Latin and read French ill, but my head was full of fancies. I was given to day dreams and used to lie for idle hours in my boat on the reedy river, thinking how pleasant it would be to be this or that." At the age of seventeen, he published his first poem, "To a Polar Star," in the *Nassau Monthly*. With only vague thoughts about a career, he lacked ambition, energy, and discipline, and his weak health often served as his excuse. During his senior year at the University of Pennsylvania, his father became seriously ill and Mitchell remained at home. After a few months, he was given the choice to give up college or repeat the year. He was only "too glad to escape the hated mathematics to hesitate," and as a result, he never received his undergraduate degree. Soon his father insisted that he choose a career. When Mitchell proposed entering a chemical factory, his father objected, saying he had no capital to give and proposed a mercantile life instead.[30]

John Mitchell felt strongly about medicine as a career. In one of his lectures on the impediments to studying medicine, he stated that although there was a general impression that of all the departments of learning, medicine exacted the least amount of education or capacity, just the opposite was true. Despite the fact that medicine was "so full of imbeciles," it was "an art which most of all demands a good education and a sound and discriminating judgment, talent to acquire knowledge, memory to retain, and tact to apply it; and that kind of moral ascendency which inspires confidence in one's self, and an almost implicit faith in others." He did not encourage young men to enter medicine without "suitable preliminary learning. It is so multifarious and vast a science as to task fully the time and the capacity of the finest intellect and the most accomplished scholar. No man can reason justly on the circulation of the blood, or the mechanism of respiration, who does not comprehend the laws of hydraulics and pneumatics; and he who does not understand the French and German languages is denied access to some of the richest stores of medical literature."[31]

With his father as the ideal, Mitchell saw medicine as a profession beyond his reach. Charming manners, a certain buoyancy and sweetness of temper, masculine beauty, and even the charm of a modulated voice were things that Mitchell noted in discussing his father's perfection. In terms of carefulness and swift decision making, he had no equal. He was the best physician his son ever knew. This idealization was both a blessing and a curse, causing Mitchell to feel inept by comparison and almost certain to fall short of such a high standard of excellence. Mitchell felt no deep desire to enter the medical profession, but some time passed and his father more distinctly insisted that he choose a career. When he finally said that he wanted to be a doctor, John Mitchell reacted with disgust: "You have no appreciation of the life. You are wanting in nearly all the qualities that go to make success in medicine. You have brains enough, but no industry."[32]

When Mitchell entered Jefferson Medical College in 1848, the annual *Announcement* included the following information: The session lasted for four and a half months, beginning in the middle of October. Six hours of lectures were given, four days each week. The anatomy rooms were kept open throughout the session, and the clinic was open on appropriate days during the entire year. For an additional fee of ten dollars, students could also attend the Pennsylvania Hospital to observe various medical and surgical procedures. Without additional cost, they had the privilege of attending the college dispensary and clinic to observe the practice of medicine, including diagnosis, prognosis, therapeutics, surgery, and obstetrics. In order to graduate, a candidate had to be at least twenty-one years old and of good moral character. He had to attend two complete courses of lectures and exhibit to the dean of the faculty lecture tickets or other evidence of attendance. He had to study medicine for no less than three years, attend at least one course of clinical instruction, present a thesis in his own handwriting, and successfully complete an examination before the faculty.[33]

The 1848–49 *Announcement* also included a recommended reading list, and the following entry appeared under the heading "Obstetrics, and Diseases of Women and Children": "Meigs's Philadelphia Practice of Midwifery, or Velpeau's or Churchill's Midwifery; Meigs's edition of Colombat de l'Isere on the Diseases of Women; or Meigs on Females—their Diseases and Remedies; and J. F. Meigs on the Diseases of Children." Clearly, Charles Meigs was the major figure and driving force behind gynecology and obstetrics at Jefferson, and he was also a close friend of the family. Mitchell wrote that Meigs was of all his father's colleagues "most near of all of them to genius" and "to me ever an interesting man, full of scholarly talk and the gossipy chat into which the obstetric doctor is apt to fall."[34] As a family friend and a professor at Jefferson, Meigs had an early and deep influence on Mitchell. A closer look at two of the books on the list, Meigs's 1845 translation of Marc Colombat's textbook *A Treatise on the Diseases and Special Hygiene of Females* and Meigs's own textbook on females, reveals what Mitchell and the other medical students were learning about women at Jefferson Medical College. This gynecological discourse is worth examining since it captures so well the predominant medical view of women at the time— one that formed the foundation of Mitchell's attitudes and later treatment of women.

Colombat's *Treatise* is a long one, almost six hundred pages, and begins with the following definition of a woman: "Feeble and sensitive at birth, and destined by nature to give us existence and to preserve us afterwards by means of her tender and watchful care, woman, the most faithful companion of man, may be regarded as the very complement of the benefits bestowed upon us by the Divine Being; as an object fitted to excite our highest interest, and presenting to the philosopher, as well as to the physician, a vast field of contemplation."[35] One of the things that Colombat and the other doctors imagined when they contemplated the female body was referred to as the reflex theory or "sympathies" of the womb. Because the womb maintained a sympathetic relation with the rest of the body, shocks to and irritation of the womb might cause disease in other parts seemingly remote. Moreover, this intimate hypothetical link was two-directional. Any imbalance or shock to the nervous system might cause pathological reactions in the womb and alter the reproductive organs and cycle. The womb recorded and the body reflected moral impressions; there-fore, even such activities as the theater, novels, political excitement, and spicy dishes might cause breakdown and disease.

In describing the young pubescent woman, Colombat noted her delicacy of features, melodious voice, and her rounded and full breasts that establish at this time their sympathetic correspondence with the womb. Her language be-comes more touching and pathetic, and her languishing eyes announce a mix-ture of desires and fears. There is heat in the genital parts that provokes the aphrodisiac sense, and sympathetic irradiations of the uterus produce the impres-sion of "touching melancholy, a charming bashfulness . . . the necessity of lov-ing . . . and . . . if it remains unsatisfied, a source of multiplied disorders and derangements." Colombat emphasized the amount of prudence and sagacity required to govern an organization so delicate and mobile, and "into what depths of the heart the physician ought to seek and detect the principle of so many unnatural shocks." Irregular menstruation might cause hysteria, convul-sions, catalepsy, spasmodic diseases, chlorosis, and consumption. The first treat-ment Colombat prescribed, sounding a little like a rest cure, was prolonged isolation, fresh and dry air, nourishing food like rich soups and roast meats, and iron. In more difficult cases, the blood must be directed toward the uterus through foot and hip baths, enemas, fumigation, cups around the pelvic area, bleeding, or four to six leeches applied to the internal surface of the thighs or on the outside of the labia majora.[36]

At the approach of puberty, Colombat advised that young women should be removed from boarding school to be constantly watched. The intimate relationships formed at school, reading romances, and frequent visits to the the-ater constitute powerful agents that could "tear the veil of modesty, and destroy, for ever, the seductive innocence which is the most charming ornament of a young girl. . . . Like a delicate plant, withered by the rays of a burning sun, she fades and dies under the influence of a poisoned breath." For girls who are cold, apathetic, and indifferent, he prescribed the opposite plan—more theater and more romances. His final counsel represented another erroneous but power-ful nineteenth-century physiological concept called "limited energy," which imagined the female body as a closed system with a restricted amount of energy. A woman's complex and delicate reproductive system was constructed and put into good working order between the ages of fifteen and twenty-five, so it was critical that she not divert energy away from this critical process in order to study, attend school, or work outside the home. Colombat warned that literary studies, abstraction, and meditation, which concentrate all the vital forces on the organ of thought, are "very prejudicial to females."[37]

In 1848, three years after his translation of Colombat, Meigs published his own book, *Females and Their Diseases; A Series of Letters to His Class,* a text of more than seven hundred pages that sounds conspicuously like Colombat's in tone and content. For example, Meigs also finds the transition from girl to woman to be quite miraculous: "The little hipless creature that you leave at home in January, as a child, is found when you return in November to have changed into a woman. . . . The round and swelling limbs and the panting bosom have taken the place of that angular, and lean and awkward form that you left behind at your departure, and the whole creature . . . has been transmuted as by the stroke of a magician's wand. Does this cost nothing of life-force, life-effort, life-expenditure? Is not this great and sudden transformation, and loss, a stage of crisis and danger?" Meigs understood a young woman only in terms of reproduction and motherhood, declaring that the "only arithmetical calculation she requires is the relation between one dozen eggs at twelve and a half cents, and three dozen eggs at the same rate; and the unknown quantity she ought to look for is, the proper gentleman whom the fates and sister three have in store for her as her future lover." He also demonstrated for his students how best to talk to mothers. The doctor should say, "I wish to shock you; I wish you to learn that unless you change the treatment, you will lose her. She will die, madam! . . . I am more than serious, I am grieved. I saw a sweet creature within a year . . . done to death by mere schooling. . . . I tell you that to rack her little brain learning Latin is nonsense. She can't learn it, in the first place. She can only try till it makes her sick, and then she'll give it up." The emotional intensity of Meigs's objections to the education of young women and the fact that he wrote for publication in such an unapproachable and dramatic way reveal much. His tone and discourse were not only pervasive but highly respected and admired. Such a tone was heard as valid and effective in and out of Mitchell's home, and provided a standard for the next generation of doctors. Meigs felt that curing the sick was "next in goodness to the mission of Christ," and he ended the book with a plea to his students to look on the medical profession not as a business, "but as a great Morality—not as a trade, but as a Mission appointed by God, for the benefit of the children of men."[38]

These beliefs and attitudes about women saturated the atmosphere of Mitchell's home and medical school. Regina Morantz-Sanchez refers to Jefferson Medical College as "a bastion of male privilege which did not open its door to women until 1961."[39] Clearly, Mitchell's lifelong obstinacy in opposing women's education was rooted firmly in the early and emotional hold of the idealization of men like his father and Meigs, and erroneous concepts like womb sympathies, limited energy, and the inheritance of acquired characteristics. Nervous and insecure, Mitchell memorized the facts of anatomy and physiology and at the same time wholeheartedly embraced the patriarchal ideology. Working ten to fourteen hours a day and brooding over the bones, he drank gallons of strong coffee and took cold showers at night to fight off the fatigue. No longer alienated by ennui, detachment, or dreaminess, he strongly identified with his father and by extension his professors, and strove to become just like them.

John Mitchell insisted that his son become a surgeon, and so he was placed in the office of Dr. Mütter at Jefferson. However, the blood and pain initially horrified Mitchell and he fainted at operations: "I saw, indeed, the last operations without anesthetics and the first in Philadelphia with them. The terribleness of the woman held by strong men, the screams, the flying blood jets and the struggle were things to remember."[40] He enjoyed Dunglison's lectures on physiology although Dunglison, like the others, gave didactic talks with little or no illustration, experimentation, or clinical presentation. He attended Joseph Pancoast's lectures on anatomy, where Pancoast, whom Mitchell regarded as a surgical genius, talked about the relationship between anatomy and surgery.

Alongside the stress and struggle to make up for lost time and prove his worthiness, there was some fun. In contrast to Mitchell's father, who used ether in childbirth, Meigs violently opposed it. To prove his point about its deadly effects, Meigs had a large billy goat brought into the lecture arena before a class of three hundred students. Ether was administered to the goat, it fell senseless, and in a few minutes the goat's death was announced. The supposed corpse was carried to a room at the halfway landing of the main stairwell. However, after the lecture while the students were descending the stairwell, Meigs's assistant opened the door and out came the goat, very drunk and charging through hundreds of laughing students. "Billy and the students went downstairs in one wild confusion," and Mitchell's father was never weary of asking Meigs about "this patient's health."[41]

There were also parties, dances, and assembly balls. In a letter to his older sister, Elizabeth, who was visiting in Boston, Mitchell wrote about falling in love with a Miss Chapman: "I can sympathise with you—since I am in Love myself—not half, or quarter, but wholesale, neck and heels in, beyond the reach of Doctor or Humane society." In the same chatty letter, he sent news of their brother Walsh's bravery. It was January and John Mitchell had taken his three younger sons—Walsh, Chapman, and Edward—ice-skating at the Fairmount Dam. Walsh and Chap skated off together. Suddenly, John realized that the "ice was in motion." A mass of ice about five acres in size had broken away from the main cake and was moving toward the dam. He picked up Ned, jumped to safety, and removed his skates, but when he attempted to go back to rescue the other two boys, the gap was too wide. Hundreds of skaters were trapped, some "falling over the dam, some leaping madly into the water—some—walking or tumbling along the slippery edge of the dam and others wringing their hands in despair—women yelling—children bawling, men cursing." Walsh, realizing that no one could help, pulled Chap to the edge and ordered him to jump, but Chap was frozen with fear and sat down on the ice, unable to move. Walsh threatened to strike him if he did not climb on his back. Finally, with Chap clinging to his back and clutching his shoulders, Walsh grabbed his feet, and together they leapt into the crashing ice and rapid water and waded to the shore. Their father, "half distracted," found them at the tavern wrapped in blankets and blue with cold. Mitchell, pleased to have such a story to counter so many others where Walsh had been foolishly reckless, wrote, "Wally certainly—behaved most gallantly—Cool and brave—So he is a hero—and has been christened Commodore in memory thereof. . . . I hope that in future you will have a little more respect at least for your Brother—Do you hear?" Mitchell also sent bits of gossip about friends and mutual acquaintances. Vanarsdale was going out again, "but the ladies won't speak to him—at all—He thinks of joining the Benedictines." Mitchell had seen Selina Lawrence and "she asked for you. How I hate hypocrisy."[42]

Only a few months after writing this letter, Mitchell broke down with liver trouble and severe jaundice due to overwork and lack of exercise. This was the first of several breakdowns that he would experience, but through rest, a proper diet, and physical activity, he persisted and overcame the illness and exhaustion. This experience of breakdown and recovery would become a pattern in his personal life and the foundation of his belief in the rest cure and camp life for patients suffering from exhaustion and nervous illness.

In addition to attending lectures at Jefferson Medical College, Mitchell worked in James Booth's chemistry laboratory, and for one summer he reluctantly worked in the apothecary shop of Fred K. Brown. He and his classmate

Thomas Bache participated in a research project under the direction of Dungli-son to determine the effects of exposing excised frog hearts to a vacuum.[43] Through this animal experimentation, Mitchell grew accustomed to the cutting and bleeding and overcame his horror of surgery. He even asked if he could assist at the surgical clinics. In March 1850 he submitted his thesis, "The Intes-tinal Gases," and graduated from Jefferson Medical College. John Mitchell, with his son in the audience, delivered the "Charge to the Graduates." Although he had expressed no strong desire to become a physician and later noted an early preference for literature, Weir Mitchell reached the end of his medical educa-tion feeling mentally and physically stronger and with fewer doubts about his career choice. Along with his youthful fascination with his father's laboratory, he developed the ability to focus and a genuine interest in his studies. He might finally be able to gain his father's trust and respect, and there was no "truer, better way of serving God and man" than by entering this splendid brother-hood, and "making yourself what you ought to be."[44]

2

LETTERS HOME

In October 1850 Weir Mitchell and his sister Elizabeth sailed for England on the clipper ship *Tuscarora*. According to the plan, Elizabeth would spend the fall and winter months with their sister Saidie Neilson, who was living with her family in Liverpool. Mitchell, after a few days there, would travel to Manchester, then London, and finally Paris to study. In the spring Elizabeth would join him, and together they would travel through Europe before returning to Philadelphia in September.

During the twenty-one-day voyage, there was some wretched seasickness, a fire onboard, and a violent forty-eight-hour storm. Mitchell wrote that "at each fresh puff we careened under it till our bulwarks touched the water and at times vast waves crashed over the bow and along the deck. Below stairs it was a matter of moment to cross the cabin, and when any thing broke loose from its lashings, there was wild waltzing to wilder music." Only one other passenger was aboard the ship, a Mr. Williams, and Mitchell wrote that he was "quite in love with himself" and provided "grave statements of his own feelings about twenty times a day." Stuck for six long days in St. George's Channel beating against the winds, "which commonly means not—that you beat anything or any body, but that you are beaten," Mitchell could smell Liverpool a league off and described the city as wrapped in mist and smoke with a "look of chronic Jaundice."[1]

He spent the next day with his brother-in-law William Neilson while he attended to various business matters in the city. They dined on sole, mutton-chops, Stilton cheese, ale, and an octave of sherry, all for two shillings. Mitchell heard "cotton talked" and "saw men with peony complexions—which by the bye gives to any mans face however handsome a low bred expression. Those I was introduced to (some prominent men) had a cordial but boisterous manner speaking in a tone which often in the streets makes me jump as two talkers pass by me." While walking alone in the city, Mitchell noticed how the "architectural grace" of the buildings was destroyed by the dirt and damp, and the "white gets leaden and black gets blacker so as to make what would be with us a fine city, nasty—and ugly here—what strikes me most—as I walk, are the donkeys." He was surprised by the number of fat men and the "ugliness of the women and by the height to which they lift their dresses—Here and there you see one with her dress fastened to her waist by a hook called a 'Page.' Our women who have little feet seem as anxious to hide them as these who have not feet but yards are to show them. Yesterday I asked a gentleman the way—He said there's a police man and walked on. So I gained a wrinkle." Brother and sister took the obligatory trip to Chester to see the Roman walls—twenty feet high, made of red sandstone, and surmounted by a beautiful walk that commands a view of the "queer quaint and olden" town and the Snowden Hills. "A large part of these walls is overgrown with ivy," Mitchell wrote, "which seems to be the natural dress of everything out of doors in this damp climate." They traveled to Bangor, Wales, staying at the Penrhyn Arms, and after a pleasant dinner "Sis says her head feels queer which is not to be wondered at as she has been drinking beer and wine."[2]

After Mitchell left Liverpool, Elizabeth became increasingly unhappy. Saidie was seven months pregnant and gave birth to a daughter in January, but rather than being helpful, Elizabeth seemed to be in the way. She was told that her manners were "very French" and her accent "somewhat Irish."[3] Unhappy and lonely, she tried to convey in letters home her sense of being ignored and unwanted in her sister's home.

Mitchell also filled sheet after sheet and complained about being "quite done up by excess of letter writing which gets to be hard work." He wrote different types of letters depending on the audience: the letters to his mother were relaxed and sentimental, whereas letters to his father were deferential and often strained by Mitchell's habitual effort to impress him. Early in the trip he told his mother, "Tell Father I will write when I have any thing worth telling." The letters addressed to his brothers or sisters contained detailed, playful descriptions of the sights and were often signed "Weiree." At home, the whole family gathered to hear Weir's letters read aloud. Matilda wrote that the family listened with "deep interest to every thing connected with our absent one; now and then your Father would signify his approbation, and the pleasure it gave him to hear of your welfare by some well timed remark, indeed your letters please him greatly."[4]

Taken together, Mitchell's letters home paint a candid portrait of his personality and emotional life, revealing both his attention to detail and his immaturity. He was hotheaded and romantic, impatient and high-strung, and still a little nervous about the direction of his career. He was writing some poetry and occasionally incorporating verse into the letters. He felt deeply grateful for the grand-tour opportunity and labored to satisfy his mother's emotional needs, please his father by seeing things through his eyes, and express affection and concern for the younger children by sending long, detailed descriptions and stories addressed directly to them. On a couple of occasions he ended with, "Number and keep my letters."[5]

In one letter Mitchell described his departure from a spot just outside Manchester called Woodlands, the countryseat of Alexander Henry, a cousin on his mother's side. A few minutes before Mitchell left, Henry handed him an envelope, stating that the enclosed gift was meant for medical books and instruments. Mitchell refused it several times, even placing it on the table, but Henry took his hand and "laughing forced the paper into my closed fist, telling me he had made up his mind; that I should vex him if I thwarted him further, and that he meant to make me take it." They drove to the station where Henry waited with Mitchell for the Birmingham train, shaking both of his hands warmly, wishing him well, and explaining that the gift stood for family love and friendship. Once on the train, Mitchell discovered that the envelope contained a note for one hundred pounds. What Mitchell feared most about accepting this gift was his father's disapproval: "You, my best friend, Dear Father, will appreciate my feelings, because you know my independent notions and may remember that I waited often until money which you owed me was offered, rather than ask for it."[6]

In the same letter, after a detailed sheet about other matters, Mitchell returned to the scene with his cousin, closing with, "Pray read carefully my first sheet— It is put less strongly than it happened." He was proud and independent of all except his father, and this gift was especially difficult to accept because on his first night at Woodlands there had been trouble. He had been playing billiards with Henry's son, and at ten thirty Henry came into the room, put out the lights over the table, and said it was time for bed. Mitchell, quick to resent such curt treatment even from an older man and a wealthy relative, immediately relit the lights and went on with the game. Henry left the room laughing. Although this billiards story does not appear in the letters home, Mitchell included it in his autobiography, where he also wrote, "Mr. Henry was the most dictatorial man I ever knew."[7] Mitchell's stubborn streak had served him well in medical school, when it took every bit of his obstinacy to buckle down and learn to concentrate. In this situation with a relative on his mother's side, he had gotten off to a bad start, and his sensibilities made it hard to make peace by accepting the gift. In future years Alexander Henry would demonstrate repeated kindness to the Mitchell family, especially after John Mitchell's death. During the Civil War, when the family was experiencing financial difficulties, Henry established a lifelong annual income of $1,200 for Matilda Mitchell.

In Liverpool and Manchester after visiting various hospitals, Mitchell somewhat disparagingly told his father that he saw nothing worthy of imitation, only "some instances of surgery which would be deemed reckless at home." In London he stayed with Mitchell Henry (Alexander's son), who was assistant surgeon at Middlesex Hospital. Henry introduced him at various hospitals and accompanied him to medical meetings and lectures. Mitchell wrote that at the Middlesex Hospital he saw a contrivance to keep windows open in a way that prevented any draft downward on the beds, and the walls were plastered with special cement that was almost devoid of absorbing power. In Philadelphia there had been talk of building a Jefferson Hospital, so Mitchell was especially keen to tell his father about hospital improvements and innovations.[8]

———

On November 12 Mitchell attended a meeting of London's Royal Medical and Chirurgical Society, the established forum for the discussion of controversial issues, where he heard the "most acrimonious debate on Ovariotomy." The evening's topic was and continued to be one of the most contentious medical issues of the century. Mitchell's career ran parallel to the development of ovariotomy, and no doubt the storm of debates helped to shape his later decision to treat female patients with rest rather than surgery. A brief look at this meeting and its sequel helps to contextualize Mitchell's decisions about the kind of physician he would become and the kind of medicine he would practice.

Nearly two hundred society fellows and visitors attended the meeting, which opened with a paper by W. E. Duffin describing a successful case of ovariotomy. The surgery was performed on a thirty-eight-year-old dressmaker, "urgent in her desire" for the operation, whose cyst made her appear to be eight months pregnant. Chloroform was administered; a three-inch incision was made midway between the umbilicus and the pubes, and 130 ounces of fluid were removed. The collapsed cyst, which contained a smaller cyst the size of an orange, was drawn through the incision and its pedicle secured by ligatures. The patient took opium for six nights, was kept on a light diet, and was given enemas. The ligatures came away on the fifteenth day. The wound healed, the abdomen resumed its natural shape, and her recovery was complete.[9]

Dr. Robert Lee, a fellow of the Royal Society and lecturer in midwifery at St. George's Hospital, had always opposed ovariotomies and followed this single successful case study with a brief overview. The early surgeries, difficult to diagnose and performed without anesthesia, often uncovered no ovarian disease and resulted in death. However, because the surgeries were performed in private homes, statistics were difficult to come by and the outcomes almost impossible to determine. After inquiry and fact-finding into 130 attempted or performed ovariotomies in Great Britain, Lee was able to gain reports of 108. In 37 cases either no cyst or tumor existed or removal was impractical, and the operation was abandoned. Of these 37 operations, 14 were fatal. Of the other 71 cases, 24 proved fatal, and in 14 of these fatal cases, the patient died during the operation. Overall, the mortality rate for the 108 cases was 35 percent.

In the animated discussion that followed Lee's report, Caesar Hawkins stated that it "is well known that the operation has been very frequently attempted, and it is generally believed that a considerable proportion of the operations have been fatal." He asked Bird and Walne, two doctors who were known to frequently perform ovariotomies, to provide statistics so that the society might determine the propriety of the surgery. Dr. Bird spoke, attempting to defend, among other things, the forty to fifty times he had made abdominal incisions merely to complete a diagnosis.

As the discussion continued, the point in question became the suppression of unsuccessful ovariotomies. Dr. Phillips stated that while no man was bound to publish, "if he publish his successful experience, he is then morally bound to publish that which is not successful. He cannot honestly garble it, if the truth must be told; and the truth means the whole truth." He continued, "For myself, I feel utterly unable to advise a patient to submit to the operation for the extirpation of an ovarian cyst. If I turn to one side, I am assured that the operation is little short of murder; if I turn to the other side, I am told it is comparatively harmless." Dr. William Lawrence, twice president of the College of Surgeons and the one who most impressed Mitchell, was the last to speak. Referring to ovariotomy as a "perilous proceeding," he expressed serious doubt regarding the propriety of admitting it into the catalogue of approved surgical operations, and questioned whether such a proceeding could be continued without danger to the character of the medical profession.[10] Mitchell told his father that "Lawrence spoke best and with a degree of caustic irony which is seldom equalled, he spoke of those who withhold unsuccessful cases."[11] Significantly, the London meeting was debating only ovariotomies performed for physical disease, yet the overall tone and message remained decisively critical.

Mitchell attended this meeting in 1850. Just one year later Lee returned with additional statistics. Many of the same doctors were present; the room was even more crowded, with standing room only after many had been turned away, and the discussion was even more contentious. During the course of this second meeting, it became clear that Dr. Bird would remain firm in his unwillingness to share information about his unsuccessful ovariotomies; he defended opening the abdomen as part of his diagnosis and attacked Dr. Lee's work. Lee referred to an analysis of 162 ovariotomies published in the last volume of *Medico-chirurgical Transactions.* In 60 there was no tumor or removal was impractical; 19 of these proved fatal. Of the remaining 102 where the operation was completed, 42 proved fatal, and the condition of the 60 patients who recovered from the surgery was imperfectly known. Lee also spoke regarding the problems of comparing ovariotomy and other great operations, such as amputation, hernia, and the ligature of large arteries for aneurism, concluding that such an analogy was not possible. Great operations were necessary because of impending death, whereas in ovariotomy, as his table confirmed, the patient's life was in no immediate danger and she might live for years with palliative treatment rather than radical intervention. Dr. Lee clarified his opposition based on the difficulty of diagnosis and the high mortality rates, and stated that ovariotomy appeared to be "an act of the greatest cruelty."[12] Regardless of the public nature of the controversy and a mortality rate of around 40 percent, ovariotomies increased in number and purpose as the century progressed.[13]

Many doctors viewed ovariotomy as a major breakthrough in surgical medicine that was both experimental and therapeutic. Especially with the discovery of anesthesia in the 1840s, gynecologists began to abandon treatments such as pessaries, leeches, injections, cauterization, and tapping, and pursued abdominal surgery instead, allowing for some of the first explorations of the interior of the human body. Even before ovariotomies for physical disease became more acceptable, doctors in Britain and particularly in the United States were re-moving non-diseased ovaries in what was called a "normal ovariotomy" (or "oophorectomy" in Great Britain) for a variety of mental disorders, including hysteria, epilepsy, and nymphomania.

The controversy regarding ovariotomy in the United States was every bit as heated as what Mitchell witnessed in London, and opponents were no more successful in controlling its widespread use. Many within the medical field, espe-cially neurologists and alienists, condemned it. Some even referred to ovari-otomists as "belly rippers." Dr. Elizabeth Blackwell referred to ovariotomy as "the castration of women" and sexual surgery as a kind of vivisection that cor-rupted the doctor's moral sense. It could only encourage doctors to treat women brutally, like the animals of their experiments, as if they were nothing more than "clinical material."[14] Still, the use of anesthesia made it painless, removing the scene of the screaming patient, which had been a psychological barrier for many physicians. Some patients and their relatives were anxious for relief and begged for such surgeries. Eventually, antiseptic methods and improvement in technique reduced the mortality rate substantially.

Mitchell's father felt strongly that his son should become a surgeon. While Mitchell experienced some difficulties with surgery in medical school, he had overcome his earlier aversion and in Paris he took a course in surgical training. His father wrote that he was glad he was studying operative surgery. Perform-ing ovariotomies and other gynecological surgeries was a lucrative business.[15] When Mitchell returned to Philadelphia, he did extensive experimentation on animals for almost a decade, performed operations, and worked as a contract surgeon during the Civil War. Such diverse and prolonged experiences would provide a high level of skill. However, before the age of thirty Mitchell switched from surgery to general medicine, writing that although his father was "very anxious" that he become a surgeon and he had trained for it in Paris, he had "neither the nerve nor the hand which was needed in those days for these oper-ations. At last, I deliberately gave it up and turned my attention to general med-icine much to my father's disappointment."[16]

One early biographer concluded that Mitchell's slight tremor and nervous temperament led to a lack of precise muscular control and thus the decision to abandon surgery.[17] Richard Walter is right to question this conclusion, stating that Mitchell's handwriting at the time was compatible with the performance of finely skilled motor movements, and that the idea that his "'nervous tem-perament' led to a lack of precise muscular control is most improbable."[18] Most convincingly, Elan D. Louis, after analyzing Mitchell's handwriting and tracing the onset and development of his tremor, concludes that at the time Mitchell made the decision to pursue general medicine rather than surgery, his handwriting reveals no indication of tremor. The tremor began in Mitchell's early forties, but even at the age of fifty, his tremor would still be considered mild. By the time of his death, however, his handwriting had been "reduced to a tremulous scrawl."[19]

While it may not be possible to determine the exact reasons, at a young age Mitchell decided not to become a surgeon. Although he still performed surgeries, when the time came to treat nervous disease after the Civil War, he made use of physiology and neurology instead. No evidence supports the accusation that he frequently performed gynecological surgery.[20] Rather, more than once he warned against such surgery, writing, "I know of many, far too many, cases where physicians have advised and women have consented to the removal of ovaries under these conditions [melancholia], and where no relief has come about in consequence of the operation."[21] Distancing himself from this lucrative but questionable procedure, he preferred the more conservative treatment of rest, massage, and a high-caloric diet. The contentious debate about widespread use of ovariotomy provides an illuminating context in which to consider Mitchell's decision not to become a surgeon, his creation of the rest cure, and its therapeutic success and limitations. As late as 1897 he was still defending this decision, when he stated that for many cases of hysteria, surgery gained nothing or made the patient worse: "Everywhere throughout this country men and, I fear women, are doing an amount of pelvic surgery which I am free to characterize as reckless."[22]

While still in London, Mitchell also attended a dinner with the doctors James Paget, Richard Quain, and William Carpenter at the house of Dr. William Jenner. Overall, he was not impressed by the appearance, class, or education of the London physicians, even men like Jenner and Paget. Ever loyal to Philadelphia, he told his father that the London medical profession was "not in a very amicable state, and, far more like what it is in New York than with us. One reason for it, may be that very few of either physicians or surgeons are of more than barely respectable birth. Taking them as a whole they are a vulgar looking set but especially the purely scientific men, like Carpenter, Bowman, Paget, etc who having no patients are not brought into contact with wealth and rank."[23] Regardless of their demands and insolence, treating wealthy patients refined the physician's character and modified the vulgarity of low birth. On the other hand, contact with poor patients made some physicians rude, careless, and ill-tempered.[24] General practitioners or practicing apothecaries who treated minor illness were even worse than the scientific men. They were not well educated, and Mitchell heard that they were often "culpably ignorant." Only London required a special examination to practice medicine. The profession was much more unregulated outside the city. Scottish diplomas were obtained with little or no trouble and allowed one to practice anywhere except in London.

Before leaving London, Mitchell spent an afternoon at the Hunter Museum, where Paget was the curator. There he saw the beautiful preparations of Hunter, Cooper, and Owen. He made a second trip to St. Bartholomew Hospital, where he saw nothing new and witnessed a "most bungling operation" and an amputation. He had been away for six weeks, but his thoughts were still of home. He asked his father about the size of the new class at Jefferson Medical College and asked him to send his introductory lecture and a daily paper now and then. He closed one of the many letters he wrote in November with, "I am waiting most anxiously to hear from you, very sincerely—Your son, W. Tomorrow night will see me in Paris."[25] This letter contains the last trace of any genuine homesickness. Paris—where "nothing in London can bear comparison, for example, with the view from the Madeléine"—would be much more than he expected.[26]

Mitchell spent a night in Dover "rather than miss a look at the cliffs" and crossed the Channel through a "blow which made all sick but me." The night train to Paris arrived just as morning was breaking, and there were "some 50 women cleaning the streets. Women scavengers—Good God—A few moments and I cross a boulevard. Then ring and kick and crack the whip at the porte cochére and at last—I get in. Paris is waking as I turn in, higher than I ever did before—I wake at 12." After café au lait and an omelet, he set off "to seek some atom of life in this world, which I can talk to."[27] He found Mr. and Mrs. Walsh and their daughter, Theresa, at home, and they gave him a warm welcome. He then found his friend Barnet Phillips, who had taken a few days off to help him get settled. Phillips had even kept a room disengaged, but Mitchell wanted to look around. After seeing seven other rooms, he returned to the one Phillips had chosen, located at 47 rue St André des Arts in the Latin Quarter, the area where the other American medical students lived and just a short walk to the École de Médicine. It was a large and comfortable room with two tall windows, three mirrors of different shapes, armchairs, a lounge with cushions, and a table, bureau, and washstand. The bed stood in a recessed area that included folding doors, so it could be shut off to make the main room into a parlor.

After shopping for wood, coal, and candles and locating a washerwoman, Mitchell fell into a pattern of rising at seven, drinking café au lait, and visiting the hospitals. At eleven he returned to his hotel for a meal of beefsteak *avec pommes de terre*, chops, omelets or cold meats, or all of these at no extra charge. Also, there was fruit and *vin ordinaire* because "no one drank water." Dinner was served at six and consisted of soup, fish, beef or chops, poultry, salad, vegetables, wine, cheese, nuts, and fruit. He always sat with the French boarders, including Charles-Philippe Robin, the histologist. He had a difficult time comprehending the discussions and lectures and began taking French lessons with a teacher "*qui ne parle pas l'anglais.*" He told his mother, "I shall not study much in the evenings, and for a time I shall frequent places where good French is spoken as the theatres etc. My time here looks only too short for the work to be done."[28]

He immediately fell in love—with the gardens, fountains, palaces, the Louvre, the Tuileries, and Notre Dame. He found that the willowy, trim, and petite women with "the neat foot in the neater shoe the—tasteful costume, and the modest down looking eyes, which fall before a look, lend charms to which England can lay no claim." Seeing all this, "you begin to love Paris with all the love which enthusiastic admiration can inspire." He had thought the English women ugly, and "it was like going from—Brobdingnag to Lilliput if one looks at feet and hands only—Nothing can be more charming than to see the young girls of the better classes in the street." Still, it was more than the girls and young women that attracted him. He loved what he called the "classic soil" of Paris. His favorite café was the same that Voltaire and Rousseau had frequented. Walking in the morning, sporting a scarlet fez cap with a blue silk tassel, he noted the clack clack of the sabots, the "queer cries" of the street merchants, the bakers with their four-feet-long loaves of bread, and the troops—the artillery, infantry, and cavalry—in red pants and dark jackets. Paris was a city where "every turn brings one to something new and pleasant—Often I stop to watch the Jugglers, and funny fellows, who collect crowds at the corners, and perform wonderful tricks. At night it is even as beautiful this great city. . . . The view from the bridges is exquisite at night—You can see thousands on thousands of lights, and the whole river looks barred with great long golden tracks of light—while you can hear from afar the sweet sad chimes of the many churches."[29] The passionate delight of these letters, so different from the letters written in England, reveals how much Paris nourished his romantic and aesthetic sensibilities. The city provided a rich and stimulating environment, and like never before, he was alive to the excitement and good fortune of being privileged and young.

Mitchell enjoyed the cafés and the theater, and at the same time he pursued his studies aggressively, attending eye clinics and courses in auscultation, microscopy, and pathology. It is sometimes said that he studied with Claude Bernard. Actually, although Bernard would become his hero and guide, when he went to hear him lecture, Mitchell was "greatly edified by hearing a lecture an hour long, scarce a word of which could I comprehend."[30] As his proficiency in French improved, he went to a clinic on diagnosis and operative surgery, watched innovative cataract surgery, and gained experience with the catheter. He remarked to his father, "I have seen Ether used once in labour by Dubois but he was afraid of it."[31] Regarding the private courses, he wrote:

> It is a little surprising that these private courses are forbidden strictly, and yet take place by dozens—. My course on operative surgery is with Velpeaus Interne in the dead room of La Charité—Now we dare not touch the unclaimed subjects (strange to say) except to make post mortems since all these belong of right to the dissecting rooms—of the schools. Those bodies which are claimed are allowed to remain long enough for examination, and then placed in coffins and given to their friends for whose benefit a piece is sawed off of the lid of the coffin to correspond with the face. Being thus recognized the lid is nailed up and the body is buried—almost immediately the funeral starting generally from the hospital—We make good use of the interval and commonly leave little save the head intact.[32]

With a portion of Alexander Henry's gift, Mitchell ordered an expensive microscope and set about examining and drawing specimens. Although microscopes had been around since the seventeenth century, technical improvements early in the nineteenth century should have moved them from the periphery to the center of research. Yet, despite its importance to histology and pathology, the microscope remained an unfamiliar instrument. "Joseph Lister would have been an unusual medical student in the 1850s in owning his own," according to W. F. Bynum, "and fewer still would have kept them after qualifying."[33] Microscopes were especially slow to cross the Atlantic. Even as late as the 1880s, there were just a few in use in U.S. hospitals. Harvey Cushing wrote that it is "difficult, to-day, to realize that up to this time [1887], far from there being a laboratory, there was no microscope, except Osler's, in use in the University [of Pennsylvania] Hospital. To be sure, Dr. Fussell, a classmate of Dock's, had been taught to make microscopic examinations of sputum, but up to this time clinical microscopy in the hospital may be regarded as a thing unknown."[34] Mitchell's decision to purchase an especially fine instrument in 1850 was cutting-edge, underscoring both his growing interest in experimental medicine and his farsightedness.

The critical tone of the London letters was gone. The correspondence makes it clear that while Mitchell was engaged in the medical work, he was even more at home in the Parisian atmosphere of beauty and exploration. At last he was on his own, and he had a great deal to learn about many things. It did not take him long to realize that a few years of lectures at Jefferson Medical College fell far short of the French system of medical training.

Parisian medicine was completely reformed after the French Revolution. Two divisions were created: the university division focusing on theory, and the hospital division focusing on clinical medicine. The trademarks of the Parisian system were innovations in clinical and anatomical correlation and a tradition of bedside teaching.[35] With Mitchell's medical education at Jefferson Medical College in mind, a brief look at the French system in general and Jean-Martin Charcot in particular reveals just how basic the American system was by comparison. Although Mitchell and Charcot met only once or twice in the early 1870s, they had much in common and influenced each other's research.[36]

Charcot had entered the Paris Medical School in 1843, five years before Mitchell entered Jefferson Medical College. When Mitchell arrived in Paris, however, Charcot was still in medical school. At the university, first-year students focused on natural history, physiology, and pharmacology, and second-year students focused on anatomy and physiology. Pathology was the focus during the third year, and hygiene, therapeutics, and forensic medicine were the focus in the fourth year. The curriculum included a heavy emphasis on anatomy and dissection, and the École Practique, the site of dissection, was located directly across the street from the medical school. In 1848 an American student, A. K. Gardner, described it as "a shocking spectacle to an unprofessional observer," where four thousand subjects of all colors, ages, and conditions are annually used for anatomical purposes. Each day at twelve o'clock the bodies are distributed and by "perambulating the several buildings, the various parts of the human organism, the nerves, muscles and blood-vessels may be easily examined, and studied. Here, the assiduous student may be seen, with his soiled blouse, and his head bedecked with a fantastic cap. In one hand he holds a scalpel, in the other a treatise on anatomy. He carries in his mouth a cigar, whose intoxicating fumes so hurtful on most occasions render him insensible to the smell of twenty bodies, decomposing, putrefying around him."[37] Running parallel to the official system was a second curriculum consisting of the private courses and tutorials that Mitchell mentioned in his letters. Before 1862 all specialty teaching was done through these private courses, requiring extra fees. As Mitchell told his father, they took place by the dozens. In 1853, for example, the number of such private courses had reached one hundred.[38]

After completing the fourth year, the Parisian medical student took five examinations, defended a thesis, and was awarded a diploma for *docteur en médecine*. Still, many wanted to continue, and the hospital provided a complicated system to select externs and interns, fill postgraduate positions to run the clinical services, and eventually, in an intensely competitive system, select hospital faculty. While the group of externs was large, the selection of interns was more exclusive. The fortunate few who were selected did four one-year rotations at different hospitals and were provided a small stipend and room and board in the hospitals. They had the opportunity to visit patients each morning with a staff physician. Charcot became an extern in 1846, an intern in 1848, and did his final internship year at the Salpêtrière in 1852.[39] He became an associate professor in 1860. In 1862 he returned to the Salpêtrière, never to leave, and in 1872 he was appointed professor of pathologic anatomy. Ten years later the Paris medical faculty created a chair especially for him, professor of diseases of the nervous system. While Mitchell and Charcot both won international reputations as world specialists in nervous disease, it is clear that they did so in distinctly different ways. Although Charcot experienced some setbacks, he always worked within the French system, and step-by-step he became the first European professor of clinical neurology. In contrast, Mitchell worked largely outside any system. Various rejections and sociohistorical events forced him to create his own clinical opportunities.

In Paris, totally immersed in his new life, Mitchell complained to his mother about the whole business of letters of introduction. For starters, every time he had to pay a visit, he had to walk some two miles. He wrote, "Imagine therefore what a bore it is to be asked to dine—, to call, and so end it. Item kid gloves 30–62 cts, à discretion. Item a card; value unknown—Item a dinner; Item its consequence; a headache,—Item—Bored to Death! *Cost* of a letter of Introduction $1.24—I wish mine all in the fire; but I will go on delivering them like a postman until my patience gives out or my legs fail me."[40] Initially, he had been in the habit of dining with the Walshes on Sunday evenings, but after a time he began to dine with William Pearce and Robin every Sunday at the Café Magny. He especially enjoyed Robin, an uninhibited and daring bachelor who always ate and drank for three. He had only one eye, and in class when asked why he told students to use their two eyes but he only used one, he responded by gouging out his glass eye. On one occasion Mitchell and Robin went to a dinner party with "half a dozen men and two females." At about 11:00 p.m. a game of cards was proposed. Robin had only twenty francs, but he had been drinking champagne and insisted on playing. Mitchell wrote that he chose not to play but stayed to watch until 6:00 a.m. The card game went on all the next day, finally ending that evening. When it was all over, Robin, who lived on "some inconceivably small sum made by teaching," had won about eight thousand francs. He invited his friends to celebrate at the Café Anglais, where Mitchell taught the headwaiter how to make tomato salad.[41]

With Pearce, "one of the best of fellows," Mitchell attended a masked ball at the Grand Opera, and he wrote home that there "never was such a jam," with masked women and costumed men who were not allowed to mask. "On, on we elbow along—women of every class save the best. Men of the best, down to any man who can raise ten francs." Pushing, poking, making fun, where it is possible to speak to every woman, but "above all don't lose your temper." "Madam will you do me the honour to move. Am I in your way? Yes!—Well so much the better, Monsieur bete Anglais—A laugh, and on again." A thousand forms are flying around, "bowing, and waving to delicious music—A thousand glowing costumes. Tis like the wind on a bed of nodding flashing tulips. I look again. They dance the 'cancan.' Fast. faster—Imagine the dance of witches in Tom O'Shanter. Imagine, I want adjectives." At 4:00 a.m. Mitchell and Pearce left the ball and went to a café with many of the others who ate and drank, some heavily, and one fell "asleep with his chin on a tumbler—They covered him up with napkins, poured wine down his neck, blacked his face, and then sang or roared—a song—around him. . . . So you see what one of these famous balls consists of."[42] Even though Mitchell's letters describing his social life were not addressed to his father, John Mitchell read all his letters. It is unlikely that he found such stories entirely amusing. And when, after a month, Mitchell made his desire to remain abroad explicit, asking that his request receive fair and thoughtful consideration and not be misunderstood, the long detailed letters describing the balls and card games could not have helped his cause.

One morning at the great state hospital the Hôtel-Dieu, Mitchell followed Auguste Chomel on his rounds. He was discussing smallpox with a case before him in the pustular stage, and he asked Mitchell to examine the patient. Fifteen days later Mitchell came down with the disease, was in bed for two weeks, and spent another week convalescing. He also caught an eye infection and was leeched twice. Because he was very ill, his neighbors Pearce and Phillips slept alternate nights in his room, nursing him and performing "every menial office." After his friend Bache had a new pillow made for him, Mitchell wrote, "Never Again Talk to me of men being selfish." Theresa Walsh paid him a visit, and every morning Mr. Walsh walked the two miles to inquire about his health. Slowly he began to recover without any scarring, but he continued to experience indigestion and weakness that combined to "deprive me even of the privilege of walking the hospital wards, as I become wearied almost at once," as he explained to his father. "But happily, Paris is full of diversions of just the right sort for a languid convalescent. I stroll to the Luxembourg and study the pictures of modern French artists or—loiter away delightful hours in the grand old Louvre." To his brothers he wrote, "I had such a crooked dismal swamp of a X-mas that I think I ought to have another all to myself. I got two presents on X-mas morning—one was a dose of salts, and the other a box of pills. I thanked kriss kringle and swallowed the insult."[43]

The illness consumed almost a month of an already too short stay, and Mitchell felt that his time was running out. In February he asked Elizabeth to remain in Liverpool until May: "For me, the little I have done here is childs play—I have learned next to nothing—I feel unsettled and instead of a year of fair work which could show results what have I to exhibit?" He asked her to say nothing against his plan: "If you say ought, aid it and not oppose it, dear Sister however much it may hurt your inclination." He repeated his wish to his father to remain abroad, explaining the new plan. He would still travel with Elizabeth, but then she would return to Philadelphia, and he would return to Paris until November. Because of two gaps in Parisian instruction in the diseases of women and pathology, he would then travel to Vienna to study. With such good reasons to stay, he pleaded with his father, "I have learned something, in some branches I hope much—but I have not learned as much as I expected."[44] But Mitchell's father did not change his mind.

It was not the additional expense to which John Mitchell objected. Rather, as he had explained in an earlier letter, he wished to see his son "at regular work as early as possible, that you may be firmly fastened in business before I may be removed, or otherwise incapacitated for your use.—I also believe that a year's absence is almost too long for safe business habits."[45] John Mitchell had already experienced one serious bout with illness and he worried about another. In his mind, his son's year abroad had already put his family at some risk. Throughout the establishment of his career and large family, John Mitchell failed to acquire any substantial savings or investments. His "precious son" was his investment in the future, and everyone in the family knew and expected that if something happened to the father, Weir would assume the full responsibility to support his mother, Elizabeth, and the four children who remained at home. He must return to Philadelphia as originally planned.

On the other side of the Channel, Elizabeth was still unhappy and most anxious to join her brother. In a letter to her father, she wrote that the people in Liverpool were just as he had described them: "They seem to me to look upon Americans as their inferiors intellectually, to which of course I will not accede and show fight."[46] Elizabeth may indeed have asserted her own ideas and showed a little "fight," and when Saidie and her friends told her that her manners were "very French" and her accent "somewhat Irish," they were criticizing her. Left to herself much of the time, she had no sense that she was wanted at her sister's house, and without other invitations, the depressing days and months dragged on. Writing in her letters that they thought of her as "ugly and disagreeable," she was impatient to leave and burst out, "Would to God I had the gift of beauty that I might at least please and not weary everyone with my presence."[47]

The reasons why Elizabeth was unwanted at her sister's house are not clear. Even as a young girl, Elizabeth was remarkable for her memory and wit. Mitchell wrote that his sister was never "seriously near to marriage, despite many chances, for her personality was very attractive and her talk always brilliant. Even when young, she was an unusual person." Saidie later recollected that Elizabeth always seemed so much an "elder and graver person, not in the least beautiful, but with fine gray eyes and a small sensitive mouth and tiny hands and feet." What is clear is that at times Elizabeth's father and brother disapproved of her behavior, calling her obstinate and emotional and sometimes threatening to withdraw their affection. She was expected to comply with the conventions of being a single woman and devote her life to others, if not as wife and mother, then as a caretaker. Mitchell wrote that "as a young person, she was sensitive, imagined slights or neglect, and was of a perilous temper and at times immensely obstinate." He also noted her "rapid skill in repartee which, like a sharp weapon, tempted her to use it too freely."[48]

Elizabeth was intelligent, articulate, and well-read, and given another setting, things might have turned out differently for her. Although not easy, it was not impossible at this time for women to exist independently. Early in 1851, for example—at the very time Elizabeth was stuck in Liverpool—just two hundred miles away, Mary Ann Evans left her Coventry home for London to associate with the likes of Herbert Spencer, Harriet Martineau, and George Henry Lewes. Evans was another young woman who had an overbearing father and brother, loved books, and was not pretty. But when her father died, he left her just enough to live independently. In London among progressives and free thinkers, she began her transformation into George Eliot, the great Victorian novelist. Mitchell often commented on his sister's wit, keen power of analysis, remarkable memory, and brilliant conversation, but the evidence does not suggest that he ever thought of her as someone who could write essays or novels—like some women were doing at the time—or that he ever encouraged her to do so.

There is slight information about Elizabeth; for the most part, she remains hidden and elusive. Rather than photographs, what remains are the many crisscrossed letters that aptly symbolize her problems with voice and identity. But there is a character in one of Mitchell's novels that is "a deliberately careful portrait of my sister Elizabeth in later days—often the words are hers."[49] Through this character one gets to know Elizabeth a little better, and it also suggests what might have gone wrong at Saidie's house in Liverpool.

In *When All the Woods Are Green*, Anne Lyndsay has delicate features, and her mouth and large gray eyes are her only beauties. In her relationship with her sister-in-law, Margaret, there is tension, irritation, and some rudeness. Margaret has established her identity by adopting an attitude of moral superiority. Intimidated by Anne's strong voice and wit, she represents her as an oddity to the rest of the family. From Margaret's conventional point of view, there is something questionable and inappropriate about Anne. Her provocative comments interrupt the even flow of conversation, and she is a bad influence on the children. The novel's narrator (sounding much like Mitchell) is ambivalent, displaying both affection and displeasure and commenting that Anne never learned "the power to restrain her fatal incisiveness of speech. She could hurt herself with it as well as annoy others, as she well knew."[50]

The Lyndsays are on holiday, camping in the wilds of northern Canada. Margaret insists that on Sundays there be no fishing and no novel reading. When one of the boys complains that it makes for a dull day, Anne agrees, saying, "I confess to a certain amount of sympathy with the unemployed. It is a Sabbath lockout." When Anne remarks that she loathes a certain man, Margaret reacts with emphasis:"He is a clergyman.""That only makes it worse," Anne responds. "I have heard him preach. Don't you think a man who has no humor must be a bad man?" Books are Anne's constant companions. She "devoured books, and digested them also, with the aid of a rather too habitual acidity of criticism; but what was in them she never forgot." She is even particular about how she arranges them, stating, "When I come home and find Swinburne in among the volumes of Jeremy Taylor, and Darwin sandwiched between Addison and the 'Religio Medici,' I get frantic and say things." When they are discussing the last book they would read before dying, Margaret believes there can be only one answer, the Bible. Anne responds, "Oh, that is not one book. Why call it a book? It is the books of many men."[51] But in Mitchell's novel Anne is no radical: she makes sacrifices, stays close to home, and attempts to be useful. This is the particular lesson that Elizabeth had to learn at Saidie's house in Liverpool.

When Elizabeth was fifteen her father wrote, "Present my thanks to Mr Kummer for his kind letter. If you could see, my dear Lizzy, how much pleasure his favourable report of you gave us both, you would strive every day more and more to deserve it. To do well is all the return you can make to us for the years of anxiety expense and trouble you have cost us." Although intelligent, spirited, and articulate, Elizabeth was threatened by the loss of her family's love and support, and she eventually bent her will in submission to their demands. Without money or beauty, she came to realize and accept her dependence on them and fulfill their expectations regarding her purpose and duty. In an April letter that Mitchell wrote to his father, just after the word "sister," a section is neatly excised. After the excision, Mitchell continues, "I shall have been engaged at my studies only Dec—Jan. feb, march—and April since she will reach this about May—January I lost through sickness so that after all I shall not have had a very long time. Sisters arrival will of necessity suspend my studies in a great measure. Do not think me ungrateful, but I only wish to keep you from being disappointed with me when I return." But Mitchell's plea to delay Elizabeth's arrival was not successful. After six months in Liverpool, she was allowed to travel to Paris. Mitchell wrote his father, "You wonder that I have not sooner brought Sister to Paris, and you seem to suspect me of being unwilling to receive her, and of thinking her in my way—what led you to this belief—I can not imagine." In closing the letter he wrote, "I believe however that you will find Sister much improved. She made a sacrifice of self to duty, this last winter which has reacted on her self with good effect."[52]

Around June 1, Mitchell and Elizabeth left Paris for three months of travel in France, Italy, Switzerland, and Germany. After just a week they met Christopher Johnston, a high-spirited young man from Baltimore. The three decided to travel together, and Mitchell wrote home that Johnston was a "good backer in a quarrel—and yet not prone to such." But even the incidents described in the letters home suggest that both Mitchell and Johnston were happy to quarrel and thoroughly enjoyed a good scrape and a dangerous situation. From Rome Mitchell told his father, "We resist impositions stoutly and take no impudence, besides speaking our minds pretty freely."[53]

On one occasion the three travelers stepped out of a stagecoach while the horses were being changed. Mitchell wrote, "The driver, a surly German immediately whipped up his seven horses and started off. This was a little too much . . . a piece of impudence and rather unprecedented. I flew at the horses and seized the off shaft horse, endeavouring to stop the team while the brute whipped them furiously—They dragged me some twenty paces." Johnston scaled the box and "had the coachee by the collar, and was about to strike as he knows how," when Mitchell stopped him. The coach stopped; the three passengers got back in "quietly—our antagonist looking very silly—and not at all enjoying the laughter of some swiss officers who saw the scene."[54]

In Naples when the Procession of the Host was paraded in front of the palace and "every soul in the street knelt," including King Bomba, Johnston "very nearly got himself into trouble by refusing to kneel. I of course did kneel." A few days later there was an incident that Mitchell described as both "unpleasant" and "amusing." A cabriolet driver urgently pursued them for a fare, and at last Johnston said "something rather rough" to which the driver replied "with a brief phrase not possible to repeat, and Johnston, who was hot headed . . .

jumped in behind and seized the man . . . by the back of the neck and jerked him over backwards and hammered him savagely for a half minute, until the frightened horse was stopped by the police." The Naples police took Johnston and Mitchell to the palace guardroom, where they were retained for many hours. Eventually, after a letter was sent to the American minister, they were released with "a very distinct warning from the police and our minister, that we had better leave Naples, since the man who had been so savagely beaten would be sure to stick a stiletto into the back of one of us on the first occasion." But they chose not to leave. A few days later there was a third incident in Naples, which Mitchell described as "another uncomfortable illustration of the nature of the country." When bargaining for boats to Capri, two men took hold of Elizabeth to lift her into their boat. Mitchell did not speak Italian, and after failing to persuade them in English and French, he struck one of the men, who fell backward into the bay. And so they were again warned to leave. Despite two warnings in three days, they remained in Naples. Mitchell wrote that this was "at a time when adventure was still possible and interesting things chanced which now would never be met with."[55]

Mitchell, Elizabeth, and Johnston traveled together through June, July, and half of August. Their most remarkable adventure, another essential ingredient for a successful grand tour, was the day they spent in the French Alps. Many writers and poets have attempted to capture the sublimity of this experience, and in one of his last letters home, Mitchell attempted to express his own delight in the thrill and danger of the climb and the awe-inspiring scenic beauty.

At Chamouni, in a valley 3,400 feet above sea level, with Mont Blanc just to the south, the three travelers set out with the guides and mules at 5:00 a.m. At 7:30 they rested at the large lake of ice called the Mer de Glace. Securing cognac, ham, cheese, and bread, they set out again, crawling at times with "elastic limbs and chests inflated with the exhilarating air of the ice bound mountains." Tracking upward, they leaped over small crevices; if wide they searched for a bridge of ice, sometimes walking half a mile to get across a crevice twelve feet across. Here they saw a *moulin* no more than twelve feet wide but three hundred feet deep and formed by streaming water: the "roar was awful the scene perfectly unique— So odd to see a great brook bounding with a roar into a hole and disappearing— like the damned in groans and darkness." After "a kind of walking fearfully fatiguing," they reached the base of Montanvert at noon and witnessed "dome like elevations all covered with snow or—ragged peaks of startling size shooting up out of the eternal snows."

Resting again to prepare for their final ascent, they found the path hugging the mountain in half-moon zigzags, and at moments "every muscle was strained to climb some mighty boulder. Now we hung poised on a path two inches wide and gazing downwards at the mighty sea of ice below." At last they gained the edge of the Jardin. Mitchell, with a whoop of joy:

> rushed up the green turfed bank and threw myself full length on the grass beside a superb spring which here gushes out from the mountain. Next I seized the cognac flask . . . and after one long draught sunk back—decidedly better. In a few moments Jn and Sis reached me— . . . seizing our bag of provender we munched away at cheese sandwiches and while the cognac played also a fair role—everything tasted delicious and the brandy seemed such nectar as I can never hope to taste again. . . . Around us and above lay a superb green turf happily called the garden and all gay with flowers of such ethereal hues as are seen only here near the sun and among the snows—. . . . No life was in sight—we alone were the only atoms of thought and motion in this awful scene so still so lovely.

The descent provided its own kind of intoxicating danger. At one point Johnston flew past while dislodging stones and snow, finally seizing a ledge and checking his wild tumble. Mitchell concluded, "Thus ended the most terrific feat I have ever undertaken. How Sis stood it I know *not* since J. and I were wearied soul and body to such state that sleep was impossible."[56] The next day they left for Geneva, visited Cologne, then traveled in Germany on the Rhine, visited Aix la Chapelle (Aachen), and parted with Johnston, who was off to study in Vienna.

In Paris letters were waiting. Their father had been ill again, and this news increased Mitchell's anxiety and unhappiness about going home. Arriving in England, he was only reminded of how much he had enjoyed Europe, especially Paris—the Latin Quarter, his friends, the food, the nightlife, and its experimental and expansive atmosphere. As far as his medical education was concerned, while he had learned a little, it was just a little. So much remained to study and know. He was returning to Philadelphia as a young man who, ready or not, was expected to share his father's large medical practice and, in the event that something happened to his father, assume complete financial and emotional responsibility for a large family.

3

THE YOUNG PHYSIOLOGIST

In 1851, when Mitchell returned to the United States, there was little pressure, support, or pay for physicians to do research. It was not expected or rewarded. Therefore, until late in the nineteenth century with only a few exceptions (such as William Beaumont's experiments on human digestion and the discovery of anesthesia), Americans made few contributions to medical knowledge. Mitchell wrote that in the days of Robley Dunglison and Samuel Jackson, a physiological lecture was "a more or less well stated resumé of the best foreign books, without experiments or striking illustrations. It was like hearing about a foreign land into which we were forbidden to enter."[1] Sitting on hard wooden benches in a large lecture hall required a great deal of imagination in order to comprehend the active functions of living organisms. Even decades later, there were fewer than a dozen full-time physiology professors in American medical schools.[2]

Mitchell, recalling the first time he saw the living, moving heart of an etherized animal, wrote that "the swift certainty of the successive motions of this bounding thing . . . filled me at once with a fresh conception of the delicacy and wonder of the vital mechanism amidst which I had been moving, so to speak with but the slightest realization of its marvel and mystery."[3] After his time in Paris, experimental medicine was what Mitchell wanted to do, and it would become his great adventure. Pushing aside the warnings and risks, he did everything in his power to engage in the process of making medicine scientific. Out of step with his practical colleagues who focused on patients, gave limited time to lecturing, and were doubtful and even suspicious of research, Mitchell, at the age of twenty-two, began to spend afternoons, evenings, and summers in the laboratory. This early experimentation prepared him well to successfully engage in a major research project and publication, which in turn became the launching pad for his career.

Not everything went smoothly during these years, however. In fact, when Mitchell applied for an internship at Pennsylvania Hospital and was rejected, it was the first of many he would experience. Due in part to bad feelings between his father and members of the board, his failure to gain admission was Mitchell's first taste of the way social pressures and politics would determine the course of his career. Instead of becoming a resident, he obtained a position as a physician to the poor at the Southward Dispensary.[4] Within a year, he began to lecture in physiology at the Philadelphia Association for Medical Instruction, also known as at the Summer Association, and he established a laboratory in the Philadelphia School of Anatomy building. With the use of his new microscope, chemical analysis, and vivisection—as well as the help of other Jefferson graduates, including Jacob Da Costa, George Morehouse, and John Brinton and their students— he began a series of experiments.[5] Only through such grit and conviction would American medicine advance beyond the widespread and often debilitating practices of heroic medicine that included cupping, blistering, purging, and bleeding.

In his historical novel *The Red City*, Mitchell addressed heroic medicine through his representation of the great bleeder Benjamin Rush. The novel is set in Philadelphia during Washington's second administration and contains a detailed section on the 1793 yellow fever epidemic. Benjamin Rush believed that massive bloodletting and large doses of mercury cured yellow fever. Making frequent appearances in the novel, Rush always profusely bleeds his patients. Arriving to examine one patient, he states, "I must bleed him at once. Calomel and blood-letting are the only safety, sir. I bled Dr. Griffith seventy-five ounces to-day. He will get well." The patient, who is also the novel's wisest character, fights with Rush and tears the bandage from his arm, shouting, "Take away that horse leech. He will kill me." The narrator comments, "The doctor bled everybody, and over and over." Rush believed that the unifying factor underlying all disease was vascular tension and that bleeding was the way to relieve it. In addition, he understood the body to contain about twice as much blood as it actually did. He often bled patients until 80 percent of the body's blood was removed (and trained others to do likewise). When colleagues pleaded with him for milder kinds of treatment, he was obstinate, and "for those who disputed his views of practice he had only the most virulent abuse."[6]

According to the medical historian John Duffy, Rush generally had little interest in pathology and research. He was convinced that massive purging was the cure for all disease, and "over considerable opposition, his views carried the day. Rush's success in promulgating his thesis meant that for years to come . . . massive purging and bloodletting were to characterize American medical practice."[7] Rush was the only physician to sign the Declaration of Independence. His success as a doctor was due to a number of factors unrelated to his skill, including his political activism and role in the American Revolution. Both Mitchell in his novel and Duffy in his medical history are careful to respectfully point out Rush's importance—Duffy noting that by 1800 he was considered the greatest physician in America. Both also note the great misfortune of his immense and enduring medical influence.

Rush's heroic treatment would dominate American medicine for fifty years, until finally by the 1840s things began to change. Bloodletting was on the wane and calomel had lost its role as the "Sampson of Materia Medica."[8] Physicians with better information were engaged in more cautious and moderate treatment. Although there was a wide gap between Rush's heroic therapy and this new moderation and belief in natural healing, there was just as wide a gap between these two approaches and Mitchell's preference for a scientific understanding of physiological function and illness. Mitchell was in Paris for only six months (from November 23, 1850, to June 1, 1851), and he lost almost a month to illness, but the time was critical in shaping his point of view regarding the importance of experimental medicine.

Claude Bernard's famous question—"Why think, when you can experiment?"—aptly symbolizes this transitional period in nineteenth-century medicine. When Mitchell described Bernard's philosophy and methodology in his 1857 review of *Leçons de physiologie expérimentale*, he was describing his own as well. Bernard's kind of research and experimentation was what he had been doing since his return from Paris. He wrote, "Certainly a more remarkable union of the inductive and experimental powers has rarely been met with in the same mind," noting that in Bernard's approach, "the very disappointments which so often wait upon experimental inquiries, become the starting-points of new researches." Traditional practitioners often scorned those interested in research and experimentation, but Mitchell preferred Bernard's flexibility and frankness to the traditional dogmatism. Bernard "invites us to the closest psychological intimacy, so that we see, as we follow him, how he came to think of this or that point . . . how it failed . . . and how then he varied the conditions, and began anew.

Such a method of relation and teaching may be unfitted for the ordinary learner, but for the physician, it gives to the story of a scientific research, the variety and fascination of a voyage of adventure." Mitchell noted the poor yield of attempting to discover the function of an organ by mere inspection of its anatomical arrangements: it is "rare that mere structural study of dead tissues, however aided by the lens, will enable us to assign to any given organ a certain function." In defending the necessity of vivisection, he wrote that if "we are to study successfully the workshops and factories of the body, we must study them while active and alive. . . . As it deals with life, it demands the aid of vivisection at every step. The knife of the operator lays bare the living, active organ, and enables us . . . to carry the torch of analytic chemistry into the midst of an organism still throbbing with vitality."[9]

In concluding the review, Mitchell openly acknowledged the controversy surrounding vivisection. First, in terms of moral objections, he hoped that animals possessed a lower grade of nerve organization, releasing them from the intensity of suffering that humans would experience while undergoing similar operations. Referring to Bernard's occasional use of chloroform, he noted that it might have been used more often since in most cases it was advantageous. Second, some professionals opposed vivisection due to its susceptibility to error, but this particular objection applied to all research, and the better the means, as was the case with vivisection, the less the chance of error. Rather than laying aside an improved means, Mitchell saw the real problem in the predispositions and assumptions of the observer, since "we reason upon facts which we have actually assisted to create. The results of vivisection, as of other means of research, may be turned but too easily into the ready channels of our own preconceptions." He argued for diligence in following the hints offered where nature pays out "her secrets miserly, in the hard coin of anguish."[10]

Grasping the extraordinary possibilities of experimental physiology, for twelve years Mitchell rarely left Philadelphia "except for a week in summer. It was my habit to get through my work at three or four o'clock; to leave my servant at home with orders to come for me if I was wanted and then to remain in the laboratory all the evening, sometimes up to one in the morning, a slight meal being brought me at evening from a neighboring inn."[11] The summers spent in the city were hot ones, and he often noted being baked and boiled, with his brain simmering in its case. He experimented with opossums, muskrats, pikes, pigeons, frogs, turtles, dogs, rabbits, ducks, and chickens. This productive period resulted in presentations at the Academy of Natural Science and a number of clinical papers published in such journals as the *American Journal of the Medical Sciences* and *Transactions of the College of Physicians of Philadelphia*.

———————

As a partner in his father's large practice, Mitchell was kept busy during the morning and early afternoon hours seeing patients. His father had never fully recovered from an 1855 stroke, and as the decade progressed, his health worsened. He became much thinner, stopped smoking cigars and drinking wine, and after attacks in 1856 and 1857, spoke with a speech impediment that interfered with his lecturing and public speaking.[12] As his father's health worsened, Mitchell took on more and more responsibility. In a letter to one patient's brother, he wrote that he had used ether in her delivery, "against the advice of one of my friends, the very excellent physician who has previously attended her." She came through it splendidly with little pain, in a shorter period than usual, and without other complications. He explained that "young men like myself, however confident they may be of right judgement, feel so deeply the heavy responsibility of disregarding the dicta of older men that a termination so happy as this one becomes doubly grateful."[13]

In 1856 Mitchell became a fellow of the College of Physicians of Philadelphia. He had been told there was "some bitterness of feeling between the highly successful Jefferson Medical College and the University of Pennsylvania." And because the latter held the largest number of college fellowships, he had been told that he "should get into that body with difficulty. Whether there was any vote against me or not, I do not know, but I remember with a certain awe, the first meetings I attended in the little picture house, as it was called, on Pine St."[14] Mitchell could little imagine that he would give the address on its hundredth anniversary and that for a period of time he would become the college's most important member.

The same year that Mitchell joined the college, he fell in love. He explained to Elizabeth that he had been resolute to visit Mary Middleton Elwyn many times, but work had interfered with his plans. Finally, early one morning with "half a sleep half a wash," he took the first of many two-and-a-half-hour train rides to the lovely Elwyn country home called Reculver, thirty miles west of Philadelphia, near West Chester. Mary's father, Alfred Langdon Elwyn, had graduated from Harvard and received his medical degree from the University of Pennsylvania. He did not practice medicine, however, and was known instead as a philanthropist and author. Both parents welcomed Mitchell warmly, and he and Mary walked for miles that evening with "the moon for a lantern—and *such* a moon." About this walk in the moonlight, he told his sister, "Well, my dear, I came again thereby, and thereafter to that *summum principium* of—human knowledge. Kane—knows it, ask him." In closing the same letter he wrote, "Of course in my way of open chat with you I have many little things to talk about but some how—there is an idea of most damnable publicity about letters."[15] Elizabeth responded immediately to the news, addressing him as "My darling Weir," and writing, "I wish all the time I could be at home with you, for you, dear old boy, are my future. I cannot tell you what you are to me and just now I feel as eager to be with you, I feel as if I could almost fly to you."[16] While Elizabeth always expected her brother to marry, she was now completely dependent on him and did not hesitate to stake a claim for his continued affection and support. Their sister Letitia was engaged, and Elizabeth wrote her best friend, Bessie Kane, "I am glad anyone thinks Tish is doing well. *I* think it the greatest case of, throwing away, that I ever have met with in my life long experience. I cannot yet put on rose couleured spectacles when thinking of it, and see nothing pleasant about it to compensate us for the loss of Tish."[17]

On Sunday, April 4, 1858, John Mitchell died of typhoid pneumonia. Just the previous Sunday he had been in better health than usual. The prominent neurologist William Hammond had dined with the Mitchells, and John had "laughed, chatted, joked and told Scotch stories, appearing to enjoy Dr Hammond's society." Just a few days before that, he had walked seven miles in an afternoon and evening. But on Monday he experienced violent chills and profuse vomiting. After mustard plasters and limewater and brandy, he dressed and paid one visit on Tuesday, but again experienced violent vomiting. When Mitchell examined his father, there was pneumonia on his left side, his pulse was weak, and his eyes were infected. John felt that that his condition was hopeless. What "can you do with a ruined stomach, a weakened nervous system, and a lung scarred by old pneumonia—You would not expect to cure anyone else in such a position— Do not let your hopes—mislead you." On this same day, Mitchell found him "engaged in passing a stomach tube down his own throat—This operation he repeated twice—directing me to hold a feather at the aperture of the tube, that we might observe—whether or not much gas escaped."[18]

On Thursday evening Mitchell and his father, who had asked to see certain medical books, had their last medical talk. They discussed the purposes of pain and how different it would be if patients could describe their illnesses in some detail. Smiling, John remarked that "we should have more autobiographie of disease in our literature." Mitchell wrote that "his brain never acted more clearly. . . . He twice corrected some of us for errors in pronunciation, and— reminded me that he was to have *iced* water, not ice water." He also remarked that he was "glad to escape death by the brain and too the inevitable and bloody war he foresaw between north and south." He died on Easter, and that morning, he kissed his children and made his wife promise that Weir's wedding would not be delayed.[19]

When Alexander, the oldest Mitchell son, died, Weir assumed his position as oldest with reluctance. In contrast, when his father died, he assumed the position of family head without hesitation. While he mourned the loss, he was free of the constant scrutiny. After his return from Europe, he had worked closely with his father and saw more clearly "his wants of character." John Mitchell had lived "very freely, after the Virginian method or want of method," as Mitchell put it, and his "generosity and southern indifference to expenditure fell with heavy burdens in days to come on me and others; of this I do not complain." As suspected, there was no ample estate to support Matilda, the three sons, and Elizabeth. Also, Mitchell and his father had worked as a team, and without his father's authority and fine reputation, Mitchell lost patients and his practice dropped from $2,000 to $1,000 a year.[20]

Although the next few years would prove financially difficult, Mitchell felt invigorated by the challenge. He married in September, six months after his father's death, and Mary was soon pregnant. "From that time on," he wrote, "my practice slowly increased and I was enabled still, at great cost of such labor as few men give, to carry on some of my scientific work." The responsibility of two families, a medical practice, and teaching and research did not drain away Mitchell's energy; rather, he discovered untapped sources of vitality and drive. He was happy in his own developing abilities, writing, "My own morale developed late and brought me a great desire to do right, to help others, and an intense ambition to be at the top."[21] In the same year as his father's death, Mitchell presented nine papers at the Academy of Natural Science on topics such as the blood of the sturgeon, reflex and conscious action, the inhalation of cinchona, and the effect of mucus on urea. The next year he presented six papers, dealing mainly with results from his experimentation on opossums, muskrats, frogs, and fish. In this early work he made some contributions, but they mainly served as an informal internship in physiology that advanced his education and refined his methodology. He was still searching for that special topic that would result in groundbreaking research and publication.

Mitchell and William Hammond had been collaborating on various projects. In one they experimented on frogs, a cat, a large pigeon, and themselves with sassy bark, known as an ordeal poison used by African tribes to prove guilt or innocence.[22] They also experimented with curare, also known as "woorara" and "urari." A vegetable extract used by South American Indians on arrows, curare paralyzed muscles but had no effect on pain. Bernard had been experimenting with it since 1845.

After a trip to the Rocky Mountains, Hammond told Mitchell that he had successfully used Bibron's antidote for rattlesnake venom. After obtaining several rattlesnakes from the Pennsylvania Alleghenies, Mitchell began to test the antidote. Although the results were negative, in the true tradition of Bernard's approach, Mitchell's disappointment became the starting point for new research. He was both surprised by the lack of information about rattlesnakes and fascinated with the composition and production of the venom. "After destroying many animals," he began to realize that he "was working in the dark" and needed definite knowledge about the nature of the venom, the mode of its formation and ejection, and its effects. Later he explained, "The information which I desired was yet to be created. It existed in none of the books, and even so much of it as had been acquired by Fontana with regard to the viper, might not be true of the rattlesnake."[23] Systematically, through long hours in the lab and extensive vivisection, he tested and retested the effects of the venom on numerous animals. This intimate and dangerous relationship with venomous snakes would continue off and on for the next forty years.

In his review of the previous research, Mitchell explained the reasons why such work had been so spotty, including fear, the cost and difficulty of purchase and transportation, the mortality of caged specimens, and the lack of laboratory facilities. But he was determined to overcome these obstacles, writing, "Surrounded by a haze of the strangest popular beliefs, the serpent venom got no fair examination until the researches of Francesco Redi, whose essay, originally in Italian, 1669, is now before me in Latin form, Amsterdam, 1675."[24] Mitchell identified with Redi's determination to replace metaphysical explanations with empirical research. With every decollation and dissection, Mitchell demonstrated his fearless crusade to reverse a tradition of superstition and prejudice through control and scientific progress. With every pigeon, rabbit, cat, and dog that he watched die, he was impressed with the action of the rattlesnake venom, a viscous substance that was pale emerald green, orange, or yellow in color and "seemingly indestructible by time." Mitchell preserved a sample of dried rattle-snake venom for twenty-two years and wrote that it "proved as poisonous as that removed yesterday." Throughout this dangerous work, he frequently employed the words "remarkable," "profound," and "virulent" when referring to the "terrible energies of these poisons."[25]

Mitchell was also impressed with Felix Fontana's "Treatise on the Venom of the Viper," published in 1767. Fontana advocated an inductive approach, writing that "great care should be taken not to confound what we imagine, with what is pointed out to us by observation." In the introduction Fontana stated that he had conducted more than six thousand experiments, had more than four thousand animals bit, employed upward of three thousand vipers, and used pigeons, rabbits, fowls, guinea pigs, cats, dogs, and frogs. Fontana had severed heads and tormented snakes in order to enrage them. For example, he had "removed a considerable portion of the skin from the backs of four vipers, and had them bit by seven others, from which they actually received several blows of the teeth. . . . Again I irritated another viper, by pricking it on the body with a pointed iron, and afterwards made it bite a piece of jagged glass."[26] With Fontana as his guide, Mitchell set out to perform similar experiments. He spent an amazing amount of time in the lab, noting that for almost two years he devoted a portion of each day to his rattlesnakes.

This intense and hazardous work resulted in the publication of *Researches upon the Venom of the Rattlesnake* in 1860, a record of the habits of the *Crotalus* in captivity, the anatomy of the venom apparatus, and the physiology and toxicology of the venom. With the publication of this important research, Mitchell gained an international reputation. In 1886 he would make another major contribution in collaboration with Dr. Edward T. Reichert and publish *Researches upon the Venoms of Poisonous Serpents*. Mitchell and Reichert proved that rather than a single poison, snake venoms possessed tissue-destructive and neurotoxic properties. In addition to these two major studies, Mitchell published approximately fifteen additional articles on snakes, and he is cited often in Laurence M. Klauber's 1956 definitive study *Rattlesnakes: Their Habits, Life Histories, and Influence on Mankind*.

When Mitchell decided to work on venomous snakes, he entered a world saturated with myth and superstition. Snakes, because of their evolutionary success, ancient histories, and mesmerizing effects, infuse any present moment or starting point with past beliefs and attitudes. Harry Greene writes that snakes, with their lidless eyes once dubbed "peepholes into hell," are "natural puzzles, suggestive of things that haunt and inspire us. . . . Snakes are sinuous, supple eroticism exaggerated by paired, intricately ornamented sex organs."[27] In the shape of the uraeus, caduceus, cockatrice, and basilisk and an abundance of other icons on jewelry, pottery, tombs, and temples, the widespread imaginary function of snakes speaks to a seemingly irresistible preoccupation with their tubular, limbless shapes, movement, and powers of enchantment. They slither, burrow, swim, and climb. Looped and coiled with unblinking stares and forked tongues, they possess rattles, facial pits, and hoods and engage in open-mouth threat displays, spitting, hissing, cloacal popping, molting, bluffing, death feigning, and combat dancing.

To a degree, Mitchell was aware of their mesmerizing effects, writing, "Without carefully reviewing this mass of strange opinions and superstitious conceptions, it is not possible to appreciate the service done by Fontana in clearing the ground for modern research and in setting at rest a host of minor absurdities." In order to legitimate himself as a scientist, Mitchell was determined to continue in Fontana's footsteps and unravel "the united web and woof of popular and scientific beliefs as to venomous serpents."[28] Yet, despite his attempt to be objective and to do this research without preconceived ideas, Mitchell was imaginatively and subjectively engaged. His early exposure to Christian myth and British literature had shaped the "ready channels" of his preconceptions, just as he had explained in the Bernard review. Embodying powerful symbolism, snakes are both belly-crawling brutes and creatures of allurement and eroticism. Mitchell's preconceptions affected the way he interacted with the snakes in the lab, and the way he observed and represented them in his writing.

In his 1860 publication *Researches*, as others had done before him, Mitchell employed the conventional language used to name and describe snakes. He referred to the "sheath" of the rattlesnake fang as the "vagina dentis." He referred to the fang as a "singular weapon," writing that the "point of this singular weapon is brittle, but of an exquisite fineness." The fang must be "fully erected" in order for the duct to work properly; moreover, reserve fangs lie one behind and below another in the snake's mouth, each smaller and less developed, but always ready to replace a damaged fang. He wrote that the poison gland is so constructed that it "resembles very strikingly, in section, the appearance of a small testicle." When the blow is given, the "poison is ejaculated," and in snakes that are "perfectly fresh, healthy, and undisturbed for some weeks in summer, the first gush of their venom was sometimes astonishingly large." After the whole process, "the work of an instant," the "serpent's next effort is to disentangle itself from its victim."[29]

Suggesting human sexuality, these descriptions of the snake's venom mechanism are too striking to ignore. Words explicitly associated with sexual organs and sexual intercourse become interchangeable with the anatomy and toxicology of the rattlesnake. The metaphors at play create a sense of penetration, ejaculation, and withdrawal and sustain ideas about the snake's phallic power. Rather than ornamental, metaphor is often the controlling mode of thought. In this case it advances an understanding of the venom apparatus through familiar sexual terms and images tinged with sin, shame, and lust.[30]

Richard Shine writes that unlike many Eastern cultures that worship snakes, Western society has generally shunned the snake. Even naturalists accepted the notion that snakes were "somehow wicked. In the 1700s, Linnaeus wrote of their 'cold body, pale colour, cartilaginous skeleton, filthy skin, fierce aspect, calculating eye, offensive smell, harsh voice, squalid habitation, and terrible venom,' and Francis Buckland wrote in 1858 that 'serpents are the most ungentle and barbarous of creatures.'"[31] Scientific names for rattlesnakes such as *Crotalus horridus*, *Crotalus terrificus*, and *Crotalus lucifer* also illustrate the extent of the fear and negative attitudes. Although a deeply entrenched hostility toward snakes did not originate in scientific discourse, it did find a home there. Researchers like Mitchell would make new discoveries and at the same time perpetuate the old myths, substantiating Fontana's conclusion that "man" is "incapable of attaining the truth, in any other way than of passing through errour."[32]

In a long footnote in the 1860 *Researches*, where Mitchell ostensibly intended to demonstrate the "great tenacity of life on the part of snakes," he wrote:

> Immediately after the head has been cut off, the body writhes slowly along the floor, or, if hung up, returns on itself, twining the pendant trunk around the tail. If, when the body is entirely fresh, we seize the tail, the headless trunk frequently returns on itself, in the effort to strike the offending hand. Occasionally, this movement is so perfectly executed, that the bleeding and headless trunk smites the operator's hand before it can be withdrawn. In one or two instances, persons who were ignorant of the

possibility of this movement, have been so terrified at the blow which has greeted them, as to faint on the spot. To hold thus the headless snake, has been made a test of firmness in some parts of the West; and few have been found composed enough to retain the tail until the innocent, but ghastly stump, struck the hand.[33]

Rather than the tenacity of life on the part of snakes, this scene conveys the profound fear and fascination that humans feel toward them. The rattlesnake's headless body posed no physical danger, but Mitchell clearly marks the stump's symbolic power to create terror, to cause loss of consciousness, and to become a test of firmness and will. In 1889 he returned to this same scene, writing that the "nervous mechanism which controls the act of striking seems to be in the spinal cord, for if we cut off a snake's head and then pinch its tail, the stump of the neck returns and with some accuracy hits the hand of the experimenter— if he has nerve to hold on. Few men have. I have not."[34] Even though it was a stump, a harmless object of reflex motions and no longer a living organism, the scene attests to the power of cultural beliefs and attitudes to control conceptualization and experience.

Throughout his various publications on snakes, Mitchell frequently employed narrative, metaphor, and anthropomorphic description, and at times, especially when writing for popular audiences, he conveyed his admiration and regard for them. In *The Century Magazine* he wrote, "Snakes have always seemed to me averse to striking, and they have been on the whole much maligned. Any cool, quiet person moving slowly and steadily may pick up and handle gently most venomous serpents. I fancy, however, that the vipers and the copperhead are uncertain pets."[35] In the *Atlantic Monthly* he noted the "singular expression" of the rattlesnake and wrote that the "attitude of a large rattlesnake when you come suddenly upon him is certainly one of the finest things to be seen in our forests." The whole posture is "bold and defiant, and expressive of alertness and inborn courage."[36] He described the mutual compatibility of snakes, writing, "I have had, in a single box, from ten to thirty-five snakes, and have never observed the slightest signs of hostility towards one another. Even when several snakes were suddenly dropped upon their fellows, no attempt was made to annoy the newcomers." Because snakes were disinclined to eat in captivity, other animals were often welcome cellmates. The smaller birds "soon became amusingly familiar with the snakes, and were seldom molested, even when caged with six or eight large *Crotali*. The mice—which were similarly situated—lived on terms of easy intimacy with the snakes, sitting on their heads, moving round on their gliding coils, undisturbed, and unconscious of danger."[37]

In addition to this "easy intimacy" between rattlesnakes and other animals, Mitchell noted similar behavior between rattlesnakes and humans. A young friend had taken the active fangs from a rattlesnake, supposing that in doing so he had disarmed the snake for life. He had handled it freely for three months and was not bitten. Mitchell wrote that on "opening the mouth, I pointed out to him the new and efficient teeth which had taken the place of those he had removed." Another story concerned a tavern keeper in Philadelphia who had two large, "perfectly wild" rattlesnakes in a box: "Coming into his bar-room early one morning, he found his little daughter, about six years old, seated beside the open snake-box, with both serpents lying in her lap."[38] In these scenes, the rattlesnakes are touched and handled in a nonthreatening way and respond in a benign manner, contradicting other stories regarding their vicious and combative natures. Mitchell's reading audiences varied, but whether published by the Smithsonian Institute, the *Atlantic Monthly*, or the *New York Medical Journal*, his books and articles convey dramatic and lively impressions of the behavior and emotional life of snakes in some of his most lucid and engaging prose.

———

Still, alongside Mitchell's anthropomorphic descriptions and the clarity, expressiveness, and figurative quality of his writing, stands the reality of the pain and violence of his experimentation. Unlike Fontana, Mitchell did not estimate or chose not to disclose total numbers, but over a forty-year period he also destroyed a great number of animals. In the 1860 *Researches* he cited experiments that involved the death of approximately 150 animals, including 100 pigeons and reed birds and 20 dogs. In addition to the experiments actually cited, Mitchell frequently noted that they were selected from a much greater number.[39] In the first paragraphs of his 1868 article "Experimental Contributions," he noted that this particular investigation involved a large expenditure of birds, dogs, and rabbits. And in the 1886 *Researches*, Mitchell and Reichert stated that in all they used 200 living rattlesnakes, cobras, copperheads, and coral snakes. The largest was a rattlesnake that was over eight feet long and weighed nineteen pounds. Approximately 250 other animals were destroyed in the experiments cited in 1886, mainly pigeons, rabbits, and cats. In the conclusion to chapter 3, the authors noted other experiments, "too numerous for detail." In concluding chapter 6 they wrote that the experiments had been "supplemented by many others" and "frequently repeated."[40]

Previous researchers usually obtained their venom by killing the animal and compressing the gland. Mitchell noted that this was perhaps the best procedure if snakes were abundant and "if the head be cut off rapidly and suddenly, without allowing the snake to bite at any object, and thus exhaust its venom."[41] But snakes were not always available. Early in 1861, for example, Mitchell wrote Jeffries Wyman, "I fear that my snake promises will fail you this year at least— Virginia fails to export even serpents and nowhere else can I be secure of a supply. For the present I have turned to other work."[42] Again, while it is difficult to arrive at a total number or even determine how Mitchell acquired or disposed of the animals, his experimentation involved a great expenditure of snakes, birds, frogs, rabbits, cats, and dogs. According to Susan Lederer, before 1866 "concern about animal welfare was almost exclusively a private matter." Although some states had enacted statutes prohibiting cruelty to animals before the Civil War, there is little evidence that these laws were well-known or enforced.[43] Thus, when Mitchell began his animal experimentation in the 1850s, he was unrestrained by any laws or regulations.

He frequently cut off the heads of rattlesnakes, mentioning decollation at least seven times in the 1860 *Researches.* About one such decollation, he wrote, "The snake's head was next cut off. Placed on a plate, it bit eagerly, but threw out no venom, even when I galvanized the anterior temporal muscle after removing the cuticle."[44] In order to decrease the number of deaths and increase the venom, when the snakes were indisposed to eat, he force-fed them, using milk, flies, grasshoppers, and later raw beef chopped fine that was passed into the belly of the snake through a large glass tube. For force-feeding and extraction of venom, he used the snake loop and invented other special tools and instruments to better manipulate and control their bodies and fluids. On several occasions he tasted the venom, once by design and at other times by accident when engaged in collecting it by sucking it into a pipette. He noted the odors and smells of snakes and was constantly observing and handling them. In dealing with the acute and chronic poisoning caused by the venom in all the animals—the dogs, cats, rabbits, pigeons, and frogs—he was continually confronted with their urine, feces, vomit, blood, mucus, and pus.

Because of their relatively large size, dogs lived longer after being bitten, and when the venom was "long in killing the animal," Mitchell had more time to observe and record the toxicological effects. On one occasion, a white mongrel weighing seventeen pounds was placed in a cage with a large snake and struck twice. The dog "suffered terribly, and during two hours whined and yelled incessantly." On another occasion, a young terrier was lowered into a box containing a fresh snake, and the snake struck twice without effect. When the third blow took effect, "the dog cried out, as though in great pain. Within five minutes he was trembling in every muscle. At the twentieth minute he was so much better that I subjected him to a second bite." Another dog was "bitten by three snakes, so as to be the more profoundly affected . . . the artery was cut across, and the dog allowed to bleed to death." Birds, of course, were much more susceptible to the venom, but there was hardly time to observe the results. Mitchell wrote that so minute "was the quantity required to kill a small bird, such as the reed-bird, that under certain circumstances these little creatures became very delicate tests of the presence or relative activity of the venom."[45]

Anti-vivisectionists strongly objected to allowing animals to die long and painful deaths. However, for many years Mitchell believed that the investigation of the physiological effects of the venom precluded interference or contamination by anesthetics. When Mitchell's brothers were in the army and stationed in places such as Florida, Panama, and Granada, the correspondence reveals that he requested and they shipped turtles, various poisons, and roots to him in Philadelphia.[46] Curare was one of the poisons mentioned. Regarding its use on a frog, Mitchell wrote that this "active agent possesses the power to paralyze the motor nerves, and to leave the muscles in a highly irritable state. The animal was thus placed in the same condition as though the whole motor nervous system had been removed by dissection, without serious injury to the remaining parts." For many years Mitchell believed that curarization was a huge help in his research, but anti-vivisectionists saw it as the worst kind of cruelty. Feelings were especially fierce regarding such experimentation on dogs. Long and painful deaths were a large part of Mitchell's early experimentation, and he conscientiously recorded the details in charts and summaries. The 1860 *Researches* contains a "Table of Symptoms in Eight Rabbits" that records the "duration of life after bite," "early local symptoms and place of wound," "general symptoms," and "mode of death." The time of death ranges from twelve minutes to nine hours.[47]

Generally, anti-vivisectionists believed that the use of sentient creatures for scientific knowledge was barbarous and immoral. Animals existed so that humans might practice sympathy and mercy. Physiologists, however, drifted into materialism and even nihilism. Many anti-vivisectionists feared that the experimentation on animals would lead to human experimentation. Lederer argues that

American opposition to animal experimentation cannot be understood apart from the expectation "that unrestrained experimentation on animals would culminate in the scientific exploitation of vulnerable human beings."[48] Some called for a complete ban on vivisection. Others recommended properly conducted experiments that would include the use of anesthesia, the immediate killing of the animals after the experiment, and the obligatory use of an additional anesthetic with curare.

On the other side of the debate, empirical philosophy fueled the argument in favor of vivisection. Knowledge was gained only through observation and experimentation, and vivisectionists frequently noted the contradiction of those who farmed, fished, hunted, and ate animal flesh and at the same time condemned vivisection. A few even pointed out the hypocrisy of those who attended the anti-vivisectionist meetings in the skins of mammals, exotic furs, and the plumage of birds.[49] Bernard wrote, "It would be strange indeed if we recognized man's right to make use of animals in every walk of life, for domestic service, for food, and then forbade him to make use of them for his own instruction in one of the sciences most useful to humanity."[50] In *The Development of American Physiology*, W. Bruce Fye examines the obstacles faced and contributions made by the four pioneers of experimental medicine—John Call Dalton, S. Weir Mitchell, Henry P. Bowditch, and H. Newell Martin. As one of the first, Mitchell eventually found himself in the spotlight of a fierce vivisection controversy that would last throughout the century.

In contrast to the anti-vivisectionists, many members of the scientific community applauded Mitchell's research. In 1861 the European physiologist Charles-Edouard Brown-Séquard wrote, "I am very happy to see that you do so much for Physiology, and I congratulate you sincerely for the advances this noble science owes to you already. You and your friend and scientific partner, Dr. Hammond, are the most original Physiologists of the United States."[51] In 1866 Dalton presented "Vivisection: What It Is, and What It Has Accomplished" to the New York Academy of Medicine, subsequently published in the *Bulletin of the New York Academy of Medicine*. In a short list that included Mitchell along with Harvey, Boyle, Lavoisier, John Hunter, Beaumont, Bell, and Magendie, Dalton summarized the beneficial results of vivisection. He wrote that Mitchell's publication *Researches* had "no superior in medical literature for the clearness and elegance of its style, the abundance of its material, and the precision of its results." It "would be difficult to find a medical treatise which should illustrate more fully than this the judicious caution and reserve which guide the physiological experimenter, and which enable him to avoid the sources of error that lie in his way."[52] Oliver Wendell Holmes also wrote to Mitchell to say how impressed he was with the number and variety of his experiments that formed such a major contribution to zoological knowledge and animal chemistry. Holmes was a professor of anatomy at Harvard from 1847 to 1882, and during that time he published poems and novels and was best known for his "Breakfast-Table" essays. He had been a friend of Mitchell's father and visited their home when Mitchell was a boy. After John Mitchell died and even before the publication of *Researches*, Holmes had written that "it gives me pleasure to renew my acquaintance with the father in the son, and if at any time I can serve you I shall be most happy to do so."[53]

At the same time that Mitchell was deeply involved in his research on rattlesnakes, Holmes was writing a novel about them. *Elsie Venner* was initially published serially in the *Atlantic Monthly* as "The Professor's Story," the first number appearing in December 1859. In order to give the story some credibility, Holmes had kept a rattlesnake for several weeks to study its movements. He also made use of a number of reports of snake-children, including an 1846 story in the *Boston Medical and Surgical Journal* about a girl with flexible muscles, cold skin, and a low pulse.[54] In Holmes's novel, just before Elsie's birth, a rattlesnake bites her mother, and the venom flowing into Elsie's blood makes her more like the rattlesnakes she often visits than the human beings who sense and fear her cold still eyes, wild beauty, ominous birthmark, and snakelike behavior.

In the novel, however, before telling Elsie's story, Holmes spends an entire chapter on the influence of heredity on character and appearance. As a Harvard professor, he had observed two different types of manhood, describing the first as robust but inelegant, with uncouth or at least common features: a "mouth coarse and unformed,—the eye unsympathetic, even if bright,—the movements of the face are clumsy, like those of the limbs,—the voice is unmusical." This first youth is "the common country-boy, whose race has been bred to bodily labor. . . . The hands and feet by constant use have got more than their share of development,—the organs of thought and expression less than their share." The other type of manhood is slender, with a smooth, often pallid face, regular and delicate features, bright and quick eyes, and lips that "play over the thought he utters as a pianist's fingers dance over their music." This second group of young men comes from the "*Brahmin caste of New England*." American scholars come chiefly from this privileged order, "just as our best fruits come from well-known grafts." The New England aristocracy resulted from the repetition of the same influences generation after generation "which not to recognize is mere stupidity."[55]

Mitchell agreed with Holmes's views regarding heredity, and he wanted to establish them as scientific fact. In 1859 he wrote to Holmes—as "one whose sympathy with my object is already pledged"—about his plan to investigate the "physical statistics of our native born white race." During the previous summer Mitchell had submitted this plan to the Academy of Natural Science. He wrote that it had been approved, actively aided by the academy members, and sanctioned by the Smithsonian Institution. He wanted to obtain the physical statistics for undergraduates from the principal colleges and a similar set of statistics for factory workers and mechanics. He had already examined five hundred mechanics. Holmes agreed to gather the statistics for the college students. Later he wrote, "I have not forgotten your statistics. . . . It is doubtful whether I shall do anything with them. Until you want them I will keep them with the chance that I may get a popular article out of them."[56]

Mitchell also sent Holmes a poem, hoping that he could get it placed in the *Atlantic Monthly*. Holmes wrote back to say it was "a poet's poem,—warm, flushed even—perhaps at some points a little over-heated." And he thought the *Atlantic* editor, James Russell Lowell, might find two faults with it, its length and its similarity to Tennyson.[57] Three of Mitchell's poems from this period appear in his *Complete Poems*—"The Hill of Stones: A Legend of Fontainebleau," "Herndon," and "Elk Country." It seems likely that "The Hill of Stones" is the one he sent to Holmes.

Eleven pages long and written in blank verse, "The Hill of Stones" recounts the mythic origins of Fontainebleau's rocky formations. This early example of Mitchell's poetry is noteworthy for its treatment of sexual difference, representing attitudes that will resurface later in his medical writing, clinical treatment, and novelistic representations of women. While his attitudes were born at home and nurtured in medical school, it is interesting to consider in what ways the extensive vivisection may have sharpened and hardened them. In the poem there are two worlds: the king and his court and the Diana-like queen and her maidens. The forest women, scornful of men and happy to live apart, harm no one through their self-sufficiency and festive celebrations. But many knights enter the forest and attempt to capture them. When the knights fail, they are turned to stone. Eventually, one knight does prevail, and the queen and her maidens are transformed into a "tumbled heap of dreary rocks." In the polarity that opposes nature to culture, these independent women pose a threat to the social order. Nature is most often represented as female, and through a set of associations of nature with females and mother earth with *mater,* attitudes toward women, animals, and nature merge. Man must subdue and control this valuable but volatile resource. Mitchell saw women as impulsive and instinctive creatures that needed to be counteracted and neutralized. No legitimate space existed outside heterosexuality and motherhood. Ironically, alongside this patriarchal mandate stands the imposing figure of the queen, the only spirited character in "The Hill of Stones." In her outspoken and fearless resistance, she becomes a prototype for Mitchell's unruly female patients who will later refuse to rest and be silent.

In addition to his friendship with Holmes, another bright spot in Mitchell's life at this time was meeting Phillips Brooks. Male friendships were most important to Mitchell. Through correspondence, gift giving, and gracious hospitality, he worked hard to nurture a number of special friends. Of the many bonds he formed with men such as Hammond, Holmes, William W. Keen, John S. Billings, John Cadwalader, and William Osler, the deepest and most intimate relationship was with Brooks.

After graduating from Harvard and studying at the Theological Seminary in Virginia, Brooks became rector at the Church of Advent in Philadelphia in 1859. He was an instant success. Just a short time after his arrival, Mitchell heard him preach and sought him out, and they were immediately attracted to each other. Imaginative, eloquent, handsome, and over six feet three inches tall, Brooks drew large crowds with his preaching. According to one biographer, "He was the joy and the pride of the whole city." While not without critics, many found his energy, sincerity, and intelligence inspiring and referred to him as a "force" and "a prophet."[58] In 1862, when Brooks became rector of the prestigious Church of the Holy Trinity in Rittenhouse Square, he moved to a residence near the Mitchells. He had dinner with them several times each week, and it was his habit to stop by in the evenings and smoke and chat in Mitchell's study before the fire.

Brooks formed an equally close bond with Elizabeth. Whenever he was away, he wrote her at least once a week. Mitchell wrote that Brooks "continually sought her counsel and criticism," and that no one influenced his opinions as much as this "remarkable woman." During the summers, Mitchell and Brooks went boating on the river and took several canoeing and hiking trips together. One summer they traveled by canoe from Moosehead Lake to the sea by way of the Allagash and St. John Rivers, a trip of well over four hundred miles. Mitchell wrote that Brooks was "a very strong man, and his physical force was a source of admiration to our stalwart guides." He enjoyed the swimming, paddling, and hiking, but he did not hunt or fish, and he "had a great dislike to killing even a troublesome insect."[59]

It is remarkable that Mitchell found time to make new friends and write poetry given his work and many family responsibilities. He told Elizabeth, "Indeed you do not know the hundred cares upon me or you wd know that my heart must be writing letters to you when I cannot." His mother, Matilda, would say to her other three sons, "What would you boys do without your brother Weir?" Mitchell's role as surrogate father was especially clear in the case of Edward, or Ned as he was called, who was the baby of the family and fourteen years younger than Mitchell. Ned was doing well as a student at the University of Pennsylvania. He spent a lot of time reading at home on the sofa, and even though he was the gentlest and most affectionate member of the family, he still seemed to break something every day, "always old glass or—Sevres china."[60]

But there were more serious problems with Walsh, who was seven years younger than Mitchell. Walsh had joined the army in 1857, and after John Mitchell's death the following year, the correspondence indicates that he began to gamble, borrow large sums of money, and engage in a number of altercations. Matilda told Elizabeth, "Looking over Weir's account-book I see he has paid in the last month 300 dolls. debts for Wallie." Walsh had been a troublemaker as a boy, often the ringleader in neighborhood scrapes and feuds. When he was fourteen, the day-watch took him into custody for kicking a woman who was passing the school playground. Although Walsh said it was an accident, the constable asserted that it was intentional. Joining the army provided a more legitimate outlet for Walsh's aggression. While stationed in Panama in 1859, he was wounded in a duel after pitching a cup of hot coffee into another soldier's face. A few weeks later he told Mitchell, "Casanova died and with him his story. Now whether I killed him or the fever is a mystery to me. . . . I have the swords. They are yours." In the same letter he wrote that he had a fistfight with a father after accidentally stepping on his infant's fingers in a crowded train. He scolded Mitchell for taking him so seriously regarding his visits to the ladies and joked about marrying a Spanish woman: "The fact is that the older I grow, the more fond I am of ladies society. So dont take a thing in earnest old fellow, when it has the shadow of a joke connected with it. '*It sounds boyish.*'"[61]

While Walsh was home on leave, Mitchell hoped to obtain a lieutenancy in the Keystone Regiment for him, writing, "Beyond that I have a scheme to get for him a line appointment so that he is likely to have a chance at the only trade he was ever meant for. Everyone is struck with his resolute look and handsome face—wh is no longer sallow but red and fair and browned a good bit. A handsome dog." Mitchell explained that Walsh was "so unlucky as to emerge from scarlet fever at nine with epilepsy. This never got entirely well until the war. It left him a strong-willed, unruly, excitable person. . . . He was, even as a lad, conspicuous for courage, a lover of danger, the only man, save one, Percy Sargent, I have known who delighted in peril."[62] By blaming epilepsy, Mitchell justified the violent behavior, preserving his belief in heredity and defending the family honor.

Elizabeth was also causing problems. She made disparaging remarks about Mitchell's wife, Mary, and the way she managed the house. Mitchell destroyed two of Elizabeth's letters that had caused him to weep "inwardly after my heathen fashion." He told her, "I can not help feeling when I reflect on it that a most baseless jealousy has been the shadow of yr. life not only now but always. . . . If as I doubt not has been the case our dear Father ever pointed out to you the shoals on wh. he conceived that you might drift—recal all that he said to you— and this is not asking too much." He continued:

> My own study and estimate of a Christian training and its value if it have any is not formed by me fr. watching how it acts on people like my wife who began young with it and have not by nature those iron faults to bend wh. are the growth of natures such as yours or mine. . . . I do miss among Christians the evidence of its utterly penetrating their daily life, of its marking their manners and clothing with its unselfishness the whole of their life of relation to others. How sharply I have looked at this in the men who are mixed up with me in life you cannot conceive. . . . Now please don't say this is a personal attack—You don't to the parson.[63]

Standing apart, identifying himself as a "heathen" and demanding the respect of a parson, Mitchell criticized Christian hypocrisy. Evoking their dead father and repeating the old threat of shoals and shipwreck to drive home his message, he told Elizabeth to guard her character.

Despite the problems with Elizabeth and Walsh, these were some of Mitchell's best years. He had become a prominent physician and family man who found time to maintain an extensive correspondence, write poetry, and create lifelong friendships. His marriage and the birth of two sons gave him much happiness. Due to his creative energy and determination, he had turned a handful of rattlesnakes into a major research project, and he would later describe this risky research as one of the most important works of his life.[64]

4

WAR'S AWFUL HARVEST

In 1860, when the Summer Association closed, Mitchell lost his teaching position in physiology, and this was the last formal teaching post he would hold. This same year he became an attending physician at the Pennsylvania Institution for the Instruction of the Blind. In 1861 he was elected a member of the Boston Society of Natural History, and the next year a member of the American Philosophical Society. Early in 1861 the Harvard professor Jeffries Wyman wrote to say that just that morning he had received a letter from Charles Darwin requesting a copy of Mitchell's book *Researches upon the Venom of the Rattlesnake.*

For Mitchell, the decade began peacefully enough. Given the various activities and responsibilities that filled his days, it was not difficult to push aside thoughts of the impending war. Ten years of hard work had paid off, especially his work with rattlesnakes, and Mitchell and John Call Dalton were widely acclaimed as America's leading physiologists.[1] Focused on his research, medical practice, and wife and family, Mitchell was as vigorous and content as he would ever be. However, the next few years would produce several events that hijacked his plans and expectations, shaking his confidence and altering the direction of his career.

Because of his family roots in Virginia and his dislike of Lincoln, Mitchell was not inclined to commit to the Northern cause. Referring to Lincoln's presidency as "the reign of Abe Lincoln the first," he asked, "How can people call Lincoln a patriot, or even *honest.* The connection is a degradation to the adjective."[2] Regarding African Americans in the army, he told Elizabeth, "Do you see that we have now black officers—commissioned I mean. Did you hear that

Othello was forbidden in Boston because it was presumed to be insulting to the culled pussons—Also that in the negro regiments they wear white crape on the arm?" He continued, "Do you know that the aristo. darkies decline all association with the plebs who enlist? . . . If I were a nig I shd. go in for it all but being white I decline—For my part I think all sides are insane—I have sympathy with something of all—entire sympathy with none."[3]

Expressing similar views, Mitchell's youngest brother, Ned, told William Keen, "Thank Heaven! Lincoln has only two more years to tyranize over the weakest people on Earth, and then a day of retribution will come, when usurpers will find that we are *free*, not to be ruled by a renegade. Abolition may be right, Keen, as you have often tried to teach me, but it is casting out devils in the name of the devil." A few months later, Ned told his mother, "This morning I had the felicity and honor to escort around the Hospital his Majesty Abraham Lincoln, and of all uncouth, clumsy and ragged looking specimens, Mr. L. was the greatest. He went all over the place, shaking hands with every one in it, and his manner showed very evidently that he only came for the effect of the thing, and that he did not care a button about the soldiers or their sufferings."[4]

All three of Mitchell's brothers had joined the Union Army. Ned had joined as a medical cadet, Walsh was in the 6th Pennsylvania Cavalry, and Chapman enlisted in the 15th Illinois. Dalton, Bowditch, and Billings along with many other physicians had volunteered. Mitchell had to do something. In 1862, with all three of his brothers away, he decided to refuse a position as brigade surgeon in the U.S. Army and work as an acting assistant surgeon in Philadelphia instead. In this way he could maintain his income from private practice, stay close to his family, and at the same time work at a military hospital each day for an additional eighty dollars a month.

In October 1862 Mitchell began his work as a contract surgeon at the old armory building at Sixteenth and Filbert Streets. Once he began, his ambivalence about the war did not dampen his enthusiasm for the new clinical work. Unlike many of the other military surgeons, he was particularly interested in injuries to nerves. From all around the city, physicians began to refer nervous cases directly to Mitchell. In a kind of nightmarish substitution, human beings replaced the animals of his earlier experimentation—many of them very young men with torn flesh, shattered bones, burning pain, and phantom limbs.

William Hammond, Mitchell's friend and collaborator in poisons and venoms, had resigned from the chair of anatomy and physiology at the University of Maryland and rejoined the Army Medical Department. In April 1862 he became surgeon general. Hammond saw the great potential of bringing Mitchell's knowledge of anatomy and physiology to bear on gunshot wounds and injuries to nerves. He also knew that Mitchell liked to write, was good at it, and would capture this pioneering work in smooth and lucid prose.

When the Filbert Street hospital proved too small, Hammond moved Mitchell to a second hospital on Christian Street. But it also proved inadequate, and Hammond created a third hospital of four hundred beds at a suburban estate on Turner's Lane. When Mitchell and George R. Morehouse were transferred there, Mitchell requested that Keen join them. Turner's Lane Hospital was devoted entirely to nerve injury and disease with the exception of Dr. Da Costa's ward for heart cases. All the doctors worked long hours, discussed the cases in great detail, and took endless pages of notes. Mitchell wrote:

> The cases were of amazing interest. Here at one time were eighty epileptics, every kind of nerve-wound, palsies, singular choreas, and stump disorders. I sometimes wonder how we stood it. If urgent calls took us back into town, we returned to the hospital as if drawn by a magnet. In fact, it was exciting in its constancy of novel interest. . . . The victims of nerve-wounds were often men worn out from fever, dysentery and long marches; hence some of the symptoms of nerve-wounds we described have never been seen since in like intensity. The statements in regard to causalgia—burning neuralgia—were received in England with critical doubt. That hospital was, as one poor fellow said, a hell of pain.[5]

Challenged and roused by this "hell of pain," Mitchell told Elizabeth, "No physiology this summer but splendid hospital work and I thank God—heartily such wonderful results that I am sometimes amazed. It is such a pleasure to see men who have drifted hopeless and helpless from Hosp—to Hospital with dead limbs or moveless below the waist—to see them walking about and grateful even to tears."[6] Like so many, Mitchell initially failed to fully grasp the immensity of the Civil War and how it would change things, but he did quickly understand the incredible clinical opportunity born through this tragic event.

Other affairs did not stand still during the intense clinical experience at Turner's Lane Hospital. Somehow Mitchell still found time for his letter writing, sending off five to eight letters every two days, all the time hating it with

"an increasing fervour." In the correspondence, the stories about Walsh's indis-
cretions were replaced by cryptic references to more serious problems. Mitchell's
mother wrote to Elizabeth, "I suppose Weir told you all about Wallie. . . . Where
his money goes is not for me to say tho' I may have my own opinion on the
subject." And again she wrote, "I hope that Lizzie you remember what I told
you about not mentioning Wallies little secret to *any body*. Weir thought I ought
not to have told you." Mitchell, referring to Walsh in a letter to Elizabeth,
wondered, "Can a man be dragged up out of such a deep of moral degradation?
Perhaps a man with a keen sense of shame would despair where one more cal-
lous mt. not."[7]

Right at the time that Mitchell began to work at Turner's Lane, another event
occurred that dwarfed all worries about Walsh. Weir and his wife, Mary, were
living at 1226 Walnut Street. After she gave birth to their second son, she caught
diphtheria and seven months later died. There is little information about the
months leading up to and following Mary's death. Her mother took the children, caring for both in the summer and the baby, Langdon, full-time throughout his first year. Speaking of the "infinite pain" and "sorrows of association"
of the old house, Mitchell moved to 1332 Walnut Street. Elizabeth moved in
with him to manage the new household. On the first anniversary of Mary's
death, Mitchell wrote of his agonizing memories and the need to escape, hoping to go to Cape May with Da Costa. He told Elizabeth, "If I could blot from
my mind the very memory of the hours of Marys illness I believe I wd do it—
It was such a cruel time."[8]

In the spring of 1863, Samuel Jackson resigned as professor of the institutes
of medicine at the University of Pennsylvania, and Mitchell decided to apply for
the position. In a letter to Wyman asking for a recommendation, Mitchell wrote,
"Of my opponent I have nothing to say but that he is a gentleman and that
we are both *said* to teach well—But I shall feel it just a little hard if—it should
happen that I am beaten by one who has never added a leaf to the crown of the
mistress in whose service I have spent so many hours of welcome labour—You
will know how I feel and why the heaviness of the stake makes me so unscrupu-
lous a beggar."[9] In addition to Wyman, Mitchell gathered endorsements from
Holmes, Hammond, Louis Agassiz, Joseph Henry, and Samuel Jackson himself.
His supporters understood the value and need for original research in American medicine, and Hammond stated that he did not know Mitchell's superior
in physiology in the United States. Still, the board of trustees at the University
of Pennsylvania saw it differently, and the chair went to Francis Gurney Smith.

Smith, who was ten years older than Mitchell, had an undergraduate degree and medical degree from the University of Pennsylvania and possessed greater private influence. As was customary at the time, only three of the twenty-four board members at the University of Pennsylvania were physicians. Several belonged to the same Protestant Episcopal Church as Smith. He had lectured at the Summer Association for a decade before becoming a professor at Pennsylvania College, was a popular teacher who did little research, and derived most of his income from his practice, student fees, and the editing of medical textbooks, including William B. Carpenter's *Principles of Human Physiology.* He also served as editor of the *Philadelphia Medical Examiner* from 1844 to 1854. At a time when little distinction was made between the transmission of old and the discovery of new knowledge, social factors influenced the trustees. Smith did little research in physiology, and it would take him twelve years to establish a physiological laboratory at the University of Pennsylvania.[10]

For Mitchell, the rejection was a profound disappointment and setback, another bitter taste of the power of family connections and social forces to determine the path of his career. His supporters wrote to express how sorry they were. Henry wrote, "I am very sorry to learn that you have lost the election but you and your friends have the satisfaction of knowing that you deserved it." Dalton wrote that the loss was not all on Mitchell's side.[11]

During Mitchell's campaign for the chair of physiology, another personal tragedy began to unfold. Although Mitchell's brother Ned was nineteen when he enlisted as a medical cadet, emotionally he was younger than his years. Mitchell felt the role of surrogate father most strongly with Ned. His first letters home were from the U.S. General Hospital on Fifth Street in Philadelphia. He was transferred to Douglas Hospital in Washington, and finally to a number of Southern locations, including Hilton Head, South Carolina, St. Augustine, Florida, and Beaufort, South Carolina. Because Hammond was surgeon general and because other doctors in the various military hospitals knew Ned's famous brother, he was given some extra attention, such as a horse to ride and letters of introduction. At first he wrote upbeat letters and seemed enthusiastic about the hospital work and his medical studies, but then in the wards of Douglas Hospital he contracted diphtheria.

The first time Mitchell met John Shaw Billings was at Ned's bedside at Douglas Hospital, where Billings was the attending physician. Although Ned survived diphtheria's acute stages, his frequent and carefully dated letters convey his deteriorating health over the next two years. When he was well enough, he worked in the wards, but complications from the diphtheria persisted. There were abscesses on his thigh, arm, and head, and chills and coughing, and he continued to take a gram of quinine each day.

Congress had approved the formation of the U.S. Army medical cadet corps in 1861 in recognition of the need for medical assistants. The corps consisted of medical students, like Ned, who enlisted for one year as noncommissioned officers to dress the wounded, perform as ambulance attendants, assist with postmortem examinations, prepare medicines, and do various administrative tasks such as issuing clothing. When there were staff shortages or a heavy influx of casualties, however, the cadets made treatment decisions, took personal charge of wards, and assisted with and even performed surgeries. While these clinical experiences provided a rare opportunity for the cadets, the pay was insufficient and most of them depended on money from family and friends to meet their expenses.[12] Ned was always in need of money, explaining his expenses in detail and often asking for help. At one point he told Elizabeth that he regretted that her letter did not contain a "'greenback' or two as my financial condition at present is not flourishing; my cash on hand amounting to $00.35, with my Mess bill due, and the wash woman clamorous!"[13]

Maintaining contact with his family was of the utmost importance to Ned. Unfortunately, due to the irregularity of the mail and his frequent moves, he did not receive many letters from home. Still, he continued to write about his experiences and observations. From Beaufort, for example, he wrote his mother that there were two regiments doing guard duty, one white and the other black. These two regiments occupied the same barracks and bunks alternately. Every day when the guards were changed, "you may see marching through the streets a squad of half black and half white soldiers. . . . The whites following the others and the whole lot in charge of a Negro Sergeant who gives his orders and instructions the same to both parties!" Ned had seen this repeatedly and wrote that it was "much to my disgust. . . . The 'freedman,' alias 'contrabands,' alias 'chattels,' alias 'slaves' rule the ranch here and woebetide the unhappy individual who happens to butt against them in the newly received ideas of liberty, said liberty being the right to steal whatever they can lay their hand on and to have their own way generally." The black soldiers even talked of their plans to buy the confiscated land in the area and make a freedman's town of Beaufort. Ned finished this section, which he had marked throughout with numerous exclamation points, by writing, "In my next letter I will give you some more items of 'Negropolis.' I wish some of our abolition friends would pay me a visit. I think I could give them some new ideas on their pet subject."[14]

Increasingly and pathetically, the letters reveal Ned's loneliness and at times an almost desperate need to hear from someone in his family. After waiting and waiting to hear, in June 1863 he wrote, "I begin to believe that I am being gradually forgotten at home." This same year Assistant Surgeon General DeWitt C. Peters published an article titled "The Evils of Youthful Enlistments, and Nostalgia" in the *American Medical Times*. In it he wrote of the young men who were too immature in mind and body to join the army. They were susceptible to physical disease and mental disorders, especially after a few months when the "bright anticipations" wore off in the face of hardship and homesickness. He defined nostalgia as "a species of melancholy, or a mild type of insanity, caused by disappointment, and a continuous longing for the home. It is frequently aggravated by derangement of the stomach and bowels, and is daily met with in its worse form, in our military hospitals and prisons, and is especially marked in young subjects."[15] In another article, "Nostalgia as a Disease of Field Service," Dr. J. Thomas Calhoun wrote that as the war dragged on, the initial enthusiasm died away and many yearned to go home, longing "for the luxuries to which they had been accustomed, a good bed, a cheerful fireside and the delicacies of the table." And he asked, "Is it strange, then that men have sickened, and I doubt not died, from home sickness?" Battle action was one remedy for nostalgia. Calhoun also advocated a liberal furlough system as a way to deal with serious homesickness.[16]

Ned did not have battle action or a chance at a furlough to relieve his loneliness, but he struggled to put a positive face on things. He often said that he was in excellent health and never felt better. He tried to locate the briar roots and turtles that Mitchell requested. He sent oranges to little John and shared the news that Walsh had been mentioned in the paper as the "gallant aid of Gen. Reynolds." As part of his valiant effort to appear strong and optimistic, he informed Mitchell that the trip from New York to Hilton Head was "a very pleasant voyage down. I was not at all sea sick, and enjoyed the trip hugely." But in less than two weeks he wrote his mother that "the sea voyage from New York depressed my very much, and when I arrived here I was almost used up." The same month he told Mitchell, "It is very lonely here. I have no companions at all and very few books."[17] Throughout the fall and into December, in almost every letter he expressed his keen desire to permanently return home when his term expired in January. In October he went home for a visit and wrote several weeks later, "I do not want to go through another year of Cadet service, and in fact I have set my heart on returning in Jan, and will be much disappointed if I cannot do so." Still, Mitchell wrote that he wanted Ned to reenlist as a cadet and stay at least until May. Ned was "sick at heart" and begged, "Please do not advise me to remain."[18] In 1863, for the first time, Ned spent Christmas alone and away from his family. A few months later, early in 1864, he died. He was twenty-one, blind, and partially paralyzed as a result of the diphtheria—a mere skeleton.

In his autobiography Mitchell wrote, "Of Ned I can hardly speak." He referred to his death as "one of the most acute regrets of my life." Ned was "very simple, of gentle temper, imaginative, subject to moods of gravity," and "of all of us, the most earnest and perfect character. He was during my life at Crawford's and at college, the petted baby, and was then a beautiful creature with a certain rare spiritual look which troubled one to see."[19] Like so much about the Civil War, thoughts of Ned and his "delicate masculine charm" haunted Mitchell. In a poem, he wrote that Ned was never far from any one day's thoughts—all the years "take him no further from me. . . . A little duty done; / A little love for many, much for me, / And that was all beneath this earthly sun."[20]

Mitchell's ambivalence about the war persisted. He struggled to come to terms with these feelings, but in place of the satisfaction and calm that comes with certainty, some of the old unsettledness remained. When his brother Chapman was offered a majority in a black regiment and wrote for advice, Mitchell explained that he was not opposed to black troops "now that we have them," and that Chapman "must be controlled by the status of such officers in the West—the army feeling and the advice of Major Wilson."[21] In 1863, as a special inspector of the general hospitals of the army, Mitchell was ordered by the War Department to inspect the military prison at Fort Delaware, an eighty-acre island some ten miles below Newcastle. His comments before and after the trip reveal some of his vacillating feelings. Before the inspection, he wrote Elizabeth, "A thousand ill—12000 on an island which shd hold 4000—The general level 3 ft *below low* water mark. 20 deaths a day of dysentery and the living having more life on them than in them. Occasional lack of water and thus a christian! nation treats the captives of it sword. . . . I am more of a democrat than a republican and not enough of either to please either."[22]

After spending two days at the prison, Mitchell found things better than expected. The prisoners were well fed and given fresh water, and he felt that the reports spread by the "copperheads" were untrue. He wrote:

> I smelt 900000 smells—saw dying men and scurvy, dined with the commandant, and so home to report things not so bad as the secesh. had said in fact vastly better, and not so bad as the ultra republicans and sinners wish—vide J. Frazier who says we shd. open the dykes and drown them out ... and a visible regret in the minds of secesh friends who on hearing all this must resign the joy of cursing us for barbarians who kill their captives by slow means. Meanwhile—the locality is a bad one not fit for a prison depot.[23]

Although the location was "a bad one," the North supplied food and water to the Confederate prisoners. Fresh water was brought to the island from the Brandywine Creek in tugs, but rather than go to the wharf for water, the prisoners dug wells in the moist soil and in this way maintained and spread disease. Mitchell reported that with winter approaching, the men were in dire need of warm clothing. Old army uniforms were sent from the Philadelphia arsenal, but at first the Confederates flatly refused to wear the U.S. uniforms. When the cold weather gave them no choice, Mitchell commented on the comical effect of their appearance in dress uniforms and musicians' outfits from the War of 1812.[24]

At the beginning of the war both sides had returned captured surgeons, but as this was no longer the policy, Mitchell found more than forty surgeons confined in the Fort Delaware prison, and some had been his classmates at Jefferson Medical College. He gave them tobacco, books, and money. He always felt that the Union and Confederate physicians and surgeons were poorly treated during and after the war—their valuable contributions, bravery, and numerous sacrifices never recognized in any appropriate way. Later he attempted to commemorate with bronze tablets the field hospitals and the sites where Union doctors were killed or wounded at Gettysburg.

———

In contrast to his ambivalence about the war, Mitchell clearly understood the medical opportunities at Turner's Lane, and although harried and exhausted, his passion for research relentlessly drove him on. He was observing and writing about things like phantom limbs, or "sensory ghosts" as he called them, and burning pain or causalgia, phenomena that others had often overlooked or dismissed as female weakness and hysteria.[25] In August 1864 he wrote Elizabeth, "I so much dread to find increasing practice—or other cause removing from me the time or power to search for the new truths which lie about me so thick."[26]

Searching for the new truths was a circular process for Mitchell. The writing brought structure and clarity to the work and provided a permanent record. But it also created more questions and sent Mitchell back to his patients for answers. As a result of this amazing eighteen-month period of research and writing, Mitchell produced a number of valuable articles and books. In 1864 he coauthored with Morehouse and Keen "Reflex Paralysis," "On Malingering, Especially in Regard to Simulation of Diseases of the Nervous System," and *Gunshot Wounds and Other Injuries of Nerves*.[27] A striking aspect of *Gunshot Wounds* is the rich narrative detail of the case studies, which name and bring to life so many of the soldiers. It soon became the authority on nerve injuries, discussing various methods of treatment such as blistering, leeches, cautery, electricity, and hypodermic injections, and presenting the first distinct descriptions of "causalgia" and "phantom limbs," terms that Mitchell coined. In 1867 Mitchell published "On the Diseases of Nerves, Resulting from Injuries." In 1872, after devoting considerable time to substantial revision and additions, he published *Gunshot Wounds* under a new title, *Injuries of Nerves and Their Consequences*. The American Academy of Neurology reprinted *Injuries* in 1965, referring to Mitchell as the father of American neurology and stating that each study "of peripheral nerve injuries incident upon major wars since the American Civil War has drawn upon Mitchell's account of his own experience. None has had the impact of Mitchell's." According to Dr. R. L. Richards in the *Archives of Neurology*, Mitchell's description of burning pain "was so good and so accurate that even today, 100 years later, it can still be read and accepted as a true clinical picture of the condition."[28]

After Mitchell treated several soldiers experiencing burning pain, he wrote that this intense pain "had never been described except by my colleagues and myself." He wanted to call it something else, and Robley Dunglison suggested the word "causalgia."[29] Soldiers, when they could speak, often described causalgia as "mustard red-hot," or as "a red-hot file rasping the skin." Although symptoms, intensity, and duration varied with individual cases, there was the "glossy skin," deep red or mottled in patches, "perfectly free from hair," and without wrinkles—skin that shined as though skillfully varnished. According to *Gunshot Wounds*, "Nothing more curious than these red and shining tissues can be conceived of." Often the nails became curved and thickened. In one case the body sweat became "copious and intensely acid, so that an odor of vinegar could be smelt at all times in the neighborhood of the man. . . . The same unpleasant symptom existed to a less degree in others; while in a single instance the odor of the sweat was disgustingly heavy, and resembled the smells from a bad drain." The slightest jar, touch, sound, exposure to air, presence of light, or advance of the surgeon seemed to cause excruciating pain.[30] Patients frequently mentioned the relief found from wetting the hands and pouring water into the boots. Many soldiers broke down. One moaned and wept "incessantly" and "constantly prayed us to amputate the arm."[31]

In *The Body in Pain*, Elaine Scarry discusses pain's resistance to language, writing that at first pain monopolizes language, becoming its only subject, and complaint becomes the exclusive mode of speech. As the pain deepens, sounds anterior to learned language displace the coherence of complaint. Just at the moment when the need is most acute, cries and groans supplant learned language.[32] Mitchell, in completing the various Civil War publications spanning an eight-year period, must have known that he was attempting to reverse the de-objectifying work of pain, writing, along with Morehouse and Keen, that causalgia was "a form of suffering as yet undescribed, and so frequent and terrible as to demand from us the fullest description."[33] Through direct and indirect discourse he conveyed the soldiers' words and borrowed their metaphors. Through his own words as physician and artist, he attempted to construct a language that communicated the devastating effects of this type of nerve injury.

———

One evening while discussing amputation and lost limbs with Henry Wharton, Mitchell mentioned hearing about a man who had lost both legs and both arms in the fight at Mobile Bay.[34] This conversation inspired him to write a short story about such a person. While puzzling over a name, he saw "Dedlow" on a jeweler's sign and, thinking that a good one, called the story "The Case of George Dedlow." Published in the fall of 1866, it was the first of many Civil War stories and poems that Mitchell would write.[35]

George Dedlow is a doctor's son who is studying medicine at Jefferson Medical College when the war begins. He becomes an assistant surgeon with the 10th Indiana Volunteers, and he is shot for the first time south of Nashville when traveling alone to obtain quinine and stimulants for his command. Both arms are hit and fall helpless, and "within an hour I began to have in my dead right hand a strange burning . . . as if the hand was caught and pinched in a red-hot vise. . . . At length the pain became absolutely unendurable, and I grew what it is the fashion to call demoralized. I screamed, cried, and yelled in my torture."[36] This passage marks the moment at which pain shatters Dedlow's ability to speak, the moment when pain actively destroys language, replacing it with cries and groans and the onset of hysteria. In a rebel hospital near Atlanta, Dedlow's wounds are dressed, but his hand remains "alive only to pain." Finally, after six weeks of this torture, the doctors decide to amputate.

After a period of imprisonment and thirty days of furlough, Dedlow returns to his regiment as a captain only to be wounded again at the Battle of Chicka-mauga.[37] Without forewarning, both of his legs are amputated, and he wakes to the experience of phantom pain. Then, in Nashville "in one of the ten thousand beds of that vast metropolis of hospitals," his remaining arm, infected with gangrene, is amputated. "Against all chances," he tells the reader, "I recovered, to find myself a useless torso, more like some strange larval creature than anything of human shape. Of my anguish and horror of myself I dare not speak."[38] Moved to the Stump Hospital in Philadelphia, he sees hundreds of amputees, but none like himself. The story ends awkwardly when Dedlow attends a séance and is momentarily reunited with his lost legs. Mitchell did not intend for the ending to be taken seriously. He had no patience for séances and satirized such meetings again in *The Autobiography of a Quack*. In fact, many years later, after attending one of Mrs. Piper's séances with William James, he wrote that the interview lasted for two hours "and absolutely not one thing came out of it. . . . The impression made upon me was of a fraud and I thought a very stupid one." It was a "babble of utter nonsense" and "inconceivable twaddle."[39] Mitchell was attempting to end the short story with a bit of cynical humor.

After writing "The Case of George Dedlow," Mitchell gave the story to Mrs. Caspar Wister to read, who in turn gave it to her father, Dr. Furness. In the meantime Furness sent it to Edward E. Hale, the editor of the *Atlantic Monthly*, and to Mitchell's "surprise and amusement," he received a check for eighty dollars along with the page proofs. When the story was published anonymously as the lead article, many readers thought it was a true account. A few even collected money and tried to visit Dedlow at the "Stump Hospital" located at Twenty-Fourth and South Streets in Philadelphia.[40]

Phantom limb syndrome was first described in "The Case of George Dedlow." This is the only time that a medical condition was explained first in Mitchell's literature. All other literary representations of neurologic conditions appear after he had discussed them in his medical writing.[41] And he was not necessarily comfortable with this aspect of the short story. His dismissive comments, its anonymous publication, and its parodic ending suggest that he did not fully realize the significance of this innovative and richly detailed piece. Five years after its publication, he made his discomfort clear in "Phantom Limbs" in *Lippincott's Magazine of Popular Literature and Science.* In this article he did not exactly state that he authored "The Case of George Dedlow." Rather, he used the third person singular to create distance between himself as a physician and the author of the story. He wrote that "the author" took "advantage of the freedom accorded to a writer of fiction" to describe certain astounding psychological states. The "author" never imagined that his jeu d'esprit and "humorous sketch, with its absurd conclusion, would for a moment mislead any one."[42]

While Mitchell did not realize the story's significance, readers did. Lisa Long writes, "The story became a phantom limb; Mitchell's subsequent statements would make it into a fraudulent version of reality, but his readers' responses suggested that it conveyed new and troubling information about postbellum bodies and identity."[43] The story, combining detailed medical information with the immediacy of first-person narration, relates the hysteria of causalgia and phantom limbs that Mitchell encountered at Turner's Lane. Although "fiction," the story conveyed knowledge about Civil War injuries that was every bit as real as phantom limb pain. And "The Case of George Dedlow," perhaps Mitchell's best fictional work, is the one that subsequent generations have continued to read.[44]

One of the interesting things about Mitchell's Civil War output is the affinity between the literary and medical writing. He seems driven to make and remake language in an attempt to represent what was happening at Turner's Lane. Instances of intertextuality are numerous where passages repeat themselves and reappear. Using vivid description, metaphor, and narration, both the medical and literary writing deal extensively with causalgia and phantom limbs, and some of the cases are the same. The case of Joseph H. Corliss, age twenty-seven, appears three times in Mitchell's writing—in *Gunshot Wounds,* in *Injuries of Nerves,* and in "The Case of George Dedlow" (as the hysterical Dane). Dr. Richards writes that this case "can still serve as a model case history illustrative of true causalgia."[45] Corliss's pain:

was so severe that a touch anywhere, or shaking the bed, or a heavy step, caused it to increase. . . . He keeps his hand wrapped in rags, wetted with cold water, and covered with oiled silk, and even tucks the rag carefully under the flexed finger-tips. . . . He will allow no one to touch his skin with a dry hand. . . . He keeps a bottle of water about him, and carries a wet sponge in the right hand. This hand he wets always before he handles anything; used dry, it hurts the other limb. At one time, when the suffering was severe, he poured water into his boots, he says, to lessen the pain which dry touch or friction causes in the injured hand. . . . He thus describes the pain at its height: "It is as if a rough bar of iron were thrust to and fro through the knuckles, a red-hot iron . . . with a heavy weight on it, and the skin was being rasped off his finger-ends."[46]

The "as if" construction employed in this passage is characteristic of descriptions of pain. Scarry writes that this projection into metaphor, with a weapon on the other side though moving toward the body, "by its very separability from the body becomes an image that can be lifted away, carrying some of the attributes of pain with it."[47] By recording the soldier's experiences and words, Mitchell gave visibility and voice to human pain, attempting to transcend its mastery of the body.

Another soldier, S. Johnson, enlisted in 1861 at the age of eighteen and was wounded twenty-one months later by a ball that entered just below the level of the teeth. The ball went backward and inward and most likely lodged in the spinal column, and he experienced total motor paralysis of the arms and legs. After a couple of months in other hospitals, in July 1863 he was transferred to Turner's Lane. The clinical terms in the following passage hardly dispel the horrible image of the emaciated and rigid body: "A more wretched spectacle than this man presents can hardly be imagined. He lies in bed, motionless, emaciated to the last degree, and with bed-sores on both elbows and both hips. His hands lie crossed on his chest, perfectly rigid; the fingers extended; the skin congested and thin; the nails curved; false anchylosis of all the joints of the upper limbs; the head and neck rigid, with acute pain in these parts on movement." There is a "monkey-like appearance" to the hand, with the "thumb rotated outward, and its nail looking upward and even toward the forefinger."[48] Despite his protests and prayers to be left alone, Johnson is treated with massage and a high-caloric diet. Finally, in October he begins to improve: his appetite becomes voracious, he gains weight, and he can voluntarily cross his legs. In January his hands have lost their smooth, shiny look, and the nails are less curved. He is given electrical treatments and etherized daily; his adhesions are forcibly broken, and the massage continues. By late February Johnson can walk a few steps, and by March he walks well without any aid. After almost a year of paralysis and causalgia, he is discharged, slightly shuffling but with nearly the entire use of all his limbs. In this case, a successful outcome required eleven months of treatment, and its four major components—rest, a high-caloric diet, massage, and electricity—would later constitute Mitchell's trademark method of treatment, the rest cure.

The small ball that blasted through Johnson's jaw and lodged in his spinal cord was most likely one of the Civil War's famous "Minié balls." Before the war, because the traditional smoothbore musket had a maximum range of about 250 yards and an effective range of about 80 yards, close-order formation was necessary to concentrate the firepower of such inaccurate weapons. In 1848, however, Claude E. Minié invented a spinning conical bullet; then James H. Burton made a cheaper and better version. These bullets not only increased the already high number of casualties, but also exacerbated the kind and extent of the physical injury and pain.

With a range of 1,500 yards and extreme accuracy at 350 yards, a .58-caliber Minié ball fired from a Springfield or Enfield musket could penetrate six one-inch pine boards. Officers on both sides, trained in a tradition of close-order infantry assaults, were slow to register these differences in range and accuracy. Casualties multiplied and injuries worsened, and the pain was unbearable. Because the soft lead flattened and broke apart upon hitting the human body, the destruction of tissue, bone, cartilage, and vein was massive. While the entrance wound was the size of a thumb, the exit wound could be the size of a fist, and when it hit the arm or leg, the ball could shatter the bone from a distance of six to ten inches.[49]

In the case of William S. Sylvester, a farmer, age twenty-two, a Minié ball entered his face an inch below the left eye, passing backward and outward and injuring the eye, ear, and jaw. His mouth was locked, an abscess formed at the posterior wound and discharged freely, and he experienced total palsy of the muscles of facial expression. His brow and lid hung, the cheek was flabby, and his mouth pulled toward one side. Irritated by his inability to cover his eye with the lid, he learned to roll the eye upward to cover the iris, supposing that he had then closed the lid. For the remainder of his life Sylvester would suffer from complete facial palsy. In noting such extensive effects of the Minié ball, Mitchell, Morehouse, and Keen wrote "that a ball in thus passing may radiate effects, so to speak, upon tissues at a distance of an inch at least, is seen commonly enough, where a Minié, gliding over the sciatic nerve, palsies the limb as terribly as though the nerve had been in the very track of the ball."[50]

More than 620,000 soldiers died between 1861 and 1865, and another 500,000 were injured, a cost as great as all the nation's other wars combined. One-third died from battle wounds, and over 94% of battle wounds were caused by gunshot. Amputation was the Civil War's most common surgical procedure, and approximately sixty thousand were performed.[51] Most were over in two minutes, including closing the arteries and preparing a skin flap. The surgeons had little or no understanding of antiseptic procedures, so postoperative septicemias and gangrenes caused a high death rate among the amputees. Mitchell described "hospital gangrene" as a slight flesh wound that "began to show a gray edge of slough," and within two hours it widened at the rate of half an inch an hour and deepened, "until in some horrible cases arteries and nerves were left bare across a devastated region. . . . Instant removal to the open air of tents, etherization, savage cautery with pure nitric acid or bromin, and dressings of powdered charcoal enabled us to deal with these cases more or less well, but the mortality was hideous—at least 45 per cent."[52] In an attempt to suggest some small part of the carnage and torture, Mitchell wrote extreme violence onto the body of his fictional character George Dedlow. As a symbol of the war's costs, Dedlow becomes a composite figure for the half-million Civil War soldiers who went home disfigured and chronically ill.

In Mitchell's writing it is not amputation or the loss caused by amputation, but always the pain that creates the hysterical thrashing, screaming, and crying. Dedlow, before his first amputation, experiences burning pain for six weeks with "the humerus broken, the nerves wounded, and the hand alive only to pain." Finally, the doctors prepare to amputate. Dedlow, with his hand "red, shining, aching, burning, and, as it seemed to me, perpetually rasped with hot files," watches "with a sort of eagerness." Although the pain of the operation without anesthesia (or even alcohol) is severe, "it was insignificant as compared with that of any other minute of the past six weeks." Such burning pain exploits the nervous system, replacing all other physical sensation and invading consciousness with a kind of nerve torture that shatters the body's discipline and coherence. After the amputation, Dedlow experiences elation and wonder. He points to the arm on the floor and says, "There is the pain, and here am I. How queer!" Feeling "instant, unspeakable relief," he falls into a deep sleep.[53] In this scene, amputation marks the end of his hysteria, not the beginning. Regarding such causalgia, Mitchell, Morehouse, and Keen wrote, "We have again and again been urged by patients to amputate the suffering limb."[54]

It is important to note that soldiers who grew anxious and irritable were diagnosed as "hysterical." The "rattling of a newspaper, a breath of air, another's step across the ward, the vibrations caused by a military band, or the shock of the feet in walking," increased the pain, until finally "the patient grows hysterical, if we may use the only term which covers the facts." In *Gunshot Wounds* several case studies illustrate this hysteria. David Schively, age seventeen, was shot in the chest and again in the head at Gettysburg: "Both hands are kept covered with loose cotton gloves, which he wets at brief intervals. He is . . . nervous and hysterical to such a degree that his relatives suppose him to be partially insane. It is difficult even to examine him properly on account of his timidity, and his whole appearance exhibits the effects of pain, want of rest, and defective haematosis."[55] Another soldier, A. D. Marks, age forty-three, was wounded in the neck and in the chest at Chancellorsville on May 3, 1863. On July 5 he "lies on his back, anxious-looking and pain-worn. The left arm rests on a pillow. It is cold, mottled, and swollen. . . . The whole arm and hand, except its back part, is, as he says, alive with causalgia. . . . He constantly prayed us to amputate the arm." Injections of morphine were given near the scar twice a day and provided great relief, but on August 14 the warm weather increased Marks's pain to such a degree that he became hysterical, moaning and weeping "incessantly."[56]

In the narratives—both the forty-eight case histories in *Gunshot Wounds* and the short story—it is not a loss of manhood resulting from amputation that causes hysteria. Some amputees experience phantom limbs, and sometimes this experience creates its own kind of pain that causes hysteria. But many soldiers become hysterical without amputation. It is always the pain, with or without amputation, that causes the hysteria. It is significant that Mitchell repeatedly witnessed hysterical soldiers. Up to this time, many considered such behavior intrinsically feminine, the result of a wandering and faulty womb. Based on these case histories, hysteria becomes a disease of the nervous system, impartial to sex and requiring neither emasculation nor a faulty uterus to thrive. The creation of the rest cure did not originate with notions of feminine decorum.[57] Rather, the rest cure was born out of the extended period of rest necessary to allow the soldier's body to repair damaged nerve tissue.

In the short story, when Dedlow loses all four limbs, Mitchell pauses to explain his nerve irritation theory or how for many months the great mass of men (over 80 percent) who undergo amputations consciously feel that they still have the lost limb. He writes that "the nerve is like a bell-wire. You may pull it at any part of its course, and thus ring the bell as well as if you pulled at the end of the wire; but, in any case, the intelligent servant will refer the pull to the front door, and obey it accordingly." The amputee does not merely imagine the phantom limb. Rather, the nervous system transmits electrical signals from the nerves of the stump to the spine to the brain. The brain refers such messages to the lost parts to which the "nerve-threads" once belonged. The phantom limbs are grounded in chemical and electrical signals sent to the brain, and the fact that the brain misunderstands the signals makes them no less material and sentient. The impressions that create the "phantom limb" continue while the stump is healing and stop when the stump is completely healed and healthy. In some cases this complete healing never occurs, while in others the impressions and sense of the lost limb come and go, so that the man "loses and gains, and loses and regains, the consciousness of the presence of the lost parts."[58]

In the last chapter of *Injuries of Nerves*, Mitchell writes that nearly every man "who loses a limb carries about with him a constant or inconstant phantom of the missing member, a sensory ghost of that much of himself, and sometimes a most inconvenient presence, faintly felt at times, but ready to be called up to his perception by a blow, a touch, or a change of wind." Mitchell describes curious symptoms, such as amputees with lost legs who get up during the night to walk, men who experience erections after castration, and a lost thumb that cuts into an absent palm. In approximately a third of the leg and half the arm amputations, the foot or hand is felt to be nearer to the trunk than the extremity of the other limb, and at times it approaches the trunk "until it touches the stump, or lies seemingly in its interior,—the shadow within the substance."[59]

In "Doubtful Arms and Phantom Limbs," James Krasner writes that recent experiments by V. S. Ramachandran "with neural remapping show that the apprehension of phantom limbs can be incited by the habitual acts of other parts of the body." Because of the interpenetration of cortical regions, a smile, for example, can create the illusion that an amputated hand is still there. In his article, published in 2004, Krasner writes that neurological theories for phantom limbs have "now" superseded the psychological explanations associated with hysteria and femininity that remained significant well into the twentieth century.[60] Krasner makes no mention of Mitchell's Civil War writing regarding phantom limbs. However, it is clear that Mitchell provided a neurological explanation; his theory that phantom limbs were not imaginary remains true.

Yet, according to Ramachandran, there are problems with Mitchell's nerve irritation theory.[61] Maps for such things as vision and tactile and somatic sensations exist in the brain, and these maps can and do change. Although they are mainly stable throughout life, "they are also being constantly updated and refined in response to vagaries of sensory input." Based on this idea that brain maps change, a partial explanation for phantom limbs is that they occur with remapping, the result of a kind of cross wiring.[62]

At the U.S. Army Hospital, Dedlow, as a mere torso, is surrounded by hundreds of cases of epilepsy, paralysis, St. Vitus's dance, and nerve wounds. With any great change in the weather, he might see a dozen convulsions at once, sights from which he cannot escape. He is disturbed by the variety of suffering around him: "One man walked sideways; there was one who could not smell; another was dumb from an explosion." One man had palsy of the rhomboids, and when he lifted his arms, his shoulder blades stood out like wings and "got him the sobriquet of the 'Angel.'" Each one, in fact, "had his own grotesquely painful peculiarity." With no arms and legs, Dedlow is reduced to a "fraction of a man." Ironically he notes his lack of things to do and can only reflect on both the drastic alteration to his sensation and physiological rhythms and the "perfect quiescence" to which his body is reduced.[63]

Again, Mitchell's medical voice breaks through to present his theory of the relation of the mind to the body. In losing four limbs, Dedlow has lost four-fifths of his body weight and as a result eats little and sleeps little. With only about one-fifth of his body remaining, he is less conscious of himself: "About one half of the sensitive surface of my skin was gone and thus much of the relation to the outer world destroyed." His heart beats only forty-five times per minute (down from seventy-eight). A large part of the receptive central organs are idle and degenerate rapidly, and all the central ganglia that give rise to movement are also at rest. Thus much of what is left is functionally dead, and Dedlow remarks, "This set me to thinking how much a man might lose and yet live."[64]

Throughout his discussion of Dedlow as a quadruple amputee, Mitchell is arguing that there is no such thing as pure spirit or mind. His theory of lost limbs firmly contradicts a discourse of prosthesis that defines essence "in terms of what a body can do instead of what a body is." From this point of view, identity is firmly located in the amputee's "ability to perform physically demanding tasks," where "artificial limbs articulate a sort of functionalist work ethic—all the amputee needs to be essentially himself is a working body."[65] This view of artificial limbs maintains the very separation of mind and body that Mitchell challenged in his Civil War writing, where the entire physiological and neurological reality that constitutes the human mind (brain and body) involves surface contact, body weight, heart rate, and other vital functions. Such integrated activities of nerve cells throughout the entire body, which compose phenomena attributed to the mind, cannot be recovered using artificial limbs. While artificial limbs might represent the possibility of anatomical replacement, they cannot simulate the sensation or epistemology of the natural body encompassing the entire nervous system, including all the nerves, even the tiniest nerve fibers in the farthest extremities from the brain. Dedlow concludes that "a man is not his brain, or any one part of it, but all of his economy, and that to lose any part must lessen this sense of his own existence."[66]

Like many others, Dedlow is "greatly eased by having small doses of morphia injected under the skin of my shoulder, with a hollow needle, fitted to a syringe."[67] At Turner's Lane, in order to attempt to manage so much pain, Mitchell, Morehouse, and Keen made heavy use of narcotics. They began their article "On the Antagonism of Atropia and Morphia" by acknowledging this "incessant use" of hypodermic injections, "which alone in many instances seemed able to overcome the anguish of certain forms of neuralgic distress." At certain times "the resident surgeons made every day from twenty to thirty subcutaneous injections. In one case half a grain to a grain of morphia was injected thrice a day, and the man finally recovered after having used nearly four hundred injections."[68] The resident surgeons, passing through these wards with their narcotics and hypodermic syringes, would see "anguish and troubled faces before them, and leaving behind them comfort, and even smiles. The picture is not overdrawn, since, perhaps, few hospitals have ever embraced at one time so many cases of horrible torture." Mitchell wrote that the "pains of traumatic neuralgia are so terrible that we are usually driven at once to the use of narcotic hypodermic injections, without which it would often be impossible to relieve such cases." Narcotics chiefly helped by enabling the soldiers to bridge over the many months needed by the body to reconstruct and restore the nerves. In numerous cases narcotics were "the saving of a number of nerves and of many limbs which otherwise must have been sacrificed for the purpose of relieving unendurable pain."[69]

Mitchell does not refer to the possibility or occurrence of drug addiction in the Civil War writing. Given his propensity to experiment on himself and to sample various drugs and poisons, he most likely experimented with various narcotics at this time. Each day he confronted the "torture" of causalgia, phantom limbs, and gangrene. He saw hundreds of mangled bodies in excruciating shock and pain—a raw and fierce corporeality that created unique clinical opportunities. Only this war could provide such opportunities, and in one sense Mitchell was in the right place at the right time. Yet it was "a hell of pain" and he was done in by the death of his wife and brother, the horrors and complexity of the war, the loss of the university professorship, and the constant strain of overwork. These intense years eventually consumed his strength and vigor. In March 1864 he resigned his position as attending physician at the Pennsylvania Institution for the Instruction of the Blind. A few months later, ill and exhausted, he took a two-month leave of absence from Turner's Lane and sailed for England.

5

WIND AND TIDE

Overall, the trip to London and Paris did little to improve Mitchell's health or lift his spirits. Among the wealthy class of Londoners, he found considerable sympathy for the South and outright hostility for the North. In the various clubs and resorts that he frequented, he did not meet a single person "who was not our enemy.... All the literary folk of England, the banking class, the professions, and generally the titled classes were against us so that it became at last too depressing for a man in search of renewed vigor." He knew no one, and amid the "young fashionables, guardsmen and diplomats," he described himself as a "lonely, somewhat depressed man."[1]

On the Saturday night before the battle of the USS *Kearsarge* and the CSS *Alabama*, Mitchell overheard a group of men betting heavily on the *Alabama*. He was especially taken with one of the young gamblers, and, calling him aside, advised him to change his bet. The *Alabama*, built in secrecy in northwest England in 1862, was a Confederate raider that had captured or burned sixty-five Union merchant ships. The *Kearsarge*, built in Maine in 1861, pursued Confederate raiding ships in European waters, and it finally caught up with the *Alabama* in Cherbourg Harbor. One hour after the start of the battle, the *Alabama* surrendered and then sank. Forty-one of its crew members, including the captain, escaped capture when a private British yacht rescued them. Mitchell, in his poem "*Kearsarge*," wrote that the guns of the two warships were heard in the churches along the English Channel as the summer winds stole through the windows, and "passed the oaken door, / And fluttered open prayer-books / With the cannon's awful roar." After the battle Mitchell dined with the young gambler, and over the wine "ventured to ask him whether he had lost much the night before." But the gambler had changed his bet and won £3,000. He told Mitchell, "You saved my life.... It will pay all my debts and set me free."[2]

Back in Philadelphia, as the war raged on, Mitchell's health deteriorated. A clause in the Draft Act of 1863 allowed men to be exempt or to resign from the military by paying a substitute to serve in their place. Mitchell paid $400 for a substitute to serve a three-year term and resigned his position at Turner's Lane. He explained to Keen, "I have been ill or should have written before. Just after your traps arrived, per porter, I took a big diphtheria + a double quinsy—a droll mixture—but it nearly ended me. And now here I am at the close of February—just beginning to feel that I shall' ever be myself again. There is a great hiatus full of aches and nausiaus doses—mustard plasters, slow, long, lazy days of convalescence and lots of no work done—my health forced from me a resignation of my nerve hospital. It went hard—you know *how* hard." Mitchell had contracted a severe case of diphtheria, and his "double quinsy" consisted of two pus-filled growths near his tonsils. Keen, who had also left Turner's Lane, was in Paris studying with Mitchell's old friend and teacher Robin. Mitchell warned him that "in all things save morals you will profit. That is unless he has changed nucleus and cell—as to his whole economy." In the letter Mitchell also wrote about his investments, including property in California—that "fairy land of oil"—at one dollar an acre. He asked Keen to keep "a lookout on things physiological—especially when you go to Germany—write me about contraptions of all sorts." He also asked for photographs of noteworthy men in physiology and medicine.[3]

———

Although details about this year of poor health and breakdown are scarce, Mitchell wrote two literary works, *The Autobiography of a Quack* and *In War Time*, which represent some of the fears, temptations, and insecurities of the life of a doctor. In 1867, hoping to "call the attention of the public to the various devices of quacks and charlatans," he published *The Autobiography of a Quack* anonymously in the *Atlantic Monthly*. When he revised the story in 1899, he wrote that he only regretted "that it was not set at a later period when christian science could have been made to figure."[4] On the opening pages of this novella, Dr. Elias Sandcraft, the first-person narrator, is at the Massachusetts General Hospital, covered with yellow and brown spots, writing his life story, and dying of Addison's disease. As a young man, he had done poorly at Princeton College. His father was a physician, and not knowing what career to pursue, Sandcraft decided to attend medical school in Philadelphia. He paid all his fees, but he did not attend lectures, spent little time in the dissecting lab, and skipped the required yearlong internship in a physician's office. Graduating after two years, he comments, "whether you merely squeeze through, or pass with credit, is a thing which is not made public, so that I had absolutely nothing to stimulate my ambition." After graduation, he hung his sign right on the edge of an unseemly neighborhood, "where you may be drunk at five cents, and lodge for three, with men, women, and children of all colors lying about you." Only the lowliest of whites lived in the neighborhood, but it was among these broken and destitute people that the new doctor hoped to find his first patients—among the ragpickers, pawnbrokers, and thieves. He observes, "I hated filth, but I understood that society has to stand on somebody, and I was only glad that I was not one of the undermost and worst-squeezed bricks." Eventually he is called to one of these filthy dens and finds a Quaker woman sitting beside a black woman stretched out on a straw mattress. Although this is his chance to act responsibly, he fails miserably, misdiagnosing measles for smallpox and making a hasty exit to lessen his exposure.[5]

After locating an apothecary who will overcharge by 10 to 20 percent and give him the difference, Sandcraft turns to selling drugs such as cod liver oil, quinine, and milk-sugar pills with various creative labels. In St. Louis he assumes the identity of a "Dr. Von Ingenhoff," a well-known German physician who, after years on the plains studying Indian medicine, treated all diseases with vegetable remedies. Sandcraft finds a partner who sits in the waiting room in various disguises gathering patient information and then slips through a sidedoor to pass on the details to Sandcraft. After this scheme is exposed, he sells electromagnetic batteries and tries out several "isms," including spiritualism. He learns to make "remarkably clever knockings, so called, by voluntarily dislocating the great toe and then forcibly drawing it back again into its socket." An even more convincing noise can be produced by "throwing the tendon of the peroneus longus muscle out of the hollow in which it lies, alongside of the ankle." He often fails, but finds that the rare successes always receive more attention, since "most folks preferred to hold their tongues, rather than expose to the world the extent of their own folly."[6]

After St. Louis, Sandcraft returns to Boston, where he considers traveling as a "physiological lecturer" and frightening audiences with a list of symptoms that belong to most healthy people. Then he treats those who "are gulls enough to consult me next day. The bigger the fright, the better the pay." He loses $6,000 attempting to smuggle drugs into the Confederate States. Broke and desperate, he sells himself as a substitute in Providence, "where, as I had heard, patriotic persons were giving very large bounties in order, I suppose, to insure the government the services of better men than themselves." In order to encourage enlistment, the U.S. government paid bounties of $300 to new recruits, and men seeking substitutes could increase this amount. In this way, enlisting, deserting, and reenlisting under another name became a lucrative business. Sandcraft's first bounty amounts to $650, followed by two for $400, and the last for $700 from a Norristown editor, "whose pen, I presume, was mightier than the sword." He is finally caught malingering at the Douglas Hospital in Washington, where he is tried and convicted, and then sent to Fort Delaware until the end of the war.[7]

For the most part, Sandcraft is a humorous vehicle for Mitchell's exposé on quackery. This is not the case in his novel *In War Time*. Printed serially in the *Atlantic Monthly* in 1884 before its publication in book form the next year, this tragic novel contains one of Mitchell's finest psychological studies. And any reader who knows Mitchell is invited in the opening pages to make the connection between the author and the protagonist. The narrative begins at the door of the military hospital on Filbert Street, the same hospital where Mitchell began his Civil War work, and the protagonist, Ezra Wendell, is a contract surgeon as well. It is a hot, humid July day just after the Battle of Gettysburg, and Wendell and his sister, Ann, walk toward the hospital. Wendell's features are "distinct but delicate," and while his upper lip gives his countenance a certain "purity of expression," his mouth is too regular for "manly beauty." His vest is buttoned unevenly, and as two soldiers pass by, one comments, "What an interesting face!," and the other responds, "But what a careless figure! And a soldier with a sun umbrella is rather droll." Wendell is not really a soldier, but he must wear the uniform for his hospital work. Gradually, the reader comes to feel that Wendell is really not much of a doctor either, not in any ideal sense. He is resentful of any kind of criticism from his superiors, and petty annoyances bother him for days. Rather than medicine, botany is clearly what interests him—the stamen of a flower, the insect on his sister's sleeve, and the texture and color of the trunk of a paper mulberry tree. Like Mitchell, Wendell has his own microscope. He buys expensive lenses, and spends his evenings examining and drawing specimens that he gathers from the neighboring paths and ponds. His sister tries to reassure him about his unprofitable practice, saying, "You will only have to love your books and microscope and botany a little less, and study human beings more." As they walk toward the hospital, she carries a heavy basket and hurries him along because he is late again. When she asks for help, he reluctantly takes the basket.[8]

Mitchell disliked the name "Silas," and Wendell is uncomfortable with his given name, "Ezra." This slight similarity signals a deeper connection between the two. Listless and preoccupied, Wendell's moodiness and ennui are reminiscent of Mitchell as a young man—undecided about a career, unable to concentrate, and resentful of authority. When a young soldier dies, Wendell wonders if his own negligence and carelessness caused the death, thinking, "I ought never to have been a doctor." Still, he is likeable enough—described as refined, sensitive, amiable, and handsome, and "supremely happy" in a natural setting with "all his sensuous being alive to the color of the leaves, the plumed golden-rods, the autumn primrose, and the cool woodland odors." In contrast, with a "too delicate sense of the moods and manner" of those around him, he finds human nature messy and annoying. If he could have found some quiet college nook and remained a student of physiology and pathology, he would have achieved some success. But, like Mitchell, he depends on his practice and patients to pay his bills.[9]

For many physicians, treating the poor and destitute was a necessary first step in establishing a successful medical practice. This was Mitchell's experience. After medical school and a year abroad, he failed to obtain an internship at the Pennsylvania Hospital. In place of a residency, he took a position aiding the poor at the Southward Dispensary, where he "acquired experience at the cost of very great labor."[10] Both of his fictional doctors Sandcraft and Wendell, although reluctant, confront this sharp test of character—"the up-hill toil among the lower social classes"—that "makes or mars, degrades or ennobles" the physician. In the case of Sandcraft, after he fails to properly treat a poor black woman, news of his incompetence travels quickly and destroys his reputation. Wendell dislikes people who are simple or poor. But when another doctor refuses, he travels a long distance to treat a farmer's wife and three children who have smallpox. Because his senses are "steadily in revolt," such visits are brief.

Ezra Wendell possesses some of the same character flaws as one of the most famous fictional doctors, Dr. Tertius Lydgate in *Middlemarch*, whose life also ends in tragic ruin. Rather than the ideal—that alert, upright, and unerring doctor whose strict obedience to the Hippocratic Oath never wavers—these doctors possess what George Eliot called spots of commonness and represent the pitfalls and liabilities of a medical career. Wendell is careless, preoccupied, and most likely responsible for at least one patient's death. In his defense the narrator comments, "There is probably no physician who cannot recall some moment in his life when he looked with doubt and trouble of mind on the face of death."

Insightful and complex, *In War Time* feeds on the tension between Mitchell's intimacy and uneasiness with Wendell. Before his final tailspin and disgrace, he is engaged to marry Alice Westerley, the beautiful and wealthy upper-class woman that he loves with a "passion so profound, the first and the only one of his life." In the power of this love lies the suggestion that in time, because Wendell begins to test and try himself according to "his ideal of her conscience," he will rise above his weakness and instability.[11] Despite his gentle and intelligent nature, he is not given the time and ends a broken and pathetic man.

Mitchell's 1864 breakdown was just one in a string of events that caused him years of unrest. After the Civil War ended, he continued to be tossed around by circumstances he could not control. *In War Time* represents his feelings of frustration and self-doubt at that time. He later wrote that in the novel Alice Westerley and Helen Morton were pure creations and Colonel Morton resembled one of his relatives, but Wendell was drawn from life: "The doctor, yes, I drew him from life, but of course it is like taking a man with certain characteristics and putting him in a new position. That is fair enough."[12] Elizabeth Stuart Phelps sent Mitchell high praise of the novel, writing, "I should do another doctor right off if I were you!"[13]

In 1868 Robley Dunglison resigned his chair in physiology at Jefferson Medical College, and Mitchell had a second opportunity to capture a university professorship—or as he put it, the opportunity to again "undergo the awful horrors of a canvass."[14] At this point he had completed the experimental medicine of the 1850s, published *Researches upon the Venom of the Rattlesnake*, and won international acclaim for his Civil War publications. The original work with phantom limbs and causalgia in *Gunshot Wounds* and the articles on malingering, morphine, and reflex paralysis were especially noteworthy because such publications were rare. William F. Norwood writes that apart from the observations of a few keen minds like Mitchell, Keen, Hammond, Hunter McGuire, and Joseph Jones, "Medical science did not gain substantially from the vast wartime experience."[15]

Mitchell was especially well qualified for the Jefferson chair, and just as they had done in 1863, several eminent scientists, including Wyman, Brown-Séquard, Joseph Henry, Hammond, Louis Agassiz, Dalton, Austin Flint, Jr., and Dunglison, recommended Mitchell for the position. Brown-Séquard, in his letter of support, described Mitchell as a most ingenious experimenter, a discoverer of very important facts, doctrines, and laws, and a "clear, forcible and learned writer," adding that "even if the vacant chair were opened to the competition of European as well as American Physiologists, few of the competitors could occupy that chair . . . as Dr. S. Weir Mitchell."[16]

Mitchell's opponent was James Aitken Meigs. His supporters were mainly Philadelphia men who were impressed with Meigs's urbanity, fine lecturing, and pleasant manners. He was already on the Jefferson faculty as an adjunct professor, and although qualified to hold the chair, it was in a different way from Mitchell. He knew the literature on physiology, used vivisection in his teaching, and acknowledged the research ethic. However, his specialty was ethnology and he spent less time with experimental physiology and original research.[17]

Of the thirteen members of the Jefferson board who were present, eight voted for Meigs and five for Mitchell. The group included lawyers, politicians, businessmen, and one physician. When Wyman wrote to inquire about what had gone wrong, Mitchell's response leaves no doubt that he was deeply stung by a second rejection. He later told his son John that at this time "the world seemed at an end for me."[18] He explained to Wyman that the board had focused almost entirely on the issue of class and political party, and that "Dr. Meigs is the son of a shoemaker here and has fought his way up with courage and intelligence." The board members were, like Meigs, Democrats and "nearly all men of the people" who had risen from the ranks, and several connected "by family and other ties have long been looking forward to using their positions to place in the faculty a member of their clique and family."[19] Incredibly, after Meigs won the chair, he made a clear distinction between science and medicine and trained his students to be physicians, warning against the dangers and distractions of scientific investigation. Fye concludes, "Meigs left no mark on physiology in Philadelphia."[20]

While awareness of the importance of physiology was slow to reach Philadelphia, changes were taking place elsewhere. In 1867 the American Medical Association issued guidelines for reforming the nation's medical institutions that included higher admission standards, a longer term of study, and dissection and clinical practice. Charles W. Eliot was elected president of Harvard in 1869. In addition to the establishment of a full-time salaried physiology chair in 1871, he abolished Harvard Medical School as a proprietary unit, installed a graded curriculum, established entrance requirements, required the university, not the medical school, to collect student fees, and began to attend faculty meetings. In 1877 Billings gave a lecture on medical education at Johns Hopkins University. He stressed the importance of original research, urged a more systematic consideration of the scientific aspects of medicine, and recommended that the baccalaureate degree become a prerequisite for medical school.[21] However, as the 1910 Flexner Report, a study of medical education in the United States and Canada, makes clear, for the majority of medical schools, reform came only with pressure and at a snail's pace.

It is sometimes said that Mitchell was a product of his time, but in a professional sense he was ahead of his time in Philadelphia, and his original research and calls for reform in U.S. medicine may have done him more harm than good. He later wrote that "in reading of Englishmen of note and their university life and their friends, I feel how much of the atmosphere of rivalry, the stimulus of congenial tastes present in those groups was lacking amid the provincial life of my city." Even as late as 1883 it was estimated that of the 1,500 Philadelphia physicians, only six engaged in occasional vivisection.[22] The rejections at the University of Pennsylvania in 1863 and Jefferson Medical College in 1868 certainly affected Mitchell's career, but also the state of medicine in Philadelphia for years to come, especially in terms of experimental medicine and medical training. Based on what Mitchell was about to do at the Orthopedic Hospital, one can only speculate about the work in toxicology, immunology, and neurology that he might have pursued with his students had he received the support, laboratory facilities, and prestige of a chair at either institution.

Instead, after the Civil War, he watched the time available for experimentation recede further due to mounting demands in consulting for nervous disease—"at home but interrupted every ten minutes—no experiments." The Jefferson chair was a last chance to achieve a primary focus on research. In many ways it was out of his control now. Sounding a little like Ezra Wendell in the novel, he closed the letter to Wyman with the following: "Of course I felt bitterly the defeat of certain intellectual ambitions, but most of all the fact that I must continue to work as hard as ever at practice and so see it year after year encroaching on the little time I can give to science."[23] Even though he would not give up experimentation entirely, from now on any "systematic research" was exactly what would be missing. The two defeats served as roadblocks, preventing him from fulfilling his potential in what had been his first love—vivisection-based research and experimental physiology. Indeed, the Jefferson rejection marked a major turning point in Mitchell's career. Not by his own choice, he would now focus on consulting and private practice. He would never acquire a chair in physiology, and this failure constituted the one major disappointment of his medical career. Characteristically, he refused to write about it entirely as a defeat, feeling instead that "a certain amount of misfortune destroys in some all the germs of success. For others, a failure is like a blow. It may stagger, but it excites to forceful action."[24]

About this same time, Phillips Brooks accepted the position of rector of Trinity Church in Boston. Brooks had been in Philadelphia for ten years, and the decision to leave came as sad news to Mitchell and Elizabeth. For most of this time Mitchell had been a widower, and Brooks spent most of his evenings at the Mitchell home. The friendship between the nerve doctor, his sister, and the Episcopalian preacher had evolved into a deep and warm intimacy.

In August 1869 Elizabeth wrote Brooks that the morning mail had confirmed her worst fears: "I think you *very much* under-rate your importance to the church in Phil and your usefulness there. You are our only strong barrier in fact the only one strong or weak against ritualism which threatens the very foundation of the protestant element in our church. Of course the Boston people are calling in their usual arrogant tones, seeing only their side of the question and I fear their wily tongues. My personal feeling in the matter I cannot talk about, of course private friendship must always go under in such cases."[25] Brooks was captivating and charming. His language was beautiful and erudite, creating a special intensity about his preaching. Mitchell wrote that at his Wednesday lectures "he used to stand away from a desk, so that his massive figure and the strength of his head had their effect, and from his great height the magic of his wonderful eyes was felt, like the light from some strong watch-tower by the sea."[26] As his reputation steadily grew, Brooks developed into one of those larger-than-life figures and became one of America's great Anglican preachers, especially in terms of his oratory skills and his widespread influence on other preachers.[27] In 1873, when fire destroyed Boston's Trinity Church, a new church was built in the city's prestigious Back Bay. Henry Richardson was the architect, Stanford White the interior designer, and John LaFarge the artist for what is considered one of the nation's most magnificent buildings. Brooks's gentle but commanding presence further enhanced this grand setting. Mitchell wrote that while he had known a number of the men who were thought to be great, Brooks was the only one who seemed "entirely great."[28] Everything about him was worthy of love and respect. Mitchell often looked forward to ending his day with a visit from Brooks, when together they would smoke and talk. The loss of his conversation and warm friendship left an empty, lonely place by the fire.

In July 1872 Mitchell's mother, suffering from asthma and insomnia in the intense July heat, fell and bruised her head. Mitchell wrote that she looked "very
ill and haggard" and took only milk and a little soup. Doctor Hutchinson was
attending, and Tish and Saidie came on alternating days. But because of the heat
in the city, Mitchell advised Elizabeth to stay away. Elizabeth was ill herself, he
reasoned, and their mother might improve quickly, making the trip unnecessary.[29] Matilda Mitchell died four days later at the age of seventy-two. Within
months of her death, Mitchell's brother Walsh, who was thirty-six, also died.
In his last letter from St. Kitts, he apologized for the shame he had caused the
family and expressed his gratitude to his older brother for his help and support.
With Walsh gone, there were no more debts to pay or disturbing stories to conceal. Mitchell placed Walsh's swords over the mantel and began to construct a
new story. Leaving behind the gambling, altercations, and rakishness, Mitchell
spoke of Walsh as a valiant war hero.

In August, on the way to Newport, Mitchell stopped in Boston to see
Holmes, who had just returned from Newport due to the death of an old servant. That day Holmes was in the mood to talk about religion. Known as a mil-
itant Unitarian who often attacked Calvinistic dogma, he said that Christianity
was a failure because of its inability to relate to contemporary social and scientific issues. Unitarianism was on the decline because of too much free thought
on the one hand and too much Episcopalianism on the other. Mitchell wrote
that the talk with Holmes was "one sided because it came so fast but was worth
hearing—much more of such talk is done in Boston than with us I fancy—I
liked his saying that Presbyterian preaching was Tubercular." Even though
Mitchell rose twice to go, Holmes talked on. When Mitchell finally left the
house, Holmes followed him outside, sitting on his top step and chatting for
another ten minutes, and "at last made chirpy remarks to me until I was out
of ear shot—and far away up Beacon st."[30]

The next summer, Mitchell would require more than a trip to Newport to
escape the heat and exhaustion. Describing his condition as "very grave neurasthenia," he again broke down and again sailed for England and France. He spent
almost two months abroad, sometimes traveling alone and sometimes with Frank
Lewis, and he saw old friends and returned to the Alps. In the letters home he

mentioned the ripening hops and wheat, the boys at cricket in open daylight at 9:00 p.m., and St. Martin's, one of the oldest churches in England, with a little square window where the lepers once stood to hear the service. He still complained about the food, writing Elizabeth that "no English cooking is as good as ours—(home) coffee atrocious," and commenting on the "droll" custom of bringing the salad after dessert. Taking the train to Dover, he slept at Calais and "enjoyed that queer old city." In Paris he revisited the Latin Quarter "and saw with strange sense of youth gone by—my old rooms. . . . I went in to see Vulpian and Robin and Charcot—and envied their laboratories." He went again to Notre Dame and the Louvre, and saw the "young—pretty girls," that "loveliest of pictures Corregios Marriage of St Catherine," the red-legged soldiers, and "graceful merry french women and meagre children."[31]

Ten invigorating days in Pontresina, Switzerland, were the highlight of this particular trip, constituting a kind of camp cure for Mitchell. Each day he walked and climbed fifteen miles up the Bernina route and along the River Inn, a spot "unmatched in Switzerland. Indeed the air 6000 ft. above the sea is like the wine of life to folks who are nervous and—bloodless." In another letter he wrote that "never was atmosphere like this—so cool and pure and so energizing."[32]

He continued the trip "steaming down the dream land—people on earth call Lake Como," to Chiavenna, Italy, and then to Milan, "fruit—Heat Cathedral—No strangers—No cholera but vast dread of it." Back in England, he visited Salisbury and Stonehenge, then "between hedge rows and under noble oaks" to Bath, Wells, Bristol, and along the rapid Wye to the "most delicious ruins" of Tintern Abbey. He stayed at the Beaufort Arms, "a hotel so tiny that it might have been—made for a baby house. Two stories ivy clad with queer stone stairways on the outside of the house—and the abbey just across the way." That evening he drank whiskey punch with two clever young Englishmen until midnight. The next day he rode on the top of the coach with handsome girls on either side, chatting "immensely as we bowled along the lovely Wye to Monmouth two hours—away."[33] In these letters Mitchell is relaxed and restored, momentarily cut loose from habit and convention in a scene of idyllic beauty. In this setting he is "a lover of the meadows and the woods" with young and lively people for companions—drinking whiskey punch and riding on top of the coach—a role quite different from the one he would soon create for himself in Philadelphia.

Phillips Brooks, after leaving Philadelphia, wrote to Elizabeth every week. In 1871 he told her:

> This is one of the evenings when I wish myself in Philadelphia; not that anything particular is the matter with Boston, but I have an evening to myself and I am tired of reading, and there is nobody in particular that I can go and see without its being a visit, which I don't feel up to. Nobody's house where I can go and smoke and be pleasantly talked to, and answer or not, as I please. I know one such house in another town where I don't live any longer. But I am not there, and I must make the best of it.

Brooks returned to Philadelphia three times during his first three months in Boston. In December 1873 he told Elizabeth, "Three weeks from to-night I hope to start for Philadelphia. Fix which night you will for me to dine with you, and I will come up to the trial without a flinch." Two weeks later he wrote, "The first beauty of the New Year is that I am coming on to see you all, and a week from to-night shall be upon my way. You do not know how much I depend upon it." In February he wrote, "Eight weeks from to-day I'll be in Philadelphia." Even after years in Boston, Brooks still kept track of the time between trips and repeatedly wrote about how much he depended on these visits. In his last letter to Elizabeth, he wrote, "Our new Chapel begins to look beautifully, and by the time you are here the walls will be almost done. . . . So don't fail to come. My love to Weir."[34] Elizabeth died ten days later, in May 1874.

Mitchell had lost his wife, two brothers, and mother. He had been a widower for twelve years. However, Elizabeth's death set him adrift. He often talked about "how terrible was Aunt Lizzys loss," telling his son John, "I was half afraid to come home again to this lonely house and I *have* found it hard. I look up fr my work to ask Aunt Lizzy a question or to say isn't this good—or I want to know how this bit of English sounds and—the wonderful face that had a world of expressions is gone away forever." Mitchell's sons were often away at school or with Grandma Elwyn at the Reculver farm, and so he was alone in the house. He wrote John, "Today I am awfully alone—a fate for which few men are so ill fitted as I—How much I yearn for you—how eagerly I shall welcome the clatter of those great feet of yours." He would never get used to "the empty chair on the far side of my table," and "no one will ever fully know what this death has cost me."[35]

John was fifteen and attending St. Paul's School in Concord, New Hampshire, a preparatory academy founded before the Civil War for the sons of the Protestant elite. For a while, Mitchell tried to replace Elizabeth with his son, writing him at least once a week, usually on Sunday afternoon when he was "free of flies in the office web," the "only day when there comes in a daylight segar—and—a very brief sense of nothing to do—which is sweet and full of comfort." These loving and warmhearted letters to John are filled with talk of books, poetry, family news, and advice. Rather than religion or romance, Mitchell urged finding comfort in books because "books you do not have to make love to in order to get the best of them and in time of sorrow—or sickness and amidst all the worries and inevitable disappointments of life they are noble help-mates—honest counsellors sweet trustful friends."[36] When the director of St. Paul's, Dr. Coit, urged John to take confirmation, Mitchell advised caution: "I think no man should publicly acknowledge himself as a member of Christ's Church until he feels sure of himself. . . . Men are no better and no worse for saying in public I believe. Some men among the best I know have never been able to do it. . . . In this matter I leave it to you—I do not want you pushed into it or talked into it—or led by mere example—It is a thing to be sure about *very very* sure."[37] Mitchell's mother had been a deeply religious Presbyterian, but his father had not been religious, and memories of childhood churchgoing and Bible reading were mainly ones of confusion and boredom. Although these feelings would change, at this time Mitchell was investing his faith in books and science. He had a pew at St. Stephen's Church where he regularly attended Sunday service, and he always went to Christ Church on Easter. But he expressed no stirring belief in Christianity. Over a year later, the subject of John's confirmation came up again. This time Mitchell responded firmly, "No matter on what your objections be founded if they exist it is enough to prevent or postpone this act. . . . Do in this matter obstinately as you please. . . . Whatever conclusion you reach you may say is my conclusion and that you are acting under my wishes."[38]

These letters to John provided a safe place, and sometimes the only place, where Mitchell could record certain feelings and events. In October 1873 he wrote, "On Saturday Prof. Dalton dined with us—He came to offer me a Professorship in the chief medical school of New York. Of course I said no—not out of pure love to Philadelphia but from dislike of change wh. means change of friends and every thing else in life. . . . Do not speak of his offer. . . . This was my third offer from New York—and—will I presume be the last—as now they must be sure I am not to be had."[39] When he was asked to join the board of trustees of the University of Pennsylvania, he told John that he said yes with some doubt because of the "savage feeling it may make among the older men of that school. Curious that the board wh once rejected me as a Professor should now think of me as their fellow and to become chairman of their medical committee and in a manner the governor of the man once preferred to me. Time makes things to turn queer corners. I leave this matter in other hands—not wanting the place or its grave responsibilities—not willing to refuse them and not quite sorry if the opposition to me prove too strong." Such cautious comments before the vote indicate a considerable residue of hurt from earlier rejections as he mentally prepared for another disappointment. At this time he also became a trustee of the old Fifth Street library, and he told John that this gave him pure pleasure because of the library's quaintness and the "flavour of romance there was to me about it in my boy days." He had spent so much time there, watching the "old fellows going in and out of the little railed in space . . . and taking off—books and journals. These I was told were Trustees—I held them in awe—and now perhaps some small boy will hold me in awe." He added, "I see you grin at the notion of anyone having me in awe."[40]

Few of Mitchell's letters to his second son survive. If there were more letters, they may have been too expressive and detailed and been destroyed by Mitchell or Langdon himself (who survived his father and older brother by two decades). Mitchell's comments to John about Langdon were often anxious and critical. While he confided in John—"I tell you everything"—he was troubled by Langdon's poor performance in school and bad behavior. There were fights and rows, and though John was not a particularly good student either, Langdon was finally expelled from St. Paul's and not allowed to return. Mitchell wrote, "Lany going to the farm—wants a fly rod—says there are bass in the Brandywine—I told him there wd be one on the bank with the B. left out— at wh. he grinned superciliously." In another letter Mitchell noted that Langdon "cultivates his oddities a little—as gardeners do their double flowers—and this is a family trait not ours. . . . Queerness is not ableness—though often mistaken for talent."[41]

After receiving the news that both sons had been in school fights, Mitchell advised John that if a blow be needed, to remove his glasses, strike hard with the fist, and never slap anyone's face: "If it be worth while to hit it is well to hit hard—I remember your good Grandfather giving me this advice. . . . What came to Lany of his row—I hope his great physical strength is not making him quarrelsome." And again, "I have been more troubled about Langdons mis-conduct than I cared to show—I am too sensitive about my boys—and the intense sel-fishness of L. upset me."[42] At Harvard Langdon was cutting class, overspend-ing, and causing trouble. Mitchell, with his firm beliefs in heredity, must have wondered if Langdon had inherited any of his Uncle Walsh's wild tendencies.

The winter and spring months dragged on. Mitchell was ill, depressed, and unable to work. On April 4 he wrote John, "I never did fancy being alone all the time and this winter and no Aunt Lizzy and the long sad—evenings has been too much for me. . . . No doubt summer will set me straight—but it's rather disgusting to be told by one and another how badly you look. . . . This is a long growl—but I tell you all things."[43] Such remarks were sincere enough, but they were also preparing John for the possibility of a second marriage. As early as 1868, Mitchell had joked about marrying into the Cadwalader family, writing Elizabeth about the three Cadwalader sisters, "I greatly enjoyed my visit and am not clear if it be Emily Mary or Maria. Couldnt you assist me." He wrote to Mary Cadwalader's friend Cassy Meredith, asking for her help in securing a half hour alone with Mary: "Respect for Miss Cadwaladers feelings has forced me to try to avoid the appearance of seeking her—and hence no end of shams and pretences which are unmanly and destroy ones self respect—. . . . But above all do not put your self out about it because soon or late I shall find my chance."[44] In the spring of 1875 he found his chance and proposed. Mary Cadwalader's brother John, who was assistant secretary of state at the time, initially opposed the marriage, but Mitchell had his way.

On April 13 Mitchell wrote his son about a "fresh hold on life" due to his plans to marry Miss Mary Cadwalader, "a lady—sweet tempered—well bred intelligent—and—only willing to quarrel with me because you boys are to be away so much." It had been Elizabeth's dying wish that he remarry. He also spoke with Grandma Elwyn, who was "fully satisfied not only that I am about to do what is wise but that for you and Lany as well it is a wise step."[45] His comments and telling repetition of the word "wise" underscore the fact that this was not a romantic alliance. He regarded this marriage mainly in terms of social status. Through marriage to a Cadwalader, he and his sons would move from the mid-dle class into Philadelphia's most elite social circle, and Mitchell would fulfill his dream of becoming a republican aristocrat, the "best of American types."[46]

Around one thousand wedding invitations were mailed. On June 23 the cou-ple wed. A week later, along with Mary's sister Maria and Mitchell's son John, they sailed for Europe. Though Mary had wanted both sons to accompany them, Mitchell would not allow Langdon to go. The plan was that Mitchell and John would share a stateroom on deck. Mitchell thought that it would be "immensely—jolly *unless*—we have a storm." Mary was anxious that both sons would come to love her, telling Mitchell that if she could not teach them to love her, she would feel only half his wife. Although John called her "Mrs. Mitchell," she thought "Mary" would be nice, and Mitchell thought "Mama" was appropriate.[47] Just nine months after the wedding, Mary gave birth to a daughter, Maria Gouverneur Cadwalader Mitchell.

After a year at Mitchell's home at 1332 Walnut Street, they moved to 1524 Walnut Street, the four-story row house and former home of Mary's family. Mitchell had an office there, and visitors were always met by a doorman in knickerbockers, red vest, and swallowtail coat with brass buttons. When Mitchell·was at home and ready to receive visitors, a sign with the word "in" was placed outside the front door; when he was away, ill, or otherwise occupied, a sign with the word "out" appeared. Visitors included patients, friends, schoolgirls who wanted an autograph, tourists, and "the beggars and pests of every prominent man's office."[48] Mitchell and his wife were fond of entertaining. As the perfect host and hostess, they gave lavish dinner parties with liveried servants, elaborate service, and sumptuous delicacies. After a meal, the fine old Madeira went round the table. Mitchell's father had also loved to entertain, but a great deal had changed since the days when houseguests asked for two-pronged steel forks and spit tobacco on the fireplace grates. Expensive wines had replaced the whiskey punch, and after dinner the men smoked fine cigars in Mitchell's study where, without the women, they could talk more freely.

Mitchell's study was just the right spot for such gatherings, a large comfortable room filled with the richness of mahogany and walnut, rare books, souvenirs, photographs, and fresh flowers. A large red rug covered the floor, and manuscripts, reviews, and magazines covered the desk and shelves. A death mask of Dante was kept in a glass-covered case; engravings, etchings, framed letters, a huge rattlesnake done in watercolors, and eventually a life-size portrait of William Harvey covered the walls. When not in formal wear, Mitchell would be dressed in his brown velvet smoking jacket, red tie, and houndstooth waistcoat and trousers. Tall and thin, dapper and charming, he was a man who never gave the impression of hurry or eagerness. In time, he began to stoop a little at the shoulders and his hands began to tremble. But with his white beard and graying hair parted in the middle, intensely penetrating blue eyes, and air of absolute self-assurance, he could hold his own socially and professionally with anyone in Philadelphia, Boston, and New York.

6

PANDORA'S BOX

When Mitchell married Mary Cadwalader in 1875, he had just embarked on what was, in terms of fame and fortune, the most successful period of his life. Although he has been best (and sometimes only) known as the creator of the rest cure, when Mitchell began to focus primarily on rest, he was in his forties and midway through his career. While there is the expected overlap, his medical life may be divided into three parts: the animal experimentation of the 1850s, the Civil War work with gunshot wounds and nerve injuries, and the treatment of mental illness beginning in the 1870s. The early and extensive vivisection provided a solid foundation in physiology for the important war work that followed. And Mitchell noted that the first indication of the great value of "rest in disease" began with his treatment of Civil War soldiers.[1]

The third phase of Mitchell's career began formally and modestly enough in 1871, when he joined the staff of Philadelphia's Orthopedic Hospital, a two-room hospital and outpatient clinic established in 1867 by Thomas G. Morton and located over a surgical instrument shop at 15 South Ninth Street. The hospital was established to treat charity and paying patients suffering from deformities such as curvature of the spine, joint disease, and clubfoot. A few years after the hospital was founded, the staff realized the relationship between some bodily deformity and nervous disease, and the Infirmary for Nervous Diseases was added to the Orthopedic Hospital. Mitchell became the first physician at the infirmary. Wharton Sinkler was the second, and they were the only attending physicians until 1879.

Largely due to Mitchell's efforts, over the next decades the infirmary became a major center for the treatment of nervous disease. William Keen wrote that Mitchell's first step in bringing about this transformation was to reconfigure the hospital's apathetic board of managers into a group of younger, more active and knowledgeable men. In 1873 the hospital moved to an old residence at the corner of Seventeenth and Summer Streets. In 1886 a separate twelve-month nursing program was established with a focus on neurologic care. In 1887 the old house was replaced by a new building with wards, thirty-six private rooms, and greatly expanded facilities.[2]

Mitchell remained the driving force at the infirmary, and his extensive clinical work and training there sometimes go unnoticed in accounts of his life. Much of the expansion and development were due to his reputation and his focus on research and publication. Like Turner's Lane Hospital during the Civil War, the infirmary provided Mitchell with opportunities for the clinical research and collaboration on which he thrived. Like a magnet attracting rare and difficult cases, he saw patients who traveled great distances to seek his help, often as a last resort. He developed a neurological department with residents and assistants like Morris Lewis, Charles K. Mills, Wharton Sinkler, and William Osler. Innovations included the teaching clinic, an expanded outpatient department where a senior physician was always in charge, and a school for massage and remedial exercise.[3] Mitchell was one of the first physicians in the United States to introduce the card index for cases, where a detailed case history of each patient was taken, followed by an extensive examination. The case-history form at the infirmary included "family history," "personal history," "causes assigned by the patient for the disease," and "sexual functions." Then a group of doctors, including the senior physician and usually an ophthalmologist and medical electrician, met to hear the case history read aloud and to make recommendations.

There are record books of the Orthopedic Hospital and Infirmary for Nervous Disease for the years 1867–1942 housed at the College of Physicians of Philadelphia. Although incomplete at times and missing for some years, the records contain a wealth of information, including patient books, casebooks, and admission and discharge books. According to these records, Mitchell began by seeing patients of all ages, from eight months to seventy-seven years, for such things as infantile paralysis, epilepsy, chorea, asthma, Pott's disease, and meningitis. In 1871, of the 160 patients he saw, two were classified as insane, and there was no diagnostic classification for "hysteria" or "neurasthenia." This began to change quickly, however, and by 1879 there were twenty-two patients with "general nervousness," thirteen with "hysteria," one with "melancholia," thirteen with "neurasthenia," and one with "night terrors." By 1889 there were twenty-nine patients with "hysteria," six with "insanity," four with "insomnia," eleven with "melancholia," seventeen with "general nervousness," three with "night terrors," and sixty with "neurasthenia." The records make clear that Mitchell's rest cure was in wide use by the various physicians at the infirmary. Patient discharge conditions were recorded as "satisfactory," "cured," "relieved," "improved," and "unimproved." And a few patients "left" without formal discharge.

According to its bylaws, the Orthopedic Hospital was intended to benefit all persons irrespective of "creed or color and . . . particularly intended to assist the indigent in obtaining a permanent cure or relief, by providing board and appliances free, or at such a cost as can be afforded." By 1906 the hospital had 120 beds for patients with neurologic problems, and 84 of these were reserved for the indigent.[4] Mitchell's concern for patients unable to pay is another aspect of his medical work rarely acknowledged. He wrote that the "influence of this clinic in Philadelphia has been very great, owing to the unusual care and the amount of attention, which could not have been exceeded, were the patients millionaires."[5] Many of the residents and assistant physicians became prominent neurologists, and four were early presidents of the American Neurological Association. Between 1889 and 1907 the members of the staff published 522 papers and articles on a wide variety of topics, largely due to Mitchell's emphasis on research and publication.[6]

Keen, a surgeon at the Orthopedic Hospital for eight years, stated that in 1871 when Mitchell began this work, there was no Philadelphia hospital with even a ward for neurological diseases. There were six such hospitals in Europe and only two in the United States. The Orthopedic Hospital and Infirmary for Nervous Diseases would become one of the most fully equipped special hospitals in the nation. In an attempt to capture Mitchell's leadership, Keen said that the "tail began by being longer than the dog and it ended by its wagging the dog."[7] While it is important to acknowledge Mitchell's innovations, it is also important to keep in mind that when he joined the staff, he was working in two small rooms above an instrument shop—a humble circumstance for a man who had published widely, earned an international reputation, and been in the running for professorships at Philadelphia's two leading medical schools. However, as with his first batch of rattlesnakes and his exceptional interest in gunshot wounds and nerve injuries during the Civil War, Mitchell sensed the opportunities and possibilities. Whether in toxicology, neurology, or psychiatry, Mitchell's mind was brilliantly suited to this type of trailblazing.

The same year that Mitchell joined the staff of the infirmary, he published *Wear and Tear; or, Hints for the Overworked*. Although this seventy-page rambling lecture regarding diet, dress, and mental hygiene stands as some of the first sociomedical writing, it can hardly be considered a touchstone for his past or future work. It was an instant hit, however, selling out in ten days and going through four editions in a year. It created considerable controversy, and while some of the harshest critics referred to its author as a quack, hundreds of people contacted Mitchell by mail and came to him with a variety of ills and complaints. For example, after reading *Wear and Tear* a lawyer from central Pennsylvania wrote to "Wear Mitchell" about deafness and headaches and then traveled to Philadelphia for treatment. Upon examination, Mitchell found that his ears were completely blocked and after syringing them, the man suddenly heard. He found that "his own voice—was terrible and the street noises thunder. After leaving me he came back faint and begged to rest awhile before venturing into the tremendous row of the streets."[8] Of course this case, a funny story and a problem easily solved, was exceptional. Increasingly there were desperate, pathetic, and even bizarre cases knocking at Mitchell's door.

When he first began this pioneering work, Mitchell wondered a little about its relative value. All the success and attention gave him reason to pause. Just what was he tapping into? He felt ambivalent about the sales of *Wear and Tear* and told Elizabeth, "I am amused to watch the wear and tear—business. It brought me 25$ yesterday. Then the day before 3—reviews. . . . No one can be more amazed at this odd little bit of success than I am—To have done so much right honest work without anybody knowing or caring and then to have one little flirtation with popular literature written about and talked about fr. Maine to Georgia."[9] He told John, "If I do any thing really of value—it does not get credit—and then somehow you hit the taste of the hour—and succeed."[10] The "right honest work" and "thing really of value" referred to Mitchell's 1872 publication of *Injuries of Nerves and Their Consequences*.

It is interesting to consider that the same writer published books as different as *Injuries of Nerves* and *Wear and Tear* in the same year. *Injuries of Nerves*, a heavily revised and expanded version of *Gunshot Wounds*, had taken Mitchell eight years to complete. When William James published his article on the consciousness of lost limbs in 1887, he referred to *Injuries of Nerves* in his first and last sentences, stating that overall he left the subject where he found it, in Dr. Mitchell's hands. One of the results of James's investigation was admiration for the manner in which Mitchell had written about it fifteen years before.[11] As Richard

Walter points out, *Injuries of Nerves* is a classic medical text, representing cutting-edge research on the anatomy of nerves, neurophysiology, and diagnosis and treatment.[12] While Mitchell was puzzled by the popular success of *Wear and Tear*, he began to understand the message, finding himself in the vanguard of yet another medical breakthrough.

In 1877, one year after the birth of Mitchell's daughter, Maria, he gave the annual oration before the medical faculty of Maryland, which was subsequently published as *Fat and Blood: And How to Make Them*. He also published two long essays in one volume, titled *Nurse and Patient, and Camp Cure*. *Fat and Blood*, another huge success, stands as the most complete description of the rest cure, with chapters devoted to "Fat in Its Clinical Relations," "Seclusion," "Rest," "Massage," "Electricity," and "Dietetics and Therapeutics." These components of the cure had all been used by other physicians, but as Mitchell noted several times, they had not been combined and employed in just this particular way. Many of his patients were women, invalids, or semi-invalids, whose health had been gradually deteriorating and who had already seen many other doctors. They had been treated for various troubles and experienced loss of appetite, intense fatigue, depression, serious weight loss, spinal inflammation, migraine, and irregular or no menstruation. They had undergone water cures, braces, plaster jackets, pessaries, and cauterization and taken various drugs such as bromides, opium, and chloral.

Before anything else, Mitchell considered the possibility of organic disease. If no organic disease could be detected, he believed that patients suffering from depression, anorexia, anemia, or drug addiction had experienced a family crisis or other mental trauma that stole their energy and left them sleepless. Over time, symptoms like back pain and constipation developed and worsened. Once Mitchell had eliminated organic disease as a cause, he generally understood problems with the spine, uterus, stomach, and bowels as symptoms. He understood hysteria as the transformation of emotional trauma into somatic manifestations. Still, diagnosis was a knotty business, since nerve damage resulted in an almost indistinguishable mix of nutritive and other disorders that were the same or similar to symptoms of hysteria. A symptom such as chronic spasm might be the "child of either parent, whether it be hysteric or due to the nerve lesion, and yet as it concerns treatment, it may be of the utmost moment to reach such a decision."[13] Isolation from family and friends, complete rest with massage and electrical treatments, and weight gain would result in an increase in the color and amount of red blood cells and thus energy and wholesomeness for the body and mind.

Mitchell's first rest cure patient, Mrs. G. of Maine, was a tall, gaunt woman weighing under a hundred pounds who had been to spas and seen eminent physicians and gynecologists. She had worn spinal supports and had taken every possible tonic; yet her condition worsened until she was unable to leave her room and suffered from insomnia. Any excitement while eating caused nausea and vomiting. Any use of her eyes caused nausea and headache. After several visits and much thought, Mitchell insisted that she be secluded from friends, relatives, books, and correspondence. The key to the success of this case was the addition of massage and electricity. Mitchell wrote that "in two months she gained forty pounds and was a cheerful, blooming woman, fit to do as she pleased. She has remained, save for time's ravage, what I made her."[14]

As a treatment for eating disorders, depression, and anxiety, among other things, the rest cure spread quickly throughout the United States, England, and the rest of Europe. Part of its success was the fact that the grim alternatives included surgery, institutionalization, and drug addiction. Various doctors made changes to the rest cure to suit their individual notions and needs. For example, the actual location of a cure could vary from an expensive hotel or resort to complete isolation in a rural clinic. Some patients were very young, prepubescent girls; others were young women still living at home with their parents. There were unmarried workingwomen, physicians' wives, older women, and teachers. Finally, there were the "early feminists," as Ellen Bassuk describes them, women like Charlotte Perkins Gilman, Jane Addams, and Virginia Woolf.[15] Although some of these "New Women" left a record of their experiences, they most likely do not represent the majority of rest cure patients.

In treating an "endless" variety of illness and disease, Mitchell did not prescribe a rest cure for all patients. Several times he stated that the first decision was whether the patient needed exercise or rest, a determination that "turns up for answer almost every day in practice. Most often we incline to insist on exercise, and are led to do so from a belief that women walk too little, and that to move about a good deal every day is good for everybody."[16] But in the cases where exercise failed to help and caused additional fatigue, indigestion, and nausea, rest was needed. Some patients were thin, colorless, and perpetually weary but not hysterical. For them isolation was not an essential part of their treatment. They could rest in their own homes for two or three hours each day.

Others needed separation from the home and complete rest in a hospital or clinic for six to eight weeks.

In some cases, patients began by feigning illness to gain sympathy and attention and to manipulate and control family members. In one such case, a woman appeared to eat a chop for breakfast and no other food throughout the day. When Mitchell discovered the oranges, bananas, and bread under her pillow, she said coolly, "Well, now I am caught."[17] Mitchell simply could not abide such patients, viewing them as capricious and self-indulgent. He created the fictional character Octopia Darnell in the novel *Roland Blake* to represent this kind of couch-loving invalid. He lashed out with irritability and anger, comparing them to home predators. Over time, through inactivity and excessive self-study of "every ache and pain," these spoiled women developed serious physical problems and hysteria. Only through breaking up "the whole daily drama of the sick-room, with its little selfishnesses and its craving for sympathy and indulgence," could such women begin to get well.[18] Still, other patients had become hysterical through no fault of their own. In referring to the sickroom, regardless of whether the patient was feigning illness, Oliver Wendell Holmes described a chronic invalid "as a vampire sucking the blood of the healthy people of a household." Mitchell commented, "Strong as are his words, they do no more than briefly describe what really happens in many families."[19]

Imagine a young woman, most often between the ages of twenty and thirty, who lost color and weight, was "tired all the time, by and by has a tender spine, and soon or late enacts the whole varied drama of hysteria."[20] Such nervous instability led to a great number of hysterical symptoms and ended in invalidism. Other cures and treatment had failed, and under such circumstances "even the firmest women lose self-control." While a few patients, men and women, were ennobled by such illness, most broke down and degenerated morally as well as physically. The room was shut up and darkened; the caregiver, often a sister or mother, read to the patient since the light hurt her eyes, and often in such a suffocating atmosphere the devoted caregiver also fell ill. In these cases, removal from the home and the substitution of the devotion of a friend or relative with the firmness of a trained nurse were necessary.

The rest cure's full feeding began with milk, but within ten days the patient was eating three full meals, often two ounces of malt extract before each meal, a pound of beef daily in the form of raw soup, three to four pints of milk, and large amounts of butter. Depending on the individual case, other parts of the diet might consist of cod-liver oil (sometimes given as a rectal injection), iron, whiskey or champagne, strychnine, and aloe extract.

Electrotherapy and massage compensated for the negative effects of complete bed rest by raising the body's temperature, exercising the muscles, and bringing about positive nutritive changes.[21] The use of electricity was more like actual exercise than massage, causing contractions of the muscles, increasing the absorption of oxygen, and changing the form and color of the red corpuscles. Daily massage began with the feet, where the masseuse gently pinched the skin and rolled it lightly between the fingers. The small muscles were kneaded, and finally each foot was firmly rolled about with both hands. The ankles were massaged next and so on to every part of the body (except the face), with special care given to the loin and spine. On the first days the massages were gentle and lasted thirty minutes; gradually they were made rougher and extended to one hour. Applications of cocoa oil or Vaseline lubricated the skin, making it "smooth and soft and supple." Under the skilled hands of practiced manipulators, such massage stimulated the skin and its secretions, increased the flow of blood to the tissues, toned the muscles, and relieved the body's sore spots, leaving a "general sensation of comfort and ease." Patients found these massages "delightfully soothing" and complained only when they stopped.[22]

Despite the diversity of patients and range of illness, the one essential ingredient in all rest cures was the male physician. In all cases success depended on a "man who can insure belief in his opinions and obedience to his decrees . . . and it is in such cases that women who are in all other ways capable doctors fail, because they do not obtain the needed control over those of their own sex." If it were possible to reduce the feminist angst with Mitchell to one central idea, it would be this issue of control. A successful cure depended on surrender, submission, and childlike acquiescence. From Mitchell's point of view, the best doctor was the one who was perceived as forceful and godlike, especially since it was necessary to break the will of obstinate patients. Treating hysteria involved much more than altering the physical conditions. In fact, providing moral medication by directing the patient's thoughts to her lapse from duties and the selfishness of invalidism belonged "to the higher sphere of the doctor's duties, and if he means to cure his patient permanently, he cannot afford to neglect them." Apart from the physician's force of character, Mitchell usually remained vague about how he exacted such obedience, writing that it was not possible to put on paper his means for deciding "the moral methods of obtaining confidence and insuring a childlike acquiescence in every needed measure."[23]

Beverley R. Tucker did his internship at the Infirmary for Nervous Diseases in 1905 and 1906 and went on to become a neurologist and psychiatrist, and professor of neuropsychiatry at the Medical College of Virginia in Richmond. The year that Mitchell died, Tucker wrote a brief sketch of his life and then in 1936 published an article, "Speaking of Weir Mitchell." In discussing his interaction with patients, Tucker relates two interesting narratives. At the Providence Hospital in Washington, D.C., there was a case of paralysis that had puzzled several doctors in the area. Mitchell was sent for and after an examination, he asked the other doctors to step out of the room. When he joined them, they asked, "Will she ever be able to walk?" He answered, "Yes, in a moment." Mitchell had actually set her bed on fire, and soon the door flew open, and smoke and the woman rushed out and down the hallway. Another patient, "a spoiled, wealthy girl of 17," cried the whole time while Mitchell attempted to talk to her. He asked her not to cry the next day, but she cried in the same way. Then he told her that he would spank her if she cried during his third visit. She did cry, and after calling the nurse, who pulled down the bedclothes and the girl's nightgown, he did spank her.[24]

There are similar stories from other sources. For example, Mitchell took one immobile patient for a long carriage ride, stopped the carriage, and made her walk home. Another "famous story—which went all the rounds amid much laughter," was of another woman who refused to get out of bed. Finally, after days of persuasion and argument, Mitchell told her, "If you are not out of bed in five minutes—I'll get into it with you!" He removed his coat, then his vest, and finally he began to remove his pants, at which point the patient "was out of bed in a fury!"[25] When Susan Goodman and Carl Dawson retell this story in their biography of William Dean Howells, Mitchell's threat to get into bed with the patient is not playful, but rather a threat of "rape." At the same time, Goodman and Dawson conclude that Mitchell invented these various stories to demonstrate "his own magnificence," but today they would have him "defending his license to practice medicine."[26]

It is unlikely that Tucker fabricated the stories he relates about Mitchell setting the bed on fire or spanking the seventeen-year-old patient. He wanted to include them in his brief sketch because they were illustrative of Mitchell's methods. Setting a bed on fire, spanking a young woman, and threatening to get into bed with a patient are examples of the kind of risky intervention that Mitchell sometimes practiced where a dramatic act shocks the patient. This practice ran counter to the idea that doctors should not directly confront hysterical symptoms. A few years before his death, in an address to the Neurological Association in Philadelphia that was subsequently published in *JAMA*, Mitchell discussed various treatment methods. They included the use of appeals to reason and higher and lower motives, and the use of pain: "I speak here with unreserve when I say that I have seen obstinate masturbation in hysteria in the young cured by whipping. I have seen violent angers in a woman resulting in wild hysteria cured by infliction of physical pain when every other method failed. Again I have seen obstinate kleptomanias ended by like means. I have advised it in rare cases."[27] In noting the use of physical pain in the address and the *JAMA* article, Mitchell expressly made it part of the record. This may be his only mention of inflicting physical pain; it is not possible to know how often he used it or the extent of the force and violence involved.

The British physician William S. Playfair was professor of obstetric medicine at King's College, physician for the diseases of women and children at King's College Hospital, and a fellow of the Royal College of Physicians. After reading Mitchell's book *Fat and Blood* and treating several women with a rest cure, he was "anxious" to relate his "astonishing and satisfactory" results. In an 1881 *Lancet* article, he described the various components of a cure and his first four cases by way of illustration. All four patients were addicted to drugs, and for them the rest cure began as a treatment for substance abuse. Playfair explained that these women, all confirmed invalids, in a state of "hopeless misery," had gone from one doctor to another, many of them eminent obstetricians. Under these practitioners, the women were "subjected to all sorts of uterine medication, mechanical and other, with no lasting improvement, until eventually they become bedridden, or nearly so, sleepless, victims to chloral and morphia, worn and wasted, and burdens to themselves and their families." Their common symptoms included anorexia, dyspepsia, and emotional and hysterical behavior, and Playfair more than once emphasized the absolute need to remove the patient from "the morbid atmosphere of invalid habits" at home in order to "gain that moral influence over her which is really essential to success." This moral influence was ideally a mix of tact, kindness, and firmness on the part of the doctor and the nurse, which would inspire confidence and self-control in the patient. In order to illustrate his success, Playfair mailed Mitchell six sets of before-and-after photographs, intending to demonstrate through visual evidence the power of the rest cure to transform and save lives.[28]

There can be no doubt that some patients diagnosed as hysterical suffered from grave physical illness and disease that went undetected. Often placed under the umbrella term of "hysteria," some of these disorders would eventually be diagnosed as bipolar disorder, multiple sclerosis, Parkinson's disease, Huntington's disease, cerebral palsy, dementia, and posttraumatic stress disorder.[29] As early as 1875, in an article on using rest to treat nervous disease, Mitchell wrote that the "cases I speak of, some doctors like to call hysteria, but hysteria is the nosological limbo of all unnamed female maladies. It were as well called mysteria for all it name teaches us of the host of morbid states which are crowded within its hazy boundaries."[30] And there was no exact boundary between the two huge categories "neurasthenia" and "hysteria." While the more respectable neurasthenia was commonly used for exhaustion and depression, and hysteria for unpredictable and frenzied behavior, neurasthenia could progress into hysteria. An even broader label, "functional neuroses," came to encompass both neurasthenia and hysteria as Mitchell's system of cure, the "Weir Mitchell Treatment," continued to advance.

In 1881, even after thirty years of interpreting and treating sick bodies, Mitchell noted that the cases were "unfailing in interest and variety," especially the "vexing marriages of disorders." A case of paralysis "may be partly real, partly pure weakness, partly loss of power from want of belief in being able to move; or conscious mimicry may be added to palsy or to the forbidding influence of a regnant idea, or to the true hysteric may be joined ataxy of motion." There is a state of mind, especially well-developed in hysteria, "in which there exists a so monstrous development of this strange power to create disorder by thinking of it.... In this disease, indeed, we find women, and men too, passing into a mental state in which they are really much like people in dreams." They lose the power to reason and what they conceive to be takes the place of what is. They are hurt by light "or believe they are"; they cannot bear noise "or think they cannot"; they feel vibrations as pain and live "muffled lives in dark rooms, and believe they cannot walk, or even lift a hand, or move the head." Often these patients become slaves to the "tyrant ideas" or "fixed belief" that they themselves create. In answer to the question "Does the presence of the set belief create pain?" Mitchell wrote that "we are hardly wise to stamp these pains as non-existent."[31]

Treating any one of these cases was a long and arduous process. Mitchell called it a long sermon, "apt to win with a woman of intelligence, and the fools are to be dealt with by other moral drugs than these, or the honest pill must be gilded" with flattery or such better motives as will stir her conscience, "if that is to be stirred at all." Often the women were under his care for a year or more. Some were clever, ashamed of their hysteria, and wanted to get well, but others were silly, with minds "like the back of a piece of needlework with a baffling absence of pattern—women with a low, whining, bleating voice that is by itself a tell-tale of the kind of will-less ataxia which seems to cripple the mind no less than the body. These are the hard cases to relieve."[32]

Mitchell published *Lectures on Diseases of the Nervous System, Especially in Women* in 1881 and *Clinical Lessons on Nervous Diseases* in 1897. Together these books provide the most comprehensive picture of the patients seen and the treatment provided at the infirmary. In *Lectures on Diseases of the Nervous System*, each chapter illustrates a nervous disease through case studies. Here is hysteria in all its manifestations—paralysis, ataxia, mimicry, chorea, spasms, sleep disorders, aphonia, dysphagia, anorexia, phantom tumors, death spells, auras, and hysterical vomiting, choking, fasting, and defecation. Mitchell noted that some of the diseases were well-known, but others had been slighted or were almost unknown in the medical literature. Through naming and classification, he wanted to provide order to the chaos and establish his authority to treat such disorders. Working on the borderline between nineteenth-century neurology and psychiatry, he wrote that in the "tangle of named or nameless symptoms . . . amidst so much that is confusing . . . in diseases of vague boundaries like neurasthenia and hysteria, a good deal of this useful sort of secondary classification is possible."[33]

Lectures on Diseases of the Nervous System begins with the case of a sixteen-year-old girl, "rather wanting in the signs of sexual ripeness." The purpose of this reference to her sexual ripeness seems pertinent but remains vague. Some kind of alarm had caused the paralysis of her right arm, after which she cried, laughed, and suffered a slight fit. There appeared to be no deceit; rather, the "power of her belief" in her feebleness made the paralysis much worse. Mitchell was able to raise the arm, and after he ordered her to do so, she was able to raise it as well. In both the paralysis and the movement, Mitchell wrote that the agent was the same: in both, the "power of her belief" was at work. Once the patient transferred this belief to the doctor's authority, she was free to move her arm. He sent her away, "with a lightly uttered word or two as to the use of the hot iron, if she again loses power." William Osler wrote about this power of belief in Mitchell's authority. When Osler worked at the infirmary, he witnessed the workings of Mitchell's "master mind" on the men and women who flocked to his clinics. His "extraordinary success, partly due to the rest treatment, was more largely the result of a personal factor—the deep faith the people had in his power to cure."[34]

Still, Mitchell's visit with the sixteen-year-old girl ends with a "lightly uttered" threat of physical violence, and in the retelling, he creates a sense of distance from the patient. Assumptions are made and the patient is categorized. Mitchell's innovations at the infirmary in the early 1870s included taking a detailed case history of every patient before an examination. Now, less than ten years later, his approach involved "more exact ideas as to what is needed, and that unflinching purpose and action which grow out of distinct views."[35] This case is not about the importance of listening. Rather, the language suggests scenes where control, deceit, and violence might be in play. In this case Mitchell's earlier respect, diligence, and attention are replaced by suspicion, exact ideas, unflinching purpose, and sometimes threatening language. Over the years the patient records at the infirmary become less detailed or are missing completely, suggesting a change in attitude.

Another patient, Miss B., age twenty, caught a cold and lost her voice. Her symptoms gradually worsened to include at various times spasms, the inability to swallow or walk, and aphonia. After several years of such illness, Miss B. was taken to Mitchell. First, the nurse trained her to move her legs in bed, and then, while seated, she was trained to move her head and finally to walk. The lesson in walking began with creeping with "pads tied over her knees, and, lying flat on her face on the floor, without skirts, has around her a folded sheet. At an order, she tries to rise, helped by the lift of the sheet-belt held by the nurse." Gradually, Miss B. became a quadruped, then knelt, then stood in a corner or by a chair, and was well and walking in two months. Mitchell concluded, "You see that, following nature's lessons with docile mind, we have treated the woman as nature treats an infant."[36]

In one of two chapters on mimicry, Mitchell described the case of a young boy, age nine, who could not raise his head without severe pain. The scalp and spine were also sore, so the least tap caused him to cry. He kept his legs close to his body and complained bitterly about bright light, the sounds of footsteps, and the vibrations caused by the passing of carriages. But he had no fever, a calm pulse, and a good appetite, and when something caught his interest, he forgot his pain. Once Mitchell felt secure that this "actor" was "more or less consciously mimicking disease," he lifted him out of bed and "with severity, ordered him to stand up." The boy stood up and walked back to his bed. After the first day there was no further mention of his pain, and with a rough rubbing each day and some urging, he left the hospital in a week. Mitchell arranged for him to live on a farm for several months away from his "too affectionate" relatives, and there was no relapse. Another case of mimicry involved a dozen girls with spasms and convulsions, who were placed in two adjoining hospital rooms. When the doctor and manager came round, "one girl would begin to bark or twitch, then a second and a third, until on bed or floor, or seated, ten or twelve children were wheezing, barking, grunting, crowing, or in violent convulsions; while the bewildered nurses ran from one to another, presenting a scene quite astonishing to witness."[37]

One case began with an abdominal tenderness where any pressure caused nausea and dizziness. The young girl then experienced, among other things, convulsions, coma, polyuria, and constipation. Mitchell was called to the home, where the girl's mother and a nurse were attending. Each day, a long stomach tube was inserted six or seven inches up the bowel and a cup of olive oil injected, followed by one to three quarts of flaxseed tea. During the enema, one person compressed the anal opening to prevent the escape of fluid. This compression, according to Mitchell, was necessary because of the great relaxation of the sphincter, "in which a thumb could be passed without any resistance, which could be felt to arise from a muscular act." While the young girl shrieked with pain, she insisted on more water. This everyday "event" took two to four hours, leaving the patient the least exhausted of the three. Sometimes there was a stool; sometimes there was no stool for a week. At times, the scene was repeated during the night "under the wild entreaties of the patient." Called in as a consultant, Mitchell tried unsuccessfully to remove the girl from the home.[38]

Some of these hysterical patients possessed remarkable physical strength. In one case of chronic spasm, the head was bent on the breast and held there for months. In another, the thigh, leg, and foot were rigidly extended at a right angle to the body. This patient, a young, frail girl from Maryland, had been subjected to a multitude of "therapeutic experiments," but all had failed to help. Mitchell placed her at the foot of the bed and suspended increasing amounts of weight from her ankle; at one point she carried fifty pounds of weight for three hours. Ether, induction currents, and galvanism to the spine all failed to alter the rigid extension of the leg. Finally, she was cured by a "very much gentler treatment"— hypodermic injections of atropine twice a day with massage. Underlying the freakishness of such permanent spasms was the fact that they might affect any muscle of the body, and might be "so violent and lasting as to excite our amazement that, through many years, in some cases, a few groups of ganglionic cells should be competent to evolve such enormous amounts of force." Mitchell condemned both the practice of cutting the tendons in such cases and the surgeons who too often made their "diagnosis with the knife."[39]

The chapter on "Habit Chorea" in *Lectures* contains two cases. One involves a young boy, age fourteen, whose nervousness included a snap of his eyes, a roll of his head, a shrug of one shoulder followed by an upward movement of that side of his body, and contraction of his abdominal muscles. Mitchell treated the boy for a long period of time with zinc, cold douches to the spine, arsenic, and a trip to the Virginia seacoast to ride, swim, shoot, and fish. Still, the symptoms persisted until hypodermic injections of arsenic were given three times a week. After three months of this treatment, Mitchell recommended study in England, which, along with the "favoring influence of approaching puberty," completed his cure. Like other physicians, Mitchell understood puberty for girls as a critical time fraught with danger. In contrast, in this case he explicitly noted its favoring influence on the boy.

The other case of habit chorea involved M. C. G., a thirteen-year-old girl who had been nervous and irritable since the age of six and had recently undergone a rapid development of breasts and pelvis. She was coughing, snuffling, and grimacing. At times her mouth would open wide and as it closed, both eyes would shut. She had been scolded and bribed to stop these "morbid acts," which would come and go and appeared forced and voluntary. Her treatment included a special diet, light gymnastics, no school, gentle laxatives, and full doses of arsenic. The girl never seemed mortified by her "odd movements," so Mitchell administered a dose of moral medication by encouraging feelings of shame. However rudimentary, his appeal to emotions signifies his belief that such problems sprang from "consciousness." Roy Porter, in his discussion of the development of a psychological theory of hysteria, notes that around the turn of the century, leading asylum superintendents "repudiated traditional organic nosologies and medical therapeutics as misconceived and inefficacious, urging instead techniques of moral management and moral therapy. Within their theories, insanity was redefined as springing from consciousness—the intellect and the passions—thus necessitating treatment on psychological principles, by appeals to reason, humanity, and the feelings (fear and esteem, pleasure and pain, etc.). Herein lay the founding of psychiatry."[40] Mitchell was discussing the importance of moral medication much earlier, beginning in the 1870s.

In the conclusion to *Lectures*, Mitchell insisted that the rest cure was a treatment for extreme cases of nervous illness, "a plan never to be used where exercise, outdoor life, tonics, or change have not been thoroughly tested." The book's last sentence reads, "I never use it if I can do without it; but in well-chosen cases I use it, with a confidence which has become alike courageous and habitual."[41] Patients, after seeing many other doctors and trying many other treatments, came or were brought to Mitchell in desperation and as a last resort. Day after day, he dealt with women who were anxious, depressed, irrational, and manipulative. Nonetheless, at the same time he was making sweeping judgments regarding all women based on these cases.

The physician Mary Putnam Jacobi found Mitchell's overgeneralizations about women disturbing. She believed that Mitchell was permitting his constant exposure to hysterical women to influence the way he viewed women in general, and in a letter she made a point of telling him so: "I know how much authority any expression of opinion upon your part carries: and I also know how few people there are who would note, that on certain subjects, the very circumstance that has invested your opinion with such just authority, really tends to disqualify you from forming an impartial judgment. I mean your prolonged and profound study of nervous women, with all their incapacities, sophistries and essential feebleness." Jacobi felt that Mitchell "almost inevitably" based his conclusions about all women on the condition of his patients.[42] Mitchell would have been surprised by Jacobi's distinction between his patients and women in general, believing, as he did, that "the moral world of the sick-bed explains in a measure some of the things that are strange in daily life, and the man who does not know sick women does not know women."[43] But Mitchell's views regarding women preceded his treatment of them. While he may have made use of things like eating disorders and drug addiction to reaffirm his views and block any evidence to the contrary, his attitudes about sexual difference were formed early in his childhood and school years. Despite some inconsistency, these ideas did not mellow or change with time. In 1912 he told Amelia Gere Mason, "I think I know more about women than most people do . . . and I will add that no man knows much about women who has not had under his care a good many sick women. Nothing differentiates the sex as much as sickness."[44]

While Mitchell knew that men could and did become hysterical, women were much more susceptible because of biology as well as factors like climate, industrialization, and education, which played significant roles in weakening an already delicate constitution. Mitchell wrote that hysteria was a common disease, finding "in all lands and all female human nature enough conditions favorable to its growth." And, "I do not want to do more than is needed of this ungracious talk: suffice it to say that multitudes of our young girls are merely pretty to look at, or not that; that their destiny is the shawl and the sofa, neuralgia, weak backs, and the varied forms of hysteria." The situation he described was a critical one. If the mothers "are sickly and weak, the sad inheritance falls upon their offspring, and this is why I must deal first, however briefly, with the health of our girls, because it is here, as the doctor well knows, that the trouble begins."[45]

While innovative and farsighted in some ways, Mitchell held fast to the beliefs of his father and his father's colleagues at Jefferson Medical College that female bodies, "feeble and sensitive at birth," were by definition highly prone to nervous disease. In 1848, when Charles Meigs published *Females and Their Diseases* and Mitchell matriculated at Jefferson, another student, Thomas Addis Emmet, also began his studies there. Emmet, referred to as one of the founders of modern gynecology, carried the entire responsibility for surgery at the Woman's Hospital in New York, founded the American Gynecological Society and was its president in 1882, and published his *Principles and Practice of Gynaecology* in 1878. A second edition appeared in 1880, a third in 1884, and it was translated into French and German. Although published more than thirty years after Meigs's own book and his translation of Colombat (discussed in chapter 1), the Emmet volume had changed little in tone and content from these much earlier works. Emmet, threatening sterility and invalidism, wrote that around the time of puberty, "the nervous system becomes dominant in the female organization, and is as susceptible to external influences as is the barometer to atmospheric changes. . . . Whenever natural laws are disregarded, the young girl lays the foundation of a defective organization. She is liable to local disease before marriage, to sterility afterwards, or to the life of an invalid from the birth of her first child; and her enfeebled constitution will be inherited by her offspring. . . . The slightest defect in her sexual organs may, through the medium of the sympathetic nerves, reproduce functional derangement elsewhere."[46]

When viewed collectively, Meigs, Emmet, and Mitchell formed a powerhouse of influence and control. This nexus of power attained through the entanglement of morality, politics, and the female body was founded on the assumptions that womb sympathies, limited energy, and the inheritance of acquired character- istics were medical facts. Women were closer to nature, reproductive in purpose, and naturally weak and feeble. It was not enough to say that women, because they were intellectually inferior, should not study alongside men. What would be the harm in letting them try? The stakes were set very high involving noth- ing less than the survival and vigor of the human race.

Amid his forward-looking thinking about the cause of mental illness, Mitch- ell failed to question these assumptions about women's nature and bodies, and yet he might have done so. He had treated plenty of hysterical men during the Civil War. He knew that hysteria was not inherently a female disease, caused by a wandering womb. Rather, he stated that men also lose self-control: "I have many a time seen soldiers who had ridden boldly with Sheridan or fought gal- lantly with Grant become, under the influence of painful nerve-wounds, as irri- table and hysterically emotional as the veriest girl." And when discussing the causes of hysteria among women of the upper class, he referred to sociological causes, where women's lives "passing out of maidenhood, lack those distinct purposes and aims which, in the lives of men, are like the steadying influence of the fly-wheel in an engine."[47] While such a flywheel might be a career in law, medicine, or the church, possessing one was always a matter of education. Mitchell knew all this, but while he pleaded for fresh air and exercise for young women, he insisted that they focus primarily on their duty to reproduction and the family. For some of his patients, after helping them get well—and this is the real crux of the problem with Mitchell's rest treatment—he sent them back to the very situation that had caused the hysterical symptoms in the first place. He created several highly intelligent but frustrated fictional females in his novels and subdued them through romantic love and marriage.

In an 1890 open letter in the *Century*, Josephine Lazarus, speaking of edu- cated women, wrote, "It seems almost as if a new race had been created." This "new race" was what troubled Mitchell. In his address to the first class of Rad- cliffe women, he said, "A woman is *born* to a profession; a man is not. . . . The higher evolution of mind will never safely be reached until the woman accepts the irrevocable decree which made her woman and not man. Something in between she cannot be. . . . I do not fancy a middle-sex."[48] Given the frailty of female anatomy and physiology and the fast pace of urban life, neurasthenia and hysteria were accepted as natural and necessary outcomes. Doctors like Mitchell would do everything they could to help, but nature's laws were unalterable.

It is noteworthy that among Mitchell's various publications and even within one publication, he is inconsistent, moving from nature to nurture and back again. Is it anatomy, the climate, diet, clothing, lack of exercise, over- and under-heated schoolrooms, or lack of ventilation? While he wrote that he was "anxious not to be misunderstood," it is obvious that at various times he struggled with his own inconsistency, trying to find clarity and to resolve the discrepancies in his thinking. As he grew older and more prominent, however, he became obstinate and indignant. His views on gender hardened even to the touch of surveys, research, and experimentation—the very evidence that he had embraced and invested in so heavily as a young man. In *Doctor and Patient* he wrote, "I utterly distrust the statistics of these schools and their graduates as to health, and my want of reliance arises out of the fact that this whole question is in a condition which makes the teachers, scholars, and graduates of such colleges antagonistic to masculine disbelievers in a way and to a degree fatal to truth. I trust far more what I hear from the women who have broken down under the effort to do more than they were fit."[49]

Susan Mosedale refers to the "large corpus of scientific writing published in the later nineteenth and early twentieth centuries, the writings of scientists opposed to the growing impetus for female emancipation." The struggle for equality in voting rights, wages, education, and access to careers was no more threatening to scientists than other men, but "they were in an especially effective position to attack it."[50] When Mitchell joined the staff of the infirmary and began publishing on the manifestations and treatment of hysteria, he opened a Pandora's box. While there is no reason to doubt that these bizarre cases existed, one can, along with Mary Putnam Jacobi, condemn the way he used his medical authority to control women's lives. By the mid-1880s he had become one of the most prominent neurologists in the United States.[51] Because he spoke from the position of a scientist in the pursuit of truth, it is difficult to determine how mindful he was of the politics involved in his methods and his strong words against equal rights and education for women. Constantly exposed to the unpredictable nature of many patients and with the corroboration and encouragement of many colleagues, he stood firm. If there were doubts and misgivings, he did not express them.

FIG. 1   S. Weir Mitchell's father, John Kearsley Mitchell. Courtesy of the Rare Book and Manuscript Library, University of Pennsylvania.

FIG. 2   S. Weir Mitchell, 1858. Courtesy of the Rare Book and Manuscript Library, University of Pennsylvania.

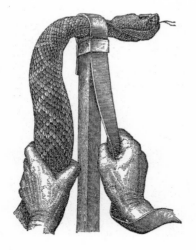

FIG. 3 The snake loop. From *Researches upon the Venoms of Poisonous Serpents,* 1886.

FIG. 4 S. Weir Mitchell. Courtesy of the College of Physicians of Philadelphia.

FIG. 5   Camping expedition in Canada around 1870. Mitchell is seated fourth from the left. Courtesy of the College of Physicians of Philadelphia.

FIG. 6   Mitchell is standing, fifth from the right. Orthopedic Hospital and Infirmary for Nervous Diseases. Courtesy of the College of Physicians of Philadelphia.

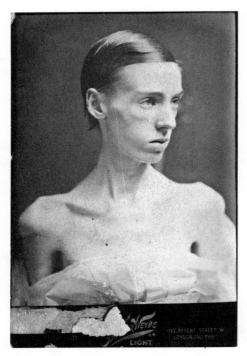

FIG. 7(a–d) Before-and-after photographs of rest cure patients sent to Mitchell by the British physician William S. Playfair, 1882. Courtesy of the College of Physicians of Philadelphia.

7(a)

7(b)

W. HUDSON, HASTINGS.

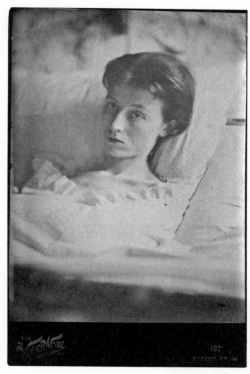

7(c)

7(d)

FIG. 7(e-f) A further set of
before-and-after photographs
of rest cure patients sent
to Mitchell by the British
physician William S. Playfair,
1882. Courtesy of the
College of Physicians of
Philadelphia.

7(e)

7(f)

FIG. 8 Mitchell's study
at 1524 Walnut Street.
Courtesy of the College of
Physicians of Philadelphia.

FIG. 9 Mary Cadwalader
Mitchell. Courtesy of the
Historical Society of
Pennsylvania.

For a long trusted nurse
S. Weir Mitchell
S-w. 1898.

FIG. 10   S. Weir Mitchell, 1898. Courtesy of the College of Physicians of Philadelphia.

FIG. 11   S. Weir Mitchell and John Cadwalader. Ristigouche River, Canada. Courtesy of the Rare Book and Manuscript Library, University of Pennsylvania.

FIG. 12 S. Weir Mitchell hiking on Mount Desert Island, Maine. Courtesy of the College of Physicians of Philadelphia.

FIG. 13   S. Weir Mitchell, around 1890. Courtesy of the College of Physicians of
Philadelphia.

7

THE APPLE OR THE ROSE

While Mitchell liked women who were pleasing and obliging, he felt that strong, clever women were disagreeable, and he avoided their company. In 1868 he told Elizabeth, "I met Miss Lena Peters at—Cadwaladers and we went a little on the war path—Robeson writes me to day asking with the kind regards of the C's if my scalp is still in place. I found the woman perfectly exquisite from her singular society training and amazing tact in talk. It was hard to say what it was that charmed one so—but you cant always just put yr finger on a butterfly—But its a gray old scalp mine and won't dry in any womans wigwam."[1] Mitchell knew what he liked, frequently mentioning his attraction to small hands and small feet and referring to stylish and well-trained women as thoroughbreds.[2] Yet, uneasy with female wit and independence, he pulled away even when captivated by an "exquisite" woman like Lena Peters.

In 1873, while in Pontresina, Switzerland, Mitchell noticed many women traveling alone. At first "they give you the bold British stare wh. says so much—but they do not otherwise annoy you . . . now and then one of them speaks and—then I sometimes find them pleasant. On the whole they are best let alone. . . . What these women want are to know how to dress and how to seem tender and feminine—for they may be both."[3] For Mitchell, the "tender and feminine" were instinctual, the defining aspects of true womanhood and the essential ingredients in female charm. He believed that careers lessened a woman's true attractiveness and made her less fit to be the "friendly lover and the loving friend." In *Doctor and Patient* he wrote, "For most men, when she seizes the apple, she drops the rose."[4] While women like Lena Peters and the British women in Pontresina certainly caught his eye, they disturbed him because they refused to yield to a man's superior strength and reason.

In the spring of 1910, when Mitchell had dinner with the Walcotts in Washington, D.C., he sat "next to a raging suffragette, and bothered her by asking if any census had been taken of the opinions of the husbands of the suffragettes." When she asked him what he thought of the whole business, he replied that it might be summed up in a few sentences: "Everything they are doing is lessening the charm, the tenderness of life, the appreciation of the woman by the man." Like Basil Ransom in Henry James's novel *The Bostonians*, Mitchell felt that "what is most agreeable to women is to be agreeable to men!"[5] Using a rhetoric of protection and naturalization, Mitchell remained unequivocal in his opposition to women's education and careers outside the home. Any woman who did not accept her biological difference and consequent duty was or would soon be broken. He sometimes created such women in his novels and whipped them into shape through love and marriage. He had a few female friends, like Sarah Butler Wister, Mrs. Caspar Wister, Agnes Irwin, and Amelia Gere Mason, and he enjoyed writing to them and sometimes depended on them for sympathy and emotional support. But nothing in the correspondence or publications contradicts his impatience and at times hostility toward independent and assertive women. A look at his views about women's education and careers reveals a resistance and increasing obstinacy that conflicted and interfered with his effectiveness as a physician.

In the nineteenth century, being agreeable to men might or might not mean being educated. At the beginning of the century, female education in the United States was intended to enhance women's fitness for marriage and motherhood. Still, the women's seminaries that began to appear in the 1810s strove to provide an education equal to that provided by men's colleges. In 1819, for example, Emma Willard founded Troy Female Seminary in New York. In 1837 Mount Holyoke Female Seminary (later Mount Holyoke College) became the first endowed institution for women's higher education in the United States. Oberlin College in Ohio, founded in 1833, was the first to accept all students regardless of race or sex.[6] In 1855 the University of Iowa became the first public university to admit men and women on an equal basis.[7] In 1865 Vassar was established, and Smith and Wellesley opened in 1875. Bryn Mawr opened in 1884 and the Woman's College of Baltimore (now Goucher) in 1885. In 1889 Barnard College, the female affiliate of Columbia, opened its doors, and in 1894 Harvard Annex was chartered as Radcliffe College with the power to grant degrees to women. Between 1870 and 1900, despite the fact that many of the nation's elite private colleges, including Harvard, Yale, Princeton, and Amherst, remained closed to women, the number of women college students in the United States increased eightfold, from eleven thousand in 1870 to eighty-five thousand in 1900.[8] For Mitchell, grasping the significance of this movement would require a radical revision of his essentialist worldview. Like so many, he failed to recognize the vast diversity of desires, needs, and ambition among half the population. Personally and professionally, he would hold fast to his narrow ideal.

Instead of offering understanding and support, Mitchell went on the attack. He referred to Vassar as one of the schools where the sentiment was "silently opposed to admitting that the feminine life has necessities which do not cumber that of man. Thus the unwritten code remains in a measure hostile to the accepted laws which are supposed to rule."[9] He went so far as to say that he "utterly" distrusted the statistics of these schools and their graduates, due to the "fact that this whole question is in a condition which makes the teachers, scholars, and graduates of such colleges antagonistic to masculine disbelievers in a way and to a degree fatal to truth." Not only would he continue to base his conclusions regarding women and education on sick women—the very practice that Mary Putnam Jacobi objected to in her letter—but he railed against any surveys and statistics to the contrary.

Previously, Mitchell had placed a great deal of faith in surveys and circulars, seeing them as a reliable way to gather information on which to base generalizations. In various letters and publications, he refers to at least five such surveys. There was his 1859 plan, submitted to the Academy of Natural Science, to obtain the physical statistics for college undergraduates and a similar set of statistics for factory workers and mechanics. He also gathered statistics on the weight and height of all the members of Philadelphia's city police, and he gathered death statistics from large cities to determine the relationship between industrialization and nervous disease. In *Lectures* he discussed a circular he designed and distributed through the Smithsonian Institution to southern states, asking about the frequency of chorea in white, mulatto, and black children. Also in *Lectures*, he included four detailed tables relating humidity, temperature, rain, and snow to the onset of attacks of chorea in Philadelphia for the years 1876–80.[10]

When it came to women and education, however, Mitchell grew increasingly unscientific. His family members simply avoided the topic, and only a few friends, like Amelia Gere Mason, risked Mitchell's displeasure by attempting to change his mind. Mason was two years younger than Mitchell. In 1851 she had earned a music degree at Mount Holyoke College and then worked as a teacher and administrator. She married at the age of forty-one and became an active member of a Chicago women's club that met in the tradition of the French salons. The club's leader, Newell Doggett, was a botanist, dancer, and the vice-president of the National Woman Suffrage Association. Mason's bouts with neurasthenia caused her to resign from teaching and periodically drove her into seclusion. In 1882, struggling with an especially devastating episode, she made the decision to travel to Philadelphia to see Mitchell.[11] After treatment, Mason was able to sustain her artistic and literary interests and went on to give presentations and publish essays and books, including *The Women of the French Salons* in 1891 and *Women in the Golden Ages* in 1901.

After their initial visit, Mason and Mitchell saw each other only half a dozen times and not at all for twenty years, but they began a correspondence that lasted for thirty years and consisted of hundreds of letters. Mason always expressed her gratitude to Mitchell for helping her regain her strength, telling him, "I feel more indebted to you than to any one else in the world." Still, four years after her treatment, she told him, "Perhaps your autocratic position with regard to invalids, who have no choice but to be patient under professional commands, has led you to overestimate her humility under masculine despotism. A woman loves strength, but not a despotic assertion of it. She may love to yield, because she prefers some other will to her own, but never to be *made* to yield, unless she belongs to a certain spaniel type.... It is a popular fallacy which I think the coming woman will dissipate."[12]

Mitchell not only felt differently, but also believed that even the authority to speak on such issues must rest with the doctors. Doctors were the ones who actually saw "how many school-girls are suffering in health from confinement, want of exercise ... bad ventilation, and too steady occupation of mind." While young girls and women might study, there must be restrictions due to their physiology and special needs. Before the age of seventeen, "overuse, or even a very steady use, of the brain is in many dangerous to health and to every probability of future womanly usefulness." The battle lines were drawn. Accusing female colleges of opposition and hostility while failing to acknowledge his own, Mitchell argued that any information derived from healthy students, graduates, and teachers was false. Yet considerable inconsistency runs throughout his comments regarding the damaging effects of education on women. What was causing the damage? Was it anatomy and physiology or diet, long hours of study, lack of exercise, and poor ventilation? He moved back and forth between the unalterable and the easily fixed, from anatomy as destiny to such things as clothing, diet, fresh air, and exercise. The American woman was too often physically unfit for her duties as a woman, he wrote, and perhaps of all civilized females the least qualified to undertake "those weightier tasks which tax so heavily the nervous system of man." He added, "While making these stringent criticisms, I am anxious not to be misunderstood."[13] Overall, in his discussions of women and education, he moved along nervously from idea to idea, losing some of his usual clarity and proceeding from generalizations to verdicts and threats.

As unacceptable as they are, Mitchell's views were widespread, institutionalized in family, church, and state. The prejudice and racism of many clergy, politicians, and doctors were conspicuous in intellectual and artistic circles as well. Explicit racist-ethnocentric views, for example, were expressed by Walt Whitman, Charlotte Perkins Gilman, M. Carey Thomas, and Edith Wharton.[14] In an article in the *Daily Times* Whitman wrote, "Who believes that Whites and Blacks can ever amalgamate in America? Or who wishes it to happen? Nature has set an impassable seal against it. Besides, is not America for the Whites? And is it not better so?" In an essay regarding suffrage, he wrote, "As if we had not strained the voting and digestive calibre of American Democracy to the utmost for the last fifty years with the millions of ignorant foreigners, we have now infused a powerful percentage of blacks, with about as much intellect and calibre (in the mass) as so many baboons."[15] In Gilman's article "A Suggestion on the Negro Problem," published in the *American Journal of Sociology*, she wrote that Negroes, the backward race, comprised "a large body of aliens, of a race widely dissimilar and in many respects inferior, whose present status is to us a social injury." Gilman identified the whites as Race A in Status 10 and the blacks as Race B in Status 4, and she wrote, "Race B in many ways retards the progress of Race A." She recommended the compulsory enlistment of all Negroes below a certain grade of citizenship into construction camps and stationery bases.[16] Significantly, when scholars acknowledge the racial attitudes in Whitman's and Gilman's work, it does not render invisible or detract from an appreciation of their contributions.

Mitchell was immensely successful, and as a prominent neurologist and writer, his vanity and arrogance grew with his stature. He had not always been so arrogant, but many years had passed since his youthful insecurity and the difficulties of the 1850s and 1860s. He was firmly and powerfully established in one of the largest medical practices in the United States, had accumulated great wealth, and achieved high social status. When he walked into a room, everyone took notice, and when he spoke, everyone listened. One admiring writer describes him as "God's gift to women. Handsome, bearded, with penetrating eyes and a persuasive manner . . . a prototype of the fashionable psychiatrist who attracts large numbers of neurotic, affluent women to his clinic."[17] Beverley Tucker wrote that even in his middle seventies, Mitchell's eyes were "youthful, blue and looked at one squarely. I never knew anyone to lie to him—no one could without being detected."[18] Mitchell's bedside manner was forceful, and the fact that it worked so well with so many patients surprised even him: "Sometimes I wonder that we ever get from any human being such childlike obedience. Yet we do get it, even from men."[19] He had seen soldiers sobbing, broken men who were hysterical with unendurable pain, and he nursed them to health through rest, diet, massage, and electricity. He listened carefully and sympathetically to these men and understood the value of validating their words and stories.

In Mitchell's writing, some of the descriptions of the conditions of his hysterical soldiers and female patients appear hauntingly similar. Several times he referred to female patients who, like the Civil War soldiers, experienced an intense sensitivity to light, noise, and touch. One young girl vomited all her food and had bowel movements only once every ten days. When Mitchell first saw this "wretched, wilted, starved creature," she was on her back "staring upwards, with glassy eyes set deep in dark rings, which faded into a sallow leathery skin, drawn tense over projecting bones. Her mouth was wide open, the jaw dropped, and the whole cavity literally lined with thrush (muguet). The skin of the body was dry, and splotched with islets of dusky red, and the bedclothes were kept off of the sensitive surface by a shelter of half-hoops." Another young girl kept her eyelids constantly closed, was said to be totally blind, and was unable to eat before 9:00 p.m. She was "a queer little shrivelled creature, tawny of tint, and the skin covered with bran–like scales." Her legs and arms were drawn up, almost hiding the "thin, ancient-looking and cunning little visage, which seemed so blind with its closed but quivering lids." Her right hip was red and swollen; her contracted thumbs had caused the palms to ulcerate, and the skin was so sensitive that even the touch of the bedding caused pain. She uttered cries of dismay and seeming terror at every approach.[20]

In the Civil War writing, Mitchell described the large quantities of drugs used to relieve pain and save limbs without reference to drug addiction. In contrast, later warnings were frequent and stern. In *Doctor and Patient* he made numerous statements about the "evil path of the opium, chloral, or chloroform habit." More than once he had seen opium addiction end in suicide. After a physician had watched a woman "roll in agony on the floor, rend her garments, tear out her hair, or pass into a state of hysterical mania," he could only conclude that no initial suffering could be as bad as such addiction. The "moral and mental habits formed under opium—the irresolution, the recklessness, the want of shame, in a word, the general failure of all that is womanly—need something more than time to cure."[21] In *Two Lectures on the Conduct of the Medical Life*, he wrote that "pain is a sad thing, but be sure that the frequent use of opiates mysteriously increases the future capacity to feel pain. Nearly always the attendant physician is in some way to blame for the opium habit. Above all, be careful in your own households. Few winters pass without bringing to me three or four morphia cases in doctors' wives."[22]

Mitchell was adamant about the need to avoid drugs. What once had been so beneficial was now poisonous. In addition to the extensive clinical experience gained through the intervening years, the shift was also due to Mitchell's different patients—the "horrible torture" of soldiers' bodies torn apart by gunshot versus the deep but invisible wounds of nervous women. Significantly, hysteria links the two groups. In *Gunshot Wounds* Mitchell referred to soldiers as "hysterical," and he employed narcotics to quiet the crying and screaming and to create time for healing. Apart from the malingerers, he felt concern and sympathy for the hysterical soldiers, a compassion that contrasts with his didactic and moralistic attitude in *Doctor and Patient* toward sick women who were "most often those who lack the power, even in health, to endure pain."[23] Successful treatment required "childlike acquiescence in every needed measure." Wise women trusted their doctors and the "wisest ask the fewest questions." He complained that the "terrible patients" were nervous women with long memories who asked questions and pointed out inconsistencies: "A nervous woman should be made to comprehend at the outset that the physician means to have his way unhampered by the subtle distinctions with which bedridden women are apt to trouble those who most desire to help them."[24] Often viewing his female patients as unreliable narrators, he was willing to help, but there were limits. Soliciting their trust and obedience and "unhampered by subtle distinctions," Mitchell did not always hear, correctly interpret, or treat the pain. Certainly this was the case with Winifred Howells.

In 1888, after eight years of illness and invalidism and various home remedies and treatments, William Dean Howells made the desperate and expensive decision to send his daughter Winifred to Mitchell—"a last effort for her cure." Winifred was twenty-five years old and weighed fifty-seven pounds. She had been treated by many physicians, including the prominent neurologist James Jackson Putnam at the Harvard Medical School, who had prescribed a rest cure that included force-feeding. Even so, Howells's wife, Elinor, opposed the decision to send Winifred to Mitchell, and the cost was staggering—around $2,000 (approximately $50,000 today).[25] According to John Crowley, there was more than a touch of exasperation in Howells's desire "to shift his domestic burdens to Mitchell's shoulders and in his belief that Winifred required some bracing discipline with her therapy."[26]

Howells believed in Mitchell. On November 25 he told his father, "If you could once see Dr. Mitchell, you would see how he differed from all other specialists, and would not have a doubt but she was in the best and wisest and kindest hands in the world." He also wrote that Mitchell did not conceal "that he thought it a very difficult case; her hypochondriacal illusions and obstinacy in her physiological theories complicate it badly."[27] For Mitchell, the first order of business was an examination to rule out any organic illness. Then he would restore her physical strength through force-feeding and treat the hysteria.

On November 30 Howells and Mitchell met for lunch in New York. Howells explained that Mitchell's hope "was in Winny's condition being hysterical, and destined to change when her body and brain were nourished. His feeding is for this end, and he will of course keep it up, whether she consents or not. It has already come to a tussle of wills, and he believes that as soon as she finds that he is absolutely unyielding, she will give in." On December 23, "Dr. Mitchell lunched with us Thursday. He says Winny has gained ten pounds, but she [is] still very obstinate in her delusions though she doesn't fight the feeding, now. On the whole he is very hopeful." On January 6, "She is still very stubborn, and has to be forced along the path to health with a very firm hand, which fortunately he has. There is none of the Dansville sentimentality in the business; she would instantly take advantage of that." In late February Mitchell moved Winifred to a clinic in Merchantville, Pennsylvania, where she died a week later. Howells wrote his father, "I telegraphed you yesterday that our poor suffering girl had ceased to suffer. It was Saturday evening, at Merchantville, near Philadelphia, from a sudden failure of the heart."[28]

Mitchell's autopsy revealed that Winifred's illness had been organic, not psychological.[29] In a few days Howells told Mitchell that "the torment that remains is that perhaps the poor child's pain was all along as great as she fancied, if she was so diseased, as apparently she was." He closed the letter thus: "All now is over, and my wife and I are united in recognizing the devoted efforts you made, in your great science, to give her back strong and well. Her death does not change our sense of this." Yet in subsequent letters Howells referred repeatedly to Winifred's pain and suffering. On June 7 he wrote Henry James, "You know perhaps the poor child was not with us when she died; she died homesick and wondering at her separation, in the care of the doctors who fancied they were curing her."[30]

Goodman and Dawson, in their biography of Howells, refer to the mysterious circumstances surrounding this case. There is no record of Winifred being admitted to the infirmary, and Mitchell's 1889 and 1890 case studies are missing.[31] These are not the only case studies missing, however; and, what is more important, Mitchell and his son John were treating patients at several locations besides the Infirmary for Nervous Diseases.

There are several references to these various treatment centers, which were located in and outside Philadelphia. First, we know from Howells's letter that there was a treatment facility in Merchantville.[32] Second, Beverley Tucker wrote that in addition to Mitchell's hospital appointments, he "was connected with many rest houses. Most of these houses were managed by ladies who had been trained under him in nervous work, even before the days of the regular trained nurse."[33] Third, when Mitchell was in Europe, John wrote to him, "I have eleven or twelve people at Mrs. Hildeburn's." Another patient is "at the Aldine and at Mrs. Van Ingan's there are an ordinary plain neurasthenic from New York, a case of hysterical neurasthenia in a man of 45 . . . and the blind child." John wrote that the child would remain for at least another month, and the mother planned to bring her back in the fall "because nobody has ever understood her properly before."[34] Finally, in Mitchell's diary for January 19, 1898, he noted that his daughter-in-law Marion was at "Mrs. Hildy's."[35]

Rather than the infirmary, it is likely that Winifred was admitted to one of these rest houses in Philadelphia. Then Mitchell sent her to the facility in Merchantville. Crowley speculates that in sending her away, Mitchell may have been hoping that "temporary exile would break Winifred's will. . . . Merchantville was a subtle form of punishment and a calculated gamble."[36] Apart from any mystery that remains, it is clear that Mitchell failed this patient. Because his initial examination failed to reveal any organic disease, he assumed there was none. Failing to listen and thinking the pain psychological, he isolated Winifred and treated the case as a battle of wills.

In contrast to the laudatory attitudes of Mitchell's contemporaries, later writers expressed critical and even damning views of the rest cure. David Schuster writes that "over the past thirty-five years Mitchell has developed a notorious reputation as a misogynist who sought to infantilize his female patients." And Schuster is right to argue that Mitchell's reputation as a misogynist is "due largely to his failed treatment of the feminist writer and intellectual Charlotte Perkins Gilman."[37] Gilman and her short story "The Yellow Wall-Paper" have wielded an impressive amount of power over Mitchell's reputation. But Julie Bates Dock has called for a reassessment of the "facts" surrounding Gilman's life and the short story, "as scholars increasingly acknowledge that literary criticism is as grounded in historical biases as the literature it seeks to interpret."[38] At the very least, a juxtaposition of Gilman's marriage, rest cure, and "The Yellow Wall-Paper" reveals that the rest cure pales in importance and impact when compared to Gilman's unfortunate marriage to Charles Walter Stetson.

Charlotte Perkins Gilman took pride in her family. Her great grandfather was the Congregational pastor Lyman Beecher; Catherine Beecher and Harriet Beecher Stowe were her great aunts, and her mother was a descendant of one of Rhode Island's founders. As a young girl Gilman made a firm decision to devote her life to social reform and felt passionately about doing the world's work. She was an avid reader and studied anatomy, physiology, geology, and history. As a teenager she earned money through illustrating and tutoring. Although she was socially marginalized by her parents' separation and her mother's subsequent poverty, she was determined to make her mark.

At the age of fifteen she took calisthenics classes, and once the Providence Ladies Sanitary Gymnasium opened, she exercised two to three times a week, often performing for her friends. Her workouts included running a mile, vaulting, jumping, climbing a knotted rope, walking on her hands, and her favorite activity, using the traveling rings.[39] Through self-discipline, study, and exercise Gilman strove to strengthen her body and mind. She valued her independence and had a deep sense of purpose that did not include marriage. She told her friend Martha Luther, "I am really glad not to marry, *I have decided*. I'm *not* domestic and I dont want to be."[40]

Despite her intentions, she met Stetson in 1882 and they married in 1884. Two months later she was pregnant. For a time Gilman was happy and busy with her new life. Stetson was attentive and affectionate and helped with the cooking, cleaning, and shopping. In the evenings they often read together, and she referred to his "ineffable tenderness." But during her pregnancy Gilman experienced considerable physical illness. Before giving birth, she also noted in her diary being "hysterical" on a couple of occasions. Although she made every effort to appreciate and enjoy her family and friends, the months after the birth of her daughter were filled with weakness and misery. In late August she recorded being "highly excited, hysterical; seeming to myself wellnigh insane."[41] In October she borrowed $320 and left Providence to travel to Pasadena for the winter, hoping to regain her energy. "From the moment the wheels began to turn, the train to move, I felt better," she noted in her autobiography, identifying her home life as the cause of her depression and hysteria. Her suspicions were confirmed in April when she returned and "the dark fog rose again in my mind, the miserable weakness—within a month I was as low as before leaving. . . . This was a worse horror than before, for now I saw the stark fact—that I was well while away and sick while at home—a heartening prospect."[42]

At the same time that Gilman was experiencing nervousness and exhaustion, she was becoming more involved in the women's movement. She became friends with Alice Stone Blackwell, assistant editor of the *Woman's Journal* and an advocate for women's suffrage. Gilman started "on a course of reading about women" and began to write a series of articles with titles like "Why Women Do Not Reform Their Dress," "A Protest Against Petticoats," and "Appeal for the Gymnasium." She divided her time between cooking, cleaning, giving art lessons, writing and publishing poems, and illustrating cards and stationery with pansies, apple blossoms, sweet peas, and wild roses. Torn by a passionate need to work and a suppressed but intense dislike of marriage and motherhood, feelings of guilt often incapacitated her. One day Stetson brought home a copy of Thomas á Kempis's *Imitation of Christ*, a fifteenth-century devotional text that counsels contemplation, self-abasement, and submission and condemns all reading, discussion, and intellectual investigation. But Gilman refused to submit, cried over her incompatibility with her husband, and had a good talk with her friend Mrs. S., who was "'another victim.' Young, girlish, inexperienced, sickly; with a sickly child, and no servant; and now very sick herself. Ignorant both, and he using his 'marital rights' at her vital expense. Ah well!"[43]

"Dismal of course, being Sunday," she wrote, "but we get up very late, so there is less of it."[44] Finally, after a particularly bad night, Gilman took her daughter, Katharine, and moved into her mother's house for a week of rest. Still, she went home each day to make Stetson's bed and clean. And the move could only be a temporary escape since Gilman's mother felt that her daughter must learn to bear it. Finally, the crying fits, frenzy, and physical exhaustion made it clear to her husband and mother that she needed outside help. Her friend Mrs. J. Lewis Diman offered her $100 to travel to the great nerve specialist, Weir Mitchell, in Philadelphia.

Just before leaving, Gilman wrote Mitchell a detailed letter of introduction, expressing her respect for him as "the first authority on nervous disease." She even began with a quote from one of his oldest friends: "To cure disease says Dr. Holmes, we must begin with the grandfathers. Here are mine." After a brief description of her grandparents and parents, she referred to her mother as "*absolutely* illogical": "In every way an exaggerated type of the so called 'feminine' qualities, love of husband home and children being almost manias." No doubt, Mitchell shook his head at this point, knowing as he did that there could never be too much love for husband, home, and children. Gilman told Mitchell about her vivid imagination as a child and how her mother, just like Mitchell's, checked "this powerful current of thought . . . telling me it was dangerous and wrong." Gilman noted her cheerful disposition before marriage: "*I could not imagine the combination of circumstance that would make me unhappy.*" But since then, "I have scarce known a happy moment. . . . This agony of mind set in with the child's coming. I nursed her in slow tears. All that summer I did nothing but cry, save for times when the pain was unbearable and I grew wild, hysterical, almost imbecile at times."[45]

When Mitchell read this letter in 1887, he had seen hundreds of young women and understood the problem to be either indulgence and selfishness or mental and physical overwork followed by exhaustion, breakdown, and finally hysteria. He imagined Gilman as a young woman who, having broken all the rules of her sex, now had to pay the price. He could help her recover her physical strength and control, but then she would have to accept her place, just as her mother had told her. Yet there were other things in the letter that Mitchell might have recognized and related to on a personal level. Gilman was doing some of the very things he was advising, especially in terms of exercise, hygiene, and diet. Like Mitchell, reading and writing sustained her, as she put it, "drawing help and companionship from books, scientific and philosophical." She mentioned physiology and philosophy, and referred to herself as a reader, writer, poet, and philosopher. But Mitchell could not glimpse any parallels with his own experiences or respond with any fellow feeling. Even some of the words that Gilman used, like "scientific and philosophical," belonged to men. According to Gilman, Mitchell thought her letter only proved her self-conceit.[46]

Gilman traveled to Philadelphia and underwent a rest cure. Although often overlooked, it is important to note that in her autobiography she writes, "I was put to bed and kept there. I was fed, bathed, rubbed, and responded with the vigorous body of twenty-six. As far as he [Mitchell] could see there was nothing the matter with me, so after a month of this agreeable treatment he sent me home." Like her earlier train ride west, the rest cure alleviated her symptoms and allowed her to regain her strength. Yet, just twenty pages later in the autobiography, Gilman writes that her short story "The Yellow Wall-Paper" was a description of nervous breakdown "beginning something as mine did, and treated as Dr. S. Weir Mitchell treated me with what I considered the inevitable result, progressive insanity." This apparent contradiction confuses the issue, since Gilman has just described the rest cure as "agreeable."[47]

It was not Gilman's experience with rest, massage, and a high-caloric diet that caused her subsequent breakdown and brush with madness. More than once in her autobiography, she states that "the immediate and continuing cause was mismarriage . . . proved by the instant rebound when I left home and as instant relapse on returning."[48] After the rest cure, Gilman returned to Stetson, but gradually the old problems returned, and she felt that she was losing her mind. In June 1888, when Grace Channing spent a few days with Gilman and Stetson in Bristol, she wrote her mother that "they just *prey* upon one another. He makes Charlotte absolutely sick. . . . This morning she is lying down, fit for nothing! And he grows as bitter and cynical in five minutes with her."[49] Finally, in "a moment of clear vision," Gilman and Stetson decided to separate. Once she was "finally free," she wrote, "I think that if I could have had a period of care and rest then, I might have made full recovery."[50]

In the autobiography Gilman writes that Mitchell told her to "live as domestic a life as possible. Have your child with you all the time. . . . Have but two hours' intellectual life a day. And never touch pen, brush, or pencil as long as you live."[51] Quoted repeatedly, these lines have become the mantra of discussions of Mitchell's treatment of Gilman. But Helen Lefkowitz Horowitz, after testing Gilman's recollection "against the record," expresses doubt about its accuracy for several reasons. Horowitz writes that Gilman may have misunderstood what Mitchell was telling her, identifying other instances of such misunderstanding on Gilman's part. Gilman did not write in her journal for three years after her rest cure. It would be almost fifty years before she would write her autobiography. She may have recalled Mitchell's advice "through a veil of distortion." For ideological and personal reasons, she may have decided to use Mitchell as a stand-in for Stetson. Horowitz notes that while many equate the home treatment in "The Yellow Wall-Paper" with a Mitchell rest cure, "it was not his regimen" and includes "many elements that Mitchell opposed."[52]

Certainly, Mitchell would have disapproved of Gilman's leaving her baby for five months to go to Pasadena. He would have vehemently opposed her taking Elixir Coca (cocaine and alcohol) prescribed by a doctor and Essence of Oats (morphine and alcohol) purchased for her by Stetson.[53] It seems unlikely, however, that Mitchell told Gilman to have the baby with her "all the time" and to never touch a pen, since he frequently recommended that a woman have a period of rest each day away from children, other family members, and domestic chores. We also know that Mitchell prescribed travel, writing, and word sketching for women. After Gilman's initial consultation with Mitchell, Stetson wrote in his diary, "Dr. Mitchell seems to think her case very serious, and says that separation from home for at least a year is very desirable." Toward the end of Gilman's rest cure, she wrote Stetson that Mitchell was recommending a year in England. Stetson noted, "He thinks the climate would do a great deal for her."[54]

Gilman needed more than a change of climate. The real problem was her eight-year relationship with Stetson, now her husband and the father of her child. She needed to separate from him and leave what she called her "wrong" and "mistaken marriage."[55] While Mitchell could and did help her recover from the exhaustion, depression, and anxiety, he could never point her in the direction of divorce. For him, divorce was not an option. There was no escaping the fact that she was first a wife and mother, however out of step she might be with a woman's natural instincts of "devotion, self-denial, modesty, long-suffering or patience under pain, disappointment, and adversity."[56]

Both Gilman and Mitchell wrote fiction and nonfiction for didactic reasons, but they did so at cross-purposes. Mitchell strove to reaffirm conservative and androcentric values; Gilman used fiction to enlighten and liberate women. In the short story "The Yellow Wall-Paper," first published in the *New England Magazine* in 1892, Gilman captures the desperate intensity of her feelings about her marriage. The first-person narrator has just given birth, and her husband, John, who is a doctor, takes her to a country home for three months to recover from nervous depression and a slight hysterical tendency. She is treated like a child, forbidden to work, and because of her nervousness, unable to be with her baby. Although writing is a great relief to her mind, John hates for her to write a word. She must be "sly about it, or else meet with heavy opposition." Her room has barred windows and iron rings on the wall. The bed is nailed down and has been gnawed, and the floor is scratched, gouged, and splintered. Someone has crept round and round on the floor like a trapped animal and worn away the wallpaper. About midway through the story the narrator writes, "John says if I don't pick up faster he shall send me to Weir Mitchell in the fall." But she does not get better and does not go to Mitchell, and in the end she, too, is creeping with her shoulder just fitting "in that long smooch around the wall, so I cannot lose my way." After John breaks down the door, she tells him, "I've got out at last. . . . And I've pulled off most of the paper, so you can't put me back!" John faints and falls to the floor, but she just crawls over him and continues to creep around the wall.[57] In 1890, the year after Winifred's death, Gilman sent Howells a copy of "The Yellow Wall-Paper," which he described as "blood curdling." In 1920 he included it in his anthology *The Great Modern American Short Stories*, writing, "I shiver over it as much as I did when I first read it in manuscript."[58] Howells may have wondered if his daughter's final days were anything like the narrator's in "The Yellow Wall-Paper."

Like Gilman, Jane Addams was born in 1860 and died in 1935. She was also one of Mitchell's rest cure patients in Philadelphia. Allen Davis, in his biography of Addams, notes the difficulty in the 1880s for women to remain independent and self-actualizing. It was "much easier to become a deficiency-motivated person who was dependent, other-directed, and sensitive to other people's approval. . . . Practically every social pressure guided a young woman toward that model."[59] Jane Addams's family made large demands on her time, and in her essay titled "The College Woman and the Family Claim" she wrote that it had "always been difficult for the family to regard the daughter otherwise than as a family possession."[60] As Addams gradually broke away from familial demands, she realized that she was physically stronger after visiting the poor than after attending a tea, lecture, or art exhibit.

Like other members of the first generation of American college women, Addams found life after college somewhat pointless. There were few careers available to educated women, but these individuals needed activity. They had to struggle to invent and construct new public spaces for themselves as teachers, doctors, and reformists. Addams, along with Ellen Starr, did just that in found-ing Hull House in 1889, a settlement house in Chicago that became so many things, including a training ground for professional women. In addition to serv-ing as Hull House's executive director, Addams was a member of the Chicago school board and for a brief time the garbage inspector for the nineteenth ward. She was the first woman president of the National Conference of Char-ities and Correction, the first head of the National Federation of Settlements, the first vice-president of the National American Woman Suffrage Association, a president of the International Congress for Women at the Hague, the first president of the Woman's International League for Peace and Freedom, and the winner of a Nobel Prize. Gilman, who spent three months at Hull House in 1896, wrote of her, "Jane Addams was a truly great woman. Her mind had more 'floor space' in it than any other I have known. She could set a subject down, unprejudiced, and walk all around it, allowing fairly for every one's point of view."[61]

Mitchell was unable to identify with these New Women even though they shared his need for self-expression. He created and controlled his identity through his writing. It was the place where he produced a "self" and then repeatedly confirmed that he was indeed that person. This power to define reality was a large part of the reason why writing was so indispensable to Mitchell. In his own words, he recognized his female patients as "house-caged," but he sent them home to fight the same old battles.[62] His unwillingness to acknowledge similar needs and endorse women's education and careers illustrates the depth of his determination to maintain a radical sexual difference.

A rest cure, compared to other nineteenth-century treatments for hysteria such as institutionalization, surgery, or medication, appears relatively mild. Haunting the pages of Charlotte Brontë's *Jane Eyre*, Antoinette Mason and her alcoholic caretaker Grace Poole—locked in the attic for twenty years—merely suggest some of the possibilities. Working from this perspective, Barbara Sicherman sees doctors like Mitchell as pioneers, not oppressors, arguing that the rest cure provided "individuals with alternatives to inaction or incarceration." Mitchell was interpreting reprehensible behavior as a sign of illness rather than sinful-ness or insanity.[63] When he ruled out the possibility of organic disease, he was turning away from the materialism of experimental medicine to help discover and create the new world of psychiatry.

Based on Mitchell's caseloads, the infirmary's discharge records, and the international popularity and staying power of the rest cure (lasting well into the twentieth century), there can be little doubt that it was of some help to many patients. Still, G. J. Barker-Benfield describes the rest cure as "the patient's descent to womblike dependence, then rebirth, liquid food, weaning, upbringing, and reeducation by a model parental organization—a trained female nurse entirely and unquestioningly the agent firmly implementing the orders of the more distant and totally authoritative male, i.e., the doctor in charge. The patient was returned to her menfold's management, recycled and taught to make the will of the male her own."[64] While certain women may have experienced the rest cure in this way, such a generalization does not describe all rest cure cases. Not all women were taught complete submission and "regressed physically and emotionally." Not all women had their arms and legs moved for them and experienced the invasion of every orifice.[65]

According to Mitchell, when he prescribed a rest cure, it was tailor-made to fit the needs of a particular patient. Some patients took the cure at home, nerve retreats, mountain resorts, or the shore. Edith Wharton, suffering from depression and exhaustion, took a rest cure in the winter of 1898 in a hotel, probably as an outpatient of the infirmary under the care of another doctor, named Dr. McClellan, rather than Mitchell.[66] She had not written poetry for ten years, and there is a story that Mitchell advised her to take up writing to avoid a mental breakdown.[67] This story is supported by correspondence written just after the publication of *The House of Mirth*, when Mitchell told Wharton, "I have a curious personal interest in your success." In a few days, Wharton responded, "Your letter gave me great pleasure."[68] Mitchell's "personal interest" may well refer to his advice to Wharton to take up writing. Jane Addams, after a breakdown, a rest cure, and six months of bed rest at home, wrote that she was glad to follow Mitchell's "prescription of spending the next two years in Europe."[69] Ann J. Lane, in her biography of Gilman, states that not all of Mitchell's patients suffered as a result of a rest cure. Certain aspects of the cure had positive value for patients. Mitchell contributed to the process of taking mental illness out of the madhouse by considering anxiety and depression seriously and attempting to treat the mind and body. He assumed, unlike others, that neuroses were treatable, and Lane writes that for many the "psychological value of receiving attention and acknowledgment that the ailment was legitimate in an environment that encouraged self-confidence was sufficient to restore some semblance of normal functioning." Through a kind of behavior modification,

Mitchell worked to restore a sense of capacity and willpower. And, in the case of Gilman, Lane identifies a kind of transference when Gilman finally received the fatherly attention that she had been deprived of as a child. In Mitchell, as the "commanding, authoritative father-figure," Gilman "finally got the attention she wanted from a father and perhaps she was thus able to engage that male power, reject it, and move out on her own." Gilman was able to transfer her need for a father to Mitchell, reject the father figure represented by Mitchell and Stetson, and through free association and resistance take the additional step of "talking it out" through her writing of "The Yellow Wall-Paper."[70]

According to Schuster, two of Mitchell's neurasthenic patients, Amelia Gere Mason and Sarah Butler Wister, were able to shape their illness and treatment to fit their personal sensibilities without passively accepting all of Mitchell's instructions. While they did not work to redefine women's roles like Gilman and Addams, they did combat the morbid thoughts and stagnation caused by their illness and return to their home scenes to live fuller, richer lives. Schuster writes that a rest cure operated on two levels: first, it insured the necessary weight gain, and second, it allowed physicians to put patients through a psychological boot camp to strengthen their minds. In this way Mitchell "inadvertently provided a mechanism that allowed patients to question patriarchal beliefs" that placed limits on women's health and social roles.[71] It is likely that a similar mechanism was at work in the case of another rest cure patient, Virginia Woolf.

Woolf was sent on four occasions for a rest cure to Burley, a private asylum in Twickenham, a place her nephew and biographer Quentin Bell described as a "kind of polite madhouse for female lunatics."[72] Woolf wrote, "I cant conceive how anybody can be fool enough to believe in a doctor. . . . My life is a constant fight against Doctors follies, it seems to me."[73] In her novel *Mrs. Dalloway*, Woolf represented her thoughts about physicians and the rest cure through the character of Dr. Bradshaw, who was based on her personal physicians, George Savage and Maurice Craig. Ellen Bassuk writes that the unwillingness or inability of early feminists "to form idealizing transferences to their physicians may have provided a vehicle for escaping traditional domestic roles." Their refusal to acquiesce "ensured greater personal growth and the potential for identifying and working through conflict rather than putting it to rest."[74] Hermione Lee argues that there can be no doubt that the development of Woolf's political position, "her intellectual resistance to tyranny and conventionality, derived to a great extent from her experiences as a woman patient."[75]

Virginia Woolf was a brilliant writer and a key figure in the twentieth-century modernist movement. Gilman and Addams, as reformers and feminists, played major roles in creating new theory and praxis. Mason, a wealthy woman who never had children, was a critic and socialite. Wister was an essayist and "homemaker," but her home was an eighty-two-acre estate called Butler Place, and she was Mitchell's cousin, someone he referred to as his "kinswoman." Making generalizations about the rest cure based on a small number of women remains problematic, yet one common element does emerge: intelligent and articulate, these women needed and relentlessly pursued avenues of self-expression and transformation.

As a literary physician, Mitchell understood the value of voice and self-expression as well or better than anyone did. He viewed language use as immensely important and repeatedly recorded a personal need to write; he understood in conscious and explicit ways the personal, social, and professional consequences of having a strong voice and an education. Many of his female patients possessed the same need, but they were stifled in domestic space, struggling to find meaningful outlets for their creativity and intelligence. Evelyn Ender writes that the impossibility of verbal symbolization characteristic of the hysterical patient begins with her inscription into a tradition that relentlessly denies to women the ability to move from impressions to the realm of thought and language. Hysteria is "a vivid reminder of the fact that, for certain categories of subjects, consciousness remains secret not because of a choice but as an imposed condition."[76]

At the age of fifty-nine, Virginia Woolf was hearing voices again. Her husband, Leonard, took her to Brighton to see Dr. Octavia Wilberforce. When Wilberforce asked her to undress for an examination, Woolf responded, "Will you promise, if I do this, not to order me a rest cure?" Wilberforce responded that when she had had this trouble before, she had been helped by a rest cure, and that should give her some confidence.[77] Even then, in 1941, Mitchell's rest cure was the most suitable treatment available to Woolf. But her great fear was that she could no longer write, and the day after this consultation she drowned herself in the River Ouse. While there were complex reasons for the suicide, Woolf's writing was of the utmost importance to her. Judith Fetterley argues that the "struggle for control of textuality is nothing less than the struggle for control over the definition of reality and hence over the definition of sanity and madness."[78] In the sexist culture of the nineteenth century, the stories that doctors and women told were not merely alternate versions of reality; rather, they were incompatible and could not coexist. An "exile from language" could be devastating. It denied women's intellect and substituted instead the social imperative called "duty."[79] When Mitchell restored women's bodies but denied their minds, he contradicted his own theory of the mind and body as one. Unable to recognize the great differences among women as a group, he judged all women according to a single type, and criticized and sometimes harmed those who did not fit his ideal.

Writers like Gilman, Woolf, and Wharton picked up the themes of silence, breakdown, and treatment and wove them into the literary fabric. Gilman stated in her autobiography that the real purpose of "The Yellow Wall-Paper" was to reach Dr. Mitchell and "convince him of the error of his ways. I sent him a copy as soon as it came out, but got no response."[80] She also wrote that she later heard that he had changed his treatment as a result of reading it. But nothing in Mitchell's papers or publications corroborates such a change, and given the rigidity of his views and his obstinacy, it seems unlikely. Still, it would be difficult to exaggerate the impact that one patient and a short story has had on his reputation. While he was not working in isolation and his attitudes were hardly original, he has come to symbolize the forces that attempted to defeat the New Women and early feminists. Gilman and "The Yellow Wall-Paper" have been used to transform Mitchell into a legendary villain for many scholars, casting a shadow over his contributions in experimental medicine and neurology, and obscuring the importance of the rest cure as a revolution in therapeutics and a bridge to psychiatry.

8

THE LITERARY PHYSICIAN

Looking back over the years, Mitchell was, for the most part, pleased with the view. The hurt of losing the chairs at the University of Pennsylvania and Jefferson Medical College had all but healed due to what he had accomplished since that time. The expansion and growing prestige of the Infirmary of Nervous Diseases provided endless clinical opportunities that fed the success of the rest cure. This happy union was matched in his personal life by his marriage and children (two sons and a daughter). There was also the trusteeship at the University of Pennsylvania and an impressive list of publications. Even so, when he turned fifty in 1879, he looked back only momentarily.

Mitchell began to spend less and less time in Philadelphia. Counting his fishing trips, summers at Newport and then Bar Harbor, and numerous trips to Europe, he was spending half the year away from the infirmary and private practice. Increasingly, he focused on writing literature. Early in his career, Oliver Wendell Holmes had encouraged him to "remember Hall and Goethe and make the most of both your talents by either of which I have no doubt you can achieve a reputation."[1] But others warned him that patients would distrust a doctor who wrote poems. He submitted a few poems and stories that appeared in the *Atlantic Monthly* and *Lippincott's Magazine*, but fearing what others might think, he published anonymously or used the pseudonym "Edward Kearsley." At the same time, writing remained immensely important to him. In the autobiography he wrote, "If I had not had to earn my own bread and that of others in my youth, it is probable that I would have given my life to literature."[2] He told John, "At 15—I came near to being a merchant—Later I hankered after—manufacturing chemistry—and all along played with the notion of literature as a life pursuit—but all thro. life it has been to me a real comfort for to sketch with words is even more useful than with pencil, more useful and—as pleasant. So all along I have never let go of literature and the skill of pen I have won has been of great value when I came to put the graver things of science on paper."[3] Now, at fifty, wealthy and powerfully established, he could really express his desire to write literature.

Spending half of each year away from the city's dust and heat, it was Mitchell's habit to write all morning and then walk or ride for two to three hours in the afternoon. From June to October, shedding his identity as a physician, he worked diligently to become a poet and novelist. He often spoke about this double life of winter doctor and summer writer, especially about the abrupt transition between the two. He told Harvey Cushing, "I often reflect with some interest on the influence upon a man of sudden changes of occupation. On my return home I find myself fully taken up by patients and consultations, and by more or less of public duties connected with institutions. I think I could no more have written the Lycian Tomb in winter than I could have flown. I wonder how many men we are, after all." In another letter he wrote, "I have scribbled verse ever since I left home—or rather it has scribbled itself—as if my imagination was kicking up its heels like a colt for joy at my holiday."[4] It was not fame exactly that he was chasing, although he certainly enjoyed that. But even more than seeking fame, he was finally able to indulge his passion for creative writing. Officially, he referred to writing literature as summer play, but the evidence belies such statements. This is especially true in terms of the amount of time he spent drafting and revising, and, perhaps more telling, the disappointment he felt at not succeeding fully. Often his novels were two or three years in the making. And in the case of at least five (*Roland Blake, Hugh Wynne, Constance Trescot, The Red City*, and *John Sherwood*), he paid to have the entire novel privately printed before publication. He felt that he could revise a novel best in print, and he called these copies "trial prints."

There is another exception to Mitchell's typical characterization of literature as summer play. Dr. R. S. Woodward had asked him along with other scientists and men of letters for information regarding the mental processes in their work. In Mitchell's response, he compared his experimenting with snakes to writing literature, equating the mental labor needed for science with that of poetry. When he began examining venom, the matter was constantly on his mind: "Ideas about snake poison . . . occupied my mind incessantly. I took it to sleep with me and woke to think about it and found it hard to escape it even when in church or conversing with people. It is something like being haunted, this grip a fruitful research gets upon you. . . . You seem to be like a cat with a mouse-hole, watching for the mouse idea to come out." The process is not "unlike that which is present when in fiction or verse you wait, watching the succession of ideas which come when you keep an open mind." Scientific research involved immense curiosity, the formation and rejection of hypotheses, the testing of these experimentally, and above all unfailing energy. Writing poetry was just such a process of formation, rejection, and selection, a "continual summoning of thoughts, clothing them in suitable language . . . felt as an immense joy by the creator of the expression." But Mitchell was frustrated at the similarities he was uncovering and finally admitted some bewilderment: "After all I have said, there lacks some definition of the scientific mind as opposed to or different from the purely poetic mind. That is, the difference between Shelley, we will say and Laplace or Newton."[5]

While doing science and writing poetry seem to be different, some of the differences are actually located in the rhetorical strategies that scientists employ to write about their work.[6] Writers of scientific discourse often delete the agent by writing in the passive voice, remove the relevance of time and place, and imply that the observation did not originate in a human observer but in the world. The observation is presented as if it were as real as nature itself. Often the narrative of discovery is omitted or described as mechanical rather than vital. Dr. Woodward felt comfortable believing that the differences between scientific and literary methods were more external or superficial ones of subject matter and environment. The internal dynamics required "the same type of mind," and he stressed the use of a lively imagination and the ability to call up a flood of images or multiple hypotheses in scientific work.[7]

Mitchell's letters to Woodward were dictated, but he added a handwritten postscript to the last one, saying, "My statement is too cold blooded. . . . In highest verse the sense of complete capture is felt as a friend says like a physical orgasm—a kind of mind rapture—I keep copy of this—it is all private confidential of course." Woodward, citing Edgar Allan Poe and James Clerk Maxwell as examples, responded that while there was a difference between Shelley and Laplace or Newton, there were a number of instances where poets had been fine mathematicians and mathematicians had been good poets. Imagination was the common factor between writing literature and doing science. Regarding the poet's "mind rapture" to which Mitchell referred, Woodward could appreciate it to some degree, but he did not think such rapture surpassed that of the mathematician or physicist, "who finds that a single hypothesis or a single differential equation will bring order out of the apparent chaos of the phenomenon he may have under consideration."[8]

Imagination, according to Mitchell, was the soul of science. In science "there are times when, starting from facts, imagination is on the wing. It casts its treasure at the feet of reason." To elaborate this point he referred to Edward T. Reichert's research with starches. Reichert had demonstrated that a plant may be identified by the way its starch cells appear under polarized light. Just give Reichert "one little cell, and he says, 'that lily, that tulip.'" And noting the immense contribution this makes to the law of individuality, Mitchell prophetically continued, "Well, here the wild-winged thing, poetic imagination (mine) comes in. All men are unlike. . . . Some day we shall say, 'that globule came from John, that from Susan.' The wild flight after the proving . . . may be hopeless, but seen with the eye of imagination the page reads clear. Each of your billion blood corpuscles is itself and each is you and since time began no other corpuscle was ever the same as any other. That is science on the wing."[9]

———

Mitchell could look back at the history of science, see its amazing evolution, and marvel at its achievements, but he could not see literature in the same way. Blocking his view was his rigid sense of etiquette and decorum, which increasingly gained the upper hand after his second marriage. When he began to write literature in earnest in the 1880s, he was a different man from the experimenter of the 1850s and the author of "The Case of George Dedlow." His exhilarating sense of "science on the wing" did not make its way into this later period of writing poetry and novels.

A friend wrote that in Mitchell's home, "Correct manners were known and practised. The good social traditions of Philadelphia which are a by-word survived here, for he was their defender and embodiment; his home set the conservative standards of the city."[10] The control and propriety that Mitchell maintained in his personal life, anchoring him in the safe harbor of respectability, deadened his appreciation of irony and ambiguity. Caught in a static web of good society, he strove to shape character and plot according to essentialist ideals. His approach was deductive, and he created narratives mainly in the framework of the romance tradition.

Mitchell said it best himself when he wrote that in his literature he was no "psychological fisherman in deep waters." While there are a few exceptions, like Ezra Wendell and the eponymous hero Constance Trescot, for the most part the fiction assumes or dismisses passion and desire without any messiness. When he wrote to thank William Dean Howells for a copy of *The Rise of Silas Lapham*, he also thanked him for "the wholesomeness" of all of his work and remarked that Henry James was falling off in this regard. He told Mason, "As for standards of morals and taste. I vaguely feel that there must be one somewhere, and confess to the additional belief that my standard is the correct one." In 1912, by which point most of his fiction had been written, he told Mason, "I agree with you about the modern fiction. I do not like it, and am happy that I never wrote a line that a girl might not read."[11]

Using contemporary standards to determine if a literary work is "good" or "bad" is a subjective process. And it fails to consider how the literature of a particular time and place acted on and influenced its readers to either sustain the status quo or bring about new ways of seeing things.[12] Several of Mitchell's novels and stories were widely read, and their "wholesomeness" was a major reason for their popularity. While his message was not subtle, many readers enjoyed it and found it comforting. Through his literature Mitchell understood perfectly that he exercised a fair amount of power in conveying his values and worldview. Friends and strangers wrote to applaud his success. *Hugh Wynne, Free Quaker* made Mott's "Better Seller" list, which was very close to best-seller status. It placed second on the *Bookman* bookstore best-seller list; *The Adventures of François* was tied for tenth. Even before the publication of *Hugh Wynne*, Sarah Orne Jewett had written with high praise, telling Mitchell about "the great pleasure your stories have given me. . . . I do not know when I have enjoyed anything so much as I have *Roland Blake*. . . . Your Miss Octopia is wonderfully true— altogether a perfectly drawn character. I read her with hungry delight! And . . . as for the drawing of the marsh country and the tide inlets, I am afraid you do not half know what a beautiful picture you are giving away between these brown book covers." Jewett wrote of the delicacy and the charm of his fiction, and after the publication of *Hugh Wynne*, she wrote that it was "at the head of the procession." She asked, "How did you happen to be such a writer and such a Doctor too is what this instructed person would like to know!"[13]

Mitchell dedicated a volume of poems to James Russell Lowell and mailed him a copy of the book. In a thank-you note, Lowell wrote back that the poems "The Swan-Woman," "A Medal," and "The Miser: A Masque" were "particularly fine and even masterly." Mitchell told Mason that Thomas Bailey Aldrich had written to say that there were two great American novels, *Hugh Wynne* and *The Scarlet Letter*: "By George! A. does not speak lightly; it took me in the throat. I have many such letters from men who do not print their opinions." He told Woodward that Charles Eliot Norton had referred to his poem "Ode on a Lycian Tomb" as "the high tide of American verse and one of the great English elegies."[14]

Yet others were not so impressed. In London the *Athenaeum* referred to the "Ode on a Lycian Tomb" as commonplace and not worth reprinting. When Macmillan printed a thousand copies of a volume of Mitchell's poetry in England, only nineteen sold. One London reviewer stated that Mitchell had shown "conclusively that he is no poet. He lacks quintessential emotion, he has not the lyric touch, even his thought (and the verse is thoughtful) is not beyond the compass of the average cultured and reflective mind, and there is a conspicuous lack of metrical ease and felicity." While many praised *Hugh Wynne*, a reviewer for the *Friends' Intelligencer* in Philadelphia stated that the novel was a polemic that misrepresented the spirit of Quakerism and glorified the man who fights. Hugh was just one of many gallant knights "who mounts and sallies forth, without fear or reproach, who is also in love, who engages and slays his enemy, and returns in triumph to his lady . . . a figure known in literature for centuries. Mitchell's hero is simply one of this class." If honor and honesty truly prevailed, there would be no occasion for fighting—"that fine figure on horseback with sword and pistol cannot be made an ideal."[15]

When a reviewer for Chicago's *Evening Post* wrote that Mitchell's prose stories fell "short of interest because of a want of vivid incident," Mitchell wrote Mason, "How curious it is that people don't take the larger meaning." And when the reviewer referred to "The House Beyond Prettymarsh" as "banal," he wrote, "I hate the word. What the story is the critics miss." The next year *The Nation* reviewed *John Sherwood, Ironmaster*, a novel that sold ten thousand copies in six months, and criticized the style as awkward and the speech as thick. Mitchell countered that the critic had misunderstood the main point and that "the capacity to feel the tone and the general trend of a novel is one which I have missed always in the 'Nation's' reviews."[16]

Mitchell asked his son, "When shall we have the true critic who helps us to see the hidden beauties rather than to grin at the obvious demerits?" He told Howells that "one would be willing to pay a really good one." To Mason he wrote in frustration, "Criticism is not in this country." Unsigned reviews especially irritated him, and he waged a small war by writing letters and an article condemning them. He told one editor, "What I mean is this. Without signature there is no career for critics; with signatures, when those belong to people of known critical force, a man is compelled to consider what is said. If I had my way I should not allow a single line of bibliographical notice without this essential addition."[17]

But what Mitchell really wanted was praise, not criticism. In order to shelter himself, he let his wishes be known and constructed a fortress of intimate friends and "his people," as he called his family members, who filtered or refuted negative comments. They discussed only friendly reviews, and his wife supported him with a "warm bath" of honeyed words and glowing praise. Even Mason, throughout her thirty years of correspondence, exercised care and caution in her "semi-critical comments," as she referred to them. Yet all along Mitchell felt that he was quite open and accepting of criticism, telling Mason, "My wife says I have one supreme virtue—a thoughtful open mind to all forms of criticism. It is true, and I cannot comprehend the defensive sensitiveness of some men—Tennyson! nor the indifference of Browning! to all criticism."[18]

Mitchell's novels, especially *Roland Blake*, *Hugh Wynne*, *The Red City*, and *Westways*, belong to the tradition of genteel and historical romance, a genre that reemerged in the United States briefly, from about 1890 to 1910. A romance follows a quest-trial-marriage plotline, where the young and handsome hero confronts some problem or obstacle. The plot unfolds through his attempts to overcome the obstacle, whether that is the enemy in war or a single villain, and in the end he is victorious and wins the beautiful young maiden. Many of Mitchell's novels follow this basic outline; all but two of his thirteen novels end in marriage, and rather than featuring realistic individuals, each narrative repeats a set of archetypes and stylized figures. While cases of obsession, paranoia, alcoholism, and hysteria do appear, with the exception of *Constance Trescot*, they are understated and take a backseat to the allegory. Mitchell felt that this caution regarding the medical detail of disease was a matter of discretion and good taste. He wrote, "I believe that my medical opportunities have been of great value to me as a writer of fiction, and in every one of my books will be found a picture of some form of disease. The great art in this work is to conceal the knowledge which a doctor has of these cases and to use only enough to interest without disgusting."[19]

With few exceptions, the novels stay clear of introspection, skepticism, ambivalence, and sexuality. There is no stream of consciousness and certainly no gross naturalistic detail. The genteel values that Mitchell personally embodied were the ones that his good characters embraced, celebrated, and were rewarded for. He often chose the American and French Revolutions and the Civil War as settings, and in two of his novels Quakers play major roles. His historical and domestic spaces provide clearly defined scripts for men as sons, husbands, and public figures and for women as daughters, mothers, and wives. He fiercely rejected the realism and naturalism of his day, seeing it as coarse and vulgar, and stating that the straining after realistic precision often injured the larger purpose of fiction or drama. He wrote, "If there is one literary label I hate more than another, it is the word Realist." In a lecture on "Novels and Novelists," he referred to books that were "needlessly painful, distressingly horrible," using Thomas Hardy's *Tess of the d'Urbervilles* as an example and referring to the "realistic atrocities of Zola, and even Tolstoi." He cautioned against a realistic portrayal of illness, writing, "Depend upon it, the novelist had better fight shy of the realities of illness, if he means to preserve the entire decorum of his pages. Here no man may dare to be realistic."[20]

Owen Wister, in his eulogy of Mitchell as a literary writer, explained, "It is preposterous to suppose that any Balzac or Flaubert or de Maupassant knew more of evil and sorrow and pain than Dr. Mitchell. Four years of mutilated soldiers and fifty of hysteria, neurosis, insanity, and drug mania, unrolled for him a hideous panorama of the flesh of the mind and the soul. But when in one of his books he makes a Doctor say:'Who dares draw illness as it is? Not I,' he gives the clue to his fiction."[21] Wister meant to defend Mitchell, but instead he identified the very problem he wished to deny. It was decorum's check on Mitchell's fiction that made it popular but not great. The 1866 short story "The Case of George Dedlow" was an exception because of its synthesis of medical detail and first-person narration. Wister's comment—"Consider what we should have had if Balzac or Flaubert or Zola had known what Dr. Mitchell knew about women"—is richly ironic in terms of lost opportunity.

When Amelia Gere Mason tried to explain the difference between realism and idealism, and substance and form, Mitchell responded that that there was "no such thing as real and ideal in true literary art. The realist is a *mere* naturalist, but the *high* naturalist is an 'in-seer.' Your true novelist is both pure observer and philosopher. The only true realist is an idealist." He told Mason that another friend had spoken of a general absence of passion in his novels and complained that Hugh Wynne's passion for Darthea was "sadly invisible." He responded, "How could an old man writing for his children speak of his passion for their mother?" Mason told him, "I have always noted that you put very little of yourself in your work, though much of your own observation, or *objective* experience. That is modern and scientific, but to my mind the divine spark lies in the personal life. . . . You are a bit afraid of emotional writing, and rightly enough, as things go. This is *not* a criticism." Mitchell was annoyed. In a few days he responded, "You say I do not put myself into my books! No real man of force puts himself into his books entire. . . . What do you call emotional writing? I want to understand that! I have no sense of being afraid of emotional expression. Tell me bluntly where this fails?" Mason immediately retracted her statement: "I do not recall what I said about emotional writing. The words might be misleading, as emotional writing is, much of it, very bad—weakly sentimental. I meant, probably, powerful emotions dealt with powerfully. I certainly did not mean a criticism." Mitchell, writing with the reserve of a gentleman, would avoid any "scenes of passion easily vulgarized" and "tempting opportunities to be excessive."[22]

While Mitchell refashioned himself as a literary physician, giving increasing amounts of time to doing the historical research for the novels and their writing, he continued to assure his colleagues that medicine was his real work, dividing his activities into scientific work, clinical labors, and "literary play in the summer." In order to capitalize on his medical position and endow his literary pursuits with a special kind of authority, he often placed "M.D." after his name on the title pages of his novels. Later, after receiving honorary degrees, he placed "LL.D. Harvard and Edinburgh" after the "M.D.," infusing his fiction with the prestige of such honors. He told George M. Gould that the "literary M.D. is one who still adheres to and honours his profession and even relates the two things. My own medical experience has been in my novels invaluable and they have had—success, as a test, in so many editions."[23] While literature provided the freshness of a new beginning for Mitchell, medicine empowered him to speak with authority.

Mitchell thought of writing as "mental gymnastics" and felt that words appearing on the page were necessary to give definition to ideas: "For me this has always been the case, and whether it be a mere literary statement or a problem in toxicology or medicine, it only grows clear to me on the written page, and perhaps only then after repeated efforts to put it in words."[24] While the use of the word "mere" again illustrates his inclination to assign a secondary status to literary pursuits, he was quick to identify the benefits of reading and writing literature for physicians. Changing the nature of one's mental activities rested and refreshed the mind. In a *JAMA* article on the poetry of Dr. Ronald Ross, who won the Nobel Prize for proving that mosquitoes transmitted malaria, Mitchell began with Ross's epigram: "These verses were written in India between the years 1891 and 1899, as a means of relief after the daily labors of a long, scientific research."[25]

Charles Darwin also noted the joy he had once taken in literature, especially Shakespeare, Wordsworth, and Byron, but along with his taste for painting and music, he had lost this pleasure. Even fine scenery did not provide the exquisite delight it once had. Darwin wrote that as an older man he could not "endure to read a line of poetry; I have tried lately to read Shakespeare, and found it so intolerably dull that it nauseated me." His mind had become a kind of "machine for grinding general laws out of large collections of facts," and this loss of the higher aesthetic tastes was a loss of happiness and probably "injurious to the intellect, and more probably to the moral character, by enfeebling the emotional part of our nature."[26] Mitchell reproached Darwin for abandoning the aesthetic side of his nature, believing that it was a common defect in scientific men. The mind, like the body, needed exercise of all its parts. Literary activity constituted a type of mental exercise that ultimately allowed the work of science to be pursued more effectively.

The Canadian William Osler also believed that literature was an essential ingredient in the life of a successful physician. Although he did not write poetry or fiction, he was an ardent reader and his essays and addresses are packed with literary allusions. Born in 1849, Osler was the youngest of eight children of parents who had traveled from England to a frontier station in Ontario, Canada, to serve as missionaries. In 1871, at the age of twenty-two, he was awarded the degree of doctor of medicine and master of surgery from McGill University. After two years of postgraduate work in London, Berlin, and Vienna, Osler joined the McGill faculty as a lecturer. He was hired because he knew how to use microscopes, was passionate about research, and had taken advanced scientific training. With his own money he purchased fifteen Hartnack microscopes from Paris and offered the first course in microscopy and histology in Canada. He was promoted to professor at the end of his first term. Michael Bliss writes that Osler had "impressed practically everyone with the range of his achievement and his idealism. . . . Not only was he ubiquitous in the journals and at meetings, but in most of his work he was good—observant, logical, steeped in the literature, and apt at any time to toss off *bon mots* from Shakespeare."[27]

When Alfred Stillé retired from the chair of the theory and practice of medicine at the University of Pennsylvania Medical School in 1884, William Pepper succeeded him. That left Pepper's chair of clinical medicine vacant. In its first 120 years, the University of Pennsylvania Medical School had appointed only one faculty member who was not a Pennsylvanian or an alumnus, and most professors were both.[28] So it was exceptional when Osler was asked to let his name stand as a candidate. Osler was in Leipzig when he received James Tyson's letter. At the same time Mitchell and his wife were abroad, and as a University of Pennsylvania trustee, Mitchell was asked to interview Osler. Mitchell was fifty-five and Osler thirty-five. They met on July 6 in London. It is often said that Mitchell's intention was to observe and test Osler's personal comportment and social graces. When Osler ate a piece of cherry pie, he passed the test by disposing of the cherrystones with his spoon. In truth, when Mitchell met and recognized Osler as a kindred spirit, it was about more than the proper disposal of a cherrystone.

After their London meeting, Mitchell did everything possible to secure the Pennsylvania chair for Osler, writing numerous letters to insure the appointment. From Paris he wrote James Wilson that "Osler is in all ways the best man—He has every social need his age is 35—He has won distinction as an investigator and writer—and will therefore add to our illustriousness—and—as to competence as a teacher if any one can be believed he must be a really unusual instructor. . . . If you think well of it Tyson would put together *all* there is in Osler's favour and see that all concerned saw it. I see that unless we are pretty active we shall be saddled with Bruen."[29] Despite the fact that Osler was a foreigner and the dark horse, he won the chair.

When Mitchell helped to bring Osler to Philadelphia, he performed a delicate and valuable service. Osler's credentials and testimonials were impeccable. He was publishing in journals and presenting at meetings, and he had just been elected a fellow of the Royal College of Physicians of London. In Osler's love of research and physiology and his familiarity with the microscope, still rare at the time, Mitchell saw himself as a young man. Henry H. Donaldson, referring to this time as the "prehistoric period in physiology in the United States," wrote that when he entered the College of Physicians and Surgeons in New York in 1880, one could receive a degree in two years by "attending endless lectures and taking quizzes with a preceptor. There was a dissecting room—but no laboratories." The first course in histology was offered that year in "a deserted ice-cream saloon, during the lunch hour, and with microscopes—mostly French models—which Prudden had borrowed from his friends. . . . It was the one bright spot in the year."[30] Considering Osler's noteworthy contributions, including his role in reforming medical education in the United States, Mitchell's efforts were fully rewarded.

Throughout Osler's years in Philadelphia, Mitchell served as his mentor and friend. When the new 110-bed Infirmary of Nervous Diseases was completed in 1887, Mitchell helped secure Osler's appointment there. Much of Osler's previous work had been pathological, but at the infirmary he shifted to neurology and therapeutics. The afternoon clinics from one to four-thirty were divided among Wharton Sinkler, Mitchell, and Osler. Bliss writes that for five years Osler "read Mitchell's books, talked intimately with him about the rest cure, and pondered the secrets of his success."[31]

Already passionate bibliophiles, together Mitchell and Osler inspired each other to new heights regarding the significance of the history of medicine. They became especially intense in their pursuit of medical books and all things related to William Harvey. Shortly after his arrival, Osler became a fellow of the College of Physicians of Philadelphia and a year later was placed on its library committee. Even after leaving, he maintained an active interest in and continued to make significant contributions to the college library.

The lifelong bond that formed between Mitchell and Osler exemplifies a deep-seated and enduring homosocial tradition in the medical profession. Proud to be members of this elite international brotherhood, they understood the need to preserve its history. They grasped the importance of research and experimentation. They also stressed the value of wide reading in literature and philosophy in order to build character and compensate for what medical school did not provide. Both men admired George Eliot, and were particularly fascinated by Dr. Tertius Lydgate in *Middlemarch* and Eliot's ability to capture their own sense of the doctor's fine character, youthful aspirations, and vulnerability. This engaging portrait represented the young doctor's everyday struggles, which were not included in medical publications like the *Lancet*. Mitchell noted that Shakespeare left no finished portrait of the doctor, Molière only a caricature, and Thackeray failed to draw him. There seemed to be "some insuperable difficulty" in creating a doctor who seemed at home with the other characters, except "the marvellous delineation of Lydgate in 'Middlemarch.' He is all over the physician, his manner, his sentiments, his modes of thought, but he stands alone in fiction." Mitchell told a group of graduating nurses that "it has always seemed strange to me that the finest, truest drawing of a physician . . . was the work of a woman who had had no long or varied knowledge of physicians. . . . Lydgate in 'Middlemarch' is a doctor inside of a man. Others there are, but this stands alone."[32] Osler also referred to Lydgate in many addresses and essays, but he felt that the main lesson to be learned was the absolute necessity of avoiding scheming, self-serving women like Rosamond Vincy and marrying obliging women instead. Both Osler and Mitchell had been careful to do just that—they had learned the lesson of Lydgate's marriage as they understood it.

After Mitchell's first wife died of diphtheria, he did not remarry for thirteen years. When he did, he was forty-six and viewed his second marriage to Mary Cadwalader, who was thirty-four, mainly in the light of social status. Osler, at the age of forty-three, married Grace Linzee Revere Gross, who was thirty-seven. She was the great-granddaughter of Paul Revere and the widow of the prominent Philadelphia physician Samuel W. Gross. Before Gross's death, Osler had been a frequent visitor to the Gross home and had come to know Grace Revere well. She had been properly brought up with every social skill, "including warmth, charm, outward self-assurance, and precisely the appropriate amount of assertiveness." When Bliss describes her as "childless, reasonably good looking, with fair hair, a fine complexion, sparkling blue eyes, and an erect carriage, albeit a bit square-faced and beginning to add flesh," it sounds a little like he is describing an aging horse. And he states that Grace "knew her place as a doctor's wife, which was to be a helpmate—and Osler knew she knew it, for he often told medical friends that widows, being broken in, made the best wives." Osler also told a friend that he would like Grace: "She is an old friend of mine and I feel very safe." Bliss speculates that he "probably meant safe from the wiles of designing, ambitious, domineering, or unreliable women. He would avoid Lydgate's fate in *Middlemarch*."[33] Grace Revere, like Mary Cadwalader, was an American blue blood, wealthy and refined, and both these women became exemplary doctors' wives.

In *Middlemarch* many readers wonder why Lydgate is not attracted to the heroine, Dorothea Brooke, since she possesses youthful beauty and intelligence and wants to sacrifice her life to some great cause. Lydgate does feel that Dorothea is a "good creature" and a "fine girl," but she speaks with more energy than is expected of so young a lady, and she does not look at things from the proper feminine angle: the "society of such women was about as relaxing as going from your work to teach the second form, instead of reclining in a paradise with sweet laughs for bird-notes, and blue eyes for a heaven." "Women just like Dorothea had not entered into his traditions," and Lydgate feels that she

is too earnest: "It is troublesome to talk to such women. They are always wanting reasons, yet they are too ignorant to understand the merits of any question."
He feels, however, that it would be "quite safe" to fall in love with "a creature
like" Rosamond, who has "just the kind of intelligence one would desire in a
woman—polished, refined, docile." Lydgate gave only a limited amount of analysis to love because he "felt himself amply informed by literature, and that traditional wisdom which is handed down in the genial conversation of men."[34]
Rosamond has small hands and feet and perfectly turned shoulders, just the
attributes that Mitchell was so fond of. The rich irony in George Eliot's representation is that—before her marriage—Rosamond is just the type of woman
that Mitchell found so attractive and represented in his medical writing and
novels as the feminine ideal. Lydgate does marry Rosamond, but the marriage
destroys him. It is his myopic view of women that Eliot satirizes so well.

Osler was less susceptible to feminine charm than Mitchell, and women like
Rosamond simply scared him. Haunted by Lydgate, in fact, Osler wrote, "This
well-drawn character . . . may be studied with advantage by the physician; one of
the most important lessons to be gathered from it is—marry the right woman!"
He also wrote, "Would that Lydgate existed only in fiction." Women like Rosamond posed a threat to the medical profession, and Osler gave his students
plenty of warnings. In one address, he contrasted the goddess Aphrodite to young
earthly women and told the young men, "The mistress of your studies should
be the heavenly Aphrodite. . . . Put your affections in cold storage for a few years,
and you will take them out ripened, perhaps a bit mellow, but certainly less subject to those frequent changes which perplex so many young men. Only a grand
passion, an all-absorbing devotion to the elder goddess can save the man with
a congenital tendency to philandering, the flighty Lydgate . . . upon whom the
judgment ultimately falls in a basil-plant of a wife like Rosamond."[35]

Following in the old monastic tradition, Osler worked hard to keep his medical students away from women and marriage, stating that "a young man married
is a young man marred."[36] He advised celibacy. Instead of using a competitive
exam, he personally selected his interns, who had to be unmarried as a condition
of their residency. Reginal Fitz likened the life of Osler's interns to that of monks
in a monastery. After Osler's own marriage, Mr. and Mrs. Osler always gave a
group of interns keys to their home. According to Harvey Cushing, "It was
another custom of the household to give a plain gold ring to each of these 'latch-
keyers' to wear as a form of protection against any designing and matrimonially
minded Gretel they might encounter while sojourning on the Continent."[37]

In his professional life Osler was immensely successful. His book *Principles and Practice of Medicine* was a pathbreaker, becoming the leading English-language textbook in internal medicine for students and physicians for half a century. William W. Keen wrote that wherever Osler went, "The wheels began to go 'round,' things began to be done, and all for the good of the profession and of the community. . . . Weir Mitchell and William Pepper were of the same type, and when this powerful triumvirate were gathered in Philadelphia they had no rival in the country or possibly the world over."[38] After five years, however, Osler decided to leave Philadelphia for Baltimore to assume the most desirable medical position in the United States as physician in chief and professor at the newly formed Johns Hopkins Hospital. His final duty at the University of Pennsylvania was delivering the farewell address to the graduates. Titled "Aequanimitas" and now a classic in the literature of advice to young physicians, Osler most likely had Mitchell in mind when he described the imperturbability and equanimity of the ideal physician.

In 1884 Mitchell published his first novel, *In War Time.* He became a visiting physician to the Insane Department of the Philadelphia Hospital and was elected the first president of the Philadelphia Neurological Society. In the span of a few years, he received an honorary LL.D. from Harvard and the University of Bologna, and was elected president of the College of Physicians. He helped found the American Physiological Society and became the first president of the Congress of American Physicians and Surgeons. Along with the hospital appointments, consultation, and a huge private practice, there were the "many rest houses" that Beverley Tucker referred to. And Tucker noted that Mitchell had one of the largest consulting practices in the United States, and that his income from practice at times reached $100,000 a year.[39] Mitchell's son John left Harvard without a degree, then received his M.D. from the University of Pennsylvania and traveled to Vienna for a year of study. Mary Mitchell had hoped that Langdon would attend law school. When he chose a career as a poet and playwright instead, Mitchell told John, "I am not Philistine enough to stop him— Then I distrust my uncritical heart and pray God he wake not at 40—a man who finds he took a wrong road. The whole business has been to me a sad perplexity." Recalling his sister Elizabeth's problems with Langdon when she was alive, he wrote, "I think more and more of dear Aunt Lizzy and her difficulties with this duck in her hen house."[40] While Langdon would eventually redeem himself in his father's eyes, there was another duck in the Mitchell henhouse that would do some permanent damage.

———

In 1873, after having a severe stroke at the age of fifty-four, Walt Whitman moved to Camden, New Jersey, to be near his brother George. In April 1878 Whitman wrote his sister that a friend had taken him "over in the coupé to Philadelphia," where he "went and saw the great Dr Mitchell, I was very well pleas'd with him—I am to go again."[41] In a few days Whitman saw Mitchell a second time and began to improve after these two visits.

Shortly after Osler's arrival in Philadelphia, his old friend, the Canadian psychiatrist Dr. Richard Maurice Bucke, asked him to become Whitman's physician. Bucke worshipped the poet and was a member of his inner circle. Years before at a dinner in Montreal, Osler had heard him compare Whitman to Darwin, Buddha, and Mahomet. As a favor to Bucke, Osler began to care for Whitman. When Osler was busy or away, John Mitchell went in his place. Later Osler wrote that he "sometimes went to Camden with Dr. J. K. Mitchell, always taking a greeting of some sort as a book from Dr. Weir Mitchell."[42] A number of references in Whitman's correspondence and biography indicate that John made frequent visits to Camden. Mitchell, his son John, and Osler did not bill for their services. Even Langdon visited the poet, who sent him home with a gift for his father. About Langdon, Whitman said, "I liked the boy . . . it was his first visit—he seemed bright, intelligent."[43]

While Whitman was not destitute, he lived modestly, and there were various ways the Mitchells helped him. On April 15, 1886, for example, Talcott Williams and Thomas Donaldson arranged for Whitman's annual Lincoln lecture at the opera house on Chestnut Street. Mitchell was one of two to give $100 anonymously for his tickets.[44] After writing Traubel to inquire about hiring a nurse and stating, "It is needless to say that you may count on me," Mitchell paid $15 a month for two years for Whitman's nurse.[45] He sent money to help with expenses and various subscriptions. In 1890 Whitman's lecture at Philadelphia's Contemporary Club was followed by addresses by Mitchell, Furness, and Gilder.[46] That same year there was a lecture and birthday party for Whitman at Reisser's restaurant, where a dinner of Delaware shad, chicken croquettes, and roast beef was served to more than fifty of Whitman's friends, including men and women. With John in the audience, Mitchell was one of the speakers to follow the main presenter, Robert Ingersoll.[47] Such social and cultural events in

Philadelphia were part of a larger fund-raising effort to benefit and acknowledge the great American bard. Whitman died in 1892.

When Horace Traubel was around fourteen years old, he met Whitman, and for almost twenty years he served as Whitman's nurse, secretary, and friend. From 1888 to the year of Whitman's death, Traubel took extensive notes of their daily conversations, transcribing the notes each evening. During Traubel's lifetime, he published the first three of nine volumes of *With Walt Whitman in Camden*. The remaining volumes were published over the course of the twentieth century, the last in 1996.

When Traubel's first volume was published in 1906, there were comments regarding all three doctors. There was only one comment regarding John— "The young man Mitchell did not take me by storm—he did not impress me." The comments regarding Osler were positive except for his too-constant joviality. The passage regarding Mitchell was less so:

> I know J. K.'s father somewhat—Weir: he is of the intellectual type—a scholar, writer, and all that: very good—an adept: very important in his sphere—a little bitter I should say—a little bitter—touched just a touch by the frosts of culture, society, worldliness—as how few are not! . . . It is true Mitchell has written poems—a volume at least or two—I am moved to second you when you say they don't come to much (I guess they don't)— they are non-vital, are stiff at the knees, don't quite float along freely with the fundamental currents of life, passion. But then you know that in our time every fellow must write poems—a volume at least—and a novel or two—otherwise he can't qualify for society: he writes, he writes, then he gets over it all—recovers.[48]

Mitchell immediately sent Osler a copy, writing, "I think you will be amused at his comments on me and my son and many of our friends. You got off very easily. How he failed to perceive that you too have 'the cold frost of culture' I do not know. Perhaps you have not." Mitchell was upset, explaining to Osler that Traubel was not a gentleman and that "Walt did not care much about people who did not crown him with praise. He had indeed a fine appetite for flattery and could digest any amount of it."[49]

In the second volume of *With Walt Whitman in Camden*, published in 1908, Whitman tells Traubel that Mitchell "is my friend—has proved it in divers ways: is not quite as easy-going as our crowd—has a social position to maintain: yet

I don't know but he's about as near right in most things as most people. I can't say that he's a world-author—he don't hit me for that size—but he's a world-doctor for sure—leastwise everybody says so and I join in."[50] If Mitchell read this passage, it did nothing to appease his indignation.

After Mitchell's death, other interesting comments were published in the subsequent volumes of *With Walt Whitman in Camden*. For example, in volume 4 Whitman tells Traubel, "Mitchell of late years has been bitten with the desire to compose, compose—that curse of curses: has written volumes: very bad, too—awful in their inadequacy: but personally he is a man to meet, to know."[51] According to Traubel, Whitman made this comment in 1889. Another comment referred to a dinner party that Mitchell gave for James Russell Lowell that same year. When Traubel asked Whitman if he had been invited, Whitman laughed "outright. 'What! to a dinner to James Russell? I guess not. My presence would spoil the soup. . . . Weir puts on some of the lingo of authorship: does more or less in a small way: stands for refinements, proprieties, the code, all that: he seems to be more ambitious for fame as a writer than as a doctor, but I have my doubts whether he'll acquire an immortality in either direction.'" Traubel asked if Mitchell was his friend: "Yes, I think so: I like him: he is cordial, easy-going, demonstrative: I realize emotions for him as a man that I do not realize for him as an author." Traubel said, "I doubt if he ranks you high as an artist." Without hesitation, Whitman responded, "I doubt it myself: indeed, I know it: know it, not because of what he has but because of what he has not said."[52] In 1887 in *Doctor and Patient*, however, Mitchell had named Whitman and Thoreau as two of a handful of writers who when read outdoors do not seem "to have gotten their nature-lessons through plate-glass windows."[53] Perhaps Whitman was unaware of this public praise.

It seems unlikely that the relationship between Whitman and Mitchell was ever one of trust and mutual admiration. It does appear that Mitchell was the first to open fire. In Mitchell's novel *Dr. North and His Friends* (published after Whitman's death and before Traubel's first volume), one of Dr. Owen North's closest friends, the "great scholar" Clayborne, refers to Whitman's poetry as "commonplace" and "trash." He says that Whitman was no poet and was "so vain that he had no power of self-criticism. No man is great who has lost power to be self-critical. . . . He was matchless in his vanity."[54] Then, after the first volume of Traubel's biography appeared, Mitchell scattered a number of comments throughout his correspondence that conveyed his sense of being ill-treated by Whitman. As late as 1911, when Charles Norton Eliot wrote soliciting contributions for

Walt Whitman as Man, Poet, and Friend, Mitchell responded, "I am sorry to say that I have not altogether agreeable reflections in my mind nor perfectly pleasant memories in regard to the poet. . . . I did a great many things for him of which I have never talked, and some of them things involving pretty large expenditures. If Traubel rightly reports him as saying the things he did, I prefer to forget all about the man and, as is too often the case concerning poets, to know him only in the future through his verse."[55] Although Mitchell often mentioned gift giving with his friends, he never mentioned the inscribed copies of *Leaves of Grass* that Whitman gave him and John.[56] When John Jay Chapman described Whitman as a "tramp of genius," Mitchell responded, "As to Walt Whitman you are beautifully correct—I knew him well and for years he lived on me and others. He was welcome—I believe he left savings and decreed—a tomb!—I asked him once if he did not think himself a greater poet than Shakespeare. He said, 'I have often considered that question but never could quite make up my mind.'"[57] The year before Mitchell died, he told Mason, "Whitman has no place for me. I think I have told you what my relation was to his life and how entirely ungrateful he seemed to me to have been, if I may trust his biographer."[58]

It would be difficult to imagine poetry as dissimilar as Whitman and Mitchell's. Although Mitchell could be present and emotive, often expressing sorrow, regret, and resignation, the rolling lines of Whitman's free verse appear especially fluid and expansive by comparison. Whitman's diction, repetition, and use of the phrase instead of the metrical foot create a vigorous kind of energy and joy, whereas Mitchell's highly structured lines are deliberate and tight. He intentionally used antiquated diction and syntax to age his language, and the exacting meter and end rhyme are its most pronounced aspects. He defined poetry as "the most elevated thoughts in the most condensed form of the best language, told to the music of rhyme and rhythm."[59] His enthusiasm was for form and structure. He admired and found pleasure in the old-fashioned workmanship of technical control, which took precedence over variation and innovation. As a child Mitchell had made fun of his father's "antique taste" and slyly quoted the new verse "so as to trap him into admissions."[60] Now, while Whitman was revolutionizing the poetic world, Mitchell, like his father, preferred the old poets.

Whitman's dismissive comments condemned writing that Mitchell had labored long and hard over. The comments that Mitchell was "a little bitter" and touched by the "frosts of culture," and that his poetry was "non-vital" and "stiff at the knees," roused his worst fears. He had been reduced to "every fellow" whose motivation to write was both a form of social aspiration and an illness from which, after a volume of poetry and a novel or two, he would recover. Mitchell did not recover, however, and even after he realized that his poetry would fail to receive any critical acclaim, he continued to produce it. He wrote, "About certain medical gains which the world owes to me, I am serenely sure of their value, eye strain headaches, rest treatment, etc., but of the relative value of my verse I have no assurance. It cost me immense labor and gave me equal pleasure. It has no sales—but what verse has?"[61] Just below a thin skin of frost and worldliness there was hypersensitivity, and even though Mitchell frequently stated a desire for criticism, he was not equipped to digest it. Even though he referred to writing literature as "summer play," it was immensely important to him. After his death, John wrote that his father "was two or three people—a poet and a scientific man certainly. His scientific work was always helped—and corrected—by his high imagination—although his critical faculty, or the expression of it at least, was sometimes a bit hindered by his feelings."[62]

9

COMBAT ZONES

Mitchell's sensitivity to criticism did not inhibit his aggressive engagement in debate and controversy, especially as he grew older. In fact, he believed that it was his duty as a famous neurologist and prominent citizen to pilot the ship and maintain the correct course. Given his status as a "professional giant," he felt obliged to do so and became even more absolute and self-righteous about his beliefs. He fortified his war of words with his reputation as the great nerve doctor and his popularity as a fiction writer. For various audiences, whether New Women, anti-vivisectionists, or alienists, he was able to take advantage of his skill as a writer, employing a number of rhetorical weapons and tactics to contend with his adversaries. Some of the battles were more heated than others, and some he ultimately lost.

When William Osler left for Baltimore in 1889, there was no medical school at Johns Hopkins University. Although the university opened in 1876 and its hospital was completed in 1889, there had been difficulty raising the funds for a medical school. Even after Hopkins president Daniel Coit Gilman made a formal appeal, stating, "Only a man of large means and of large views will be likely to appreciate the situation," no such man responded. Instead, a group of women, realizing a rare opportunity, did respond. M. Carey Thomas, Mary Garrett, Mamie Gwinn, and Bessie King organized the Women's Medical School Fund in order to raise the money. All four women had fathers who were or had been Hopkins trustees. More importantly, Garrett's father, John Work Garrett, was the head of the Baltimore and Ohio Railroad, and when he died, she inherited a huge fortune.

As the group's spokesperson, M. Carey Thomas approached President Gilman and told him that the Women's Medical School Fund (also known as the Women's Fund Committee) would contribute $100,000 to the Johns Hopkins Medical School if it would admit women on an equal basis with men. Although almost seven hundred people had contributed, Garrett's contribution would be close to half the total. In 1890 the Hopkins board accepted the $100,000, but stated that the school could not open until an endowment of $500,000 was raised. *The Nation* immediately criticized the board's decision to admit women. As a response to *The Nation's* criticism, in February 1891 the *Century* published "Open Letters: On the Opening of the Johns Hopkins Medical School to Women," including letters from Mary Putnam Jacobi, Carey Thomas, and Osler in support of the decision. Then, in 1892 Garrett offered to donate an additional $300,000 with the stipulation that the medical school would be a graduate school with high admission standards and that it be open to men and women.[1]

Carey Thomas served as the chief negotiator in bringing about this thorny and complicated end, often traveling from Bryn Mawr to Baltimore and staying up all night to prepare for the difficult meetings. These were not "cool business arrangements between rational intelligences," according to Helen Lefkowitz Horowitz, but more like "a performance of Italian opera at its most fevered."[2] Thomas wrote that many of the trustees and especially President Gilman preferred never to have a medical school than to have one that admitted women. But rather than fight in the open, they fought "in the dark with treachery and false reasons. Trustees, doctors, professors (Mr. Gwinn and Father leading our forces) became involved in a tangle of hatred, malice, detraction that beggars description."[3] The movement to allow women to attend Johns Hopkins Medical School involved more than a few women and their fathers on the East Coast, however. There was much more at stake, certainly, and committees of the Women's Medical School Fund emerged in fifteen cities, including Chicago, San Francisco, St. Louis, and New Orleans.

Mitchell, as Osler's close friend and a faithful reader of both *The Nation* and *The Century*, watched this drama unfold with great interest. Along with many others, he did not want women admitted to Johns Hopkins Medical School. Given the difficulty of raising the money and the uproar over the Women's Medical School Fund, he hoped to lure Osler back to Philadelphia. But this time, rather than using an article, a public address, or a public letter, Mitchell used a novel—serialized right in the middle of the controversy—as an opportunity to voice his feelings about women doctors. Serialization of *Characteristics* began in December 1891 in *The Century* and ran through July of the next year.

The hero of *Characteristics*, Alice Leigh, is twenty-four with an "unusual force of character," who strongly believes that a woman "of fortune and intellect" should have a career. In fact, she is depressed and unhappy without one. No one in the novel understands better than the older Mrs. Vincent, who "had once this disease, and pretty badly—the hunger for imperative duties." When asked if she were cured, she replies, "Yes; by marriage. It is what you call a heroic remedy." Alice wants to be a doctor, and she goes to Dr. Owen North for advice. Owen, who often sounds just like his author, is thirty-seven and an assistant surgeon in the army. Alice tells Owen that rather than music and sketching or helping the poor, she wants to study and practice medicine. While he does not want to "wound this gentle girl, with her honest longings, and her despair as to the meagerness of mere upper-class life—its failures to satisfy the large mind and larger heart," at the same time he cannot imagine this "handsome, high-minded girl with her exquisite neatness and delicacies of sentiment and manner amidst the scenes and work which belong to the life of the student of medicine." He cannot reconcile the two, which are so "inconsistent with his ideal of the highest type of womanhood," and he bluntly tells Alice that women are not as good as men of like education at doctoring. In fact, women doctors are not good for themselves or society: "I never saw a woman who did not lose something womanly in acquiring the education of the physician. I hardly put it delicately enough: a charm is lost." "Women lose something of the natural charm of their sex in giving themselves either to this or to the other avocations until now in sole possession of man," and the worst part is that women "fail to realize what they have lost."[4]

In Mary Putnam Jacobi's long letter to Mitchell (discussed in chapter 6), it is clear that she had read *Characteristics* in the *Century* and was upset by his critical comments regarding women doctors. Apropos of the Johns Hopkins debate, she asked where or when he had "as yet met women physicians who have had 'the same education as men'? I at least know of none such." She continued, "At the risk of manifesting an egotism which you may still further explain by the deteriorating effects of medicine," she cited her essay on cold pack and massage in anemia that was published a "year before the appearance of your little book on Fat and Blood" and contained a good many precise researches and suggestions, "which proved to be quite identical with many of yours." Jacobi wrote that she "had begun" the theory of rest and in many cases had already carried it out: "It is not necessary to comment upon the extraordinary success of your little book, while mine, which was experimental as well as theoretical, has scarcely ever been heard of." She also mentioned her work with nutrition in connection with menstruation and her work with pelvic disorders and the endometrium. She cited these three examples of her contributions, although unrecognized for the most part, because they directly touched on the question of female capacity. She finished this long letter by asking Mitchell a question: "Have you ever had an opportunity of watching a woman originally 'charming' deteriorate under the influence of medicine? If not, how do you know that those whom you have met, medical and charmless,—were not always so, even before they had taken the fatal plunge? . . . I would not venture to write so long a letter, were it not that I believe you will soon be at Newport and at leisure for idleness."[5] Mitchell would have found Jacobi's heavy irony and freedom of expression irritating and read the word "idleness" as close to an insult. Still, Jacobi was, arguably, "the most significant woman physician of her time."[6] Her letter was preserved with Mitchell's papers, which was not the case with the letters of Charlotte Perkins Gilman.

Jacobi's medical training was exceptional.[7] She was the first woman to attend the New York College of Pharmacy and graduated in 1863. In 1866, a few years after receiving her M.D. from the Female Medical College of Pennsylvania, she sailed for France, intending to take another degree. Initially rejected by the faculty of the Paris École de Médecine—in which no woman had ever set foot—Jacobi persisted, and on her first day entering the historic amphitheater as the first woman student in 1868, the predicted riots did not occur. Her six years in Paris included the winter of the Prussian siege, marked by acute suffering and near starvation, and the months of the Communist occupation. Jacobi graduated in 1871, winning a bronze medal for her thesis and returning to New York with a medical training superior to many men in the profession.

Upon her return, Jacobi accepted the position of lecturer at the Woman's Medical College of the New York Infirmary for Women and Children, founded by Elizabeth Blackwell, and from 1873 to 1889 she held the position of professor of materia medica and therapeutics. In 1872 she organized the Association for the Advancement of the Medical Education of Women, serving as president from 1874 to 1903. In 1876 she won Harvard's Boylston Prize for her study *The Question of Rest for Women During Menstruation*, which served as a rebuttal to Edward Clarke's *Sex in Education: or, A Fair Chance for the Girls.*[8] Although Jacobi's essay and prize won her admission to numerous medical societies, she was denied membership to the Obstetrical Society because she was a woman. In 1894 she became actively involved in the women's suffrage movement, also working at the time to expand educational opportunities for African Americans and to protect American Indians. She prepared more than one hundred papers for medical societies, and through her writing and work, she raised the standards of the medical education of women and played a major role in dispelling the nineteenth-century myth that women were unfit for the medical profession—a myth that Mitchell worked aggressively to sustain.

After her letter was sent, Jacobi and Mitchell stayed in touch. Jacobi wrote to Sarah Butler Wister, "When you see Dr. Mitchell, be kind enough to give him my regards, and say that I am more than ever impressed by the force of his personality. I have recently felt it in a personal interview."[9] In 1900 there was a seventieth birthday party for Jacobi's husband, Abraham, one of the leading pediatricians in the United States. Mitchell wrote a poem for the dinner celebration, and Mary Putnam Jacobi wrote in thanks for the "really beautiful poem with which you honored his birthday feast. . . . Who so fitted to appreciate a physician, as the poet who is also a physician,—or the distinguished physician who is also so thoroughly a poet?"[10] Mitchell, in turn, praised Jacobi for her work, writing, "Thanks for your book. . . . The essay on Hysteria is a wonder of this kind of brain work and most interesting. . . . I reason with difficulty on these complex questions with which your mind seems to play." He wrote that her essay on tumors was the "best in the literature and this is simply true."[11] Apart from irreconcilable differences about where women belonged and women as doctors, Mitchell and Jacobi had much in common. In terms of tone, neither was one to understate the message. They could speak and write with force and passion. They both believed that the nervous and reproductive systems were interrelated, and that women suffered more than men did from hysteria. Both stressed the importance of good nutrition for good health. Both grounded their work in physiology and neurology and were adamant defenders of vivisection. Jacobi "idealized experimentation," and it remained central to her identity and practice as a physician.[12] She never abandoned her original ideals, always maintaining that science-based research held the key to women's empowerment and liberation.

Unlike Jacobi, Mitchell's fictional character Alice Leigh in *Characteristics* surrenders her desire to become a doctor. Even though on the novel's last page she plucks the rose "to pieces leaf by leaf," she agrees to marry Owen North, wondering, "Is this the end? . . . Of me, of my life, of it," becoming a bit hysterical, bursting into tears, and sobbing like a child. "I meant to have done so much," she says.[13] Clearly, as seen in this novel and others, Mitchell realized the frustration women felt. In his novel *When All the Woods Are Green*, the narrator comments about Rose Lyndsay that "at times the discontentment of a life without the definite aims of a man's career distressed her."[14] In the novel *Circumstance*, Mary Fairthorne states that "to feel as strongly as I do and to be absolutely without voice or influence is most unpleasant." In the same novel Margaret Swanwick, who reads her husband's law books and helps him get through law school, obviously possesses the better legal mind. In subtle but substantial ways she is the stronger partner in his practice.[15] While Mitchell understood the deleterious effects of frustration and distress on the body and mind, he remained firm in his belief regarding the unsuitability of careers for women. What Dr. North in *Characteristics* believed, Mitchell captured succinctly in the line, "For most men, when she seizes the apple, she drops the rose."[16] He told Mason that "as to women M.D.s, what North says is what men—and nice men—think."[17] Not just feminine charm and beauty were lost. In 1889 he wrote that coeducation was "abominable for many reasons, but, for physiological reasons, I think it foolish and absurd; as for the others, I think it needless. You put a woman—a girl—in a class with men—or lads. Her wants and her menstrual disabilities she is forced by modesty to hide, or control, or defy. If in women's colleges the silently accepted standard of health and endurance is that of man, how must it be where the groups are of both sexes, and the effects of shame are intensified by the fear of a masculine smile." In this article, Mitchell held fast to the idea of menstruation as a disability, projecting his own feelings of fear and shame onto women. He called coeducation abominable, foolish, absurd, and "utterly wrong" and concluded by referring the reader to the papers of George Romanes, Mrs. Lynn Linton, and Edward Clarke.[18] No doubt, Mitchell was frustrated and troubled by the outcome at Johns Hopkins and Carey Thomas's formidable victory. In 1882 Mary Putnam Jacobi, Emily Blackwell, and Marie Zakrzewska had offered an endowment of $50,000 to Harvard Medical School if it would accept women. The offer was considered, but when outraged faculty threatened to resign, it was rejected.[19] In light of the fact that women were not allowed to enter Harvard Medical School until 1945, the victory at Johns Hopkins appears even more stunning.

In the 1880s, in addition to two books of poetry and three novels, Mitchell published more than fifty scientific books and articles. On several occasions throughout the years, he took time out of his busy schedule to write children's literature. In 1864 he collaborated with Elizabeth Wister Stevenson on *The Children's Hour* to raise money for the Sanitary Commission. In 1866 he published *The Wonderful Stories of Fuz-Buz the Fly and Mother Grabem the Spider* with illustrations by Philadelphia physicians. He published *Prince Little Boy, and Other Tales out of Fairyland* in 1888 and *Mr. Kris Kringle: A Christmas Tale* in 1893.

While many of his articles in the 1880s were short (only one to three pages in length), there were approximately twenty substantial ones, including two on tendon reflexes titled "Physiological Studies of the Knee-Jerk" and "The Tendon-Jerk and Muscle-Jerk in Disease, and Especially in Posterior Sclerosis." These two were written in collaboration with Dr. Morris J. Lewis, a resident at the infirmary. Mitchell told John, "M. Lewis and I are about to revolutionize the ideas concerning tendon reflex."[20] In the midst of this fruitful period of such diverse topics and genres, Mitchell did not forget about his rattlesnakes.

He liked having rattlesnakes in his lab, and when away from the city, he would write to remind his assistant to "milk" the snakes for venom. Still fascinated after decades of observation, he selected adjectives fit for leaders and warriors to describe these "heroic" animals whose "attitude is fine and warlike."[21] While traveling in Tangiers he made a point to see the snake charmers and wrote, "The business is queer enough. . . . The charmer a lithe swarthy moor with a serious and even sad ascetic face—arose and began to dance slowly, invoking Allah as he spun around. At last he took out a dozen green snakes wh. were clearly innocent. . . . Then he took out a big brown snake and him I at once knew as a poisoner. . . . It is part religious appeal to an old belief—part humbug as to the charming. . . . It was profoundly interesting to a Brother 'Sapengro' like myself."[22]

One afternoon in 1882 when walking up the front steps of a house, Mitchell glanced down and saw a rug that was "made of rope, one corner of which was partly torn off and slightly resembled a serpent. Suddenly there came into my mind the idea that the poison of serpents must be double and not a single poison." At the time the prevalent view was that snake venom was a single poison that varied with the species. Mitchell went home and "asked to have dinner put off and for ten or fifteen minutes wrote down the reasons why snake poison must be double."[23] The next day, in order to prove his hypothesis, Mitchell contacted Edward T. Reichert, professor and head of the physiological laboratory at the University of Pennsylvania. It took them five months to split the venom and conclude that various combinations of poisons in venomous snakes explain the differences in their power to destroy tissue and kill. Together they published articles and a major study titled *Researches upon the Venoms of Poisonous Serpents* in 1886.

In *Researches* Mitchell and Reichert stated that they used two hundred living rattlesnakes, moccasins, copperheads, and coral snakes. The largest rattlesnake was over eight feet long and weighed nineteen pounds. Cobra venom was obtained from India. Approximately 250 other animals were destroyed in their experiments, mainly pigeons, rabbits, and a few cats. In the conclusion to chapter 3, they noted other experiments "too numerous for detail." In concluding chapter 6, they wrote that the experiments had been "supplemented by many others" and "frequently repeated."[24] This extensive experimentation placed them front and center in the vivisection debate.

Public debate about vivisection began to emerge in the 1860s. In 1866 in New York, Henry Bergh organized the American Society for the Prevention of Cruelty to Animals. In 1867 in Philadelphia, Caroline White organized the Pennsylvania Society for the Prevention of Cruelty to Animals. In Britain the anti-vivisectionist movement culminated in the 1876 Cruelty to Animals Act. Thus by the 1880s the vivisection controversy was well established. Mitchell's experimentation with animals began in the early 1850s and continued more or less through several decades. During that time, although his few references to the issue are terse and cryptic, they indicate that he dealt with his share of condemnation. In 1868, in the *New York Medical Journal* article titled "Experimental Contributions to the Toxicology of Rattlesnake Venom," he wrote that his investigation had required a large expenditure of birds, dogs, and rabbits: "To men of science, I need not say that the torture inflicted has been used with all possible thoughtfulness, while at the same time I must add that it was usually impossible, in these experiments, to avail myself of chloroform, which would have introduced into my investigation new and obscuring elements. I have said these few words in apologetic preface, only because I respect the motives of the many ignorant and well meaning persons, who have recently sought to take away from us the chief aid of the modern physiologist."[25] In 1877 he referred to the potential harm done to laboratory investigation "by the war which hysterically acute consciences are making against vivisection."[26] In the 1880s, in addition to the experimentation, Mitchell chaired the committee of the Medical Society of the State of Pennsylvania that addressed the anti-vivisection issue. In 1885 he was responsible for outlining the rules governing vivisection adopted by the University of Pennsylvania trustees.

The war with the anti-vivisectionists was being fought even within Mitchell's family. When he invited his favorite cousin, Sarah Butler Wister, and her son, Owen, to hear him speak at the Centennial Anniversary of the College of Physicians, she refused, writing, "Owen must answer for himself. For my own part, I am sincerely sorry that I cannot be present. It is needless, I hope, that I shd. say . . . that every honour paid you seems a cause of personal pride and gratification to me. But the present occasion is official and so is yr. share in it and the College has taken a position as regards vivisection, wh. is a real moral issue to me, that prevents my having any thing to do with the celebration even in the remotest way."[27] Coming from Wister, such strong words must have been especially irritating.

Philadelphia was a center for anti-vivisection agitation, and few who performed animal experimentation were spared the attacks. Dalton, Curtis, Martin, Bowditch, and Mitchell were all threatened.[28] Keen had always been an active and impassioned defender of vivisection, and in 1912 he published a fiery pamphlet titled *The Influence of Antivivisection on Character*. On its first page Keen reproduced a copy of a letter that he received in August 1910, postmarked Los Angeles, which read, "Arch-Fiend: I read with horror you[r] article in the Ladies' Home Journal on vivisection. I hope your mother if she is living will die in the most terrible torture, and if she is dead that her soul will never know rest for having given life to such a vile monster as you is the nightly prayer of a dozen women who indited this."[29] After reading the pamphlet, Mitchell wrote to Keen:

> Your pamphlet kept me up late last night. It is a wonderful piece of absolutely complete work. I do not see how those people can ever have the insolence to talk again. I could have furnished you with some competent material in addition from my own experience when women whom one would have supposed to be decent went about among my patients announcing me as unfit to have the charge of children. Then I have a standing grudge against the Rev. Tomcat because, without any knowledge of what he was doing, he signed that anonymous paper of Mrs. White in which an attack was made plainly upon me.[30]

Such accusations and attacks were a bitter pill for Mitchell to swallow, thinking as he did that instead of condemnation, he should be honored for his scientific contributions. Nevertheless, by 1912 Mitchell's initial experimental methods were condemned by those on both sides of the debate. In the pamphlet, Keen wrote that "many of the instances cited in antivivisection literature are taken from researches—such as Magendie's—which were made before anesthetics were discovered, over sixty-five years ago. The rest in which real cruelty was inflicted, and which if done now would be condemned by all modern research workers as freely as by the antivivisectionists themselves, were done almost wholly on the Continent, and often by persons who are now dead." Keen took special care in his use of the words "many," "almost," and "often" in this passage. He was aware of the fact that Mitchell was familiar with chloroform and ether before his animal experimentation began in the 1850s, experimented with animals in the United States and not on the Continent, and was not dead. Keen concluded the pamphlet with the following: "Dr. S. Weir Mitchell, when visiting the Antivivisection Exhibition in Philadelphia, put the matter in a nutshell when he said to one of the guides, 'Your exhibition is not quite complete. You should place here a dead baby and there a dead guinea-pig with the motto, Choose between them.'"[31]

Many physicians who defended vivisection expressed their opposition to any form of outside interference in medical research. Still, a comparison of Mitchell's 1860 *Researches upon the Venom of the Rattlesnake* with Mitchell and Reichert's 1886 *Researches upon the Venoms of Poisonous Serpents* indicates that significant reform had taken place. For example, in the 1886 *Researches*, Mitchell and Reichert were careful to state at least three times that anesthetics were always used in these experiments, and when "animals were subjected to chronic poisoning they were kept under the influence of narcotics, since it had been learned that these agents did not affect the results."[32] The 250 animals cited in the experiments were most often killed, thus avoiding long and painful deaths. There was no mention of the use of curare, a drug Mitchell had utilized extensively in his earlier experimentation. Most of these animals were pigeons and rabbits, and no dogs were cited in any of the experiments.

In 1895 Agnes Irwin, the first dean of Radcliffe College and a member of Mitchell's social set, invited him to address the first class of Radcliffe students. In Mitchell's novel *Characteristics*, Dr. North tells Alice Leigh, "Try to think it is my life you are busy with." When Mitchell spoke to the Radcliffe women, he focused on this same theme. Speaking with his usual clarity and directness, he made it clear that a woman's primary duty was to serve: "First, let me state my creed. I believe that, if the higher education or the college life in any way, body or mind, unfits women to be good wives and mothers there had better be none of it." It is significant that he was not merely speaking of marriage, since a "vast number of women who do not marry [like his sister Elizabeth] come to have, at some time, charge of households or of children not their own. This surely is *the natural* life of woman." While he wanted "independence as a human right" and wanted "women to be free," he no more wanted them "to be preachers, lawyers, or platform orators, than . . . men to be seamstresses or nurses of children. I want freedom within the noble limitations of sex." He did not hesitate to praise women as long as they lived according to a certain narrow standard of healthy and "natural" female behavior. He defined a woman's nobleness: "To be homeful for others, and to suggest by the honest sweetness of her nature, by her charity, and the hospitality of her opinions, such ideas of honor, truth, and friendliness as cluster, like porch roses, around our best ideals of home. It is instinctive, and civilization kills our instincts." He strongly advised—to this impressive group of young and, no doubt, wealthy women—competency in household matters such as sewing, cooking, washing, ironing, bookkeeping, and hygiene. He spoke of men who came to see him who had married "sweet girl graduates" who knew about mathematics and literature but nothing of household management. One of the men "declared, in fact, that he had to run the house himself."

In this address, Mitchell did provide some good advice regarding diet, eyestrain, excessive tea drinking, the stress of exams, and especially the benefits of being outdoors and walking, skating, and bicycling. He advised reading poetry and novels right before bedtime, saying that "a fine brain-clearer is a novel which captures attention, and almost as good as a cold bath to sweep out the thoughts of the day." Yet overall, in this address he was less persuasive than he might have been about the importance of diet and exercise. In having the honor to speak to the first generation of Radcliffe students, he did less good that he might have. While he did not go so far as to tell the women to go home, he did make it clear that home was where they belonged, their own or someone else's, to serve, entertain, and nurse because "a woman is *born* to a profession; a man is not." He repeated one of his favorite warnings: "I never saw a professional woman who had not lost some charm. There comes a little hardness, less thought as to how prettily to do or say things; affected plainness of dress; something goes." He closed with the "irrevocable decree" of sexual difference: "Something in between she cannot be. . . . I do not fancy a middle-sex. . . . I hope I have not been extreme or brutal. . . . I see the wrecks come ashore to sail the seas of success no more. Is it any wonder I wish to warn those who are sailing or about to sail on treacherous seas? I hope, my dear Dean, and you, ladies, that no wreck from these shores will be drifted into my dockyard. Sometimes I can refit the ruined craft. Alas! sometimes I cannot."[33]

M. Carey Thomas struggled with her intelligence and her identity as a young woman. Although her father opposed it, she attended Cornell University in 1875, having passed the entrance examination with almost the highest mark. She was one of twenty women in a class of 240 and resided at Sage College, the new residential hall for female students. After graduation she applied to the graduate program at Johns Hopkins University, where the board of trustees had just debated coeducation, was divided on the issue, and finally decided to make arrangements for special cases. Thomas was admitted as a candidate but barred from graduate seminars and advanced instruction, and withdrew after a year in frustration and self-doubt. A few women were studying at German universities and, determined to become an English professor, she decided to go there and study comparative literature. First she went to the University of Leipzig, where women were allowed to attend lectures but not receive degrees. The University of Göttingen, on the other hand, barred women from lectures but seemed willing to grant them degrees. So, at Göttingen after extensive research and writing, Thomas submitted a thesis, a technical study and comparison of *Sir Gawayne and the Green Knight* and twelfth-century French poems. However, after all her work, the faculty refused to examine her.

She then traveled to the University of Zürich, which had been open to women since the 1860s and was a "female educational mecca." Zürich would accept her thesis, but she needed to meet additional requirements in Old English and Old German. She also had to prepare a second paper on English literature, take a half-day written exam, and a three-hour oral examination in German. During the oral examination she was tested in Anglo-Saxon philology, English and Anglo-Saxon historical grammar, German philology, Gothic, High German, German literature, Middle German, and English literature. After the exam, she was asked to leave the room, but only for five minutes. She returned to the news that she had passed summa cum laude, a very rare honor according to Horowitz, one that some professors had never witnessed and no woman in any field had ever received at Zürich.[34]

Thomas was fully committed to the cause of women and education. She became professor of English and dean of the faculty at the Quaker-founded Bryn Mawr College in 1884, and in 1894 she became its president. Along with her friends Mary Garrett, Mamie Gwinn, Bessie King, and Julia Rogers, she founded Bryn Mawr School in 1885 in order to prepare young women for college. Like Mary Putnam Jacobi, Thomas was forced to prove beyond any doubt the power of her intellect, and she had the determination, family support, social status, and financial backing to do so. She was equal to the task of being Mitchell's foe in the fight over higher education and careers for women.

In her 1891 open letter in the *Century* in favor of women attending Johns Hopkins, Thomas stated that for women and men "intellectual activity is the keenest of possible lifelong pleasures and a safeguard against a multitude of evils." Regarding women physicians, in contrast to a man, a woman "will be less ready to secure physical health for her patients at the expense of intellectual development, and less hopeful of so securing it. She will prescribe sheer idleness as a remedy neither for the indispositions of girls in their teens, nor for the ill-health of college students." She argued that it was wrong to restrict women studying medicine to female colleges. At Johns Hopkins the curriculum would be graduate studies (a demand of the Garrett-Thomas negotiations), and the "difference between graduate and undergraduate coeducation is seldom sufficiently insisted on." At the graduate level any disadvantages of coeducation are at a minimum; the advantages are at a maximum in terms of influence, range of activity, and national importance. To exclude women from association with their most successful contemporaries is to "exclude them from the delights of intellectual competition and the possibility of fame."[35] Thomas's focus on education as an end in itself for women created a message that was radically different from anything Mitchell and others of his caste were telling young girls and their mothers.

In 1900, when Thomas published a monograph titled *Education of Women*, she used extensive documentation, charts, maps, and statistics to outline the history of and dispel the various objections to the higher education of American women. She referred to it as a national movement that had passed beyond the experimental stage and "can no longer be opposed with any hope of success. Its results are to be reckoned with as facts." In terms of health, conduct, competition, and identical curriculum, all arguments "against the coeducation of the sexes in colleges have been met and answered by experience."[36] According to Horowitz, this publication sealed Thomas's "position as the nation's leading authority on the higher education of women." Thomas had become a celebrity, was called "an extraordinary woman," and, along with Jane Addams, was said to have the most influence over girls.[37]

In 1892, when the University of Pennsylvania opened its graduate school to women, Thomas was asked to address the audience to commemorate the occasion. Mitchell was in attendance.[38] This was three years before his Radcliffe address. Thus he was well-informed, had seen the surveys and statistics, discussed the issue in his novels, and knew the reasons why education was good for women. He refused to retreat. It would be difficult to overstate the importance of women like Carey Thomas, Jane Addams, and Mary Putnam Jacobi in fighting this battle in the face of such passionate irrationality. Considering what someone like Thomas, Addams, or Jacobi would have said to the first class of Radcliffe students, Agnes Irwin's decision to invite Mitchell says much about her own myopic view regarding women and education.

In February 1909, Provost Charles C. Harrison invited the president-elect, William Howard Taft, to speak at the University of Pennsylvania. Mitchell, thinking that "it would be well that he should fall into the hands of those who would make his stay pleasant and show him something of the better side of our social life," invited the Tafts to come on Sunday and stay at the Mitchell home as long as they wished. Mitchell heard nothing. Finally Taft wired "the day before his arrival, to my amusement, that he would come on the train from Cincinnati; and he appeared at my house at a little after seven in the morning. I was scarcely down stairs in time and met him in the entry." The afternoon of the same day, a friend lent Mitchell an automobile, and he drove Taft and his daughter Helen to Bryn Mawr College, where Helen was an undergraduate. Mitchell wrote, "I was able to meet my old antagonist, Miss M. Carey Thomas, with reasonable friendliness. In fact, what we differ about is, not what she wants the girls to have, but what I want them to have in addition and what she thinks perfectly useless."[39]

Mitchell was in constant demand as a speaker, and over the years he delivered numerous addresses. The audiences varied and the topics were diverse. In an address in New York City, for example, he talked about the "degeneracy of athletic contests" and the "absurd amount of time" and "excess of interest and energy" they consumed. He wondered why there was this all-absorbing interest in bodily contests and a "general indifference to the triumphs of the mental athlete." Just a few years prior the universities had been on friendly terms, but "how is it now? Yale and Harvard quarrel; Princeton and the University of Pennsylvania revile one another; the virus of accusation and hatred rises from the student to the whole teaching staff; and what has done this? The present athletic craze."[40] Mitchell never lost his effectiveness, and he continued to give provocative talks right up to the time of his death. In 1909, after he spoke at the dedication of Osler Hall in Baltimore, Harvey Cushing wrote that "it was a great success. Weir Mitchell was at the top notch of his best form."[41]

Around the time of his Radcliffe address, Mitchell was invited to travel to Chicago and give the keynote address for the semicentennial celebration of the American Medico-psychological Association (formerly known as the Association of Medical Superintendents of American Institutions, and later known as the American Psychiatric Association). Asked to survey the status of American psychiatry for the past fifty years, he firmly said no when first asked, understanding that it was "customary on birthdays to say only pleasant things." If he were to speak at all, he must do so without pretense or equivocation. The association persisted, however. Mitchell finally agreed, but he began the address by explaining his initial refusal.

Given the association's insistence that he speak to its members, it was his duty to "greatly use a great occasion" and to speak "without mercy" and "boldly with no regard to persons." He had done extensive research in preparing the address, and because his findings were grave and censorious, he had also called on a jury of his peers to "modify or give force" to his findings. Writing to thirty neurologists and consultants, he had asked three questions: Is the asylum management of the insane as good as it can be in the United States? What faults do you find with it? And what would you change? Twenty-four replies were printed in the published version of the address. Mitchell spoke in the first-person plural throughout, focusing on three major problems: isolation, administration, and lack of original research. In 1890 there were 120 public and some 40 private asylums in the United States (not including insane wards of county almshouses or sanitariums), and the patients in the 160 hospitals numbered around 90,000. While the problems began with the hospital boards, which "age rapidly, and acquire young the senile characteristics," they did not end there. Mitchell told the doctors that compared with the "splendid advance in surgery, in the medicine of the eye, and the steady approach to precision all along our ardent line, the alienist has won in proportion little." Isolation was the main reason: "You live out of range of critical shot; you are not preceded and followed in your ward work by clever rivals, or watched by able residents fresh with the learning of the schools." "Where," he asked, "are your annual reports of scientific study, of the psychology and pathology of your patients?" The absence of "competent original work" was the worst symptom of the torpor of the asylums. "What is the matter? You have immense opportunities, and seriously, we ask you experts, what have you taught us of these 91,000 insane whom you see or treat?"

Good general practitioners knew that what they must deal with is "not a disease, but a disease plus a man. This is deeply true of insanity. Nowhere is it more needful to study the human soil in which the disorder exists." Poverty, risk, and fear send many patients into asylums. Many more are sent by people quite able to have their friends treated outside, but they hold the widespread belief that "there is some mysterious therapeutic influence to be found behind your walls and locked doors." In and of themselves, asylums are not curative; rather, "asylum life is deadly to the insane." Mitchell criticized the use of mechanical restraints, locked doors, and barred windows—that "quasi-prison business"—as unnecessary and even harmful for many of the patients. "I presume that you have, through habit, lost the sense of jail and jailor which troubles me when I walk behind one of you and he unlocks door after door. Do you think it is not felt by some of your patients?" He criticized their quiet submission to hospitals being called "asylums" and physicians being called "medical superintendents": "Some of you allow your managers to think you can be farmers, stewards, caterers, treasurers, business managers, and physicians. You should urge in every report the stupid folly of this. . . . Insist to your managers that you are physicians and no more." And again, physicians of the insane need to maintain contact with the outside, "with the world of sane men, having consultations outside, seeing us and our societies."

Mitchell concluded with a sketch of his ideal hospital for the insane. There were no walls but railings hidden by trees and shrubs, grounds with flowers and woods, a farm with a vegetable garden, and no barred doors. Rather than waiting in "one of your vast, melancholy, unsympathetic parlors," we wait in a "small room as pretty as taste can make it" and are met by a "well dressed head nurse neat in cap and apron, pleasant and kindly." Wanting it to appear as similar to the outside world as possible, the ideal hospital consisted of grouped cottages with no bars or locked doors. At this point Mitchell paused and said, "I can see you smile." This hospital would have a library, reading rooms, billiard and amusement rooms, a gymnasium, tricycles and bicycles, tennis and croquet, workshops, and schoolrooms. Those patients who refused to work would watch the others work. The senior physician, a trained neurologist living in the city, had no business cares because there was a steward for purchases and care of the grounds and gardens. The resident physicians lived in the house, and there was an electrician, nurses trained in massage, and consulting visits from outside neurologists regarding difficult cases. Because patients spent most of the day in the society of the nurses, they were the most important part of such an organization. But Mitchell had often received letters expressing dismay and disgust about nurses whose refinement was "little above that of the cook or maid." He noted that this ideal hospital was being tried with some success at Elwyn Asylum, the Pennsylvania Institution for Feeble-Minded Children, but could not be achieved in state hospitals because "incredible folly has put most of them remote from cities." He ended the address by asking that they try not to be "merely hurt or disgusted by the verdicts of my fellow neurologists and myself. . . . Fifty years hence . . . another will possibly stand in my place and tell your history, and to him and the bountiful wisdom of time I leave it to be declared whether I was right or wrong."[42]

Mitchell had done his homework, and his clear and well-organized address caused an immediate uproar that resonated for the next fifty years. Some of the psychologists responded by both accepting the justifiable criticisms and pointing out Mitchell's mistakes and ignorance of the real problems and obstacles. For the most part, the association appreciated the value of such a critique, inviting prominent neurologists to give seven of the next eight annual addresses. Also, the Pathological Institute of the New York State Hospitals and the Association of Assistant Hospital Physicians were founded the next year. Fifty years later, in *One Hundred Years of American Psychiatry*, this address was referred to as "Mitchell's diatribe" and called "extraordinary" and "a blistering verbal chastisement" in terms "biting in their condemnation."[43] Richard Walter notes that the address has frequently been a subject for quizzing in the psychiatric section of the American Board of Psychiatry and Neurology exam.[44] Resented by many, the address remains a landmark in American psychiatry.

———

In the address to the American Medico-psychological Association, Mitchell criticized the alienists for failing to perform a "complete physical study of the insane," which would include recording lesions, studying secretions, blood counts, temperature, reflexes, the eyeground, color-fields, and all the rest involved in daily examinations.[45] In his 1897 book *Clinical Lessons on Nervous Diseases*, Mitchell provided some of the details regarding the patient and the diagnosis that he found missing in the alienists' casebooks. This publication was a final attempt to record his battle with nervous disorders.

Each chapter in *Clinical Lessons* is a lecture on a disorder such as melancholia, insomnia, false sensations of cold, spurious pregnancy, spinal curvature with mental aberration, and hysterical contracture. In style and tone, the three-hundred-page book is different from earlier ones like *Wear and Tear* and *Doctor and Patient*, which were written for lay audiences as well as physicians. Here Mitchell is direct and matter-of-fact. There is none of the rambling chat that mars some of his early medical writing. Patient ages vary from three to sixty-seven years old, and, as if to make a point about men and nervous disorders, over forty of the sixty-nine patients discussed are male. Treatment of the cases often includes some version of a rest cure, but here it is used in open wards rather than private houses. Certainly, the cases reveal the rich clinical material and bizarre symptomatology seen at the Infirmary of Nervous Diseases, the scientific use made of its wards and laboratory, and the various therapeutic methods employed.

A running theme throughout *Clinical Lessons* is the compounding of hysteria with one or more organic diseases. In the case of a man with erythromelalgia or "red neuralgia," a rare disorder that Mitchell first described in 1872, the patient also developed hysteria and spinal lesions. One woman, twenty-two, walked "as a jointed doll endowed with life might walk—a succession of jerky, abruptly ended movements, with sway of head and body back and front or to right and left." This case combined hysteria, anemia, and locomotor ataxia due to organic disease of the spinal cord, demonstrating the combination "of three distinct maladies" and the diagnostic confusion that grave hysteria brings to the study of organic disease.[46]

Many of the book's sixty-nine cases were treated with some form of rest, diet, massage, and electricity, but a number of other procedures were employed as well. In cases of sciatica, Mitchell used counterirritants such as dry cups, sometimes as many as three dozen forming a double or triple row around and over the notch and down the leg, along the nerve branches to the ankle. The cups were applied for thirty minutes, but not long enough to cause blistering. Flannel bandages, splint rest, and ice were also used, and if needed, Mitchell preferred hypodermic injections of cocaine as the best narcotic for sciatic pain.

Surgical procedures included nerve stretching and sectioning and tendon clipping. It was important to complete such surgery in a timely manner because the state of long-contracted limbs could alter the joints beyond repair, and the leg "bent at an angle of 45°, is brought, by section and the screw, to a much larger angle, but cannot be made straight enough for use. . . . Under these circumstances there may arise a question as to the propriety of making the leg straight by an operation that will leave it rigid." After referring to a few successful ovariotomies performed by others, Mitchell warned, "I know of many, far too many, cases where physicians have advised and women have consented to the removal of ovaries under these conditions, and where no relief has come about in consequence of the operation."[47]

Several of the cases in *Clinical Lessons* illustrate the bizarre manifestations of nervous disease. Chapter 6, "Subjective False Sensations of Cold," for example, concerns the case of a fifty-seven-year-old lawyer from Kansas who felt the cold so intensely that he wore three suits of the heaviest wool underwear, three pairs of heavy wool socks, felt boots over his ordinary boots or shoes, and a flannel bandage around his abdomen. At night he slept under five double blankets with the room temperature at eighty degrees or, after an unusually bad day in court, at ninety or ninety-five degrees. In the summer he did away with one of the suits, but even then his sensations of cold were "positively painful."[48]

The chapter titled "Rotary Movements in the Feeble-Minded" deals with the case of a sixteen-year-old female who had just arrived from the almshouse. She was noisy, restless, and nervous and liked to set things on fire. Her most "interesting symptom" was her dervish spinning. Many times each day she walked to the center of the room, rested on one heel with the toes raised, and rotated with extreme rapidity, "her dress rising like the governor of a steam engine," her arms either clasped on the chest or widely extended, and her right foot beating the floor to keep up the rotation. While spinning, her eyes remained closed and her place on the floor changed but little. The duration varied from fifteen to thirty minutes, and there was no evidence of vertigo. After a half hour's spin she was able to walk away on a perfectly straight line. No evidence suggested that she was under the influence of any imperative impulse, nor were the movements forced. Mitchell wrote that the motion, which seemed like a natural act, was so "inconceivably rapid that two of us failed to count the rate of the spin."[49]

In the chapter on hysterical contractures, twenty-five pages are devoted to the story of E. M. H. who, after a head injury at the age of ten, experienced almost five years of a freakish parade of symptoms including paralysis, contracture, and near death on several occasions. For twenty-seven months she was unable to move her hands, and she learned to write with a pen held in her mouth. At times she could move her head only from side to side, was unable to swallow, and her tongue hung to one side in such a way that her teeth rubbed off its skin. At other times she was fed entirely by the bowel and had the embarrassing symptom of violent protrusion of the rectal mucous membrane. Her joints, after thirty-two months of flexion, were deformed, and her knees had contracted and hardened. She would improve and then relapse.

There were ulcerations in her mouth and throat. At one point blood exploded from her nose and mouth, and she had such violent convulsions that men had to hold her down. She became totally deaf, partially blind, and speechless. He skin became rough and dry like sandpaper, her hair fell out in handfuls, and her emaciation was extreme. She discharged copious amounts of green and yellow pus from her ears and nose as well as other abscesses in and on her body. Attacks would cause the whole body to turn a mottled blue and the lips and eyelids to turn almost black. Her trouble began in 1890, and in 1894, as often happened with desperate and hopeless cases, she was sent to Mitchell.

Clinical Lessons includes photographs of E. M. H. writing with the pen in her mouth, samples of the writing, and two photographs of her naked body before and fifteen days after treatment under Mitchell's care. Even with the use of chloroform, it was impossible to straighten her legs forcibly. Pins could be stuck anywhere below the hips without evidence of pain. Massage and electricity were used continually, but it was not enough, and "it became obvious . . . that, however reluctantly, I must resort to surgical interference." William Keen sectioned the tendons, stretched the legs under ether, and then applied weights. Then, for the first time she was isolated from her relatives and spent the summer of 1895 in the country. In September she returned to the hospital, gained seventeen pounds, and "lost the indescribable look of watchfulness so familiar in these cases." In January 1896 Keen stretched her legs again under ether with such good results that she could stand on crutches and even walk a few steps unaided. Mitchell wrote, "As a clinical lesson in hysteria, nothing could be more instructive than this record. I have little doubt that early isolation and resolute treatment would have saved these years of distress."[50]

Clinical Lessons provides a sampling of some of the strange and freakish cases that, when in Philadelphia during the winter months, Mitchell battled daily. In this final volume regarding nervous illness, there is a little less wonder and excitement at the novelty and a little more uncertainty about the causes. In this last medical book, Mitchell wrote that "about nothing do we know less than of the true pathology and ultimate cause of the disorders which we group under the name of insanity." And again, with unusual modesty, he acknowledged that "we do not know what hysteria is."[51]

10

GREAT DOCTOR, POET, AND SALMON KILLER

Whether entertaining guests, rushing off to give an address, or conducting his
Friday clinics, Mitchell worked and played with an unrelenting intensity. His
limitless energy and restlessness clamored for activity. He appreciated rich food
and fine wine and liked to dine out. He was a member of several clubs, including
the Biological Club, a group of scientists that dined together on the second and
fourth Friday of each month; the Franklin Inn Club, a literary club that Mitchell
helped to found; the Mahogany Tree Club; the Triplets; the Round Table; and
the Charaka Club in New York, which he also helped to found and was mainly
composed of physician–bibliophiles. Mitchell admitted to having inherited his
father's tendencies to extravagance, and at home he and Mary entertained their
friends and family with luxurious dinners of champagne and terrapin.[1] On
Saturday evenings he welcomed friends into his study, where he continued to
acquire treasures such as a copy of Reynolds's *John Hunter* and Janssen's *William
Harvey*, and in marble under glass, the recumbent head of the Roman soldier
Guidarello Guidarelli. He owned numerous old manuscripts and rare books, and
during the gatherings he kept his son John busy taking them off the shelves—
Robert Burns's copy of Pope, a presentation copy of *Robinson Crusoe*, or a note
in Harvey's script. Mitchell poured the old Madeira, smoked his heavy cigars, and
read his poetry as the conversation lasted into the wee hours. Men like William
Osler, Harvey Cushing, James Russell Lowell, William W. Keen, John Shaw
Billings, John Cadwalader, and Talcott Williams attended these "Madeira parties," as Cushing called them.[2] Still, although Mitchell was very fond of Philadelphia and found New York congenial, the parties and clubs were not enough.

In 1888, along with James Russell Lowell and approximately ten other Americans, Mitchell traveled to the oldest Italian university in Bologna to participate in its eight hundredth anniversary. He would receive an honorary degree in medicine, and it was assumed that Lowell would receive one in letters. Mary did not go along, but Mitchell wrote once or twice a day, always addressing her as "Dear Polly" or "Dear Poll." Despite the huge crowds and intense heat, he enjoyed himself immensely amid what would be the most splendid pomp and pageantry of his life.

In his first letter, noting the natural beauty of the ride over Mount Cenis to Turin, Mitchell wrote that after the "stern peaks with their silver helmets of snow" the "snow clad hills always give me a 'turn.'" In the train from Turin to Peschiera, he shared a car with five Italians, "who talked explosively at intervals like 4th of July crackers." At the crowded Peschiera station he described the soldiers, cadets, and societies with their banners like an "ant nest poked up with a stick." Exhausted, he finally found a deserted Pullman and slept until arriving in Bologna at 3:00 a.m. "Ten ant nests would not describe it," he wrote. "It rained hard—busses full people here and there bags every where and the noise and bang—bang of these voices cracking like whips—I was over and over glad not to have you." Everything seemed mayhem: "No one knew anything." Lowell was described as "Professor," Mitchell as "Prof. Mitchell of Washington," and "Buenos Ayres as being in Canada. I guess the occasion is what Fanny the cook describes as 'upsettin.'" Yet, despite the commotion, Mitchell's delight is palpable in the intermingling of memories of past travels in Italy with the rich and invigorating sights of "pretty women students soldiers amusing and confusing," "endless arcaded streets," and "a dark priest or two like wandering shadows."

The next day the American contingent discovered that Lowell was not to receive a degree after all, and several of the members, including Mitchell, made a huge fuss by visiting the rector, the king's officer, and the university librarian. Mitchell wrote, "The rector had nobly fibbed to me and I learned that the Reverend evangelical clergyman, who was to have received the degree in literature, lived in Rome and was an intimate friend of the brother of the rector, upon which the whole matter became clear to me." Eventually the Americans succeeded in their goal. But Lowell was also troubled by poor health, and the others had to persuade him to stay. Mitchell served as his physician.

On the second evening before the ball, the Americans sat in a half-moon of seats in the syndic's palace window, viewing the draperies and royal arms of gold and scarlet hanging from every window. Then the "whole vast space filled with students of Italian colleges in fancy dress and caps red, blue, yellow—next came soldiers a dozen bands and last splendid creatures in uniforms all down the sides of the throne steps. Every window was full—Some 25000 people in the Plaza—thousands of red—white and blue fans going—and at last the king queen and prince whereon the bands rolled out the Hymn of Italy."

The following day various delegations from Melbourne to Harvard assembled, "represented by costumes past belief—gowns red—yellow, black hoods of all tints—orders—! one man must have had 30, splendid scarlet velvet gowns there were—all the French in yellow silks—One Hungarian in black with coral and gold button—gold lace full cravat, etc—Then we marched thro. the crowded streets to the university under flags, window draperies and no end of pretty women." Pillars were covered with lilies and roses, and the queen, "a lovely woman . . . in a changeable silk dress bonnet of straw with red roses and a vast fan," wore twelve ropes of large pearls and a tiara of diamonds "like hazel nuts for size." The prince of Naples was "a pale lad of 18—with legs too short to reach the ground—an unwholesome looking boy." The king was "very plain but has a strong face and a mustache to beat Willy Fishers—an anxious worried face."

It was the custom in Italy in the presence of royalty to wear evening dress at all times. Unaware of this, Mitchell had dressed in a black frock coat, gray striped trousers, and a pearl-colored cravat, appropriate for a morning occasion such as a wedding in the United States. Once he joined the procession to meet the royal family, he realized his mistake and could do nothing but decorate himself with a large gardenia. At dinner the same day, a waiter spilled melted meat jelly over his head, and he "bent over and let it drip on the table—such a mess— *He* said non mia culpa—and I—well it ended in nation—wh. was patriotic at least. 6 waiters made my toilette—and I returned to a laughing table of Oxford dons and—Yankees."

The next day the degrees were given, and the "greatest names in Europe were shouted in turn and applauded. Charcot, Virchow etc." Everyone was to wait until the entire list was read, but when Lowell leaned over to say, "There's your name," Mitchell rose and made his way through the crowd to the aisle. Realizing his mistake, he found a seat near the queen, who gave him "a good honest stare of examination. Then she spoke to the king who took a good look also. . . . I was in full dress of course and had nothing to look at except a splendid gardenia— was it my beauty?—As a fact for a few minutes it set every.body around us to gazing to see I presume what was the object of the handsome queens curiosity."

Finally, along with his degree, Mitchell received a ring with a huge emerald seal and greetings from both the king and queen. Because he did not speak Italian—a tongue, as he put it, he knew as well as Hebrew—many of the directions, speeches, and exchanges were lost on him. Still, despite the faux pas and confusion, for four days music and sumptuous colors and textures suffused the beautiful city, and Mitchell was delighted by the spectacle and happy to spend time with Lowell. He had traveled to Bologna when he was twenty-one, but he never imagined that he would one day stand with the most illustrious names in European science to receive such recognition.[3]

Writing from Ravenna, he told Sarah Butler Wister, "I had a good time in Bologna—but I wrote daily to Mary because the succession of pageants balls—Royal presentations etc—were bewildering—and I knew that once over they would leave on my mind only a dream of colours."[4] Joyful and relaxed, the man who emerges in the Bologna letters represents another side of Mitchell. The energy and classic beauty of Europe—the stylish men, pretty women, cathedrals, fountains and monuments, old stone and paved brick—charmed and stirred his sensual side. He was more like a man in love, not the cold, bitter man that Whitman knew, not the arrogant speaker at Radcliffe, not the man who burned letters because they contained too many free statements. His deep pleasure in the honorary degree combined with the lavish scene and recollections of his youth cast a dreamlike quality over the whole experience.

━━━━

When Mitchell returned from Bologna, he was in Philadelphia for only a few days before leaving for his annual fishing trip. He never missed these June fishing excursions, usually at the Ristigouche Salmon Club on the Matapédia River in Quebec. Eventually, he and other friends—including Lord Grey, governor general of Canada, 1904–11—leased land on the Cascapédia River, just fifty miles east of the Matapédia. The trips lasted for five to six weeks and included at least one guide, plenty of supplies and books, and the best fishing tackle and equipment available. In this way Mitchell escaped the personal and professional duties that often made him irritable and restless. He wrote that city life became "perplexing and trying by its intricacy: so many wheels must be kept moving in order to the fulfillment of social, domestic, civil and professional duties that in the hurry of well-filled lives we are rarely at rest."[5] His advice to patients to travel to the shores, mountains, and lakes to live a primitive existence for two to three weeks grew from personal experience with hiking, fishing, and camping.

Mitchell wrote about the benefits of camping in 1877 in *Nurse and Patient, and Camp Cure*, and in 1888 in the last chapter of *Doctor and Patient*, titled "Out-Door and Camp-Life for Women." Remarking that one "wants something more than a few days at dry Atlantic City or murky Cape May," he felt that the surest remedy for exhaustion and over-tasked nerves was returning to "barbarism" to live and sleep outdoors—that "hospital of the stone-carver"—in order to reverse the conditions of life. Living in a log house or a tent and escaping overheated homes often eliminated chronic throat trouble and bronchitis, aided those recovering from inflammatory rheumatism, and relieved dyspepsia. With hunting, fishing, studying geology and botany, reading, drawing, and what he called "word sketching" to occupy the morning and afternoon hours, camp life was never dull. Insomnia, jealousy, and petty concerns all faded away when one lived in the open air, rose "unstirred by imperious gongs," took a daily plunge in the lake, chopped wood, labored with the rod or gun, and with keen senses and an eager appetite enjoyed the mindless pleasures of outdoor life. Full of "harmless and health-giving enjoyments and of novel surprises," it was a "true and potent alternative" to the stress of city life. Mitchell made camp food sound delicious, the fried or broiled salmon, the trout in paper "a thing to remember," fried potatoes, a stew of wild ducks and peas, biscuits, baked beans, and onions for salad. He noted a craving for raw onions with salt among the campers. Onions were at a premium, and, in fact, "there is always a row in camp when the onions give out." Tea and coffee were easy to carry, and coffee was best when boiled with milk. But first thing in the morning the best drink was chocolate heated with condensed milk.[6]

Fearless and undisturbed, Mitchell felt most at home when hiking in the woods, finding it strangely charming to be "hand and hand with Nature all day long—in watching her gradual changes, the birth of morning, the sunrise newly dressed each day, the fading twilight, the growth of storms, the loveliness of form and color in wood or wave—all delightful."[7] To some degree he felt that everyone after a few days of camp life would gain this awareness and feel this wonder and "peace of soul." Initially, Mitchell did not fully realize the benefits of camp life for women, and he noted this error in *Doctor and Patient*, writing, "I have been led to regret that I did not see . . . that what I therein urged as desirable for men was not also in a measure attainable by many women."[8] The long list of benefits of camping and outdoor life included moral and intellectual improvement and physical exercise, which was good for the boys and the girls who may "swim, fish, and row like their brothers." Nothing so dismissed "the host of little nervousnesses with which house-caged women suffer as this free life."[9]

Mitchell's own experiences had been with men in camp. He frequently referred to the strength of character and good talk of the guides and trappers, enjoying their tales around the fire. One in particular, "a gnarled, rugged old fellow" who had been a lumberman, a beaver hunter, and a sergeant in Berdan's Sharpshooters, was now a guide and hunter and was "a keen eye with the rifle, gallant and cool in storms on the lake, a capital cook, and endlessly merry and full of good talk over the camp-fire at night."[10] Mitchell also noted how close this camp life brought him to his city friends, especially in the evenings when the punch was brewed and the pipes glowed.

Although Mitchell did not hunt, he was a highly skilled fisherman and always referred to catching salmon as "killing" them. At various times when he caught a fair number, he had them packed in ice and sent to friends. To Mrs. Charles Dow he wrote, "I trust that you will enjoy my salmon—I took it—'killed it' . . . this a.m. in a wild last wind. . . . 'To this all other things are mean—all other thoughts are base.'" To Charles L. Moore he wrote, "I have killed about 25 salmon and—am slowly getting accustomed to decent society—woods and waters."[11] Although Mitchell traveled with a large stock of supplies, he stated that this "mode of gypsying" could be done with much smaller means. He recommended several camping spots, including Lake Superior, the Adirondack woods, the woods of Maine, especially around Moosehead Lake, the White Mountains, the Alleghenies, and the Jersey shore. The annoyances and worries that seem so large in the city are cast away "in the gentle company of constant sky and lake and stream . . . as easily as we throw aside some piece of worn-out and useless raiment." In the cool quiet of the woods or the lounging comfort of a canoe, "one gets near realities. . . . Thought is more sober; one becomes a better friend to one's self." Even reading becomes a different experience in the wilderness. Sitting on a stump or lying in a birch canoe, many poets "shrink to well-bred, comfortable parlor bards." While a few like Wordsworth, Clough, and the outdoor plays of Shakespeare passed the test, "the artificial flavoring of some books is unpleasantly felt" in the woods. Word sketching or word painting—the way that John Ruskin or Emily Brontë captured a scene and its moods in words—was even more beneficial than reading. One began with small scenes and a good opera glass to intensify awareness of subtle tones of color, texture, and the play of light on water and leaves. Visiting the same spot in the morning, evening, and during a rainstorm heightened awareness of phenomena like density, shadow, and sound. Encouraging a love of accuracy, word sketching increased the power to see and articulate what is seen. Mitchell wrote that "this gentle passion for nature in all her moods is like a true love affair, and grows by what it feeds upon."[12]

The peace that Mitchell experienced was more than an escape from city life and more than an aesthetic appreciation of nature's beauty. It was not so much simplicity or solitude that he was seeking. His scientific background deepened his understanding of complex natural processes, and over the years as he finely tuned his attention to detail, he felt a kinship with things of the earth and a sense of association and belonging. In poems and novels he wrote of this intimate relationship with nature, the "delicious odor of the spruce" and the "drowsiness of noon" with its "faint, quick, silken murmurings." In poems like "Noonday Woods–Nipigon" he captured the intricacy of a moment:

> Between thin fingers of the pine
> The fluid gold of sunlight slips,
> And through the tamarack's gray-green fringe
> Upon the level birch leaves drips.
>
> Through all the still, moist forest air
> Slow trickles down the soft, warm sheen,
> And flecks the branching wood of ferns
> With tender tints of pallid green.[13]

Inspired by Wordsworth, one of his favorite poets, Mitchell found "quick-healing" and "infinite comfort" in nature.[14] Like Wordsworth, who addresses his sister in "Tintern Abbey," Mitchell addresses a "friend and lady" in "Elk Country," his poem about a trip to the Alleghany Mountains:

> To think how we wandered, bewildered
> With wood-dreams and delicate fancies
> Unknown to the life of the city.
> To tread but those cushioning mosses;
> To lie, almost float, on the fern-beds;
> To feel the crisp crush of the foot on
> The mouldering logs of the windfall,
> Were things to be held in remembrance.

Dost recall how we lingered to listen
The sound of the wood-robin's bugle,
Or bent the witch-hopple to guide us,
As one folds the page he is reading,
And felt, as we peered through the stillness,
Through armies and legions of tree-trunks,
Such solemn and brooding sensations
As told of the birth of religions,
As whispered how men grow to Druids
When the fly-wheel of work is arrested,
And they live the still life of the forest?[15]

In terms of a profound contrast between country and city life and the value of memories, Mitchell repeats Wordsworthian themes. But there are interesting differences. In "Elk Country" the speaker and his lady friend are "bewildered," and rather than the tranquility and "sensations sweet" of Tintern Abbey, they experienced sensations that are "solemn and brooding."

Such passages describing natural scenery are common enough throughout Mitchell's writing, but in his novel *When All the Woods Are Green*, nature plays the lead role. A close look at a few scenes provides more detail about Mitchell's annual fishing trips. In the novel the Lyndsay family is vacationing on the Matapédia River. The salmon are as "thick as pine-needles," and Mr. Lyndsay takes his daughter, Rose, who is twenty, in the canoe to teach her to fish and word sketch. During these excursions, they spend their time talking, while the guides paddle and gaff the salmon. For Lyndsay, the sport of fishing has all the charm of gambling without its liability. He brags of having killed ninety-two salmon and six grilse in five days and forty-two striped bass in twenty-four hours. To some, a sense of kinship with nature may seem incompatible with the sport of fishing. When Rose has her first fishing lesson, she wonders if Anglo-Saxon ideas of sport are a little hard on birds and fish. And a few minutes later, she says, "I wish I did not think the fish had a dreadful time. I have to think of pleasure holding the rod and tragedy at the end of the line." But Lyndsay explains why this attitude is misguided. First, the reason why salmon take the fly at all is a mystery, since salmon eat nothing while in the rivers. Second, compared to salmon, trout are "pigs for greediness." On one occasion Lyndsay caught a trout still bleeding from the hawk's claws, with its intestines and liver hanging in the water. On another occasion he caught a striped bass that had previously been terribly torn by a gaff. Because such injury and pain would utterly destroy human appetite and cause inaction, Lyndsay thinks that the "inference is plain enough: fish cannot be said to suffer what we call pain. . . . As we go down the scale of life, there is less and less of what we call pain, and at last, probably, only something nearer to discomfort or inconvenience." Rose—with her reel singing, some two hundred feet of line running out with incredible swiftness, and far across the stream a "great white thing" leaping high out of the water—is quickly converted as if charmed by magic. "How exciting it is!," she shouts. "I don't sympathize with the salmon at all; I am intent on murdering him."[16] On her first day she catches a twenty- and a thirty-two-pound salmon and a six-pound grilse. Later she catches a thirty-eight-pound salmon.

Even so, on a second trip Rose turns away, upset by the gaffing. Lyndsay explains that lingering hours of slow exhaustion are far worse, and "you could let the fish go; you could refrain from fishing; you need not eat salmon; several ways are open to the sensitive." He gently cautions that "we may over-cultivate our sensibilities so as, at last, to become Brahminical in our abhorrence of any destruction of life." Still, there is no strong argument in favor of the need for animal flesh. Nations live without it, and "it is quite possible that we have in time more or less manufactured both the appetite and the need for this diet. Our nearest anatomical kinsmen, the monkeys, are all vegetarians." Further, no one who actually lives on the river can legally fish; otherwise, in five years there would be no salmon ("they would go as the buffalo have gone"). The woodsmen and their families get salmon only through poaching or as gifts. Salmon fishing is a hobby and luxury of the rich. However, fishermen like Lyndsay spend significant sums of money while residing in these communities. The money Lyndsay and the other wealthy fishermen spend is much more beneficial to the local economy than any amount of salmon the native boatmen and farmers could catch. Lyndsay encourages his daughter to "fish, my dear, in peace of soul."[17]

Father and daughter also travel up the river to word sketch, and just as Mitchell had in *Nurse and Patient, and Camp Cure* and *Doctor and Patient*, Lyndsay discusses its value. Word sketching creates an appreciation of accuracy, larger insights, a careful attention to words, and a more intelligent love of art in all its forms. As they speed along close to the shore, they leave behind the white camp tents and the last of the clearings. They arrive at a desolate scene of burnt land with low underbrush and millions of dead trees. Lyndsay has been here several times and finds something strange and even beautiful about it. On a small island of grass with a natural spring, the guides put up the tent and light the smudge pot. Sitting in the tent opening, Rose looks through the field glass while her father directs her view to the dead trees on the point, focusing on their individuality and all the images and feelings that their form, color, and mood evoke. The guides are busy making the fire and cooking and serving a lunch of bacon and broiled salmon, roasted potatoes, and jam and biscuits on plates of bark. Rose and her father fetch water from the spring by twisting red birch bark into cups. With the sun behind them and Lyndsay smoking his pipe, they discuss tints and colors of silvery-gray and purple and examine the myriad dead pine, fir, and poplar, polished by storm and sun into a steely hardness. Returning to camp, the boat flies "down the swift waters, with here and there, where the billows rolled high over a deeply hidden rock, a wild roller which swept them on as with the rush of a bird through space, while Rose laughed out the joy of a great delight, for of all modes of motion this is the most satisfying."[18]

On another word-sketching trip, father and daughter concentrate solely on the water and how the "boughs leap every now and then as they drop their loads of rain." Lyndsay asks Rose to note the great drops and how "each rebounds from the surface in a little column, so as to seem like black spikes in the water. See, too, how the circles they make cross one another without breaking." Water, with its various moods and different sounds—rain falling on pine and spruce, or its patter on the flat-lying deciduous leaves—seems the one natural thing that possesses the sound of human laughter. After two or three weeks of intimacy with such sounds and scenery, there comes "a sense of being at home." In the city and other places of work and pleasure, even "the simplest lives involve some use of the art of the actor," but in the woods "we lose the resultant state of tension, of being on guard." Indifference replaces concern and worry "so that we look back and wonder how this or that should have caused us a thought, or called forth . . . irritability." We lose track of the days, the busy past fades "into dreamy unreality," and this ease of mind is due to the physical well-being that camp life provides.[19]

Mitchell's concern with the body, physical exercise, and minute observation was different from the spirituality that Wordsworth felt in nature, where "we are laid asleep / In body, and become a living soul: / While with an eye made quiet by the power / Of harmony, and the deep power of joy, / We see into the life of things." For Wordsworth, this spiritual sight, this "sense sublime," replaced the "glad animal movements" of youth, the "splendour in the grass" and "glory in the flower."[20] But Mitchell held fast to strenuous physical activity and animal movements regardless of age. He fished, walked, rode horses, and hiked, and his focus on the health and vigor of the body was the foundation of both his own well-being and long life and his medical treatment of nervous illness. Depending on the strength of his patients, he advised a rest cure or a camp cure, but in both cases he believed that restoring the body would help to cure the mind. Whether fishing on the Cascapédia or hiking on Mount Desert Island, he was practicing his own medical theory about good health. Through publications and novels he attempted to persuade others about the physical and mental benefits of a brisk and strenuous return to nature. After his June fishing trips, Mitchell went to Newport until October or November; then, in 1891, Bar Harbor became his permanent summer residence.

———

Bar Harbor is a town on Mount Desert Island in Maine. The island, 150 road miles north of Portland and more than 100 square miles in size, is incredibly beautiful, with a rugged coastline, strong tides that average ten to twelve feet, and ice-eroded mountains that form a belt across the island's center. A fjord six miles deep partially divides the mountains, and freshwater lakes and ponds are scattered throughout. In the 1860s Bar Harbor was a small village situated on the eastern side of the island, facing Frenchman Bay with Cadillac Mountain, the highest point on the eastern seaboard, at its back. Traveling there was difficult and had to be done on trading schooners or coastal steamers. After the Civil War, steamer connections increased when East Coast elites began to relocate to Bar Harbor, hoping to escape Newport's ostentation and tourism. In Edith Wharton's novel *The Age of Innocence*, set in the 1870s, Archer tries to persuade May to spend the summer on this remote island, "where a few hardy Bostonians and Philadelphians were camping in 'native' cottages, and whence came reports of enchanting scenery and a wild, almost trapper-like existence amid woods and waters."[21] By 1885 there was a railroad terminus at Mount Desert Ferry, and within a few years there was a Bar Harbor express that provided overnight train service from Boston and New York, later extended to Philadelphia, Baltimore, and Washington.

According to a social register for 1909–10, there were 221 families with private so-called cottages at Bar Harbor. Half of these summer residents were from New York, and the rest were mainly from Boston, Philadelphia, and Washington, an elite group that included physicians, bankers, lawyers, and retired military officers. Joseph Pulitzer built the first $100,000 cottage; George Vanderbilt also built a cottage; John D. Rockefeller, Jr., and Edsel Ford had homes nearby at Seal Harbor; and J. P. Morgan spent many summers at Bar Harbor aboard his yacht. Summer residents bought the waterfront and high-ground real estate over-looking the bay and mountains. Several hotels were destroyed to make room for the cottages, and these large private estates began to dominate the landscape.[22]

As was his way, Mitchell became an active member on committees and orga-nizations in the area and was the "recognized leader of the walking and talking set which was the backbone of Bar Harbor society."[23] There was a Bar Harbor Village Improvement Association that included Beatrix Farrand, John Stewart Kennedy, George W. Vanderbilt, and Mitchell as members. Much like a neigh-borhood association, the members had certain ideas about landscaping and san-itation and lobbied the town government for improvements. They planted trees and built fountains, encouraged all residents to maintain their homes and yards, and even distributed badges and rules to the schoolchildren to keep the streets free of litter. They had shacks adjacent to their estates on prestigious West Street condemned on sanitary grounds, and the Passamaquoddy Indians who lived there were forced to move to the town's outskirts. Utility lines were placed underground, and automobiles were banned until 1913. Led by Charles W. Eliot, Harvard president and summer resident, a group formed a charitable trust in 1901 and purchased approximately six thousand acres. In 1914 the land was given to the federal government and soon became Acadia National Park, the first such park east of the Rocky Mountains. Rather than a village of fishing and farming, Bar Harbor became an exclusive Anglo-Saxon resort. Many members of the permanent population refitted themselves as day laborers and domestic servants to serve the endless needs of the summer residents. Stephen Hornsby writes that "relationships between townspeople and cottagers were sometimes difficult. The cottagers were paternalist and expected deference in return. . . . Most of the townspeople were used to a fairly independent life. Deference did not come naturally, and tension was never far from the surface. . . . After a spate of burglaries in 1892, the cottagers lobbied for efficient police protection and prevailed on the town to build a jail."[24]

Hornsby also notes that by 1914, the year Mitchell died, "the glittering years of Bar Harbor were numbered." Mitchell lived there in its heyday as an elite and stylish resort, and he helped to transform the society and its surroundings into the "best" of its kind. The Harpswell Laboratory on Mount Desert Island estab-lished a biological outpost known as the Weir Mitchell Station, in honor of his exploration of the area. Bar Harbor's Jesup Memorial Library still prominently displays a bronze life-size statue of Mitchell done by William Ordway Partridge. Yet in the context of his camp cure and the novel *When All the Woods Are Green*, the part Mitchell played in radically reshaping Bar Harbor is interesting for a couple of reasons. To change people's careers and daily occupations and to modify their homes, surroundings, and transportation constituted more than infusing money into a local economy. It was not enough for Mitchell and the others to travel there and live discreetly. Like paternalistic colonizers, they gained control over and reconfigured the human landscape, and did so with the certainty that they were in the right. It was much more than what Lyndsay explained to his daughter Rose in the north woods, where the lives of woodsmen and their families remained virtually untouched by the wealthy summer visitors. If the relationships between the summer residents and the natives in *When All the Woods Are Green* represented the ideal, it was not one that Mitchell worked to realize at Bar Harbor.

Some aspects of Mitchell's life were not as easy to control as the setting at Bar Harbor. In the 1890s he lost several of his closest friends. In 1891, just a few years after the Bologna trip, James Russell Lowell died. Then, in 1893 at the age of fifty-eight, Phillips Brooks died, less than two years after he was made bishop of Massachusetts. The next year Oliver Wendell Holmes died. While Mitchell admired Lowell as a poet and man of letters and valued his friendship, it did not run as deep or as far back as his special attachment to Brooks and Holmes.

There had been a moment in 1886 when Mitchell thought Phillips Brooks might return to Philadelphia. After he was elected assistant bishop of Pennsylvania, Mitchell pleaded with him, "It seems as if every thing had been tending towards this welcome end and let me tell you dear friend that you are needed here. . . . Of myself I say nothing—I would be ashamed to speak of what is personal now, but when you left us much went out of my life and the chance of again having you near fills me with gladness. Think well before you say no—but then I am sure you will think—."[25] But Brooks declined the Pennsylvania episcopate, deciding to remain in Boston, his birthplace and boyhood home. After Mitchell met President Taft, he compared Brooks and Taft, writing that they were both physically "large" and "great" men with the same capacity for laughter and an appreciation of the droll side of things. About the comparison, "a likeness with much unlikeness," Mitchell said, "I should find it difficult to define my reasons for this, but there was something in the way of their relation to children, to servants, to the world at large, of good humored democracy, in both men."[26]

Brooks, in one of his last letters written the month before his death, told Mitchell that he had been "keeping company" with him during "two or three happy days" while reading the novel *Characteristics*: "It is a beautiful book,—so true, and wise, and human. All the world which reads it must enjoy it, but to me who feel and hear you in it everywhere, it is very precious. You must be very glad to have written it, and I rejoice with you. . . . So long since I had sight of you! The last time I was in Philadelphia you were not there. And, as you said, so many of the old friends have gone! Let us at least send one another greeting when we may, for indeed the old affection does not die nor change."[27] Brooks had published some of his sermons and a few books, including *Lectures on Preaching* in 1877 and *The Influence of Jesus* in 1879. He wrote the Christmas hymn "O Little Town of Bethlehem." Like many of his contemporaries, he published articles in the *Century* and the *New England Magazine*. Still, it was for his power as a preacher that he was best known. On the day of his funeral, the Boston Stock Exchange and many businesses closed from eleven until two. Almost twenty thousand people filed by his body, and five hundred carriages made their way across the Charles River to Mount Auburn Cemetery.[28] Mitchell was unable to attend the funeral. Soon after, he wrote Brooks's brother William about his disappointment at not being there "to look once more on that dear face. . . . You know how sure how close was the relation between Phillips and myself. His friendships were but few—and—I suspect that out of his own family he owned no stronger bonds than those wh. united him to my sister and to me. . . . Since I heard, and most abruptly, of his death I have been fit for little."[29]

Arthur Brooks began a biography of his brother, but when Arthur died in 1895, the family asked Alexander V. G. Allen, the church historian at Harvard's Episcopal Theological School, to complete it. Mitchell, his sister Elizabeth, and Brooks had written countless letters to one another; however, according to Mitchell, the correspondence was altered or destroyed. When Elizabeth died, Brooks destroyed her letters to him. When *Reminiscences* and *Letters and Memorials of Jane Welsh Carlyle* were published in the early 1880s, revealing Carlyle's impotence and domestic cruelty, there was a scandalous uproar. At this time Brooks destroyed Mitchell's letters to him, but put aside approximately two hundred letters that he had written to Mitchell and Elizabeth. When Brooks died, his brother Arthur sent the letters to Mitchell, asking for permission to use them and requesting that they be returned.

Mitchell understood the value of these letters, writing to William Brooks that Phillips "was more demonstrative in letters than in talk—and in a letter about my last book he talks out with the affectionate freedom of youth."[30] He told Mason that Brooks was "the only witty man I ever knew who kept it muzzled and let it out—and almost only—in his letters."[31] Even though, or perhaps because, he realized that there was a side of Brooks that appeared only in these letters, Mitchell refused to return them, explaining that "they were so full of things which would have given annoyance, of free statements, that on his brother's insisting on their return, I burned them. . . . I hated to, nevertheless."[32] Although Allen's two-volume biography was published in 1900 and contains numerous excerpts from letters written by Brooks to Mitchell and Elizabeth, they merely suggest the extensive correspondence that was presumably destroyed. Yet some uncertainty remains about how much was destroyed. In writing Sarah Butler Wister in 1899, Mitchell said, "I have been fussing over so much of Brooks letters as I allowed myself to give his biographer. . . . I cut out mercilessly all that is in the least degree personal." A few weeks later he told her, "I have been over-looking Rev Mr. Allen's—proofs of Phillips Brooks' life. To have been absolutely implacable as to any use of his letters to Elizabeth and to me would have been unwise—I wrote a few pages and cut out of the very—impersonal parts I had given or allowed, every thing—which I felt he might not have chosen to say. The letters were burned—as you know—my own from him I have kept."[33]

The decision to radically alter or destroy Brooks's letters was a part of Mitchell's attempt to revise the past, which he felt must fit cleanly on the straight and narrow path of gentility. In *Philadelphia Gentlemen*, E. Digby Baltzell writes, "Above all, S. Weir Mitchell was a very Proper Philadelphian: he lived on Walnut Street, belonged to the most exclusive clubs, went to Mount Desert every summer and after his first wife's death, married a Cadwalader." This was no small feat. Baltzell creates a list of approximately one hundred leading members of around sixty prominent Philadelphia families, which includes Mitchell and his father. John Kearsley Mitchell is simply identified as a "Physician" whereas Weir Mitchell is identified as a "Physician, Novelist, Psychiatrist." And it is Weir Mitchell whom Baltzell refers to as the "first family founder." This sudden ascendancy through a career in medicine is unusual: most families are founded on the wealth of trade and business, and members of the third and fourth generations win distinction in medicine.[34]

For thirty years Mitchell and Oliver Wendell Holmes had maintained a steady correspondence, affirming their mutual belief in the value of medical research, the controlling influence of inherited characteristics, and their identity as literary physicians. When Holmes died the year after Brooks, Mitchell lost his oldest friend and biggest fan. Holmes always supported Mitchell's various projects, sent him extravagant praise, and recognized the significance of his scientific contributions. There was no end to his praise for *Researches upon the Venom of the Rattlesnake*. About the publication of *Lectures on Diseases of the Nervous System, Especially in Women*, he wrote, "I keep my medical library on my shelves and your book shall find a place of honor on them if Hippocrates has to squeese Sydenham to make room for it."[35] Mitchell sent Holmes many gifts, including an ivory scimitar, inscribed with a riddle, to be used as a tool for cutting new volumes. When Mitchell and Reichert were splitting snake venom into various poisons, their largest snake was over eight feet long and weighed nineteen pounds. Mitchell sent the skin to Holmes, and he responded, "It is magnificent. . . . But what a parlous worm it was, to be sure! . . . He must have shed venom as a milch cow does her amiable secretion. . . . Well, well,—asps and vipers and copperheads, and cobras and rattlesnakes of reasonable dimensions I know, but a crotalus with the length and circumference of a boa-constrictor is a new acquaintance whose *bark*, if I may so call his integument, is much more welcome than his bite would be." He wished only that his wife were tall enough to wear the skin on the back of her cloak with the head forming a hood—"what a sensation it would make, to be sure, as she walked along Beacon Street!"[36]

Mitchell felt that he and Holmes were America's two successful literary physicians. When Holmes was asked what gave him more satisfaction, to have roused the medical profession to the perils of puerperal fever as an infectious disease (a reference to his 1843 article "The Contagiousness of Puerperal Fever") or to have written the poem "The Chambered Nautilus," he responded, "I had a savage pleasure, I confess, in handling these two Professors [Hodge and Meigs]— learned men both of them, skilful experts, but babies as it seemed to me in their capacity of reasoning and arguing. But in writing the poem I was filled with a better feeling, the highest state of mental exaltation and the most crystalline clairvoyance, as it seemed to me, that had ever been granted to me."[37]

George M. Gould, editor of the *Medical News*, was writing an article about an 1899 revised edition of Mitchell's *Autobiography of a Quack*. Gould wrote to

Mitchell with a few questions. But Mitchell, rather than answering the questions, was more intent on explaining his identity as a literary physician: "I would call attention to the literary emancipation of the M.D. with wh. Holmes and I still more have had to do. It hurts no one now to write verse (even that deadly sin) for the magazines. Twenty years ago—it would have been doubtful—A full list of all literary M.D.'s wd. be interesting—The mere literary M.D. is one who still adheres to and honours his profession and even relates the two things." In another letter to Gould, Mitchell wrote that Dr. Kraus of Carlsbad had remarked that the United States was the only country that could boast of a literary physician who remained loyal to medicine: "I rather think that in Europe a physician who wrote a very successful novel would find himself without practice; this has not had a similar influence here."[38] Both Holmes and Mitchell recorded their experience of writing poetry as intensely pleasurable. When Mitchell wrote that in "highest verse the sense of complete capture is felt as a friend says like a physical orgasm," that friend was probably Holmes.[39]

In the spring of 1892, just two years before Holmes died, Mitchell presented the Sarah W. Whitman portrait of Holmes to the College of Physicians of Philadelphia. He also wrote a poem for the occasion, in which two gods wander on the Boston Common and find Holmes as a schoolboy fast asleep on the ground. Arguing over the boy, Minerva wants him to "read the riddles of disease and Pain." Apollo cries, "Nay, mine the boy. . . . To wing the arrows of delightful mirth, / To slay with jests the sadder things of earth." Minerva responds, "Not mine to spoil thy joy; / Divide the honors,—let us share the boy!" As the portrait of Holmes took its place among those of other illustrious doctors at the college, their voices "in many a tongue" welcomed him, "though Apollo won thy larger hours, / And stole our fruit, and only left us flowers / The poet's rank thy title here completes— / Doctor and Poet,—so were Goldsmith,—Keats."[40] The reception of Holmes's portrait at the college symbolized the medical community's official acceptance of Holmes and Mitchell as literary physicians. At least Mitchell saw it that way.

In 1892 Mitchell sent Holmes a salmon from the Ristigouche, writing, "Dear Aristocrat—I commend to your despotic uses the salmon I send. He gave me a half hour of keen enjoyment on these wild waters." By way of thanks, Holmes sent back his praise: "I am jealous of all your manifold accomplishments—great experiments, great Doctor, story-teller—Poet—and great Salmon-Killer—it is too much for one Mortal, but my share in your last achievement reconciles me to your superiority and I thank you most heartily for your most welcome gift."[41]

This salmon may have been Mitchell's last gift to Holmes. When Thomas Bailey Aldrich wrote to propose that he and Mitchell spend an evening together, Mitchell replied that as friends "drop under the fatal fire of time—one must find new recruits and fill the thinning ranks. Indeed I have great need to do so in Boston: when I am there I walk with ghosts—Brooks—Holmes and Lowell. So I say yes!—heartily, I should like a good evening's talk with you over verse."[42]

I I

WINTER'S SORROW

Until his last days Mitchell invariably spoke of the many demands on his time and how busy Philadelphia kept him. As he grew older, he spent more and more time away. There were several other fine doctors at the infirmary, and when he was gone John took responsibility for the family's extensive private practice and any personal matters that required attention. John was also active in the profession. In 1895, for example, after conducting follow-up studies of the patients treated at Turner's Lane Hospital during the Civil War, he published the results in *Remote Consequences of Injuries of the Nerves and Their Treatment*. But overall, his job was to insure that things went smoothly for his father. Many years after Mitchell's death, John's wife, Anne, wrote Clements C. Fry, "You are quite right *re* the closeness of the tie between my husband and his father. I never saw a closer father and son relationship . . . although Dr. Mitchell accepted too much self-abnegation on his son's part, which really prevented a big career for my husband. Of this I can tell you, but not write."[1] If John were sidelined by illness or otherwise called away, it made life difficult for his father.

In 1891, when Mitchell traveled to Italy and Switzerland with his wife and daughter, he wrote that he had left home half dead. Anne, "who is as dear to me as a daughter," had typhoid "virulently," and John could do no work, "and so I staggered about with the modern old man of the mountain on my back all winter. Now, thank God, she is well, and I am laughing and better."[2] There were several such trips to Great Britain and the Continent during the 1890s, and though Mitchell spent eight weeks in Scotland and England in 1894 without his wife and daughter, they accompanied him on most of these trips. From Rome he wrote, "We go hence after a month of delight, flavoured by the unending hospitality of the most intelligent people in Rome. . . . Society here agreeably surprises me by its relative simplicity. There is little ostentatious show and even royalty is modest in display."[3] Shopping was a regular part of these trips abroad, especially for Mary and Maria, and Mitchell wrote John, "Mama has plunged recklessly into the shops and—emerged financially drowned. I limited myself to a pair of 150 f. delft vases wh. I send to yr—care—cheap and good."[4]

Several of these trips abroad included stops in London to visit Langdon, who was engaged to the actor Marion Lea. A native of Philadelphia, Lea had won fame in London by starring in the first English production of Ibsen's *Hedda Gabler*. Her sister Anna Lea Merritt, a painter, also lived in England and was associated with the Pre-Raphaelites. Of course, Marion's acting career troubled Mitchell and his wife. On one trip Mitchell wrote Wister that they had spent a day rowing and climbing in perfect weather, hoping "to get on easy terms with Marion. I still hold to my conditions; but apart from these, we effected our object and—made I fancy a complete capture. . . . I am free to say, and glad to say that M. has risen very much in my esteem and Mary's, and that I am much more nearly satisfied than I was. I begin to suspect that, quite apart fr. the stage business, M—may be after all the best kind of wife for L." Langdon was publishing a book of poetry that his father felt would strike a "fresh note." When Langdon read some of his plays to Mary, Maria, Marion, and his father, they "were screaming with their weird humour or troubled to tears,—and this latter by a little one act drama of the last day of Gettysburg—the scene being in a quaker farm house. A little spanish one act play kept us all immensely amused." Mitchell was strongly impressed by Langdon's intellectual growth, writing that he "is the most *interesting* man I ever knew, but apart from this he gives me now, as he never did before, a Sense of force in reserve." Langdon and Marion were to be married in England that winter, and Mitchell concluded, "I trust sometime the question as to M's continuance on the Stage will settle itself or be settled. I have put all of that question aside, for the time, and have been chiefly eager to learn to love the woman who is to be my son's wife."[5]

The following year the Mitchells were again in London visiting Langdon, Marion, and their new grandson. Looking "radiantly handsome," Marion dined with them, and Mitchell wrote Wister that they could not discuss Marion's plans since they had two other guests. His views about her life were "as decided as ever and more so since to leave her boy to a nurse and L. seems to me a needless setting aside of obvious duty, but I mean to have no shade of annoyance come between me and my son and his wife, and shall never speak out again my ever deepening beliefs."[6]

This trip to London was especially satisfying. Langdon's first play, *Deborah*, had its debut in London in 1892, and his second play, *In the Season*, the following year. Mitchell met Thomas Hardy, "a little half bald man with a quaint nose flat on the tip and queerly indented, a simple, kindly person." He was courted by his medical brothers and dined at many of the clubs, and he had the honor of giving an address and delivering the prizes at the Netley Army Medical School. At the Cosmopolitan, an old club that met on Wednesday and Sunday from 10 p.m. to 1 a.m. in Watts's old studio, the walls were covered with nude men and women, and "each man in turn told me *the* club joke that these were Watt's hims and Hers." Here Mitchell met "a lot of Lords young and old—artists, authors etc—Sir Wm Priestley took me and—I liked well its ease and social freedom." For an hour he poured over the betting book at Brook's, where Lord Sefton bet Fox that the colonies would not be independent in two years, and "they bet when Lady Betty—blanks baby will be born and—worse—things." After an afternoon at the lovely Squirreley Estate with its old garden, lawns, gray urns, and the stout old squire and his peacock, Mitchell "came away a made Tory—and am told I have a tory face—like enough."[7]

When *Hugh Wynne, Free Quaker* came out, the Mitchells had just arrived in Paris. *Hugh Wynne* was Mitchell's most popular novel. He was paid $5,000 for its serialization, which began in the *Century* in November 1896. The first printing of the book was in two volumes the following year. Despite Mitchell's claim that his literary life was "the holiday of a busy brain," it had assumed paramount importance. In a preface to the nineteenth edition of *Hugh Wynne*, he wrote that he had devoted the leisure time of six winters to doing research and collecting notes for this novel. He told Wister that he could think of nothing else while writing it. He felt possessed: "I can not do anything else and to try to write letters or to follow a church service I can not. I find if I dine out the talk seems some way to get on to the topics which are haunting my mind and about which I am apt to dream as I did last night." He referred to *Hugh Wynne* as his "infant," writing that "just now I am in the maternal excitement of completed product and this *I* have observed to be a temporary idiocy. Now that it is done I am alarmed at the courage of it. It is a great canvass—on it is the old city I love,—and there is the society of -70 to -75."[8] When Admiral Meade wrote to say that surely it was based on a true story, Mitchell told Mason, "Meade writes me that his ancestor, Wm. Coates, a stiff Quaker, married a French

Quaker of the Midi, who was over gay and never shed her Gallic ways. Their son was a Free Quaker, entered the army and was on Washington's Staff—an extraordinary coincidence, as I imagined my whole story."[9]

Hugh Wynne remains true to the oxymoronic character of the historical romance genre by describing the cultural context and events of the American Revolution and at the same time following the ancient quest-trial-marriage plot of romance.[10] With a clean dichotomy between good and evil, historical romances place fewer demands on the reader and usually provide the pleasure of a happy ending. Late in the nineteenth century they were all the rage with popular audiences. While Mitchell was taking advantage of the genre's popularity, he was also most comfortable with the romance tradition, where he found a literary home for his conservative values.

In the novel Hugh Wynne is a descendant of a noble and aristocratic Welsh family. Looking back, he narrates the story as an older man. It begins in 1765 in Philadelphia, when Hugh is twelve, and ends in 1783 with the proclamation of peace. Although Hugh's radical grandfather immigrated to America to escape political persecution, his father, John, did not inherit any revolutionary spirit. He is a rigid man of fixed beliefs, totally committed to obedience, nonresistance, and loyalty to the king. In contrast, Hugh's French mother, Marie Beauvais, is warm and gay. The extended family includes Aunt Gainor, John's sister and opposite, a powerful and wealthy woman who detests her brother's religion and politics. Hugh writes that at home he was taught the "extreme of non-resistance, and absolute simplicity as to dress and language. Amusements there were none. . . . At my aunt's, and in the society I saw at her house, there were men and women who loved to dance, gamble, and amuse themselves. The talk was of bets, racing, and the like. To be drunk was a thing to be expected of officers and gentlemen. To avenge an insult with sword or pistol was the only way to deal with it. My father was a passive Tory, my aunt a furious Whig."[11] The other important relative is Arthur Wynne, a cousin from Wales and soldier in the King's Army, who becomes Hugh's hated enemy and rival for the novel's love interest, Darthea Peniston.

Hugh encounters problems at home with his father, at his aunt's house with its temptations, in his fierce rivalry with his cousin for Darthea's love, and as a soldier, spy, and aide to Washington during the war. The novel gradually spans out from Philadelphia to include the countryside and nearby battlefields, and finally the events and progress of the war in general. Divided loyalties, one of Mitchell's favorite themes, exist at all levels, beginning within the Wynne household between father and son. Many of Aunt Gainor's close friends are Tories, and Darthea is a "fierce Tory." There are the old families—the Chews, Allens, Shippens, Penns, Logans, Pembertons, and Cadwaladers—and historical figures—like Rush, Franklin, Washington, Knox, Hamilton, and Arnold—all walking around the streets of Philadelphia, in and out of one anothers' homes, dining, playing cards, dueling, debating, and fighting the war. Men wear beaver hats edged with gold lace, velvet breeches, and silver-hilted dress swords, and the women carry linen and winter riding masks. In stark contrast, the Quakers are uniformly and simply dressed in gray, with their broad-brimmed hats and bonnets.

Tension, fear, and uncertainty saturate the first chapters of *Hugh Wynne*. Beginning with murmurs of discontent and the "devil-pot of war that was beginning to simmer," Mitchell creates a sense of how impossible it initially seemed that the colonists would ever fight or could ever win against the British. Still, "a sullen rage possessed the colonies" and the men begin to drill. John forces his son to stay away from the conflict by threatening to break with him for life. When Lord Cornwallis marches into Philadelphia to occupy the city, John "quite forcibly" expresses his joy and relief at the coming of the British troops, but Aunt Gainor says, "I will have no redcoats in my house." John's tyranny at home symbolizes the larger tyranny of the British government, and Hugh's struggle with his father runs parallel to the relationship between the colonies and England. In the novel, Hugh's dismissal from meeting is followed directly by the Continental Congress's vote for the Declaration of Independence. Like the colonists, Hugh finds it difficult and finally impossible to stay out of the war. Once he joins the army, the story becomes "a whirl of adventure." After meeting General Washington he marches with the army, and it seems "one great bewildering confusion of dust, artillery, or waggons stalled, profane aides going hither and thither, broken fences." A fine dust is "thick and oppressive, choking man and horse with an exacting thirst, mocked by empty wells and defiled brooks." And in all his life Hugh had never heard "as great a variety of abominable language." He passes "a lot of loose women in carts, many canvas-covered commissary waggons, footsore men fallen out, and some asleep in the fields—all the scum and refuse of an army,—with always dust, dust, so that man, beast, waggons, and every green thing were of one dull yellow."[12]

Soon after joining, Hugh is wounded and spends five months as a prisoner of war. His experiences are much more extreme than anything Mitchell recorded after his visit to the military prison at Fort Delaware during the Civil War. In this prison the man in charge is often drunk, and kicks and beats the soldiers. The cold of the winter months is intense, and they are given only straw and one blanket each. Snow flies through the broken windowpanes and covers the floor. Hugh writes, "At last the men ceased to laugh or smile, or even to talk, and sat in corners close to one another for the saving of body warmth, silent and inert." The room swarmed with rats that "kept well in the intense cold, and when we were given fire-wood, we cooked and ate them greedily."[13]

Generally, the conditions for the colonial army remain extremely dire, and this is the one constant theme that Mitchell is determined to convey. In contrast, the British always seem well fed, well dressed, and busy entertaining themselves. While serving as a spy, Hugh secretly approaches the windows of a ball given in honor of Sir William Howe's departure for England.[14] Hugh is curious to see if Darthea is attending with his cousin, Arthur, now her fiancé. The walls of the dancing room are covered with mirrors, and young black men clad in blue and white, with red turbans and metal collars and bracelets, stand at the doors and come and go with refreshments. Most of the women are in "gorgeous brocades and the wide hooped skirts of the day. The extravagance of the costumes struck me." The headdresses alone are a foot above the head and seem quite astonishing. It is a feast of color with "red coats and gold epaulets . . . the gold lace and glitter of staff-officers, and in and out among them the clouds of floating muslin, gorgeous brocades, flashing silk petticoats, jewels, and streaming ribbons." The air is full of an excess of powder from wig, queue, and headdress. Spurs clink and stiff gowns rustle. All of a sudden, recalled to a sense of danger and duty, Hugh sees "the camp on the windy hill" as if it "were before me with distinctness . . . the half-starved, ragged men, the face of the great chief they loved. Once again I looked back on this contrasting scene of foolish luxury, and turned to go from where I felt I never should have been."[15]

More than anything else, Mitchell meant to represent the radical difference between the British and colonial troops, and because of this difference the extraordinary mental determination and physical strength necessary to "humble the pride of England." Even so, in the last chapters conventional stereotypes overwhelm the time-bound historical information regarding life in Philadelphia and the buildup to and events of the war. Twice in the concluding pages Darthea becomes hysterical, and Hugh, her polestar, states that his "lady" is "impulsive" and will "need help and counsel and government, that her character might grow, as it did in after-years." Darthea also remains a Tory, and their marriage in Christ Church symbolizes reconciliation and harmony after the long war. When General Washington takes leave of his officers at Whitehall, he is compared to King Arthur bidding farewell to the last of his Knights of the Round Table.[16] Convention and sentiment tend to flatten the ending, muting the authentic detail and time-and-place markers and reminding readers once again of the paradoxical coupling of "historical romance."

Hugh Wynne sold more than five hundred thousand copies within a decade of its publication and went through at least twenty-two editions. Before arriving in Paris, the Mitchells had spent ten days in Touraine, where they had received no mail. Thus a stack of reviews came in one evening instead of arriving over several days or even weeks. That night Mary read the reviews aloud. A dozen or more critics felt that Hugh Wynne was in the highest ranks of historical novels. Aldrich, Mabie, and Gilder were wild in their favorable criticisms, and the novel "rained congratulations." Mitchell was referred to as the "amazingly virile doctor–author." One reviewer wrote that Hugh Wynne had none of that ambiguity that had so often marred the historical novel in the past. It was "a National novel," "brilliant and beautiful," "a great novel of its kind," a book of flesh and blood that becomes part of the nation's history. No other novel provided "so complete and comprehensive a panorama of this stirring crisis in American history." Mitchell wrote that if a man could be "mentally stunned by praise beyond the dreams of the avarice of vanity—I was." He enjoyed telling and re-telling this story, and over time the ten days in Touraine without mail grew to thirty days and rather than Maine to Florida it became a continent of acclaim.[17] When a Paris bookseller suggested that he buy the English edition of Hugh Wynne, a book that was selling well, Mitchell answered that "it was a tiresome book to me—and I never desired to read it again. Upon this the bookseller said—good gracious you are Dr. Mitchell. I saw yr. portrait. So you see this is as bad as being in a rogues gallery.... I go home a more than contented man."[18]

Mitchell had written from Zurich that one of the values of travel was the social isolation: "At home I at least have lost it and—can go nowhere with the assurance of being unrecognised." But rather than isolation, many letters written during this seven-month trip abroad tell of attending dinners, tours, clubs, and meetings with a variety of prominent and wealthy people, especially in London. As the famed American nerve doctor and novelist, Mitchell was a celebrity. At this point in his life he had little to complain about. While Mary Mitchell possessed substantial wealth, he did complain a little to Wister about all the shopping and the new tariff law: "I may have quite another form of depression when, in October, I land under the Dingley—(odious name) rule and have to pay for the garments in which my household lilies are to be made fine." On the eve of their departure, he wrote, "We are almost on the wing and—my women fold are out, engaged in a final effort to defy the tariff. . . . It has been seven months of unusual good fortune, with perfect weather everywhere—and—without any form of annoyance or any illness."[19] Mitchell's daughter and sons were thriving, one son in medicine and one in literature, and there were grandchildren. Honored abroad and content with the success of *Hugh Wynne* and his growing family, at the age of seventy he was living the good life. The haunting irony is that soon there would be family illness and even death. Less than three months later his daughter, Maria, who was twenty-one years old, died of diphtheria. It was "the tragedy of my winter's sorrow," as Mitchell described it.

There is scant information about the days surrounding Maria's illness. In his diary Mitchell wrote that Mary had diphtheria at the same time. There were four nurses and a physician attending, and Mitchell wrote that a Mr. Riter "obliges me by not placarding house—I shall not forget it or him." He felt "at sea—without compass star or hope." At times he reproached himself for not being more acutely sorrowful, for being too calm, writing that "this is one form of torture."[20] His wife, overwhelmed with grief, wished for her own death.

Diphtheria, an infectious disease caused by the bacillus *Corynebacterium diphtheria*, creates an inflammatory lesion in the respiratory tract called a pseudomembrane. The lesion, filled with blood clots, bacteria, dead skin, and white blood cells, becomes thick, leathery, and blue-white in color. It produces a toxin that travels through the blood stream, causes a reaction primarily in the heart and peripheral nerves, and can damage other organs and nerves. Death from suffocation results when this pseudomembrane obstructs breathing or when the toxin produced by the bacilli injures the heart, other organs, or the nervous system. This disease had a profound effect on Mitchell's life; in his diary he referred to it as his "special devil."[21] He had watched his first wife contract diphtheria and die. He himself had caught it twice.[22] It had ravaged and finally killed his brother Ned. Now his daughter had died. About Maria's final moments, Mitchell told Wister, "I can never lose memory of her last look of appeal for help—I had not to give—It left me with a wild desire to find the source of this misery—anger and—a brute despair."[23] A brief look at the development of the diphtheria antitoxin provides a broader context in which to view Mitchell's anguish.

In 1883 Edwin Klebs identified *C. diphtheriae* as the cause of diphtheria. In 1884 Friedrich Löffler isolated Klebs's microorganism and was able to grow it abundantly in cultures that included blood serum. Löffler inoculated various animals and concluded that the bacilli growing at the primary site produced a toxin that spread through the blood, and that healthy people may be "carriers" of the pathogenic diphtheria bacilli.

In 1888, working at the Pasteur Institute in Paris, Emile Roux and Alexandre Yersin confirmed Löffler's experiments and proved that diphtheria both multiplies on the tissues of the respiratory tract and produces a toxin that travels to other parts of the body. In 1890, in Robert Koch's laboratory, Emil Behring in collaboration with Carl Fraenkel and Shibasaburo Kitasato discovered an antitoxin for diphtheria. In 1891 in Berlin the first human trials were conducted and commercial production began; the first clinical trials commenced in 1892.[24]

In the fall of the same year, the New York City Health Department created a bacteriological laboratory. The next spring William H. Park was hired as the inspector and bacteriological diagnostician of diphtheria. Park had just created the "culture tube," which consisted of two glass tubes, one with solidified blood serum and the other with a short sterilized stick with a ball of cotton at its end. Park used forceps to rub the cotton against the pseudomembrane, tonsils, or pharynx. It was then rubbed against the surface of the blood serum, put back in its own tube, and plugged. Back at the lab, Park found that he could grow reliable cultures from the material on the cotton. In *Childhood's Deadly Scourge*, Evelynn Maxine Hammonds refers to this culture tube as no "trivial invention." It was the interface between the laboratory and the bedroom, giving physicians "direct access to bacteriological diagnosis." In 1893 Park published a paper in the *Medical Record* that carefully took physicians through the process of bacteriological diagnosis of all cases, from the mild to the severe, and "thus made it plain how it was their 'duty' to make a diagnosis using cultures."[25]

In 1894, at the International Conference of Hygiene and Demography, it was announced that children had been successfully treated with the antitoxin. Newspapers all over the world publicized this great scientific achievement. The first batch of antitoxin to arrive in the United States came from Germany. Public subscription campaigns were created to support its production and distribution in the United States. In January 1895 Hermann M. Biggs (the first director of the Division of Pathology, Bacteriology, and Disinfection of the New York City

Health Department) published an open letter titled "The New Treatment of Diphtheria" in the *Century*, the same publication where Mitchell published his short stories, poems, and serialized novels. Biggs explained that the cure for diphtheria had passed beyond the experimental stage. Its efficacy had been "thoroughly established," and it was a remedy "so extraordinary as to be without a parallel in the history of medicine."[26] In January 1895 the first antitoxin produced in the United States was made available. In 1896 the American Pediatric Society recommended that the antitoxin be used "in all cases of diphtheria as early as possible on the basis of a clinical diagnosis, not waiting for bacteriological culture." The report stated that "the benefits far outweigh the disadvantages, as to render the treatment not only proper, but morally obligatory upon the medical attendant. . . . It is certain that antitoxin has passed the stage of experiment; that it has secured a firm foot-hold as a therapeutic agent; that it is a powerful remedy in controlling diphtheria, and is here to stay."[27] Terra Ziporyn writes that by the late 1890s most medical texts and physicians were advocating the antitoxin when available.[28]

Still, there were skeptics who aligned themselves with the British tendency to ignore the evidence and dismiss the antitoxin treatment. Diphtheria was often associated with children or with members of the lower classes and immigrants. It could be difficult to identify, confused with other illnesses, or remain invisible until the late stages. Certain doctors saw bacteriology in general as a threat to their authority and clinical knowledge. In the 1890s Mitchell and the physician who attended Maria could have possessed the scientific knowledge to control diphtheria. Considering Mitchell's powerful network of friends, he could have obtained the antitoxin. But diphtheria, as Hammonds contends, was not controlled in any straightforward way by the introduction of bacteriological knowledge. Her argument that "it was not an instance of simply the right knowledge producing the right outcome," seems particularly relevant to Maria's case, where a maze of social factors, politics, and the nature of the disease itself obstructed the path from scientific knowledge to cure.[29]

Early in March the Mitchells left Philadelphia for a few days of sea air in Atlantic City. In a bath chair Mary sat in the dry sunshine as friends and family came to comfort her, including her brother John, daughter-in-law Anne, Alice Willing, and Talcott Williams. Mitchell wrote that Maria had been growing more like her mother "year by year with the advantage of such training as the larger life of my house contributed. . . . It is strange how young this sorrow stays with me—how fresh it is—There *must* be a natural, not quite unwholesome side to honest grief—This has none for me—I am physically the worse for it, and morally no better for it."[30]

Mary remained in Atlantic City, but Mitchell returned to Philadelphia, where "sad to say," he was "happier away from Mary when with her I carry a double burden— . . . A place like Atlantic City is one long distress to me—If a mans soul can be vulgarly hustled mine is there—where people stop my lonely walk and—are sorry for me." Writing to Wister, he wondered "how men who have no women friends endure certain things—Through all of tragedy women have seemed to me nearer to God than are men."[31] He was turning to women like Wister, Mason, and his daughter-in-law Anne for emotional support, and he depended on letter writing to express and control some of his feelings.

For the next several months Mary was more in bed than out. Finally in June she wrote, "I have tried in every way to get well for if I have to live, I do not want to be a bother. After Atlantic City . . . I lived in Maria's room, with all her little treasures, gathered about me,—and I felt happier there, *than* anywhere." She noted that "Dr. M looked so old, and worn, that I hated to look at him!"[32] Mitchell had gone to the Cascapédia River two weeks before Mary wrote this letter. Once there, he wrote Wister:

> I have been on this most beautiful river since June 7th and—feel day by day that it is the best thing I could have done. . . . There are 60 miles of uninhabited length of stream—The mountains 4 to 8000 feet high are clad with a noble forest mantle of mingled beech—birch—elm poplar and—dark fir and spruce—Here and there is the auburn cone of a dead fir and—now and then a mass of wild cherry in full bloom—The river is—one or two hundred yards wide and—then not over as many feet a wild—masterful,—dangerous torrent.

Mitchell's brother-in-law, the confirmed bachelor John Cadwalader, was with him, and they had spent Sunday afternoon canoeing to a little log house, where they read and talked. Finding the rapid movement and click of the white ash poles soothing, Mitchell wrote that it was a great thing "to acquire the art of mentally drifting—a greater to be able to shunt the trains of thought and to control thus the commerce of the mind." But now and then "no discipline I have learned will help and—I have for a moment one of those fierce stabs of—

hideous memories which make one know what limitless mental capacity for pain we have gained."[33]

In October Mitchell wrote his cousin Henry Charles Lea that "life had lost of late much of its flavour." Because of Mary's health, they were planning a trip to Egypt. He explained to Mason, "Now I must take my wife out of our home reminders of hours too sad to think of, too hopelessly sorrowful for even the base opinion of time to drug. . . . Also we must go because I dare not risk for this dear comrade our cold winter. I do not want to go." He wrote Richard Watson Gilder, "No one out of my house can imagine the completness of the calamity which has fallen upon us."[34]

At Bar Harbor, Mary Mitchell began riding a tricycle and Mitchell took lessons on the bicycle, writing, "Poll improves, uses the tricycle and—ah me—we are two sad old people. Except for those I love life seems over for me—and yet I am very well." In September they finalized their travel plans to Egypt, Mitchell writing John that "Mary has made up her mind that she can not face Christmas at home."[35] They would spend three weeks on a luxurious steamer on the Nile followed by two weeks in Cairo, return by way of Rome, Naples, Turkey, and Greece, spend two to three weeks shopping for clothes in London, and sail home in May. Mitchell worried that the long trip might disturb his fishing plans, but the priority was, and had to remain, Mary's health.

In Egypt, within days of the one-year anniversary of Maria's death, Mitchell posted a long letter, addressing it to the "Mitchell Children." "I am pretty nearly well of the Job malady," he wrote, "and—otherwise fine." In his customary way he wanted to share some of the sights, the "camels with their air of contemptuous superiority—Donkeys who seem to have achieved Nirvana—Veiled women coaches with fine horses—the Harem out for a drive—ahead run— bare legged footmen. . . . Amid all stalks by, straight—resolute not eager to get out of the way the . . . hated man in scarlet Jacket—who has come to stay and is by no grace of his own master—A woman said to me yesterday 'it is not what the Englishman does, but how he does it, that offends'—Cuba is our Egypt." He told Anne that Mary "buys something wherever she goes—to my delight. I have bought some good stone bugs to give away—and—a rhinoceros hide whip for J. K. to keep the family in order.—ah but I crave a sight of you all."[36]

After Maria's death, Mary refused all evening invitations, and so, when they arrived in London, she remained in her room at night. But Mitchell, rather than go "against the canons of English social life," wanted to go out. There was a dinner card from the Chamberlains, for example, "and so—I must go—says

Polly." Dyce Duckworth took him to a dinner at St. Barb's with three hundred other physicians. Mitchell was asked to speak and received a "wild welcome." He dined at the House of Commons with Sir William Priestley and lunched with John Singer Sargent. At the exhibition "Sargent has a big fat jewess—with rings and bangles, a lady mayoress, an astoundingly cruel portrait. Something has gone wrong with him—for me. . . . It seems a sad use of art—to paint a fat-ignoble looking smirking—self-pleased woman and why do it at all?" Mitchell enjoyed this trip, especially Egypt, and wrote that to be there was "to seem to be in some timeless other world. I yearn for it, now as never before for any land once seen."[37] The traveling had helped. Mary had regained some of her strength and interest in life. A year and half after the disaster, both parents had recovered from the physical pain of grief, but what had gone out of each day—what had made them feel complete and youthful—was no more, leaving sadness and confusion.

———————

After this long trip to Egypt, the Continent, and England, Mitchell spent only a few days in Philadelphia before leaving for the Cascapédia River. Except for six weeks in the fall of 1898 and these four days, he was away from Philadelphia for eighteen months. This long absence placed the entire responsibility for their medical practice on John's shoulders. The letters to John reveal much about the close, trusting partnership between father and son. From Egypt, for example, Mitchell was trying to determine the balance in his bank account after all the New Year deductions and travel drafts. A balance of $7,000 did not include the Cairo draft or John's share, "wh. is just what you had last year. Then you are to take *all* that comes in, even fr. patients who were our joint prey *till* 99— If you need more—you may have it." While Mitchell gave Langdon large sums of money to help with his living expenses, the difference in the father-son relationships is clear in the letter's last sentence: "Not a line from Lany since we left,—if his play is accepted or not I do not hear."[38]

John was hoping to win a professorship at the University of Pennsylvania. In the next letter his father wrote, "I am of course very anxious to see you a professor and do not see how you can be passed over—I could have secured your nomination but at a cost wh—wd—lessen my power to respect myself. . . . If you are beaten go at once and congratulate yr opponent. I do not quite understand the situation—there being three places." John did not get the professorship, however, and Mitchell told Wister that he left Philadelphia a "somewhat disgusted man" because of this defeat, which "on all accounts except for him is a university mistake—I did nothing to affect the result—and was glad to be absent. I think I was more hurt than John—for twice I have had a like fate and—professorships do not run in the family, it seems. They are only means not ends and—the roads are many—I did not inquire into the causes of the choices made by the faculty—They asked Jn.—to accept an assistant professorship—but this he declined."[39]

During this fishing trip, while walking, Mitchell came across a birch partridge in the woods that tripped hesitantly "with pounses up almost to my feet.—As I backed—, curious—she followed me, and—it was so pretty and—so innocent and confiding—that somehow of a sudden this tender instinctive trust filled my mind with thought of Maria. I sat down on a log and tried to *see* her face—When I opened the eyes closed in vain seeking—the brown bird with trust, curiosity—God knows what! was almost at my feet."[40] In Quebec and Bar Harbor, he would walk for hours, "what the Indians call great medicine," to disperse some of his saddest thoughts.

Both parents wanted to leave permanent memorials to their daughter. The sculptor Augustus Saint-Gaudens was a family friend, and Mary asked her husband to request a monument in honor of Maria. Saint-Gaudens replied that he was overwhelmed with unfinished orders and could not possibly do it. But then Mary wrote him directly, and whatever she said caused him to drop everything in order to create the memorial. Named *The Angel of Purity*, the white marble sculpture faced the Cadwalader family pew in St. Stephen's Church until 2004, when it was acquired by the Philadelphia Museum of Art. For his part, Mitchell wrote about his daughter in several poems. After seeing the sarcophagus Les Pleureuses in Constantinople, he expressed his grief in "Ode on a Lycian Tomb." The tomb itself consists of one woman carved into eighteen figures, representing the many moods of grief. He described the figures as "changeless stones" and "treasuries of regret" that "mock the term by time for sorrow set."[41] When he began another novel, he told Mason that it "serves to keep a sad man from dwelling upon an intolerable calamity—and on what is worse, the measureless sorrow of the bravest woman I have ever known."[42]

In his 1897 book *Clinical Lessons*, Mitchell had expressed concern that bacteriology was garnering all the attention and accolades. He warned that "amid the attractive fascinations of novel bacteriological study," doctors would lose sight of the everyday need for "incessant clinical watchfulness as to the lesser symptomatic novelties which are yet to be detected."[43] But after his daughter's death, Mitchell changed his mind. Shibasaburo Kitasato, the bacteriologist who had cultivated the tetanus bacillus and helped discover the antitoxin for diphtheria, had mentored the bacteriologist Hideyo Noguchi in Tokyo. When Noguchi rang Mitchell's doorbell just two years after Maria's death, it was more than curiosity that made him descend the stairs and open the door.[44] His decision to support Noguchi's research in toxicology and immunology sprang from deep feelings of frustration and remorse.

Twenty-four years old and close to Maria's age had she lived, Noguchi had been in charge of the library at Tokyo's Institute of Infectious Diseases. Simon Flexner and Frederick Gay, on their way to the Philippines, stopped in Tokyo to visit Kitasato, the director of the institute. Noguchi met Flexner at that time. Desperate to leave Japan, Noguchi wrote Flexner letters after their meeting, hoping for his help. Despite only a perfunctory response, Noguchi made plans to leave for the United States. His newly married friend sold his wife's bridal kimono to raise the money for the trip. Noguchi assumed that after arriving in San Francisco and traveling by train to Philadelphia, he could stay in Flexner's house and obtain a position at the University of Pennsylvania. Although Flexner wanted to help, he had only just arrived at the university himself. The year was 1900 and Mitchell had previously written Osler, "What a fine fellow is Flexner. I have him on to snake poisons, and have planned him full of suggestive ideas, for now I am at the time when I can sow and let others reap."[45] Once Noguchi arrived in Philadelphia, Flexner asked, "Have you ever studied snake venom?"

Due to the unusual combination of Noguchi's unrelenting determination and circumstance, he was given a bit of space in the old medical building at the University of Pennsylvania and a letter of introduction to Mitchell. Mitchell responded with financial support and encouragement, hoping that Noguchi would discover the antidote for rattlesnake venom. When Noguchi received a Carnegie Fellowship to study at the Statens Serum Institut in Copenhagen, he took along hundreds of grams of dried rattlesnake venom. Finally, Mitchell's dream became a reality when Noguchi and Thorvald Madsen produced a serum to counter the venom. When Noguchi returned to the States, he wrote the section on venom for the new edition of Osler's textbook and became part of the team at the Rockefeller Institute headed by Flexner. Mitchell wrote to Andrew Carnegie, "It must be pleasing to learn that your scientific bounty leads also to practical results. One of our early grants was to Prof. Flexner and

Dr. Noguchi and also we made the latter a science associate. Within a fortnight they have found a serum antidote for rattlesnake bites. The French had got one for cobra's but it was of no use for the American snakes. It is truly a very brilliant discovery, but without the liberal grants of the C. I. might have waited long."[46]

Noguchi also worked on tetanus, tuberculosis, and syphilis, gaining an international reputation and along with others, including Flexner, discovering the spirochete that caused syphilis. In 1910 Mitchell wrote Osler that Noguchi "has found means of cultivating with some preparation of liver the specific organism of syphilis. This would be the final triumph in this chain of wonderful discovery. I think this is calculated to produce enormous influence upon the civilization of the world, on the efficiency of armies and navies, and on the hygiene of the next generation or two." In 1913 Noguchi and J. W. Moore demonstrated that the syphilis spirochete caused a chronic, progressive infection of the meninges and brain and resulted in paresis. Noguchi traveled extensively in Cuba, South America, and Africa to work on a number of diseases, including yellow fever, trachoma, and Oroya fever. Vivisection was a huge part of his research, and at one point in Accra, Africa, he was experimenting with hundreds of monkeys. In the 1850s, Mitchell's animal experimentation had been frustrated by the lack of support and facilities. Now he took vicarious pleasure in Noguchi's research and experimentation. He told Osler that "of course Noguchi's splendid discovery pleases me greatly, who picked him up a starving Japanese some twelve years ago and secured him means of living work."[47]

In addition to Mitchell's revised view regarding bacteriology, another more gradual and penetrating change took place after the loss of his daughter: he began to focus more on his religious faith. Just a few months after Maria's death, he wrote to Wister that there was "a desolate—barren comfort in the belief that unchanging laws—do this or that. To recognize beneficence—in any human sense of it behind the law is the stern riddle—that lies in wait for us."[48] Up to this time, scientific knowledge had been his focus, but now he needed spiritual comfort. He wanted to believe in divine benevolence. After firmly defending the U.S. war with Spain, he published a poem titled "A Prayer, After Santiago" in *Harper's Weekly* in August 1898. After Bishop Doane read it in church, Mitchell wrote his family that the congregation broke down and "all over the church people cried—I am glad of it with a great gladness—To so reach the souls of men is worth much to me." Two of the poem's stanzas read:

O Lord of love! be Thine the grace
To teach, amid the wrath of war
Sweet pity for a humbled race,
Some thought of those in lands afar
Where sad-eyed women vainly yearn
For them that never shall return.

Great Master of earth's mighty school,
Whose children are of every land,
Inform with love our alien rule,
And stay us with Thy warning hand
If, tempted by imperial greed,
We, in Thy watchful eyes, exceed.[49]

In a few weeks Mitchell embellished the story by telling Anne that his poem "was read in churches all over the land and left with me a sense of having a grip on my dear land folk." In the letter written just three weeks earlier, however, Mitchell had written, "And now we are to see if we can govern—wild animals."[50] This remark—so unlike the poem's plea to the Great Master to teach sweet pity and love—is more akin to the 1899 poem "The White Man's Burden," where Rudyard Kipling refers to the "new-caught sullen peoples" as "half-devil and half-child." Mitchell's contradiction stems in part from his mental agitation and confusion and the changes taking place in his beliefs. In a few months he told Mason, "Oh, if I were always sure of what I want to believe, but my pendulum swings to the far limits of doubt and belief, and so will it be to the end." A year later he wrote, "A good bit of the savour has gone out of my life—certainly the keen joy in many things. . . . I have no philosophy to ease the ache of loss! I have only religion and that is cruelly shaken at each new mental disaster."[51] Mitchell was troubled by the possibility that death meant the end of the body and soul, and over the next few years he developed a strong belief in Christ and Revelation that provided some comfort and peace of mind.

In 1904, when Mason's husband died, Mitchell told her, "I can only hope that with you as with me, there exists a more and more intelligent belief in my Master Christ and in the promise of another earth that shall unriddle by and bye the many things that are dark to-day. Even the science of our time is losing the materiality and Christianity—or rather the Christ—has outlived the changing theories of men. . . . I can say that thro years of doubt I have won thro reason distinct beliefs. Pardon this too personal letter."[52] Mitchell wanted nothing to disturb this safe harbor he had reached. He intended to retain his identity as a man of science and at the same time embrace a belief in Christ and immortality. Throughout his comments regarding religion, he was careful to repeat that his faith was an intelligent one achieved through struggle and based on reason. He saw it as a "self-won theory of this world's workings," and it helped him to stay afloat after the death of his daughter and the shattering of his wife. In the last line of "Ode on a Lycian Tomb," he wrote that grief changes the "instrument o'er which his fateful fingers range." It would not be possible to bounce back from this family tragedy. When the storm cleared, the world was a different place.

12

THE NEW CENTURY

When C. E. Brown-Séquard wrote to Mitchell to say that he had used testicular extract for five years and was able to work an entire day without feeling the least fatigue, Mitchell requested a sample.[1] The request suggests that Mitchell's vigor and energy were beginning to decline. After 1902 he gave up his Friday clinics at the infirmary and resigned his position there. In 1906 he was made a foreign fellow of Britain's Royal Society, and Osler was delighted, writing that "there are only four or five Americans on the list. . . . It will be most gratifying to all your friends, and is a most welcome recognition in the country of your great service to science." Mitchell responded, "I suspect that I owe this honour far more to friendship than to anything scientific with which I can be credited as compared to a dozen men I could name."[2] While Mitchell's friends continued to speak of his yeasty mind, after fifty years of active engagement in research and experimentation, this part of his life had ended. At this point any scientific publications were short and most were done collaboratively. He continued to enjoy public speaking and among his many addresses were three to graduating nurses in Philadelphia and New York.[3] Increasingly, though, his interests focused on history and major figures like George Washington and William Harvey. More and more, he spent his quiet time writing novels. In the first decade of the twentieth century he published five novels along with several shorter pieces.

In 1904, at the age of fifty-five, William Osler wrote to say that he had accepted the position of Regius Professorship of Medicine at Oxford. Mitchell responded, "When I read your letter to my wife, she said isn't it splendid? and I—isn't it sorrowful?—for of course this does take you out of my life. . . . We shall see you I fear, but rarely and very soon you will be saying raily for really and H's will be lost all over the house, and you will say Gawd for God. . . . As to Jn. Hopkins—Perhaps you do not know that the Med. School at J. H. is or was Wm Osler."[4] Before his departure, Osler gave a farewell address titled "The Fixed Period" that was part of the anniversary ceremonies at Johns Hopkins University. Cushing wrote that there had never been such a gathering, with McCoy Hall packed to the windowsills.[5] In the address Osler stated that in science, art, and literature, men were most productive and made their most significant contributions between the ages of twenty-five and forty and were useless after the age of sixty. He joked, "Donne tells us that by the laws of certain wise states sexagenarii were precipitated from a bridge," and Trollope in his novel *The Fixed Period* discusses "the practical advantages in modern life of a return to this ancient usage, and the plot hinges upon the admirable scheme of a college into which at sixty men retired for a year of contemplation before a peaceful departure by chloroform."[6]

Although the address was a great success with the Hopkins audience, the next day the press went wild. Headlines included "Osler Recommends Chloroform at Sixty" and "Fixes Limit of Man's Usefulness at Forty: Dr. Osler Asserts Belief That Value to the World Ends Then." The *Daily News* listed some of the prominent New Yorkers like Rockefeller and Carnegie who were eligible for chloroforming; humorists predicted a boom in hair dye, wigs, and false teeth; there were invitations to "oslerizations," and the words "oslerization" and "oslerize" made their way into a number of dictionaries.[7] Bags of angry and threatening letters arrived at Osler's home, and Grace Osler, wanting to protect her husband from the hateful and abusive language, destroyed them. Osler told Arthur Thomson, "I hope my re-hashed Anthony Trollope joke of chloroform at 60 years has not been taken seriously by the English papers. The Yellow Journals here have raised a deuce of a row over it and over my jests about men of 40 and men of 60. I have had a very hard time of it, but the tempest is subsiding."[8]

In their biographies of Osler, Harvey Cushing and Michael Bliss respond differently to what came to be called the "fixed-age controversy." Cushing blames the journalists for the uproar. Bliss is more candid, understanding that Osler meant that "old people were not to be deferred to and consulted as fonts of superior wisdom. Old people were not generally venerable. Old age was demonstrably a pathological condition. In general the aged were to be shunted aside as effectively useless."[9] And, in fact, despite the letter to Thomson about his "jests," Osler stood firm and did not revise these views. He included "The Fixed

Period" in the second edition of his volume of addresses. In the preface, after he offered his "heartfelt regrets" to every man over sixty whose spirit he may have unwittingly bruised, he stated that "the discussion which followed my remarks has not changed, but has rather strengthened my belief that the real work of life is done before the fortieth year and that after the sixtieth year it would be best for the world and best for themselves if men rested from their labours." He wrote that "a very large proportion of the evils may be traced to the sexagenarians—nearly all the great mistakes politically and socially, and all of the worst poems, most of the bad pictures, a majority of the bad novels, not a few of the bad sermons and speeches."[10] Mitchell had just turned seventy-five; he had written nine novels and numerous poems and given numerous addresses during the last fifteen years. Given their friendship, it seems likely that Osler considered Mitchell while he was writing this address.

In May, at Osler's farewell party at the Waldorf-Astoria, while the wives watched from the balcony, six hundred men drank wine, three kinds of champagne, and liqueurs, and they dined sumptuously on dishes like mousse de jambon à la vénitienne, filet de bass de mer à la ferzen, suprême de volaille archiduc, carré d'agneau, pintade du printemps, gelée de groseilles, and glaces de fantasie.[11] There was endless teasing about oslerizations, and there were speeches about the Montreal years, the Philadelphia period, and the Hopkins era.

Mitchell wrote a poem in honor of the occasion, which he read aloud. Titled "Books and the Man," in the first part he spoke of books as friends, untouched by time, steadfast and generous friends who "greet us still / Through every fortune with unchanging looks." Referring to Bacon, Montaigne, Lamb, Thackeray, Raleigh, Chaucer, Cervantes, and Shakespeare, Mitchell continued, "Show me his friends and I the man shall know. . . . Show me the books he loves and I shall know / The man far better than through mortal friends." In the second part of the poem, Mitchell asked Osler to recall their first meeting at Limmer's Hotel in London:

> Do you perchance recall when first we met,
> And gaily winged with thought the flying night,
> And won with ease the friendship of the mind?—
> I like to call it friendship at first sight.
>
> And then you found with us a second home,
> And, in the practice of life's happiest art,

You little guessed how readily you won
The added friendship of the open heart.[12]

After the reading, Mitchell presented Osler with a 1744 edition of Cicero's treatise on old age, *De Senectute*, the first edition of the translated classic in North America and printed by Benjamin Franklin's press. A few months after leaving for Oxford, Osler wrote Mitchell to say that "the memories of your great kindness linger sweetly, and I shall always feel that it was the most fortunate day of my life when I met you and Mrs. Mitchell in London. How much it has meant to me!"[13]

For Mitchell, the following summer was full of illness and misfortune. Calling it the "summer of disaster," first he fell seriously ill while salmon fishing. The gallstone and liver trouble left him with "what I never knew before, necessity to think about what I eat and drink. Apart from that I should have been long ago well but for what came next." His dear friend Ned Coles was killed suddenly after a fall from a carriage. "On top of all while I was of the colour of a bad lemon and could have quoted Beppo—this damn Trust—must go and bust." Mitchell was a board member of the Real Estate Trust of Philadelphia, and in addition to suffering a heavy personal loss as a result of its collapse, he had deposited $31,000 belonging to Philadelphia's College of Physicians in the organization. In more than one letter, he insisted that he would cover the loss. He wrote to Arthur Meigs, the college president at the time, "I want it distinctly understood, and I would rather you said so to the College, that in case the rehabilitation of the Real Estate and Trust fails in any measure to make good the deposit of the College that I hold myself responsible and I wish it understood that I do this because it was through my agency that the deposit was made. I want the College to know this." Mitchell was right in the middle of a major fund-raising campaign for the college. He told Mason that the failure was "a long and rather sad story of a combination of hypocrisy, crime and weakness, in which I do not wish to dwell." It was embarrassing, and although it eventually righted itself, it could not have come at a worse time.[14]

Mitchell often remembered the awe he felt at his first college meetings in 1856 "in the little picture house, as it was called, on Pine St."[15] But that awestruck and uncertain young man was gone. Whitfield J. Bell describes the older Mitchell as a "patrician to his fingertips," a man who "distrusted democracy, denied that all men are in fact equal, and had no sympathy for the growing women's rights movement. . . . His presidential addresses to the College had the lofty tone of majesty addressing the commons." Bell also writes that perhaps no single individual in its long history did so much for the college as Mitchell.[16]

In the early 1880s, Mitchell made substantial contributions to the college, establishing, for example, the Weir Mitchell Library Fund with an initial contribution of $1,000 that was later increased to $5,000. Bell notes that Mitchell was a "great believer" in the effects of good food, wine, and cigars, and in 1883 he donated $5,000 for an Entertainment Fund, which was later increased to $7,000.[17] In 1907, when Ross donated his papers to the college, Mitchell wrote to thank him for the addition to "a medical collection of nearly ninety thousand volumes." In a few years Mitchell wrote Ross to ask for a drawing "from your hand rather than a microscopic specimen, which is apt to fade. We would put the drawing under your photo and autograph in the College hall, where there are countless such treasures."[18] Mitchell acquired a four-page letter of Robert Koch, the German bacteriologist who had won the Nobel Prize in 1905 and died in 1910, and planned to have it photographed and framed.[19] He organized lectures and various gatherings. He wrote to Keen and Billings to organize a panel on Civil War medicine that would discuss special hospitals, war surgery, malingering, and hospital gangrene—"because today an unknown horror." Mitchell asked Keen and Billings to read from manuscript or hire a stenographer, feeling that nothing could be more important than preserving a record of Civil War medicine. In the same letter he included information about the reception: "At ten there will be chocolate, coffee and claret Punch and lemonade and biscuits and segars—down stairs in the West room and Committee Room—all simple but good."[20] After the papers were read, they were published in the college journal, *Transactions*.[21] As well as advising the college to buy certain journals and books, Mitchell personally gathered countless rare books and documents for the library, established a Directory of Nurses, and served as president for two nonconsecutive three-year terms. Much of his work as president and on committees was pushing for reform and education to create a positive atmosphere regarding scientific progress and innovation. While Mitchell's contributions to the library were extensive, his greatest contribution was his long and hard-fought battle to raise the funds for a new college building.

By 1897 the college regularly received six hundred journals, contained more than five thousand specimens in the Mütter Museum, and had books stacked along the walls and on the floor. It became clear to everyone that the old building no longer met the needs of the library or the museum. In 1900 Mitchell offered three solutions to the problem: buy the adjoining property and build an annex, use the first-floor meeting room for books, or give up the Mütter Museum. None of these solutions was acceptable. After a year and no action, Mitchell approached Carnegie. Two years later, in 1903, Carnegie announced that he would contribute $50,000 toward increased space for the library if the college could raise an equal sum. In just six weeks, after contacting wealthy friends and college fellows, Mitchell was able to raise $53,000. This large sum of over $100,000 created the possibility of a new building. But Horatio C. Wood, college president at the time, feared that a new building would create serious debt and felt that it would be better to remodel and expand rather than build. The resulting debate, which was harsh and bitter at times, lasted for six years, and Bell notes that it was often "confused and contradictory, with the College rescinding at one meeting what it had approved at an earlier one. Motions were made, tabled, rejected, approved, and repealed. Attendance rose to unprecedented heights as advocates and opponents of particular proposals rallied in force. There was scant time for scientific papers."[22]

In 1905 Mitchell advised Arthur Meigs, who followed Wood as president and strongly opposed a new building, that since funds had been raised, it was time to form committees and move ahead. Although Meigs had asked for Mitchell's help, Mitchell politely ended the letter with, "All this is merely suggestive and I hope, my dear friend, that you will excuse my interference." In the spring of 1906 Mitchell told Osler that the "college will build at 17 and Pine unless it has a new fit of mental ataxia." Still, this plan along with several others came to nothing. Mitchell switched his attention to a lot on Twenty-Second Street and directed Meigs to call a meeting to accept it as the new building site. Mitchell was frustrated and disappointed, and wrote, "Should the College fail to accept this I shall abandon all further effort. We have been wobbling and wandering and as LeConte says 'The College has no adhesive majority.' It is time we settled down to something." Finally, things began to move forward. Carnegie donated another $50,000 on the condition that the college raise $100,000. Mitchell told William J. White that within days he had raised $20,000 and hoped to get the rest, "but hope though a remarkably good banker occasionally fails." He noted in the same letter that "there is a humbug University Temple or something like that up Broad Street which proposes to become a full fledged university."[23]

In a few months, by a vote of sixty-three to forty-five, the college fellows reaffirmed their intention to build on Twenty-Second Street. Architects were hired. In March the college fellows voted unanimously to approve the plans. In a few months Mitchell told Osler that the college would be free of a debt of $75,000 due to a gift from a friend, E. T. Stotesbury, and that Eckley B. Coxe (Wharton Sinkler's nephew) had purchased "the stable next to us and will hold it until we can buy it and is not this a fine ending, to my eight years of anxiety?" In the next letter he wrote, "We hope to lay the corner stone in Oct.— and this after five years of fight! I sometimes suspect myself of obstinacy!" At Christmas he wrote that the "college is now to be built at a cost of 270,000 dollars of wh. we now have $229,000 and shall get the rest given—We are to sell the old home at 150,000 with freedom to deliver it within four years—We shall enter the new home with an income of $18,000—and my dream will thus materialize."[24]

In April 1908 Mitchell laid the cornerstone, explaining to Keen, "I think we have money enough to finish the College, furnish it and leave us free of debt and with the product of the sale of our old building. It is however most desirable, and possible, tho' it is not to be publicly talked about, to obtain the whole or half of the stable lot to the south of us." Finally, in January 1909, he told Osler that "the college is rising and will be very fine. At present I want for it to finish—about 40,000." Later he explained, "We have had a great many gifts to the College. The last one a lot next door (where a stable stood). It has now been made over to the College free of charge, being really a gift of $45,000."[25] Sinkler had persuaded his nephew Eckley Coxe to purchase the adjoining lot and buildings. After Sinkler's death, Coxe offered the property rent free to the college, and asked only that some memorial be created in honor of his uncle. Mitchell suggested a garden, and in this way the quiet retreat just south of the college with its herbs, shaded benches, and pathways came to be.[26]

At the dedication of the new college building, both Mitchell and Carnegie spoke. Mitchell told the audience that if they wandered back to the iron book stacks, they would encounter eight to nine thousand volumes and one hundred thousand pamphlets. And the college was an "absolutely free library, it is open to all who would read here. A card from a fellow gives permission as freely to take books home. Here come and are welcome men and many women, physicians of every sect, reporters, the laity in search of knowledge of spas, climatic conditions, and other matters of interest. What this vast collection is to us, how essential, I need but say. It preserves for us the changing story of our history, and we are kept in constant touch with the science of all nations by the receipt of nine hundred journals."[27] The history of medicine that was housed in the college library was a national resource and treasure, and he thanked the donors who understood its purpose and value in that way. When Carnegie spoke, he praised Mitchell, referring to the completion of the new building as the "apotheosis of his career," and, perhaps with Osler's "Fixed Period" in mind, said that "nothing, no triumph, no ceremony, no honor can be bestowed upon him that can quite equal this night, at the very apex of his life."[28]

At the same time that Mitchell was fund-raising for the college, the correspondence with Osler reveals their mutual interest in all things—lecture notes, portraits, correspondence, autographs, and genealogy—related to William Harvey. After a trip through Europe, Osler wrote Mitchell that in Paris he "had a sore disappointment in a reputed Harvey portrait at Sedelmeyers,—a Jansen, 1656,—a splendid picture. I took a photograph to London and submitted it to Cust, Power and others and looked up the reputed pedigree. It could not have been a Harvey, much to my sorrow, as I had determined to take it." Mitchell found, in preparing an address, that Harvey's lecture notes "would tax the wits of the most ingeniously learned." He teased Osler, "My *Harvey* is not a lecture, but a collection of disconnected articles about the great man, some of which will be new even to you."[29]

In 1895 Mitchell and John Cadwalader helped John Shaw Billings become the first director of the New York Public Library. Then Mitchell made good use of Billings's position to help with his Harvey research. He made requests for information about genealogy and a recent owner of a Harvey autograph, writing, "I should like Mr Stevens to understand that any expense he may be put to in running this thing to earth I will gladly pay for." A few months later he wrote, "I am still very curious to know who was the owner finally of the Harvey autograph. . . . It is too important to leave undone anything which may pertain to the history of this remarkable paper. I hope you were able and had time to find other Harvey matters for me."[30]

There are many such letters to both Billings and Osler, and at times Mitchell was overtaken by the hunt and lost his usual tact and politeness. He bought a Harvey signature for a great deal of money and then went through considerable trouble to confirm its authenticity. He told Osler, "There is—in Oxford—at Merton—a letter of Harvey of which I should like to have, *at my cost* a photographic copy of exactly the size of the original." And again, "If at any time any novel Harvey matters turn up—buy them for me recklessly." When the college initiated a lecture series on great physicians, Mitchell was the first to speak on Harvey. He was most surprised by the indifference with which the discovery of the circulation of the blood "was treated even by doctors with whom he must have made it familiar, until it came out in printed form; and most strange of all, in the whole nine volumes of Bacon's works there is not an allusion to Harvey or his discovery."[31]

Fascinated with the man, Mitchell was certain that everything about Harvey had value, and he spared no time or expense. He was especially upset when the Royal Historical Manuscript Commission in England would not release thirteen Harvey letters to him. They were to be published in two years but Mitchell, at eighty-one, did not feel that he necessarily had two years. D'Arcy Power had published his *Life of Harvey* in 1897, and so Mitchell wrote to him about the letters: "Osler failed to get them for me, and I am told it will be two years before they will be printed, and in the meantime no one can see them, which appears to me rather absurd. Cannot some one get us leave to use them?" After nine months, outraged that he still could not see these letters, he wrote Osler, "I want to know at once from you what you can tell me about those letters you mentioned.... I mean to make an effort through the American Ambassador to see if I cannot break through this ridiculous situation and obtain copies of these letters. Now tell me just about what they are, why they cannot be seen, and to whom application must be made; then I will write to Whitelaw Reid and threaten a war with Great Britain in case they are not immediately forthcoming."[32] As usual, Mitchell got his way.

On Harvey's birthday Mitchell planned to speak to the Harvey Society of New York. In preparation, he wrote Osler to ask the difference between a "lesser pensioner" and a "greater pensioner" in order to determine if Harvey's father had financial difficulties in sending him to Cambridge. "By this time," he told Osler, "you have concluded that the curse of a corresponding friend has come upon you; but this cannot be helped. Do not forget about Sir Vere Isham. I much want the whole of that letter of Bishop's." The next month, while Osler was on holiday, Mitchell impatiently repeated one of his many requests, writing, "I do not like to trouble you, but nobody hesitates to trouble me and I may as well pass it on."[33]

As a result of all this research, Mitchell published *Some Memoranda in Regard to William Harvey, M.D.* in 1907 and *Some Recently Discovered Letters of William Harvey with Other Miscellanea* in 1912, which included a bibliography of Harvey's works, compiled by the college librarian Charles Perry Fisher. The bibliography

listed thirty-three editions of works by Harvey at the college and the same number at the Surgeon General's Library, and Mitchell wrote that no other library
in the world "is up to us in this matter." He mailed two copies of *Some Recently
Discovered Letters* to Osler, one to the Radcliff College library, one to the British
Museum library, and copies to several friends in London. He distributed a copy
to each college fellow and mailed copies to various descendants of the Harvey
family, including Lord Winchilsea and Heneage Finche.[34]

Still, the hunt was not over; several of Mitchell's last letters discuss various
Harvey portraits, letters, and descendants. Late in 1912 Mitchell wrote Harvey
Cushing a long, detailed letter regarding a supposed Janssen portrait of Harvey
offered for sale in Boston. Based on his knowledge of Harvey's biography and
especially his intimate knowledge of his facial features, Mitchell knew it to be
a fake. While Janssen may have painted it in 1644 at Oxford, it was not Harvey
nor did it resemble any of his brothers.[35] Proud of all the research he had done,
he told Osler, "I am a little pleased that no one can write a great life of Harvey
without some reference to me—It is something to be a bob—to that Heaven
soaring Spirit. . . . Keep an eye on any Harvey things for me and quit writing
me those half page scraps of letters—I have seven queries to put at you about
Harvey—I spare you—. Could I learn at the Herald office when Wm H—got
arms? I hear you cuss."[36]

In 1904 Osler returned to the United States to give the Ingersoll Lecture on
Human Immortality at Harvard. His address was titled "Science and Immortality," and in it he identified the prevalent attitudes toward immortality by dividing
people into three groups. The majority of people were Laodiceans, who accepted
but were indifferent about the prevailing religion. They were focused on getting
and begetting—baseball, bridge, and the price of beef, coal, and stocks. Nor, as a
rule, did this change when they were close to dying. Osler had kept careful
records of five hundred deathbed scenes, and in terms of the sensations of the
dying, ninety suffered bodily pain and discomfort, eleven showed mental apprehension, two positive terror, one spiritual exaltation, and one bitter remorse. For
the great majority, then, Osler concluded that their death like their birth was "a
sleep and a forgetting." Using Howells, Lowell, and Holmes as examples, he stated
that "the older we grow, the less fixed, very often, is the belief in a future life."[37]

Osler's second group, the Gallionians, which included scientists, deliberately
put the matter of immortality aside as something they had no means of knowing

anything about. Osler had often heard Joseph Leidy say that "the question of a future state had long ceased to interest him or to have any influence in his life." In the Christian religion man is a fallen creature, "an outlaw from his father's house," but in science man is "the end-product of a ceaseless evolution" and the "crowning glory of organic life." Osler's statement that a critical study of the Bible must weaken belief in Revelation was especially threatening to Mitchell's beliefs. Science also questioned the credibility of direct Revelation based on miracles. But Mitchell wanted to believe in Revelation. Even more than that, he wanted to believe that he would continue to exist after death. But nature, according to Osler, "so careless of the single life, so careful of the type—is so lavish with the human beads, and so haphazard in their manufacture, spoiling hundreds, leaving many imperfect, snapping them and cracking them at her will, caring nothing if the precious cord on which they are strung—the germ plasm—remains unbroken. Science minimizes to the vanishing-point the importance of the individual man."[38]

Osler's third and smallest group, the Teresians, was composed mainly of women, often lowly and obscure. They were idealists, narrow, prejudiced, "and often mistaken in worldly ways and methods," but they "compel admiration and imitation by the character of the life they lead and the beneficence of the influence they exert." Osler encouraged students of science to avoid dogmatism and denial but, at the same time, to acknowledge the value of a belief in immortality as an asset in human life—calling it "the rock of safety to which many of the noblest of his fellows have clung."[39]

When Charles W. Eliot had asked Mitchell to give this lecture before Osler, he declined, writing, "I am flattered that you should have thought of me for the Ingersoll lecture, but, frankly speaking, the subject is not one which my habits of thought or my lines of study would enable me to deal with in a way that would be satisfactory either to me or to such an audience as Cambridge would offer. Had it been some other subject I might have considered coming."[40] He told Mason, "I declined the Ingersoll lecture at Harvard and Osler gave it. He was not at his best. . . . Clever, learned, happily languaged, but as I see it, thin. And creeds? To my mind all the great religions were revelations and all suffered at the hand of man. Christ's may not be final. It seems to me the best and there I stop, since else I must go on to write the lecture I refused to give."[41]

After the publication of Osler's lecture, Mitchell remained troubled, and as he had done so many times before, he tried to reach some clarity and control through his writing. He wrote a detailed letter under the heading "To Doctor

Osler in regards to his book on 'Science and Immortality.'" Mitchell meant the letter to be a formal response and contravention. In it he wrote that "the skepticism of to-day has lost its laugh, has shed its scorn, and no longer treats this matter with the assured indifference of men, who think themselves mentally superior in point of view to such men as Faraday and Newton or can afford to smile at the faith of such men." On a more personal note, he wrote, "I have felt of late years prepared to struggle successfully with beliefs which were inculcated in my childhood and which for a long while troubled me with increasing doubt." Disagreeing with Osler's point that nature cares nothing for the single life, Mitchell wrote that the universe wastes nothing, and "I think that when you or I during long lives improve in power to act, to reason and end by constructing mental machinery of value, I say it does not seem likely that all this is going to be lost any more than the material products of nature which simply changing reappear under new forms still capable of use."[42]

Mitchell believed that over time there had been an increase in mental power and altruism, which would not have been possible without adversity, pain, and sin. God could not appear directly since that would "be so authoritative as to not admit for a moment of disobedience." The apparent desire of the Maker was that the world should grow through evolutionary conditions and the "reaction of man upon man until it rose to levels of which no human imagination may dare to predict." Still, under these circumstances God created special beings like Mohammed and Christ in order to appeal to and aid humankind. Although Mitchell saw reincarnation as incredible, still "to admit of a possible creator is to admit a possible active life post mortem—a fog or halo of speculation explained." All that is unclear would be made clear elsewhere, "as a great deal of the conduct of the father is unclear to the child."[43] In this statement, so grave and reserved and so entirely unlike letters to Osler in terms of presentation and tone, Mitchell did write the address he, uncharacteristically, refused to give at Harvard.

In 1908 Mitchell spoke to the American Neurological Association and addressed some of the criticisms and misunderstandings regarding the rest cure. He also differentiated his treatment from psychotherapy, for which there was an epidemic of enthusiasm that "just now occupies whole books and is the talk of dinner tables."[44] For Mitchell, rest and full feeding were essential to a successful cure, but for others the primary focus had shifted to mental treatment and psychic influence under the favorable conditions of rest. At the same time, Mitchell did not relinquish any credit for the "use of influential mind treatment," what he had all along called "moral medication" and "moral education" and was now calling "psychic medicine."

Sigmund Freud (who gave his Clark lectures in the United States in 1909) took Mitchell's pioneering work in psychiatry very seriously. He had written a favorable review of *Fat and Blood*, and he had several books in his personal library on the rest cure in English and German.[45] Several of the books were written by Mitchell, including *Injuries of Nerves and Their Consequences*, *Fat and Blood*, and *Lectures on Diseases of the Nervous System, Especially in Women*. The books in Freud's library help to dispel the myth that the rest cure was the fraudulent delusion of one society doctor. Rather, the list indicates that the impact and success of the Weir Mitchell Treatment on mental illness was far-reaching and long-lasting.

Although their theories and the purpose they ascribed to "talking" were different, Freud and Mitchell had certain attitudes and practices in common. In *Studies on Hysteria*, co-written by Freud and Josef Breuer, they wrote that they could not imagine delving into the psychical mechanism of hysteria with anyone who was low-minded or below a certain level of intelligence. Mitchell often spoke of the difficulty of treating foolish women and his easy success with intelligent ones. Freud and Breuer wrote that above all, the "complete consent" and "confidence" of the patient were essential. It is almost inevitable that the patient's personal relation to the doctor "will force itself, for a time at least, unduly into the foreground. . . . An influence of this kind on the part of the doctor is a *sine qua non* to a solution of the problem."[46] This need for consent and confidence corresponds to the "childlike obedience" that Mitchell required from his patients. Mitchell also believed that the causes of illness and breakdown often originated in the distant past and that transference between patient and physician was critical to a successful cure.

William W. Keen wrote that Mitchell taught him "how to observe and how to elicit, often literally to 'dig up,' histories from unobservant patients." After working alongside Mitchell at the infirmary, Charles K. Mills called Mitchell "one of the greatest of our psychoanalysts." Beverley Tucker, who also worked with Mitchell, referred to him as a "psychiatrist" and "psychoanalyst." Mitchell's patients were suffering from phobias, obsessions, mild manic and depressive conditions, anxiety, exhaustion, and schizophrenia. All aspects of a rest cure set the stage for his "truly psychotherapeutic visits. His patients told him everything as he dug into their psychogenic experiences and he patiently explained to them and suggested away their problems."[47] Mitchell wrote that while the priest hears the crime of the hour, the physician is "oftener told the long, sad tales of a whole life," and "none may be quite foreign to his purpose or needs" because the causes of breakdown are often to be found in the "remote past." The doctor "may dislike the quest, but he cannot avoid it."[48]

The critical differences between Freud and Mitchell included Freud's belief that an analysis based on Breuer's cathartic method was almost essential to treat a neurotic illness. He had adopted the habit of combining cathartic psychotherapy with rest, and even extending it at times into a "complete treatment of feeding-up on Weir Mitchell lines." This combination prevented the disturbing introduction of new psychical impressions during the psychotherapy and removed the boredom of a rest cure, "in which the patients not infrequently fall into the habit of harmful day-dreaming" (a problem Mitchell never mentioned). Freud and Breuer, commenting that one might think the excitement resulting from the reproduction of traumatic experiences would counteract the benefits of Mitchell's rest cure, wrote, "But the opposite is in fact the case. A combination such as this between the Breuer and Weir Mitchell procedures produces all the physical improvement that we expect from the latter, as well as having a far-reaching psychical influence such as never results from a rest-cure without psychotherapy."[49] But Mitchell cautioned against psychotherapy's tendency to complicate psychic medicine, saying that in "one or another form it is a world-old business." Noting the "wearisome detail of psychopathic analysis and treatment" and evoking Professor Polonius, he wrote that most of it was "simple and yet temptingly open to elaborate description." He argued that psychotherapy was "having, I fear, a tendency to create the disorders in full proportion to the cures."[50] From this perspective, some forms of hysteria could be the morbid penalty of excessive introspection rather than the consequence of denial and repression. Roy Porter has made a similar point, writing that the "protocols of Charcot's Tuesday Clinic and the Freudian couch arguably hysterized hysteria, as one might douse a fire with gasoline."[51]

Despite a mutual interest in hysteria and the overlap of some of their methods, Mitchell did not appreciate or respect Freud's contributions. Partially due to Mitchell's Victorian sexual mores and less elaborate theoretical framework, he rejected concepts like childhood sexuality, the Oedipus complex, and the unconscious mind.[52] According to Mills, Mitchell "was not given to prolonged, perplexing, and confusing methods of searching for doubtful causes in the sexual incidents of early childhood or infancy of his patients."[53] Ilza Veith writes that Mitchell "categorically rejected all sexual implication," rejecting "sexual factors as the essential cause of hysterical disturbances."[54] However, while Mitchell did not explicitly discuss sexuality in his public writing and speaking, he did not categorically reject all sexual implication. He chose not to discuss sexuality in public, but he was adept at digging up histories and his patients "told him everything" in private. More to the point, the standard case history form at the Infirmary for Nervous Diseases asked each patient to provide information about "sexual functions" along with "family history," "personal history," "habits," "causes assigned by patient for disease," and "age at onset." Clearly, sexuality was considered pertinent to the diagnosis and treatment of nervous disorders at the infirmary. The difference between Freud and Mitchell was more a matter of degree and focus. Still, in contrast to Freud's respect for Mitchell and incorporation of the rest cure into psychoanalysis, Mitchell found Freud's writing disgusting and impatiently dismissed him. As the story goes, after borrowing one of Freud's books from the college library, Mitchell asked, "Where did this filthy thing come from?"—and sent the book windmilling across the room and into the fire.

Along with the Harveiana and college fund-raising, Mitchell devoted a fair amount of time to the Carnegie Institute of Washington. Billings, a member of the executive committee and one of Carnegie's most valued advisers, helped Mitchell become a trustee and executive committee member. Mitchell later told Billings's biographer that before joining the committee, he was "quite unknown to Mr. Carnegie and I am under the impression, between us, that he thought me a person who wrote novels and knew little else about me."[55] Because of the Carnegie committee meetings, Mitchell and Billings saw each other regularly. They were sometimes seen driving around Washington, D.C., together in a ramshackle buggy with Billings at the reins. It gave Mitchell keen pleasure to be the "anonymous author of a great charity. What are poems and—novels to that? It gives me keen pleasure." He told Mason that this Carnegie work was his largest burden: "I hardly dare to look forward to what it will be when we are using 500,000 a year. It is, of course, vastly interesting and instructive—playing with other people's money."[56]

Billings, during his thirty-five years in the Army Medical Corps, had created the Surgeon General's Library and the *Index-Catalogue*. Because the *Index-Catalogue* listed medical publications only from the beginning of the nineteenth century to 1878, Billings and Robert Fletcher created the *Index Medicus* in 1879 to index the medical literature for each month going forward. In 1895 the U.S. Congress withdrew its support of the *Index Medicus*. In 1903, most likely due to Billings and Mitchell's insistence, the Carnegie Institute undertook its publication.[57] In his letters Mitchell noted other Carnegie projects, such as Robert Peary's arctic exploration and Frederick J. Bliss's explorations in Syria. He wanted to provide a grant to Edward Curtis's daughter, who published an article in *Harper's* about the music of the Moquis Indians. She hoped to travel west again and make a more complete study of Indian music and verse, and Mitchell felt that nothing "more interesting in the archaeology of the southern tribes can be found than a study of their poetry and music together." Billings had been a good friend of Mitchell's brother Ned during the Civil War. Mitchell told Billings, "I know you will want to help her for the sake of the old relationship between Curtis and yourself and my brother Ned, a thing I never cease to remember."[58] Mitchell also wanted to publish a linguistic paper by Max Müller, writing, "In my own opinion it is the papers which few read and no other people will print that are just the ones we should provide for."[59]

The correspondence between Carnegie and Mitchell tells of a warm and trusting friendship. In one letter Carnegie asked, "If you had say five or ten millions of dollars to put to the best use possible, what would you do with it? Prize given for the best answer." Mitchell responded, "I should realize the vain dream of my life,—hospital wards and rooms for my 'Rest Treatment' for the poor—a means to bridge over the time of people leaving the hospital and not yet able to work. Two millions would be enough for me. The rest would go to increase incomes of college teachers—say in the five great Eastern universities."[60] Mitchell asked Carnegie's help in restoring the cemetery at Christ Church in Philadelphia, writing that it was "a sort of little Westminster Abbey for Americans, with its half dozen signers of the Declaration buried in and around it. . . . It is not as a church I address you at all in regard to this, but as a national monument in a good deal of peril."[61] In another letter to Carnegie, Mitchell wrote, "We leave on the 9th and I shall certainly make a call on you at Dungeness and be glad of a talk on various matters which interest us both. I have read with all the interest of my Scotch blood the booklet about your movements and work in the dear motherland. Your speech at Stirling struck me as very fine and I am pretty sure that you write now and then wee bit verses—and tell no one—Any way inside of you somewhere there is a poetic corner."[62] In 1910 Mitchell told Cushing, "Carnegies 10,000,000 for science—is—indeed splendid—In all we have 25000000—Imagine it."[63]

But Mitchell did not get along with everyone as well as he did with Billings and Carnegie. In fact, he developed an intense dislike and "personal enmity," as he called it, toward "his highness" Theodore Roosevelt. And, in settling the score, Mitchell scattered several unpleasant remarks about Roosevelt throughout his diary, autobiography, and letters to insure their survival.

Much of this anger followed Roosevelt's refusal to grant Mitchell's great-nephew Richard Edwards a nomination to the Naval School of Annapolis. Mitchell had assumed that he would succeed with this request, even spending money to prepare Edwards for the examination. He tried explaining to Roosevelt that his predecessor, President McKinley, had promised to make an exception to the rules in this case. Mary Mitchell's relatives also tried to induce Roosevelt to change his mind. He, in turn, explained that he could make no exception. Appointments to the Naval Academy were under the control of Congress. Nominations were made by members of the U.S. House of Representatives and Senate. Mitchell wrote to Secretary of State John Hay, "I want to see the President for ten minutes to ask of him an appointment to Annapolis in 1902—Here, I can get none—The places are filled—and really I think I am justly entitled to be considered when in my own country, for the first time, I ask a government favour. . . . May I not rely on yr—kind and *real* aid in this matter—. . . . I am so *used* to giving rather than to asking that I approach the asking attitude with difficulty."[64] But John Hay was no help.

Several diary entries about Roosevelt's refusal were inserted into Mitchell's autobiography. For example, Mitchell asked, "Why are my services less than those of this or that admiral? They differ in kind, have involved just as much peril." A few days later he wrote, "I would like to get disagreeably even with R. It is not revenge one wants but the opportunity. Then to give it up is easy. That is the worst of getting your face slapped when time leaves you so small a margin for retributive justice. . . . R's act is honest but unfair, discourteous to me, and showed a want of sentiment."[65] The following year Bertie Adams provided an alternate appointment for Mitchell's great-nephew. And when Adams's first choice failed the exam and Edwards did well, he was able to enter the naval academy after all the fuss. Mitchell wrote Roosevelt about this acceptable outcome and received a civil letter in return. Edwards eventually became an admiral in the U.S. Navy.

The next encounter with Roosevelt did not end so well. Mitchell was vice-president of the Valley Forge Association, and along with John Cadwalader he went to see Roosevelt about making a campground at Valley Forge. Roosevelt, attempting to make amends, approached Mitchell and took both his hands in his own. Although he could not talk about Valley Forge at that very moment, he invited them to lunch the next day. Cadwalader had to persuade Mitchell to go. He was seated next to Mrs. Roosevelt and Cadwalader sat next to the president, "who talked straight through the lunch about everything in the world except Valley Forge. . . . I went out, feeling that Mr. Roosevelt had not improved the state of my feelings in regard to a man who could either forget that he had brought two busy men all the way from Philadelphia or who took this method of evading a subject upon which as proved later we were not in agreement."[66]

Mitchell was not alone in his dislike of Roosevelt. Referring to Roosevelt's "lifelong compulsion for center stage," the biographer Edmund Morris writes that "those who hated Theodore did so with passion." A fellow student of Roosevelt's at Harvard referred to him as "an excellent example of the *genus Americanus egotisticus.*"[67] Mitchell was not in the habit of playing a supporting role, and he found Roosevelt's massive ego insufferable. His dislike of Roosevelt deepened over the years. He told William Draper Lewis that he "exceedingly" disliked Roosevelt and his ways, and referred to his "personal enmity to the man, which I assure you is well-founded." He told J. William White that he so much personally disliked the man that "I have been rather careful about what I have said of him." Thrilled when Roosevelt was defeated in 1912, he wrote Mason that "above and beyond all I honestly thank God for saving the country from the rule of a man who is in my mind a demagogue and whose personal ambitions have destroyed the Republican Party." The next day he wrote Osler, "I am very happy this morning in the disastrous defeat of Roosevelt, whom I dislike personally, politically, and in every other way."[68] Rarely did Mitchell express such contempt in the public space of a letter. There were other things that upset him—the anti-vivisectionists, Walt Whitman, Marion's acting career, Langdon's extravagant spending, Osler's address on immortality—but nothing could compare to Roosevelt.

Mitchell was still thinking about Roosevelt when, late in 1912, he was asked to speak in Chicago. In December he wrote Mason, "I am terror stricken because I have accepted a request signed by some forty of your most eminent physicians to visit Chicago." They had invited him to speak at the Physicians' Club and attend a banquet in his honor. In accepting, he also asked what they wanted to hear, because "when you get a lion, you expect him to roar," and he wanted to know what to roar about. While in Chicago he also wanted to spend a day with Mason and read aloud his verse drama "Francis Drake" to her and a group of her literary friends. Mason wrote back that she did not want to tire him, that people did not enjoy listening to verse so much, and that she preferred that he give a talk about novels or drama. But oblivious and optimistic, he insisted and wanted her to understand that "what I want is to make myself pleasant to you, and whether I shall do so by reading to ten or fifty people is indifferent to me." He could give the audience a "pretty fresh sensation" and "'Drake' is better—more fetching."[69]

The subject of Mitchell's address to the Physicians' Club was Civil War medicine, and he discussed William Hammond's term as surgeon general, tent hospitals, gangrene, epilepsy, Civil War surgeons, the psychology of lost limbs, and a kind of homesickness that made men hysterical. He spoke of the regimental doctors, surgeons, and medical cadets and mentioned his brother Ned. Mitchell's major hope was that the surgeons, like other heroes and soldiers, would be recognized for their distinguished service. There had been doctors who dressed wounds with bullets flying around them, and surgeons who had operated until they fainted beside the table from fatigue. In the Union Army fifty-one surgeons were killed; thirteen were killed or wounded at Gettysburg alone. Four had died in prison, and 281 had died of disease resulting from active service. And, with Roosevelt in mind, he concluded, "Ah, when I think of the risks some of us have taken, the laboratory problems to be solved at daily personal peril, I am proud of the silence of our courage. Contrast with the thunder of the reputations made in our tiny Spanish War the tranquil, modest efficiency of that more deadly war which Reed and his officers conducted against yellow fever. I conclude that perhaps after all our way is the better. We wage no kindergarten wars!"[70] After giving this speech and reading his forty-page verse drama to Mason's friends, Mitchell returned to Philadelphia. Once there, he wrote her, "It is a calamity to be distinguished in several ways. It distracts attention, appreciation. . . . Do you think one of my hearers ran to buy 'Drake' or asked what else has he written?"[71] Mitchell knew that he could still write an engaging address on medical history, but that did not interest him so much. When he was a young boy, he had adored that "creature called a poet." Chicago was a last chance to prove his worth as one, and he was more than a little disappointed with the result.

EPILOGUE

At the age of eighty-three Mitchell began writing another novel, *Westways.* When he told Mason, she wrote back that he was brave to attempt it. "Oh, I have to," he responded, "because I can not sit down here and read all the morning and run about and play bridge all day, and I cannot walk all the time and a fellow must have something to do, and what people do with their time I really do not know." He continued to write poetry even though he had received "his lesson of neglect," feeling that the "real joy is in the use of the creative power, something like the indulgence of an instinct."[1] Overall, he felt that *Constance Trescot* was his best novel and "The Sea-Gull" and "Ode on a Lycian Tomb" were his best poems. In "The Sea-Gull" he wrote, "If I could wander on as sure a wing, / Or beat with yellow web thy pathless sea, / I too might cease to sing."[2] But sing he must. His last novel was published in 1913, the year before he died.

Mitchell frequently mentioned reading novels, including those of Edith Wharton and Henry James. He felt that Wharton was a splendid writer, but objected to her characters, especially how she felt about them. He told Mason that there "are no high-minded, well-bred, gentle folk in her books." George Darrow in *The Reef* is "a vulgar, ill-mannered blackguard. She meant him to be a gentleman; and if not, she is past praying for."[3] He wrote that *The House of Mirth* was "a great novel on the uplands of fiction," telling Howells, "It is a disagreeably sad book but—oh—very well done."[4] He wrote Wharton to say, "I take off my hat to the writer of the House of Mirth. . . . You have given me a very great pleasure."[5] He kept trying to read the novels of Henry James, what John called "depressions of America," but did so with "bewildered amazement." He wrote that "since I played cat's cradle as a child I have seen no tangle like it. To get the threads of his thought off of his mind onto mine with the intermediation of his too exasperating style has been too much for me. . . . I am too old to learn a new language and still struggle to write my own with clearness." He felt there was a large and a small way of dealing with a novel's canvas: "Thackeray had a large way. Henry James is a miniature painter to the verge of Lilliputian art, in what he says about a smile, a look, or a word of one of his characters." Finally Mitchell quit trying, writing, "I do not read Henry James, not because I do not see a certain greatness in his powers, but because this immense analysis seems to me unnatural and because I expect a novel to interest me."[6]

When Prime Minister Asquith conferred a baronetcy on Osler, Mitchell wrote, "Tell your son I killed a 45 pound salmon last week, and two days before three, 40, 39, 29, lbs. Of less importance is it that you are a Bart. What is that to me, for whom you are long ago high in the *peerage* of Friendship a lessening number alas! I can count among the survivors—four—only four. Time has terribly dealt with that splendid peerage—Lowell, Holmes, Alex, Agassiz, Brooks—and last Ch. Norton—and Aldrich; and I am last of nine children save one Sister. Therefore please to take care of the new Baronet."[7] Since his student days in Paris, friends had provided affection and stimulation for Mitchell, and he wrote, "I am rich in friends and have a talent that way." He delighted in meetings, dinners, and travel with prominent men like Holmes, Brooks, Keen, Osler, Billings, and Cadwalader. These friendships became lifelong relationships of correspondence, gift exchanges, and professional collaboration.[8] He dedicated his biographical piece on George Washington, *The Youth of Washington*, to Billings: "In Grateful Remembrance of Forty Years of Friendship." He wrote, "To dedicate it to you has given me a very great pleasure. There are few—very few entirely satisfying friendships but surely our's has been of them—and—has been through some forty years a source of happiness to me, of keen intellectual sympathies, and—without a word or act I could wish had been other than it was." Billings had always looked up to Mitchell, and in a few days he wrote his wife, "I have a very fine little letter from Weir Mitchell, which I enclose. Please take great care of it—it is better than an LL.D."[9] When Billings died in March 1913, a month after Mitchell's Chicago trip, he was devastated. Although he had his wife, sons, daughters-in-law, and grandchildren close to him, he wrote Osler, "My friends are fast falling, by the way, and this last loss was a far more serious calamity to me than would seem likely to hardened old age. . . . I grow not less but more sensitive as time runs on. The stated engagements of the Carnegie Trust once a month brought Billings and me together so often that we were not separated as busy men are apt to be. I have always dreaded the arctic loneliness of age, and now alas!"[10]

Though plagued by insomnia, the "grippe," and deafness, Mitchell believed that his mind was as active and strong as ever. Osler and Mason continued to compliment him on his energy, enthusiasm, and mental strength. After seeing him at the memorial for Billings, Osler wrote, "It was good to see you again and in such fine form. I never heard you speak more clearly and to the point than at the Billings meeting. How I wish I could see you on the river tackling a salmon! So long as you can do this do not talk of old age. You have done more in the past twenty years than many an active-minded man in a life-time."[11]

Mitchell was the president of the Franklin Inn Club, and in the years just before his death he was in the habit of sending a great salmon to its members. In June 1913 he sent the largest ever, weighing thirty-nine pounds. A friend and fellow member of the club wrote that "the steward's ovens would not hold it, and it was cut into parts before it could be baked for the use of the members, who at such times were assembled by letter and telephone to enjoy the feast."[12]

That fall, Mitchell wrote Osler that John had fallen while horseback riding and broken two ribs and his collarbone, and his condition "has been extremely grave. When he will do any work again I do not know. He was not in a satisfactory condition when the accident happened, nor has he been for a good while. He seems to be older than his years. . . . I have been obliged to ask that he be relieved of his clinics and hospital work for the winter. You may imagine what this is to me, knowing as you do the unusual affection which binds us together; there is rarely so perfect a tie in the case of John and me."[13] That Christmas, with another Civil War article on his desk, Mitchell caught the flu, which developed quickly into pneumonia. Haunted by bodies ravaged by gunshot wounds and burning pain, delirious with thoughts of the war, he spent his final moments raving about Gettysburg. He died on January 4, 1914.

It was the eve of World War I, and as Mason put it, Mitchell was "spared this senseless, appalling, inconceivable war. It seems the end of civilization."[14] John wired Osler the same day, "Father died this morning." On the telegram Osler wrote that Mitchell was one of his dearest friends and "had I been a son he could not have been kinder to me during the five years of my life in Philadelphia."[15] He inserted the telegram and Mitchell's last two letters, dated November 29 and December 20, in his presentation copy of "Ode on a Lycian Tomb." Mary Mitchell, after asking individuals and organizations to refrain from sending bouquets to the funeral, filled St. Stephen's Church with white flowers. People packed the church and spilled into the streets. Newspaper headlines read "Giant of Intellect: Noted in Field of Medicine and Scientific Research—as

Author and Poet Honored at Home and Abroad," "Quaker City Mourns Dr. S. Weir Mitchell," and "Writer and Savant, Claimed by Death."[16] Just one week after the funeral, Mary Mitchell died. John Cadwalader died within the year. Three years later John died. Osler's son and only child, Revere, who was twenty-two, was killed in Belgium after taking shrapnel in the chest, abdomen, and thigh. Osler, after living through the horrors of the war, died in 1919. Mason was right. Mitchell had escaped these long and painful years, and in many ways he had lived a charmed existence, or so he made it seem. He wrote in the poem "Vesperal," "I know the night is near at hand. . . . But I have had the day. / Yes, I have had, dear Lord, the day."

NOTES

There are at least two versions of Mitchell's unpublished autobiography, one at the College of Physicians of Philadelphia and a second, shorter version at the Historical Society of Pennsylvania titled "Second draft after original July 1, 1943." I rely entirely on the College of Physicians version, a manuscript of more than three hundred pages with two and sometimes three sets of page numbers. In citations I use the page number appearing along the top of each page.

ABBREVIATIONS

AB	Mitchell's unpublished autobiography, S. Weir Mitchell Papers, College of Physicians of Philadelphia Historical Medical Library
AGM	Amelia Gere Mason
Beinecke	Beinecke Rare Book and Manuscript Library, Yale University
CPG	Charlotte Perkins Gilman
CPP	S. Weir Mitchell Papers, College of Physicians of Philadelphia Historical Medical Library
Cushing/Whitney	Harvey Cushing/John Hay Whitney Medical Library, Yale University
DUMC	Duke University Medical Center Library, Trent Collection, History of Medicine Collections
EDM	Edward Donaldson Mitchell
EKM	Elizabeth Kearsley Mitchell
Harvard Medical	Harvard Medical Library in the Francis A. Countway Library of Medicine
Houghton	Houghton Library, Harvard University
HSP	Historical Society of Pennsylvania
JKM	John Kearsley Mitchell
NYP	John Shaw Billings Papers and S. Weir Mitchell Correspondence, both in Manuscripts and Archives Division, New York Public Library, Astor, Lenox, and Tilden Foundations
OL	Olser Library of the History of Medicine, McGill University, P100, Sir William Osler Collection
OWH	Oliver Wendell Holmes
RBML, UPenn	Rare Book and Manuscript Library, University of Pennsylvania
SBW	Sarah Butler Wister
Schlesinger	Schlesinger Library, Radcliffe Institute for Advanced Study, Harvard University
SMM	Sarah Matilda Mitchell
SWM	Silas Weir Mitchell

WDH   William Dean Howells
WO   William Osler

INTRODUCTION

1. AB, 3.

2. Osler, "Obituary," 121; Keen, "Address," 256.

3. SWM to EKM, 15 August 1856, CPP; SWM to AGM, 4 April 1900, CPP; SWM to SBW, 26 August [1897], Wister and Butler Families Papers (Collection 1962), HSP; SWM to SMM, 19 November 1850, CPP.

4. Louis, "Silas Weir Mitchell's Essential Tremor," 1218–20. Louis traces the onset and development of Mitchell's tremor through an analysis of handwriting samples, and states that "early handwriting samples reveal no tremor."

5. SWM to AGM, 4 April 1900, CPP; SWM to AGM, 30 July 1909, CPP; SWM to AGM, 25 May 1912, CPP.

6. The children's literature written by Mitchell includes *The Children's Hour* (in collaboration with Elizabeth Wister Stevenson for the benefit of the Sanitary Commission), 1864; *The Wonderful Stories of Fuz-Buz the Fly and Mother Grabem the Spider*, 1866; *Prince Little Boy, and Other Tales out of Fairyland*, 1888; and *Mr. Kris Kringle: A Christmas Tale*, 1893.

7. Metzer, "Experimentation," 303–4. Wharton Sinkler read the paper at the annual meeting of the American Neurological Society in 1896, and it was published in the *British Medical Journal* as "Remarks on the Effects of *Anhelonium lewinii*."

8. SWM to SBW, 24 September 1899, Wister and Butler Families Papers (Collection 1962), HSP; SWM to Helena De Kay Gilder, 4 April 1911, RBML, UPenn, MS 413, box 1.

9. See Strouse, *Alice James*, 324 where Strouse discusses similar problems with Burr's publication of Alice James's diary.

CHAPTER I

1. SWM, *Two Lectures*, 51, 32.

2. SWM to WO, 4 January 1909, OL.

3. SWM, *Brief History*, 9.

4. Ibid., 14, 19–25.

5. AB, 25–26.

6. JKM to SMM, n.d., CPP.

7. AB, 53, 82.

8. SWM, "Address to the Students of Radcliffe College," 21–22.

9. Neilson, "Recollections," 303. Sarah (Saidie) Mitchell Neilson's "Recollections" are incorporated into Mitchell's autobiography, pp. 296–310.

10. JKM, *Oration*, 26–27.

11. JKM, *Lecture*, 11, 16.

12. Moore, "Higher Education of Women," 296, 297. The address was subsequently published in the *British Medical Journal*.

13. Walter, *S. Weir Mitchell*, 15, 21.

14. JKM, *Introductory Lecture*, 17.

15. SWM to AGM, 22 November 1894, CPP.

16. Neilson, "Recollections," 300.

17. AB, 31–32.

18. Ibid., 53, 56–57.

19. Neilson, "Recollections," 304.

20. AB, 52.

21. Ibid., 48-49.

22. Ibid., 41.

23. Ibid., 78, 81, 55.

24. Ibid., 82, 26.

25. Ibid., 83-85.

26. Ibid., 86-87.

27. SWM to Brander Matthews, n.d., University of Iowa Libraries, Iowa City.

28. AB, 51, 58-61.

29. Ibid., 64-68.

30. Ibid., 80-81, 92, 71, 90-91.

31. JKM, *Impediments*, 10, 6, 8.

32. AB, 91-92.

33. *Annual Announcement of Jefferson Medical College of Philadelphia*. Although the *Announcement* stated that a candidate for a medical degree "had to study medicine for no less than three years," Mitchell attended for only two sessions, 1848-49 and 1849-50.

34. AB, 87.

35. Colombat, *Treatise*, 17.

36. Ibid., 4, 72, 474.

37. Ibid., 544, 562.

38. Meigs, *Females and Their Diseases*, 348, 364-65, 363-64, 661.

39. Morantz-Sanchez, *Sympathy and Science*, 67.

40. AB, 94.

41. Ibid., 94-95.

42. SWM to EKM, [15 January?] 1849, CPP.

43. Fye, *Development of American Physiology*, 57.

44. SWM, *Two Lectures*, 51.

CHAPTER 2

1. SWM to SMM, 15 October 1850, CPP; SWM to SMM, [November 1850], CPP.

2. SWM to SMM, [November 1850], CPP; SWM to Chapman, Walsh, and Ned Mitchell, [November 1850], CPP.

3. EKM to JKM, 29 November [1850], CPP.

4. SWM to SMM, [November 1850] CPP; SMM to SWM, 4 January 1851, CPP.

5. SWM to SMM, 19 November 1850, CPP.

6. SWM to JKM, 14 November 1850, CPP.

7. AB, 101.

8. SWM to JKM, 14 November 1850, CPP.

9. Record, November 12, 1850, Meeting of the Royal Medical and Chirurgical Society, *Lancet*, 583.

10. Ibid., 584, 585-86, 586-87.

11. SWM to JKM, 14 November 1850, CPP.

12. Record, November 25, 1851, Meeting of the Royal Medical and Chirurgical Society, *Lancet*, 536, 540.

13. Moscucci, *Science of Woman*, 137; Wood, "Fashionable Diseases," 48.

14. Moscucci, *Science of Woman*, 153, 124; Wood, "Fashionable Diseases," 48.

15. JKM to SWM, 20 January 1851, CPP; Moscucci, *Science of Woman*, 152.

16. AB, 108.

17. Earnest, *S. Weir Mitchell*, 34-35.

18. Walter, *S. Weir Mitchell*, 28.

19. Louis, "Silas Weir Mitchell's Essential Tremor," 1220, 1219.

20. Barker-Benfield, *Horrors*, 130. Barker-Benfield writes that Mitchell castrated women, but he provides no documentation.

21. Mitchell, *Clinical Lessons*, 45. See also "Treatment by Rest," where Mitchell writes, "For a long while too much was said of the ovary. Then the pathologic criminals were derelict kidneys. Just now the hooded clitoris is indicted. So much for the surgeon" (2036).

22. SWM, "Relations of Nervous Disorders in Women to Pelvic Disease," 1.

23. AB, 102; SWM to JKM, 21 November 1850, CPP.

24. SWM, *Two Lectures*, 35.

25. SWM to JKM, 21 November 1850, CPP.

26. SWM to SMM, [November 1850], CPP.

27. SWM to "Sisters," [November 1850], CPP.

28. SWM to SMM, [November 1850], CPP.

29. SWM to SMM, [November 1850], CPP; SWM to "Dear Boys," [December 1850], CPP.

30. SWM to SMM, [November 1850], CPP.

31. SWM to JKM, 15 January 1851, CPP.

32. SWM to JKM, April [1851], CPP.

33. Bynum, *Science*, 100, 123.

34. Cushing, *Life of Sir William Osler*, 1:284.

35. Goetz, Bonduelle, and Gelfand, *Charcot*, 8.

36. Goetz, "Jean-Martin Charcot," 1128.

37. Gardner, quoted in Goetz, Bonduelle, and Gelfand, *Charcot*, 12.

38. Goetz, Bonduelle, and Gelfand, *Charcot*, 14.

39. Ibid., 14–16.

40. SWM to SMM, 27 January [1851], CPP.

41. AB, 104–6.

42. SWM to SMM [January 1851], CPP.

43. SWM to EKM, [January 1851], CPP; SWM to JKM, 15 January 1851, CPP; SWM to Chapman, Walsh, and Ned Mitchell, 16 January [1851], CPP.

44. SWM to EKM, 2 February [1851], CPP; SWM to JKM, 3 April 1851, CPP.

45. JKM to SWM, 24 March 1851, CPP.

46. EKM to JKM, 29 November [1850], CPP.

47. EKM to SWM, 26 March 1851, CPP.

48. AB, 76; Neilson, "Recollections," 299; AB, 75.

49. SWM to AGM, 22 November 1894, CPP.

50. SWM, *When All the Woods Are Green*, 8.

51. Ibid, 66, 108, 44, 395, 131.

52. JKM to EKM, 6 November 1840, CPP; SWM to JKM, 3 April 1851, CPP; SWM to JKM, 12 May 1851, CPP.

53. SWM to JKM, [June 1851], CPP.

54. SWM to Robert Walsh Mitchell, 13 August 1851, CPP.

55. AB, 118–19, 112.

56. SWM to Robert Walsh Mitchell, 13 August 1851, CPP.

CHAPTER 3

1. SWM, "Memoir of John Call Dalton," 179.

2. Fye, *Development of American Physiology*, 5.

3. SWM, "Memoir of John Call Dalton," 180.

4. AB, 132.

5. Fye, *Development of American Physiology*, 58.

6. SWM, *Red City*, 213.

7. Duffy, *From Humors to Medical Science*, 65.

8. Ibid., 73, 70.

9. SWM, "Review of *Leçons de physiologie expérimentale*," 529–32.

10. Ibid., 546–47.

11. AB, 111.

12. SWM to Professor Dickson, 9 April 1858, CPP.

13. SWM to Captain H. M. Naglee, 1 January 1856, CPP.

14. AB, 139.

15. SWM to EKM, 15 August 1856, CPP.

16. EKM to SWM, 20 August 1856, CPP.

17. EKM to Bessie Kane, 16 August [1856], CPP.

18. SWM to Professor Dickson, 9 April 1858, CPP.

19. Ibid.

20. AB, 96, 144, 74–75, 145.

21. Ibid., 145, 74.

22. SWM and Hammond, "Experimental Examination" (both in the *Medical Journal and Review* and the *Proceedings of the Academy of Natural Science*).

23. SWM, "Treatment of Rattlesnake Bites," 270–71.

24. SWM, "Poison of the Rattlesnake," 453.

25. SWM and Reichert, *Researches*, 5, 157.

26. Fontana, *Treatise*, 108, xv, 31.

27. Greene, *Snakes*, 304–5.

28. SWM, "Treatment of Rattlesnake Bites," 269.

29. SWM, *Researches*, 8, 16, 12, 6, 27, 22.

30. For a discussion of structural systems and metaphor, see Lakoff and Johnson, *Metaphors We Live By*, 115, 146.

31. Shine, *Australian Snakes*, 176.

32. Fontana, *Treatise*, ii.

33. SWM, *Researches*, 24n1.

34. SWM, "Poison of Serpents," 507.

35. Ibid.

36. SWM, "Poison of the Rattlesnake," 453.

37. SWM, *Researches*, 3, 5.

38. SWM, "Poison of the Rattlesnake," 455–56.

39. SWM, *Researches*, 46, 57, 71, 87.

40. SWM and Reichert, *Researches*, 43, 54.

41. SWM, *Researches*, 27–28n1.

42. SWM to Jeffries Wyman, 21 May 1861, H MS c12.2, Harvard Medical.

43. Lederer, *Subjected to Science*, 28.

44. SWM, *Researches*, 40.

45. Ibid., 71, 73, 83–84, 64.

46. Robert Walsh Mitchell to SWM, 2 July 1859, CPP; EDM to SWM, 29 October 1863, CPP; EDM to SWM, 21 November 1863, CPP.

47. SWM, *Researches*, 79, 68.

48. Lederer, *Subjected to Science*, 27–28.

49. Elston, "Women and Anti-vivisection," 265.

50. Bernard, *Introduction*, 102.

51. Charles-Edouard Brown-Séquard to SWM, 20 July 1861, DUMC.

52. Dalton, "Vivisection," 35, 36.

53. OWH to SWM, 28 December 1858, DUMC.

54. Small, "Afterword," 364.

55. Holmes, *Elsie Venner*, 16–18.

56. SWM to OWH, 23 March 1859, Houghton, bMS Am 1241.1 (742); SWM to OWH, n.d., Houghton, bMS Am 1241.1 (471); OWH to SWM, 25 February 1861, DUMC.

57. OWH to SWM, 28 December 1858, DUMC.

58. Allen, *Life and Letters*, 1:598; Woolverton, *Education of Phillips Brooks*, 5.

59. SWM, "Appreciation of Phillips Brooks," 631–33.

60. SWM to EKM, [1 July 1861], CPP; EDM to SWM, 21 November 1863, CPP; SWM to EKM, [1 July 1861], CPP.

61. SMM to EKM, [3 July 1861?], CPP; JKM to SWM, 11 November 1850, CPP; Robert Walsh Mitchell to SWM, 17 April 1859, CPP; Robert Walsh Mitchell to SWM, 12 July 1859, CPP.

62. SWM to EKM, [1 July 1861], CPP; AB, 77.

63. SWM to EKM, 17 August 1859, CPP.

64. AB, 144.

CHAPTER 4

1. Fye, "S. Weir Mitchell," 192; Fye, *Development of American Physiology*, 62.

2. SWM to EKM, [1863?], CPP. Mitchell would later revise his view. In his 1891 sonnet "Lincoln," he wrote, "Most was he like to Luther, gay and great, / Solemn and mirthful, strong of heart and limb."

3. SWM to EKM, [10 August 1862], CPP.

4. EDM to William Williams Keen, 8 December 1862, CPP; EDM to SMM, 23 May 1863, CPP.

5. SWM, "Medical Department in the Civil War," 1449.

6. SWM to EKM, n.d., CPP.

7. SMM to EKM, [July 1860?], CPP; SMM to EKM, [1864?], CPP; SWM to EKM, 31 August 1865, CPP.

8. SWM to EKM, [1863], CPP.

9. SWM to Jeffries Wyman, 4 February [March?], 1863, H MS c12.2, Harvard Medical. Mitchell misdated this letter. See Fye, "S. Weir Mitchell," 195n30.

10. Fye, *Development of American Physiology*, 66–67.

11. Joseph Henry to SWM, 7 May 1863, Reynolds Historical Library, quoted in Fye, "S. Weir Mitchell," 197; John Call Dalton to SWM, 17 May 1863, Trent Collection, quoted in Fye, "S. Weir Mitchell," 198.

12. For a full discussion of medical cadets and their duties, see Hasegawa, "Civil War's Medical Cadets." Overall, 273 men served for one year or more as cadets during the Civil War. Of these men, 111 became commissioned or contract surgeons.

13. EDM to "Sister," 9 July 1863, CPP.

14. EDM to SMM, 29 December 1863, CPP.

15. Peters, "Evils of Youthful Enlistments," quoted in Deutsch, "Military Psychiatry," 374–75.

16. Calhoun, "Nostalgia as a Disease," quoted in Deutsch, "Military Psychiatry," 375–76. The *Medical and Surgical History of the War of the Rebellion, 1861–1865* records 5,213 cases of nostalgia among the white Northern troops during the first year of the war.

17. EDM to SWM, 8 September 1863, CPP; EDM to SMM, 18 September 1863, CPP; EDM to SWM, 24 September 1863, CPP.

18. EDM to SMM, 14 November 1863; EDM to SWM, 11 December 1863, CPP.

19. AB, 214, 77.

20. SWM, *Complete Poems*, 270.

21. SWM to EKM, n.d., CPP.

22. SWM to EKM, 26 July 1863, CPP.

23. SWM to EKM, 1 August [1863], CPP.

24. AB, 148–49.

25. Rylance, "The Theatre and the Granary," 267.

26. SWM to EKM, [August 1864], CPP.

27. Canale, "S. Weir Mitchell's Prose," 18n9. Reflex paralysis was first described by Mitchell, Morehouse, and Keen as a loss of motor and sensory function in an extremity that was remote from the site of injury, usually caused by gunshot wounds. Canale writes that the condition has not been recorded in modern accounts of gunshot wounds. John Fulton called "Reflex Paralysis," which was issued by the Surgeon General's Office as "Circular No. 6," one of the great milestones in the history of American neurology. However, in 1982 Russell DeJong questioned this assessment, writing that the paralysis in these cases was probably not organic and the publication of the circular was "unfortunate." Canale agrees with DeJong.

28. SWM, *Injuries of Nerves*, vi; Richards, "Causalgia," 349.

29. SWM, "On the Diseases of Nerves," 439.

30. Mitchell, Morehouse, and Keen, *Gunshot Wounds*, 101, 80, 86, 112.

31. SWM, "On the Diseases of Nerves," 449.

32. Scarry, *Body in Pain*, 54.

33. Mitchell, Morehouse, and Keen, *Gunshot Wounds*, 101.

34. For two of Mitchell's references to a quadruple amputee, see AB, 173; and "Phantom Limbs," 564. See also "Weir Mitchell's First Story," where Cavanagh writes that *The Medical and Surgical History of the Rebellion* reported on approximately thirty thousand amputations, but only 172 were double. Eighty-two of these cases involved the loss of both legs, but no triple or quadruple amputations were included.

35. For critical discussions of "The Case of George Dedlow," see Canale, "Civil War Medicine"; Goler, "Loss and the Persistence of Memory"; Herschbach, "True Clinical Fictions"; Journet, "Phantom Limbs and 'Body-Ego'"; Katz, "Flesh of His Flesh"; Long, "Corporeity of Heaven"; Long, *Rehabilitating Bodies*; Louis, Horn, and Roth, "Neurologic Content of S. Weir Mitchell's Fiction"; Michaels, *The Gold Standard and the Logic of Naturalism*, 23–25; O'Connor, *Raw Material*, 103–47; Rylance, "The Theatre and the Granary"; Schneck, "S. Weir Mitchell."

36. SWM, "Case of George Dedlow," 120–21.

37. Adams, *Doctors in Blue*, 94–95. Adams writes that Chickamauga was "one of the worst medical failures of the war." After the first of two days of fighting, 4,500 Union soldiers were wounded. When the fighting moved farther north the next day, the Confederates bombarded the hospitals, claiming that they had mistaken the hospital flags for those of battle.

38. SWM, "Case of George Dedlow," 129.

39. AB, 263–66; SWM to George M. Gould, n.d., CPP. See also the three letters (undated) written by Mitchell to William James at the Houghton Library.

40. AB, 174; SWM, introduction to *Autobiography of a Quack*, ix–x.

41. Louis, Horn, and Roth, "Neurologic Content of S. Weir Mitchell's Fiction," 403, 405. This article analyzes the extent to which neurologic topics are present in Mitchell's fiction and whether the fictional accounts of neurologic topics precede, parallel, or follow his presentation of the topics in the scientific literature.

42. SWM, "Phantom Limbs," 564.

43. Long, *Rehabilitating Bodies*, 42.

44. It appears, for example, in *Literature and Science in the Nineteenth Century: An Anthology*, edited by Laura Otis, and *To Live and Die: Collected Stories of the Civil War, 1861–1876*, edited by Kathleen Diffley, both published in 2002.

45. Richards, "Causalgia," 341.

46. SWM, Morehouse, and Keen, *Gunshot Wounds*, 109–11; see also SWM, *Injuries of Nerves*, 292–95.

47. Scarry, *Body in Pain*, 173.

48. SWM, Morehouse, and Keen, *Gunshot Wounds*, 23–24.

49. McPherson, *Battle Cry*, 473–75.

50. SWM, Morehouse, and Keen, *Gunshot Wounds*, 52–54, 35.

51. McPherson, *Battle Cry*, 854; Figg and Farrell-Beck, "Amputation in the Civil War," 454.

52. SWM, "Medical Department in the Civil War," 1446.

53. SWM, "Case of George Dedlow," 121–24.

54. SWM, Morehouse, and Keen, *Gunshot Wounds*, 105.

55. Ibid., 103, 89. Schively's case history also appears in SWM, *Injuries of Nerves*, 302; and SWM, "On the Diseases of Nerves," 463.

56. SWM, Morehouse, and Keen, *Gunshot Wounds*, 149–50, 151. Marks's case history also appears in SWM, *Injuries of Nerves*, 273; and SWM, "On the Diseases of Nerves," 448.

57. Tom Lutz makes this argument in *American Nervousness*, 32.

58. SWM, "Case of George Dedlow," 132, 133.

59. SWM, *Injuries of Nerves*, 348, 350, 359, 351.

60. Krasner, "Doubtful Arms and Phantom Limbs," 229, 231n8.

61. Ramachandran and Blakeslee, *Phantoms in the Brain*, 23. They write that according to the nerve irritation theory, "The frayed and curled-up nerve endings in the stump (neuromas) that originally supplied the hand tend to become inflamed and irritated, thereby fooling higher brain centers into thinking that the missing limb is still there."

62. Ibid., 39–40, 29, 40.

63. SWM, "Case of George Dedlow," 134–36, 137.

64. Ibid., 136, 138.

65. O'Connor, *Raw Material*, 124, 126.

66. SWM, "Case of George Dedlow," 139. See Canale, "Civil War Medicine," 16, where he writes that "awareness of one's self is of course a higher cortical brain function," and has "nothing to do with one's total body mass."

67. SWM, "Case of George Dedlow," 135.

68. SWM, Morehouse, and Keen, "On the Antagonism of Atropia and Morphia," 67–68.

69. SWM, *Injuries of Nerves*, 268–69.

CHAPTER 5

1. AB, 123–24.

2. SWM, *Complete Poems*, 287; AB, 124–27.

3. SWM to William Williams Keen, 8 February 1865, CPP.

4. SWM to George M. Gould, 9 December 1899, CPP.

5. SWM, "Autobiography of a Quack," 468–70.

6. Ibid., 591.

7. Ibid., 594–95.

8. SWM, *In War Time*, 4, 23.

9. Ibid., 17, 78, 20.

10. AB, 132.

11. *In War Time*, 17, 339–40.

12. SWM to AGM, 19 July 1912, CPP.

13. Elizabeth Stuart Phelps to SWM, 18 November 1884, CPP.

14. SWM to Jeffries Wyman, 14 April [1868], H MS c12.2, Harvard Medical.

15. Norwood, "Medical Education," 487.

16. Charles-Edouard Brown-Séquard to the Board of Trustees of the Jefferson Medical College, 16 April 1868, DUMC.

17. Fye, *Development of American Physiology*, 69–70.

18. SWM to John Mitchell, 16 November 1873, CPP.

19. SWM to Jeffries Wyman, 10 June [1868], H MS c12.2, Harvard Medical.

20. Fye, *Development of American Physiology*, 74.

21. Chapman, *Order Out of Chaos*, 128, 132.

22. AB, 232–33; Fye, *Development of American Physiology*, 76.

23. SWM to EKM, 31 August 1865, CPP; SWM to Jeffries Wyman, 10 June [1868], H MS c12.2, Harvard Medical.

24. SWM, *In War Time*, 6.

25. EKM to Phillips Brooks, 29 August 1869, Houghton, bMS Am 1594.1 (418).

26. SWM, "Appreciation of Phillips Brooks," 1:635.

27. Woolverton, *Education of Phillips Brooks*, 111.

28. SWM, "Appreciation of Phillips Brooks," 1:635.

29. SWM to EKM, 2 July 1872, CPP.

30. SWM to EKM, 27 August 1872, CPP.

31. SWM to EKM, n.d., CPP.

32. SWM to Chapman Mitchell, 9 August [1873], CPP; SWM to EKM, 15 [August 1873], CPP.

33. SWM to EKM, [15 August 1873], CPP; SWM to EKM, [27 August 1873], CPP; SWM to Chapman Mitchell, 28 August 1873, CPP.

34. Allen, *Life and Letters*, 2:45, 2:87–89.

35. SWM to JKM, [1874], CPP; SWM to JKM, 7 June 1874, CPP; SWM to JKM, 27 September 1874, CPP; SWM to JKM, 20 November 1874, CPP.

36. SWM to JKM, 16 November 1873, CPP.

37. SWM to JKM, 15 February 1875, CPP.

38. SWM to JKM, 11 April 1876, CPP.

39. SWM to JKM, 18 October 1873, CPP.

40. SWM to JKM, 28 March 1875, CPP.

41. SWM to JKM, [1875?], CPP; SWM to JKM, 16 November 1875, CPP.

42. SWM to JKM, n.d., CPP; SWM to JKM, n.d., CPP.

43. SWM to JKM, 4 April 1875, CPP.

44. SWM to EKM, 11 July 1868, CPP; SWM to Cassy Meredith, n.d., Menninger Foundation Archives.

45. SWM to JKM, 13 April [1875], CPP.

46. SWM to JKM, 13 April [1875], CPP; SWM to AGM, 30 March 1913, CPP.

47. SWM to JKM, 6 June 1875, CPP; SWM to JKM, 16 November 1875, CPP.

48. Oberholtzer, "Personal Memories," 132–33.

CHAPTER 6

1. SWM, "Evolution of the Rest Treatment," 368.

2. Keen, "Address" 257.

3. SWM, "Address of Dr. S. Weir Mitchell to the Nurse–Graduates." Mitchell gave this address, which provides an overview of the infirmary's history and services, on the first occasion that the hospital held a public ceremony for its nurse graduates.

4. Pappert, "Philadelphia Infirmary," 1848, 1849.

5. AB, 135. See pp. 132–37 for Mitchell's discussion of the Orthopedic Hospital.

6. Pappert, "Philadelphia Infirmary," 1851; Keen, "Address," 258.

7. Keen, "Address," 257.

8. SWM to EKM, [1871], CPP.

9. Ibid.

10. SWM to JKM, [1874], CPP.

11. James, "Consciousness of Lost Limbs," 249, 258.

12. Walter, *S. Weir Mitchell*, 105–10.

13. SWM, *Lectures*, 121.

14. SWM, "Evolution of the Rest Treatment," 372.

15. Bassuk, "Rest Cure," 256.

16. SWM, *Fat and Blood*, 37.

17. SWM, *Lectures*, 85.

18. SWM, *Fat and Blood*, 35.

19. SWM, *Nurse and Patient, and Camp Cure*, 31.

20. SWM, *Fat and Blood*, 25–26.

21. SWM, "Annual Oration," 14–15.

22. SWM, *Fat and Blood*, 54–55.

23. Ibid., 39, 43–44, 91.

24. Tucker, "Speaking of Weir Mitchell," 343.

25. Burr, *Weir Mitchell*, 184.

26. Goodman and Dawson, *William Dean Howells*, 294. Although Goodman and Dawson cite Burr, to my knowledge they are the first to use the word "rape" in retelling this story.

27. SWM, "Treatment by Rest," 2036.

28. Playfair, "Notes on the Systematic Treatment," 131–32.

29. Porter, "The Body and the Mind," 256.

30. SWM, "Rest in the Treatment of Nervous Disease," 94.

31. SWM, *Lectures*, 15, 60–61.

32. Ibid., 32, 31.

33. Ibid., 45.

34. Ibid., 13–14; Osler, "The Faith That Heals," quoted in Cushing, *Life of Sir William Osler*, 2:223.

35. SWM, *Lectures*, 16.

36. Ibid., 41–42.

37. Ibid., 67–68, 74.

38. Ibid., 215–16.

39. Ibid., 115–19.

40. Porter, "The Body and the Mind," 261.

41. SWM, *Lectures*, 233.

42. Mary Putnam Jacobi to SWM, 3 June [1891?], CPP.

43. SWM, *Doctor and Patient*, 10.

44. SWM to AGM, 22 November 1912, CPP.

45. SWM, *Lectures*, 202; SWM, *Wear and Tear*, 32, 30–31.

46. Emmet, *Principles and Practice of Gynaecology*, 18–19.

47. SWM, *Fat and Blood*, 28; SWM, *Lectures*, 14.

48. Lazarus, "Higher Education," 315; SWM, "Address to the Students of Radcliffe College," 21–22.

49. SWM, *Doctor and Patient*, 151–52.

50. Mosedale, "Science Corrupted," 1.

51. Walter, *S. Weir Mitchell*, 141.

CHAPTER 7

1. SWM to EKM, 11 July 1868, CPP.

2. Mitchell told Elizabeth that one woman he met was "like some finely made thoroughbred and was not even handsome." SWM to EKM, 27 August 1872, CPP. In *Characteristics*, 143, he wrote, "The woman's distress of mind was evident to me, but she had all of that self-control which belongs to the thoroughbred woman."

3. SWM to Chapman Mitchell, 9 August [1873?], CPP.

4. SWM, *Doctor and Patient*, 139–40.

5. AB, 312; James, *Bostonians*, 312. *The Bostonians* was first published in serial form by *The Century Magazine* between 1885 and 1886.

6. Goldberg, "Breaking New Ground," 196, 198.

7. Sigerman, "Unfinished Battle," 263.

8. Sigerman, "Laborers for Liberty," 313–14.

9. SWM, *Wear and Tear*, 44.

10. SWM to OWH, 23 March 1859, Houghton, bMS Am 1241.1 (742); SWM, *Fat and Blood*, 14; SWM, *Wear and Tear*, 23–24; SWM, *Lectures*, 127, 130.

11. The author gratefully acknowledges the assistance of David G. Schuster for his discussion in "Personalizing Illness and Modernity" of the life of Amelia Gere Mason and her friendship with Mitchell.

12. AGM to SWM, 30 November 1885, CPP; AGM to SWM, 27 December 1886, CPP.

13. SWM, *Wear and Tear*, 48, 35–36, 57.

14. In *Power and Passion*, 230–32, Horowitz discusses Carey Thomas's anti-Semitism. In *Edith Wharton*, 612, Lee discusses Wharton's "snobbery, racism, anti-Semitism and anti-feminism," which "are much more crudely voiced (as is almost always the case with the bigotry of intelligent people) in her private letters than in her fiction." In *To "Herland" and Beyond*, 255, Lane writes, "Although Gilman's racist, anti-Semitic, and ethnocentric ideas are most apparent in her personal writings, in her letters and journals, these biases inevitably limit and scar her theoretical work as well."

15. Whitman, *Brooklyn Daily News*, May 6 1858, quoted in Reynolds, *Walt Whitman's America*, 372–73; Whitman, *Prose Works*, quoted in Reynolds, *Walt Whitman's America*, 470.

16. CPG, "Suggestion on the Negro Problem," 176–77, 178, 179.

17. Ball, "Silas Weir Mitchell," 122.

18. Tucker, "Speaking of Weir Mitchell," 343.

19. SWM, "Rest in the Treatment of Nervous Disease," 84.

20. SWM, *Lectures*, 77–78, 81.

21. SWM, *Doctor and Patient*, 98.

22. SWM, *Two Lectures*, 47.

23. Mitchell, Morehouse, and Keen, *Gunshot Wounds*, 103; SWM, *Doctor and Patient*, 93.

24. SWM, *Doctor and Patient*, 48–49.

25. WDH to William C. Howells, 18 November 1888, in *William Dean Howells: Selected Letters*, 3:235 (hereafter cited as *Selected Letters*).

26. Crowley, *Mask of Fiction*, 95.

27. WDH to William C. Howells, 25 November 1888, *Selected Letters*, 3:235n1.

28. WDH to William C. Howells, 25 November 1888, *Selected Letters*, 3:235n1; WDH to William C. Howells, 23 December 1888, *Selected Letters*, 3:241; WDH to William C. Howells, 6 January 1889, *Selected Letters*, 3:243n4; WDH to William C. Howells, 4 March 1889, *Selected Letters*, 3:246.

29. Cady, *Realist at War*, 98. Cady writes that "Mitchell apparently ran an autopsy and discovered that nothing could really have saved Winifred. That her disease was organic, not merely psychic, and that her pain had been all too physiologically real." See also Lynn, *William Dean Howells*, 298, who writes that an "autopsy showed that her affliction had been organic."

30. WDH to SWM, 7 March 1889, *Selected Letters*, 3:247; WDH to Henry James, 7 June 1889, *Selected Letters*, 3:253.

31. Goodman and Dawson, *William Dean Howells*, 298.

32. WDH to William C. Howells, 4 March 1889, *Selected Letters*, 3:246.

33. Tucker, *S. Weir Mitchell*, 15.

34. JKM to SWM, 13 March 1899, CPP.

35. SWM, diary entries, 19 January 1898, CPP.

36. Crowley, *Mask of Fiction*, 98. For Howells's reference to the Merchantville rest home where Winifred died, see WDH to William C. Howells, 4 March 1889, *Selected Letters*, 3:246.

37. Schuster, "Personalizing Illness and Modernity," 718.

38. Dock, "But One Expects That," 52.

39. Lancaster, "I Could Easily Have Been an Acrobat," 45.

40. CPG, *Diaries*, 1:xiv.

41. Ibid., 1:331.

42. CPG, *Living*, 92, 95.

43. CPG, *Diaries*, 1:375.

44. Ibid., 1:381.

45. CPG to SWM, 19 April 1887, Schlesinger.

46. CPG, *Living*, 95.

47. Ibid., 96, 119.

48. Ibid., 98.

49. Grace Channing to Mary Jane Tarr Channing, 18 June 1888, quoted in Horowitz, *Wild Unrest*, 149.

50. Gilman, *Living*, 98.

51. Ibid., 96.

52. Horowitz, *Wild Unrest*, 139–42, 210, 178.

53. Ibid., 101, 105, 174.

54. Stetson diary, quoted in Horowitz, *Wild Unrest*, 122.

55. CPG, *Living*, 110, 97.

56. SWM, *Doctor and Patient*, 138.

57. CPG, "Yellow Wall-Paper," 656.

58. WDH, quoted in Dock, *Charlotte Perkins Gilman's "The Yellow Wall-paper,"* 91, 118.

59. Davis, *American Heroine*, 39.

60. Addams, "The College Woman and the Family Claim," quoted in Davis, *American Heroine*, 41.

61. CPG, *Living*, 184.

62. SWM, *Doctor and Patient*, 161.

63. Sicherman, "Uses of Diagnosis," 53.

64. Barker-Benfield, *Horrors*, 130.

65. Bassuk, "Rest Cure," 252.

66. Lee, *Edith Wharton*, 79–80.

67. Bell, *Edith Wharton and Henry James*, 53.

68. SWM to Edith Wharton, 2 November 1905, Beinecke; Edith Wharton to SWM, 6 November 1905, Beinecke.

69. Addams, *Twenty Years*, 65.

70. Lane, *To "Herland" and Beyond*, 118–20, 131–32.

71. Schuster, "Personalizing Illness and Modernity," 708–9, 721.

72. Bell, *Virginia Woolf*, 1:164.

73. Woolf, *Letters*, #194, 1:159.

74. Bassuk, "Rest Cure," 256.

75. Lee, *Virginia Woolf*, 179.

76. Ender, *Sexing the Mind*, 19.

77. Bell, *Virginia Woolf*, 2:225.

78. Fetterley, "Reading About Reading," 160.

79. Ender, *Sexing the Mind*, 19n25, 50.

80. CPG, *Living*, 121.

CHAPTER 8

1. OWH to SWM, 8 May 1862, DUMC.
2. AB, 129f.
3. SWM to JKM, 16 November 1873, CPP.
4. SWM to Harvey Cushing, 7 November 1907, Cushing/Whitney; SWM to SBW, 14 June 1888, Wister and Butler Families Papers (Collection 1962), HSP.
5. AB, 166–67, 162–63.
6. Hubbard, *Politics of Women's Biology*, 12.
7. AB, 156.
8. AB, 164, 158–59.
9. SWM to AGM, 24 March 1912, CPP; SWM to AGM, 2 April 1912, CPP.
10. Oberholtzer, "Personal Memories," 133.
11. SWM to AGM, 2 January 1904, CPP; SWM to WDH, 4 June 1885, RBML, UPenn, MS 413, box 1; SWM to AGM, 23 May 1910, CPP; SWM to AGM, 23 September 1912, CPP.
12. Davidson, *Revolution and the Word*, 14.
13. Sarah Orne Jewett to SWM, 19 January 1887, Houghton, Autograph File; Sarah Orne Jewett to SWM, n.d., Houghton, Autograph File; Sarah Orne Jewett to SWM, n.d., Houghton, Autograph File.
14. James Russell Lowell to SWM, 4 April 1888, Houghton, bMS Am 765 (66); SWM to AGM, 9 January 1898, CPP; SWM to R. S. Woodward, 2 September 1907, CPP.
15. SWM to AGM, 27 October 1901, CPP; SWM to Richard Watson Gilder, 4 April 1908, RBML, UPenn, MS 413, box 1; "Review of *Selections from the Poems of S. Weir Mitchell*," *Academy*, July 27, 1901; "Review of *Hugh Wynne*," *Friends' Intelligencer*, 50, no. 1 (1898).
16. SWM to AGM, 8 November 1910, CPP; SWM to AGM, 11 August 1911, CPP.
17. SWM to JKM, 14 March 1886, CPP; SWM to WDH, 4 June 1885, RBML, UPenn; SWM to AGM, 6 June 1889, CPP; SWM to Miss Porter, 3 November 1889, Beinecke.
18. AGM to JKM, 30 November 1914, CPP; SWM to AGM, 2 April 1912, CPP.
19. SWM to George M. Gould, 9 December 1899, CPP.
20. SWM, "The Poet as Influenced by His Time," CPP; SWM, "Novels and Novelists," CPP.
21. Wister, Owen, obituaries, CPP. Wister's eulogy was published in the *Philadelphia Press* on April 5, 1914, under the headline "Owen Wister Graphically Views Life of Dr. S. W. Mitchell."
22. SWM to AGM, 7 December 1885, CPP; SWM to AGM, 9 January 1898, CPP; AGM to SWM, 26 December 1899, CPP; SWM to AGM, 2, 3, 4 January 1900, CPP; AGM to SWM, 6 January 1900, CPP; SWM to AGM, 16 July 1913, CPP.
23. SWM to George M. Gould, n.d., CPP.
24. SWM, *Two Lectures*, 29.
25. SWM, "Literary Side of a Physician's Life," 852.
26. Darwin, *Autobiography*, 53–54.
27. Bliss, *William Osler*, 85, 119.
28. Ibid., 128.
29. SWM to James C. Wilson, [17 July 1884], OL.
30. Donaldson, "Early Days," 600.
31. Bliss, *William Osler*, 159.
32. SWM, *Doctor and Patient*, 75, 77; SWM, "Address to the Graduating Class," 17.
33. Bliss, *William Osler*, 192, 191, 198, 194.
34. Eliot, *Middlemarch*, 95, 289, 93, 164.
35. Osler, "Internal Medicine as a Vocation," in *Aequanimitas*, 136n1; "The Master-Word in Medicine," in *Aequanimitas*, 364–65.
36. Osler, "Nurse and Patient," in *Aequanimitas*, 155.
37. Cushing, *Life of Sir William Osler*, 1:321, 1:405.

38. Keen, quoted in Cushing, *Life of Sir William Osler*, 1:279–80.
39. Tucker, *S. Weir Mitchell*, 15.
40. SWM to JKM, 16 January 1886, CPP.
41. Whitman to Louisa Orr Whitman, 13–14 April 1878, in Whitman, *1876–1885*, 114.
42. Osler, "Walt Whitman," quoted in Leon, *Walt Whitman*, 20, 24.
43. Traubel, *September 15, 1889–July 6, 1890*, 188.
44. Leon, *Walt Whitman*, 58.
45. Traubel, *September 15, 1889–July 6, 1890*, 107; Leon, *Walt Whitman*, 149.
46. Traubel, *September 15, 1889–July 6, 1890*, 359–60.
47. Reynolds, *Walt Whitman's America*, 580–81.
48. Traubel, *July 16, 1888–October 31, 1888*, 454–55.
49. SWM to WO, [April 5, 1906], Cushing/Whitney.
50. Traubel, *July 16, 1888–October 31, 1888*, 271–72.
51. Traubel, *January 21, 1889–April 7, 1889*, 338–39.
52. Ibid., 87–88.
53. SWM, *Doctor and Patient*, 162–63.
54. SWM, *Dr. North*, 13.
55. SWM to Charles N. Eliot, 4 December 1911, in Lozynsky, "S. Weir Mitchell," 121.
56. Traubel, *October 1, 1891–April 3, 1892*, 316, 363, 396.
57. SWM to John Jay Chapman, 11 March 1898, Houghton, bMS Am 1854 (1155).
58. SWM to AGM, 17 September 1913, CPP.
59. SWM, *Two Lectures*, 25.
60. AB, 82.
61. Ibid., 188.
62. JKM to Dr. Garrison, n.d., CPP.

CHAPTER 9

1. Horowitz, *Power and Passion*, 233–38.
2. Ibid., 237.
3. M. Carey Thomas to Hannah Whitall Smith, 11 March 1894, quoted in Horowitz, *Power and Passion*, 237.
4. SWM, *Characteristics*, 234–35, 250–51, 262, 251, 264–65.
5. Mary Putnam Jacobi to SWM, 3 June [1891?], CPP.
6. Bittel, *Mary Putnam Jacobi*, 5.
7. The author gratefully acknowledges Carla Bittel's biography *Mary Putnam Jacobi and the Politics of Medicine in Nineteenth-Century America* for details regarding Jacobi's life and work.
8. Bittel, *Mary Putnam Jacobi*, 126–27. As part of the 1876 annual essay contest, the Boylston Prize Committee asked, "Do women require mental and bodily rest during menstruation; and to what extent?" The committee members, questioning Edward Clarke's conclusions in *Sex in Education*, were inviting alternate views.
9. Mary Putnam Jacobi to SBW, n.d., Wister and Butler Families Papers (Collection 1962), HSP.
10. Mary Putnam Jacobi to SWM, 6 May [1900], DUMC.
11. SWM to Mary Putnam Jacobi, 15 June [1902], Schlesinger.
12. Bittel, *Mary Putnam Jacobi*, 138, 91, 109.
13. SWM, *Characteristics*, 306.
14. SWM, *When All the Woods Are Green*, 117.
15. SWM, *Circumstance*, 116, 285, 361–62.
16. SWM, *Doctor and Patient*, 139–40.
17. SWM to AGM, 12 July 1891, CPP.

18. SWM, "Co-education," 671.

19. Bittel, *Mary Putnam Jacobi*, 135.

20. SWM to JKM, 16 January 1886, CPP.

21. SWM, "Poison of Serpents," 506.

22. SWM to JKM, 9 October [1888], CPP.

23. AB, 153–54.

24. SWM and Reichert, *Researches*, 43, 54.

25. SWM, "Experimental Contributions," 290–91.

26. SWM, "Annual Oration," 2.

27. SBW to SWM, 29 December 1886, Wister and Butler Families Papers (Collection 1962), HSP.

28. Fye, *Development of American Physiology*, 175–76.

29. Keen, *Influence of Antivivisection*, 1.

30. SWM to William W. Keen, 28 August 1912, CPP.

31. Keen, *Influence of Antivivisection*, 9, 43.

32. SWM and Reichert, *Researches*, 85, 137, 149.

33. SWM, "Address to the Students of Radcliffe College," 5, 6, 12, 18, 21, 21–22.

34. Horowitz, *Power and Passion*, 148, 152.

35. Thomas, "Open Letter," 637.

36. Thomas, *Education of Women*, 38, 15.

37. Horowitz, *Power and Passion*, 319–20.

38. Ibid., 247.

39. AB, 276–77, 281–82.

40. SWM, "Address Before the New York City Alumni Association," January 16, 1906, CPP.

41. Harvey Cushing to Henry Barton Jacobs, [May 1909], quoted in Fulton, *Harvey Cushing*, 289.

42. SWM, "Address Before the Fiftieth Annual Meeting."

43. Whitehorn, "Century of Psychiatric Research," 167–69; Malamud, "History of Psychiatric Therapies," 296.

44. Walter, *S. Weir Mitchell*, 148.

45. SWM, "Address Before the Fiftieth Annual Meeting," 424.

46. SWM, *Clinical Lessons*, 181–84, 142, 144.

47. Ibid., 288, 45.

48. Ibid., 121.

49. Ibid., 295.

50. Ibid., 249–74.

51. Ibid., 25, 242.

CHAPTER 10

1. AB, 75.

2. Fulton, *Harvey Cushing*, 226.

3. For Mitchell's description of the Bologna trip, see his autobiography (pp. 196–208) and his four letters to Mary Mitchell written in June 1888 (CPP).

4. SWM to SBW, 14 June 1888, CPP.

5. SWM, *Nurse and Patient, and Camp Cure*, 54.

6. Ibid., 46, 51, 53.

7. Ibid., 55–56.

8. SWM, *Doctor and Patient*, 155. Barbara Will points out this modification in Mitchell's thinking, but she writes that it occurred after "The Yellow Wall-Paper" had "achieved some

measure of fame." Will may be suggesting a causal relationship between the two. *Doctor and Patient* was published in 1887, however, five years before "The Yellow Wall-Paper." Will, "The Nervous Origins of the American Western," 310n2.

9. SWM, *Doctor and Patient*, 161–62.

10. SWM, *Nurse and Patient, and Camp Cure*, 57–58.

11. SWM to Mrs. Charles Dow, 12 June 1890, CPP; SWM to Charles L. Moore, 29 June 1892, RBML, UPenn, MS 413, box 1.

12. SWM, *Doctor and Patient*, 162–64, 175.

13. SWM, *Complete Poems*, 323.

14. SWM, *Complete Poems*, 312.

15. SWM, *Complete Poems*, 317–18.

16. SWM, *When All the Woods Are Green*, 103, 26, 27, 25.

17. Ibid., 101–2.

18. Ibid., 91.

19. Ibid., 104, 276, 334–35.

20. Wordsworth, "Tintern Abbey," 123; Wordsworth, "Ode," 173.

21. Wharton, *Age of Innocence*, 168.

22. Hornsby, "Gilded Age," 456–58.

23. Baltzell, *Philadelphia Gentlemen*, 221.

24. Hornsby, "Gilded Age," 465–66.

25. SWM to Phillips Brooks, 6 May 1886, Houghton, bMS Am 1594.1 (419).

26. AB, 291–92.

27. Phillips Brooks to SWM, 10 December 1892, quoted in Allen, *Life and Letters*, 2:926.

28. Woolverton, *Education of Phillips Brooks*, 1.

29. SWM to William Brooks, n.d., Houghton, bMS Am 1594.1 (419). Phillips Brooks died on January 23, 1893.

30. Ibid.

31. SWM to AGM, 21 August 1913, CPP.

32. AB, 76–76a.

33. SWM to SBW, 24 September 1899, Wister and Butler Families Papers (Collection 1962), HSP; SWM to SBW, 6 October 1899, Wister and Butler Families Papers (Collection 1962), HSP.

34. Baltzell, *Philadelphia Gentlemen*, 154, 71–77, 148.

35. OWH to SWM, 25 March 1885, CPP.

36. OWH to SWM, 1 March 1883, quoted in Morse, *Life and Letters*, 261; OWH to SWM 15 March 1883, quoted in Morse, *Life and Letters*, 261–62.

37. OWH to WO, 21 January 1889, quoted in Cushing, *Life of Sir William Osler*, 1:302.

38. SWM to George M. Gould, n.d., CPP; SWM to George M. Gould, 9 December 1899, CPP.

39. AB, 164.

40. SWM, *Complete Poems*, 408–10.

41. SWM to OWH, 20 June [1892], Houghton, bMS Am 1241.1 (746); OWH to SWM, 30 June 1892, CPP.

42. SWM to Thomas B. Aldrich, 28 December 1897, Houghton, bMS Am 1429 (3136).

CHAPTER 11

1. Anne Mitchell to Clements C. Fry, 9 February 1939, CPP.

2. SWM to AGM, 29 April 1891, CPP.

3. SWM to Arthur Meigs, 18 May [1891], CPP.

4. SWM to JKM, [May 1891?], CPP.

5. SWM to SBW, [1891?], Wister and Butler Families Papers (Collection 1962), HSP.

6. SWM to SBW, [1892?], Wister and Butler Families Papers (Collection 1962), HSP.

7. Ibid.

8. SWM to SBW, 16 September 1895, Wister and Butler Families Papers (Collection 1962), HSP.

9. SWM to AGM, 18 January 1897, CPP.

10. For a discussion of the "oddity and even paradox in the coupling of 'historical' and 'romance,'" see Dekker, *American Historical Romance*, 15–18.

11. SWM, *Hugh Wynne*, 101.

12. Ibid., 201, 255, 257, 303–4.

13. Ibid., 319–20.

14. This scene is based on an actual ball that took place in Philadelphia during the British occupation. Tory ladies and British officers zealously paid homage to Sir William Howe in a magnificent regatta, tournament, and ball called the Meschianza. Accounts "glitter through the old records like a fragment of the Arabian Nights. The English officers (André being stage manager of the gorgeous spectacle) appeared as knights, and the Philadelphia Tory belles as Turkish princesses." Davis, "Old Landmarks," 162.

15. SWM, *Hugh Wynne*, 371–73.

16. Ibid., 563, 565–66.

17. SWM to Mrs. Charles Down, 21 October 1897, CPP; SWM to Thomas Bailey Aldrich, 28 December 1897, Houghton, bMS Am 1429 (3136).

18. SWM to Mrs. Charles Dow, 21 October 1897, CPP.

19. SWM to SBW, 15 August 1897, Wister and Butler Families Papers (Collection 1962), HSP; SWM to Mrs. Charles Dow, 21 October 1897, CPP.

20. SWM, diary entries, 13 January 1898–30 January 1898, CPP.

21. Ibid.

22. SWM to William Williams Keen, 8 February 1865, CPP; SWM, *Two Lectures*, 41.

23. SWM to SBW, 9 March [1898], Wister and Butler Families Papers (Collection 1962), HSP.

24. Wood, *From Miasmas to Molecules*, 38–40; Ziporyn, *Disease*, 37.

25. I am especially grateful to Evelynn Maxine Hammonds for her detailed study of diphtheria. See *Childhood's Deadly Scourge*, 59, 75–76.

26. Biggs, "New Treatment of Diphtheria," 477.

27. Report of the American Pediatric Society, quoted in Hammonds, *Childhood's Deadly Scourge*, 135.

28. Ziporyn, *Disease*, 53.

29. Hammonds, *Childhood's Deadly Scourge*, 7.

30. SWM to SBW, 9 March [1898], Wister and Butler Families Papers (Collection 1962), HSP.

31. SWM to SBW, 3 April 1898, Wister and Butler Families Papers (Collection 1962), HSP.

32. Mary Cadwalader Mitchell to "My Dear Alice," 23 June 1898, CPP.

33. SWM to SBW, 19 June 1898, Wister and Butler Families Papers (Collection 1962), HSP.

34. SWM to Henry Charles Lea, 30 October [1898?], RBML, UPenn, Ms. Coll. 413, Box 1, SWM to AGM, 20 November 1898, CPP; SWM to Richard Watson Gilder, [1898], CPP.

35. SWM to JKM, 12 September 1898, CPP.

36. SWM to "Mitchell Children," [11 January 1899], CPP; SWM to Anne Mitchell, 15 January 1899, CPP.

37. SWM to Anne Mitchell, 11 May 1899, CPP; SWM to AGM, 10 November 1899, CPP.

38. SWM to JKM, 7 February 1899, CPP.

39. SWM to JKM, 9 February 1899, CPP; SWM to SBW, 24 June 1899, Wister and Butler Families Papers (Collection 1962), HSP.

40. SWM to SBW, 24 June 1899, Wister and Butler Family Papers (collection 1962), HSP.

41. SWM, *Complete Poems*, 394, 435.
42. SWM to AGM, [1900?], CPP.
43. SWM, *Clinical Lessons*, 145.
44. Eckstein, *Noguchi*, 88–89.
45. SWM to WO, [January 1900], Cushing/Whitney.
46. SWM to Andrew Carnegie, n.d., CPP.
47. SWM to WO, 2 December 1910, Cushing/Whitney; SWM to WO, 29 November 1913, OL.
48. SWM to SBW, 9 March [1898], Wister and Butler Families Papers (Collection 1962), HSP.
49. SWM, *Complete Poems*, 418.
50. SWM to Anne Mitchell, 4 September [1898], CPP; SWM to family, 14 August 1898, CPP.
51. SWM to AGM, 20 November 1898, CPP; SWM to AGM, 2 January 1900, CPP.
52. SWM to AGM, 17 September 1904, CPP.

CHAPTER 12

1. Goetz and Aminoff, "Brown-Séquard," 2102. They note that here is the beginning of modern hormone replacement therapy.
2. WO to SWM, 23 May 1908, "Volume of S. Weir Mitchell Correspondence and an Address," Cushing/Whitney; SWM to WO, 30 May 1908, Cushing/Whitney.
3. He spoke at the School of Nursing, Presbyterian Hospital in New York City on May 11, 1905; at the infirmary on November 16, 1906; and at the New York Hospital Training School for Nurses on February 28, 1908.
4. SWM to WO, 14 August 1904, Cushing/Whitney.
5. Cushing, *Life of Sir William Osler*, 1:665–66.
6. Osler, "The Fixed Period," quoted in Cushing, *Life of Sir William Osler*, 1:667.
7. Leon, *Walt Whitman*, 37; Bliss, *William Osler*, 324–25.
8. Cushing, *Life of Sir William Osler*, 1:669; WO to Arthur Thomson, 3 March [1905], quoted in Cushing, *Life of Sir William Osler*, 1:672.
9. Bliss, *William Osler*, 326.
10. Osler, preface to *Aequanimitas*, viii; "The Fixed Period," in *Aequanimitas*, 382–83.
11. Bliss, *William Osler*, 329–30.
12. SWM, *Complete Poems*, 418–22.
13. WO to SWM, 6 August [1905], quoted in Cushing, *Life of Sir William Osler*, 2:14.
14. SWM to AGM, 3 October 1906, CPP; SWM to J. William White, 24 October 1906, CPP; SWM to Arthur Meigs, 2 October 1906, CPP.
15. AB, 139.
16. Bell, *College of Physicians*, 171, 169.
17. Ibid., 193.
18. SWM to Ronald Ross, 22 July 1907, CPP; SWM to Ronald Ross, 3 November 1910, CPP.
19. SWM to WO, 22 December 1911, OL.
20. SWM to W. W. Keen, n.d., CPP; SWM to W. W. Keen, n.d., CPP.
21. SWM, "Some Personal Recollections"; Keen, "Surgical Reminiscences"; Billings, "Medical Reminiscences."
22. Bell, *College of Physicians*, 207, 209.
23. SWM to Arthur Meigs, 19 September 1905, CPP; SWM to WO, [1906?], CPP; SWM to Meigs, 11 April 1906, CPP; SWM to William J. White, 18 December 1906, CPP.
24. SWM to WO, 13 March [1907?], OL; SWM to WO, [6 April 1907], OL; SWM to WO, 25 December 1907, OL.
25. SWM to W. W. Keen, 29 September 1908, CPP; SWM to WO, [January 1909], Cushing/Whitney; SWM to WO, 22 December 1911, OL.
26. Bell, *College of Physicians*, 219.

27. SWM, "Address Delivered on the Opening of the New Hall," 15–16.

28. Carnegie, quoted in Bell, *College of Physicians*, 213.

29. WO to SWM, 25 July [1903], OL; SWM to WO, 22 December 1903, OL.

30. SWM to John Shaw Billings, 10 May 1905, John Shaw Billings Papers, NYP.

31. SWM to WO, 2 March 1906, OL; SWM to WO, [1906?], OL; SWM to D'Arcy Power, 20 January 1910, DUMC.

32. SWM to D'Arcy Power, 19 March 1910, DUMC; SWM to WO, 6 December 1910, OL.

33. SWM to WO, 21 March 1911, OL; SWM to WO, 5 April 1911, OL.

34. SWM to WO, 29 November 1911, Cushing/Whitney; SWM to WO, 26 March 1912, OL.

35. SWM to Harvey Cushing, 17 November 1912, Cushing/Whitney.

36. SWM to WO, 28 June 1911, OL.

37. Osler, *Science and Immortality* 11, 19, 13.

38. Ibid., 22–24, 33.

39. Ibid., 35–36, 40.

40. SWM to Charles W. Eliot, 15 November 1902, Harvard University Archives.

41. SWM to AGM, [1904?], CPP.

42. SWM to WO, [1904?], OL.

43. Ibid.

44. SWM, "Treatment by Rest," 2036.

45. Other books in Freud's library directly related to the rest cure were John Hilton, *Rest and Pain: A Course of Lectures*; Leopold Löwenfeld, *Die moderne Behandlung der Nervenschwäche (Neurasthenie), der Hysterie und verwandter Leiden: Mit besonderer Berücksichtigung der Luftcuren, Bäder, Anstaltsbehandlung, und der Mitchell-Playfair' schen Mastcur*; S. Weir Mitchell, *Die Behandlung gewisser Formen von Neurasthenie und Hysterie*, translated from the fourth edition of *Fat and Blood* by Georg Klemperer; Josef Schreiber, *Zue Behandlung gewisser Formen von Neurasthenie und Hysterie durch die Weir-Mitchell-Cur*; Leopold Löwenfeld, *The Modern Treatment of Neurasthenia, of Hysteria and Related Illnesses, with Special Consideration of Air Cures, Institutional Treatment, and the Mitchell-Playfair "Mast" Treatment*; S. Weir Mitchell, *The Treatment of Certain Forms of Neurasthenia and Hysteria*; and Josef Schreiber, *On the Treatment of Certain Forms of Neurasthenia and Hysteria Using the Weir-Treatment Regimen*. See Davies and Fichtner, *Freud's Library*.

46. Breuer and Freud, *Studies on Hysteria*, 265, 266.

47. Keen, obituary, CPP; Mills, "Silas Weir Mitchell," 69; Tucker, "Speaking of Weir Mitchell," 342, 345.

48. SWM, *Doctor and Patient*, 10.

49. Breuer and Freud, *Studies on Hysteria*, 266–67.

50. SWM, "Treatment by Rest," 2037, 2034, 2036.

51. Porter, "The Body and the Mind," 247.

52. SWM to AGM, 23 May 1910, CPP. Mitchell wrote, "I do not believe in what is called the subconscious mind."

53. Mills, "Silas Weir Mitchell," 69.

54. Veith, *Hysteria*, 218–19.

55. AB, folder 8, miscellaneous sections.

56. SWM to SBW, 19 March [1902?], Wister and Butler Families Papers (Collection 1962), HSP; SWM to AGM, 22 March 1902, CPP.

57. Cushing, *Life of Sir William Osler*, 1:418, 1:606.

58. SWM to John Shaw Billings, 17 September 1904, John Shaw Billings Papers, NYP.

59. SWM to Charles Walcott, 8 March 1905, CPP.

60. Andrew Carnegie to SWM, 14 January 1908, CPP; SWM to Andrew Carnegie, 16 January [1908], CPP.

61. SWM to Andrew Carnegie, 22 November 1909, CPP.

62. SWM to Andrew Carnegie, n.d., CPP.

63. SWM to Harvey Cushing, [1910?], Cushing/Whitney.

64. SWM to John Hay, 25 January [1901], S. Weir Mitchell Correspondence, NYP.

65. AB, 238a.

66. Ibid., 241.

67. Morris, *Rise of Theodore Roosevelt*, 118; Poultney Bigelow, *Seventy Summers*, quoted in Morris, *Rise of Theodore Roosevelt*, 118.

68. SWM to William Draper Lewis, 12 April 1912, CPP; SWM to J. William White, 6 November 1912, CPP; SWM to AGM, 6 November 1912, CPP; SWM to WO, 7 November 1912, OL.

69. SWM to AGM, 28 December 1912, CPP; SWM to AGM, 1 January 1913, CPP; SWM to AGM, 13 January 1913, CPP; SWM to AGM, 21 January 1913, CPP.

70. SWM, "Medical Department in the Civil War," 18.

71. SWM to AGM, 30 March 1913, CPP.

EPILOGUE

1. SWM to AGM, 19 July 1912, CPP; SWM to AGM, 21 August 1913, CPP.

2. SWM, *Complete Poems*, 369.

3. SWM to AGM, 22 November 1912, CPP.

4. SWM to Richard Watson Gilder, 6 November [1905], CPP; SWM to WDH, [December] 1905, CPP.

5. SWM to Edith Wharton, 2 November 1905, Beinecke.

6. SWM to J. William White, 23 September 1905, CPP; SWM to AGM, 3 October 1906, CPP; SWM to AGM, 10 September 1908, CPP.

7. SWM to WO, 28 June 1911, OL.

8. SWM to AGM, 6 February 1901, CPP.

9. SWM to John Billings, 18 September 1904, Beinecke; John Billings to Kate M. Stevens, 21 September 1904, Beinecke.

10. SWM to WO, 30 April [1913], Cushing/Whitney. John Billings died on March 11, 1913.

11. WO to SWM, [15 April 1913], DUMC.

12. Oberholtzer, "Personal Memories of Weir Mitchell," 132.

13. SWM to WO, 29 November 1913, OL.

14. AGM to JKM, 30 November 1914, CPP.

15. JKM to WO, telegram, 4 January 1914, OL.

16. Mitchell's estate was valued at $484,062 (approximately $10 million today). His investments were mainly in railway and public utility bonds. He willed his estate to his wife, until her death, and then $20,000 annually to each son. He left Gray Pines at Bar Harbor to John's wife, Anne, and a Philadelphia townhouse to Langdon's wife, Marion. Mary Mitchell's estate was valued at over $100,000 (approximately $2 million today). She left nothing to her two stepsons, John and Langdon, except one of the five stately oil portraits of Mitchell (by Holl, Vonnoh, Whitman, Beaux, and Sargent).

BIBLIOGRAPHY

Adams, George Worthington. *Doctors in Blue: The Medical History of the Union Army in the Civil War.* Baton Rouge: Louisiana State University Press, 1952.

Addams, Jane. *Twenty Years at Hull-House with Autobiographical Notes.* 1910. Reprint, New York: Macmillan, 1960.

Allen, Alexander V. G. *Life and Letters of Phillips Brooks.* 2 vols. New York: E. P. Dutton, 1900.

Annual Announcement of Jefferson Medical College of Philadelphia: Session of 1848–49. Philadelphia: Frick and Kelly, 1848.

Ball, Donald. "Silas Weir Mitchell." *Practitioner* 217 (July 1976): 117–24.

Baltzell, Edward Digby. *Philadelphia Gentlemen: The Making of a National Upper Class.* New Brunswick: Transaction, 1989.

Barker-Benfield, G. J. *The Horrors of the Half-Known Life: Male Attitudes Toward Women and Sexuality in Nineteenth-Century America.* New York: Harper and Row, 1976.

Bassuk, Ellen L. "The Rest Cure: Repetition or Resolution of Victorian Women's Conflicts?" *Poetics Today* 6, nos. 1/2 (1985): 245–57.

Bell, Millicent. *Edith Wharton and Henry James: The Story of Their Friendship.* New York: George Braziller, 1965.

Bell, Quentin. *Virginia Woolf: A Biography.* 2 vols. New York: Harcourt Brace Jovanovich, 1972.

Bell, Whitfield J. *The College of Physicians of Philadelphia: A Bicentennial History.* Canton, Mass.: Science History Publications, 1987.

Bernard, Claude. *An Introduction to the Study of Experimental Medicine.* Translated by Henry Copley Greene. 1927. Reprint, New York: Dover, 1957.

Biggs, Hermann M. "The New Treatment of Diphtheria." *The Century Magazine* 49, no. 3 (1895): 476–77.

Billings, John Shaw. "Medical Reminiscences of the Civil War." *Transactions of the College of Physicians of Philadelphia* 27 (1905): 115–21.

Bittel, Carla. *Mary Putnam Jacobi and the Politics of Medicine in Nineteenth-Century America.* Chapel Hill: University of North Carolina Press, 2009.

Bliss, Michael. *William Osler: A Life in Medicine.* New York: Oxford University Press, 1999.

Breuer, Josef, and Sigmund Freud. *Studies on Hysteria.* Translated by James Strachey. New York: Basic, 1957.

Burr, Anna. *Weir Mitchell: His Life and Letters.* New York: Duffield, 1929.

Bynum, William F. *Science and the Practice of Medicine in the Nineteenth Century.* Cambridge: Cambridge University Press, 1994.

Cady, Edwin H. *The Realist at War: The Mature Years, 1885–1920, of William Dean Howells.* Syracuse: Syracuse University Press, 1958.

Canale, D. J. "Civil War Medicine from the Perspective of S. Weir Mitchell's 'The Case of George Dedlow.'" *Journal of the History of the Neurosciences* 11, no. 1 (2002): 11–18.

————. "S. Weir Mitchell's Prose and Poetry on the American Civil War." *Journal of the History of the Neurosciences* 13, no. 1 (2004): 7–21.

Cavanagh, G. S. T. "Weir Mitchell's First Story." *Trent Collection Report* 14 (March 1982). Medical Center Library, Duke University.

Chapman, Carleton B. *Order Out of Chaos: John Shaw Billings and America's Coming of Age.* Boston: Boston Medical Library, 1994.

Colombat, Marc. *A Treatise on the Diseases and Special Hygiene of Females.* Translated by Charles D. Meigs. Philadelphia: Lea and Blanchard, 1845.

Crowley, John W. *The Mask of Fiction: Essays on W. D. Howells.* Amherst: University of Massachusetts Press, 1989.

Cushing, Harvey. *The Life of Sir William Osler.* 2 vols. Oxford: Clarendon Press, 1925.

Darwin, Charles. *The Autobiography of Charles Darwin and Selected Letters.* New York: Dover, 1958.

Davidson, Cathy N. *Revolution and the Word: The Rise of the Novel in America.* London: Oxford University Press, 1986.

Davies, J. Keith, and Gerhard Fichtner. *Freud's Library: A Comprehensive Catalogue.* London: Freud Museum, 2006.

Davis, Allen Freeman. *American Heroine: The Life and Legend of Jane Addams.* London: Oxford University Press, 1973.

Davis, Rebecca Harding. "Old Landmarks in Philadelphia." *Scribner's Monthly* 12 (June 1876): 145–67.

DeJong, Russell N. *A History of American Neurology.* New York: Raven Press, 1982.

Dekker, George. *The American Historical Romance.* Cambridge: Cambridge University Press, 1987.

Deutsch, Albert. "Military Psychiatry: The Civil War, 1861–1865." In *One Hundred Years of American Psychiatry,* edited by J. K. Hall, 367–84. New York: Columbia University Press, 1944.

Diffley, Kathleen, ed. *To Live and Die: Collected Stories of the Civil War, 1861–1876.* Durham: Duke University Press, 2002.

Dock, Julie Bates. "'But One Expects That': Charlotte Perkins Gilman's 'The Yellow Wallpaper' and the Shifting Light of Scholarship." *Publication of the Modern Language Association* 3, no. 1 (1996): 52–65.

————. *Charlotte Perkins Gilman's "The Yellow Wall-Paper" and the History of Its Publication and Reception.* University Park: Pennsylvania State University Press, 1998.

Donaldson, Henry H. "The Early Days of the American Physiological Society." *Science* 75, no. 1954 (1932): 599–601.

Duffy, John. *From Humors to Medical Science: A History of American Medicine.* Urbana: University of Illinois Press, 1993.

Earnest, Ernest. *S. Weir Mitchell: Novelist and Physician.* Philadelphia: University of Pennsylvania Press, 1950.

Eckstein, Gustav. *Noguchi.* New York: Harper and Brothers, 1931.

Eliot, George. *Middlemarch.* 1874. Reprint, New York: Penguin, 1994.

Elston, Mary Ann. "Women and Anti-vivisection in Victorian England, 1870–1900." In *Vivisection in Historical Perspective,* edited by Nicolaas Rupke, 259–94. New York: Routledge, 1987.

Emmet, Thomas Addis. *The Principles and Practice of Gynaecology.* Philadelphia: Henry C. Lea, 1880.

Ender, Evelyn. *Sexing the Mind: Nineteenth-Century Fictions of Hysteria.* Ithaca: Cornell University Press, 1995.

Fetterley, Judith. "Reading About Reading: 'A Jury of Her Peers.'" In *Gender and Reading: Essays on Readers, Texts, and Contexts,* edited by Elizabeth A. Flynn and Patrocinio P. Schweickart, 147–64. Baltimore: Johns Hopkins University Press, 1986.

Figg, Laurann, and Jane Farrell-Beck. "Amputation in the Civil War: Physical and Social Dimensions." *Journal of the History of Medicine and Allied Sciences* 48, no. 4 (1993): 454–75.

Fontana, Felice. *Treatise on the Venom of the Viper.* Translated by Joseph Skinner. London: J. Murray, 1787.

Freud, Sigmund. "Femininity." In *New Introductory Lectures on Psychoanalysis*, edited by James Strachey, 112–35. New York: Norton, 1965.

Fulton, John F. *Harvey Cushing: A Biography.* Springfield, Ill.: Charles C. Thomas, 1946.

Fye, W. Bruce. *The Development of American Physiology: Scientific Medicine in the Nineteenth Century.* Baltimore: Johns Hopkins University Press, 1987.

———. "S. Weir Mitchell, Philadelphia's 'Lost' Physiologist." *Bulletin of the History of Medicine* 57, no. 2 (1983): 188–202.

Gardner, A. K. *Old Wine in New Bottle; or, Spare Hours of a Student in Paris.* New York: Francis, 1848.

Gillen, William H., Howard D. Fabing, Simon Horenstein, Lawrence C. McHenry, Richard P. Schmidt, and Edwin D. Clarke. "Preface." *Injuries of Nerves and Their Consequences.* 1872. Reprint, New York: Dover, 1965.

Gilman, Charlotte Perkins. *The Diaries of Charlotte Perkins Gilman.* Edited by Denise Knight. 2 vols. Charlottesville: University Press of Virginia, 1994.

———. *Herland.* New York: Pantheon, 1979.

———. *The Living of Charlotte Perkins Gilman: An Autobiography.* 1935. Reprint, New York: Arno Press, 1972.

———. "A Suggestion on the Negro Problem." In *Charlotte Perkins Gilman: A Nonfiction Reader*, edited by Larry Ceplair, 176–83. New York: Columbia University Press, 1991.

———. "The Yellow Wall-Paper." *New England Magazine* 11 (1892): 647–56.

Goetz, Christopher G., and Michael J. Aminoff. "The Brown-Séquard and S. Weir Mitchell Letters." *Neurology* 57, no. 11 (2001): 2100–2104.

Goetz, Christopher G., Michel Bonduelle, and Toby Gelfand. *Charcot: Constructing Neurology.* New York: Oxford University Press, 1995.

Goldberg, Michael. "Breaking New Ground: 1800–1848." In *No Small Courage: A History of Women in the United States*, edited by Nancy F. Cott, 179–236. Oxford: Oxford University Press, 2000.

Goler, Robert. "Loss and the Persistence of Memory: 'The Case of George Dedlow.'" In *Difference and Identity*, edited Jonathan M. Metzl and Susan Poirier, 160–83. Baltimore: Johns Hopkins University Press, 2005.

Goodman, Susan, and Carl Dawson. *William Dean Howells: A Writer's Life.* Berkeley: University of California Press, 2005.

Greene, Harry W. *Snakes: The Evolution of Mystery in Nature.* Berkeley: University of California Press, 1997.

Griffith, Kelley. "Weir Mitchell and the Genteel Romance." *American Literature* 44, no. 2 (1972): 247–61.

Hall, J. K., ed. *One Hundred Years of American Psychiatry.* New York: Columbia University Press, 1944.

Hammonds, Evelynn Maxine. *Childhood's Deadly Scourge: The Campaign to Control Diphtheria in New York, 1880–1930.* Baltimore: Johns Hopkins University Press, 1999.

Hasegawa, Guy R. "The Civil War's Medical Cadets: Medical Students Serving the Union." *Journal of the American College of Surgeons* 193, no. 1 (2001): 81–89.

Herschbach, Lisa. "'True Clinical Fictions': Medical and Literary Narratives from the Civil War Hospital." *Culture, Medicine, and Psychiatry* 19, no. 2 (1995): 183–205.

Holmes, Oliver Wendell. *Elsie Venner: A Romance of Destiny.* New York: New American Library, 1961.

Hornsby, Stephen J. "The Gilded Age and the Making of Bar Harbor." *Geographic Review* 83, no. 4 (1993): 455–68.

Horowitz, Helen Lefkowitz. *The Power and Passion of M. Carey Thomas.* Urbana: University of Illinois Press, 1999.

———. *Wild Unrest: Charlotte Perkins Gilman and the Making of "The Yellow Wall-Paper."* Oxford: Oxford University Press, 2010.

Howells, William Dean. *William Dean Howells: Selected Letters.* Edited by George W. Arms, Richard Ballinger, and Christopher Lohman. 6 vols. Boston: Twayne, 1979–83.

Hubbard, Ruth. *The Politics of Women's Biology.* New Brunswick: Rutgers University Press, 1990.

James, Henry. *The Bostonians.* 1886. Reprint, New York: Barnes and Noble, 2005.

James, William. "The Consciousness of Lost Limbs." *Proceedings of the American Society for Psychical Research* 1, no. 8 (1887): 249–58.

Journet, Debra. "Phantom Limbs and 'Body-Ego': S. Weir Mitchell's 'George Dedlow.'" *Mosaic* 23, no. 1 (1990): 87–99.

Katz, Leslie. "Flesh of His Flesh: Amputation in *Moby Dick* and S. W. Mitchell's Medical Papers." *Genders* 4 (Spring 1989): 1–10.

Keen, William Williams. "Address at the Dedication of the Mitchell Memorial Building of the Philadelphia Orthopaedic Hospital and Infirmary for Nervous Diseases." *Science* 44, no. 1130 (1916): 255–59.

———. *The Influence of Antivivisection on Character.* Defense of Research Pamphlet 24. Issued by the Bureau on Protection of Medical Research of the Council on Health and Public Instruction of the American Medical Association. Chicago: American Medical Association, 1912.

———. "Surgical Reminiscences of the Civil War." *Transactions of the College of Physicians of Philadelphia* 27 (1905): 95–114.

Klauber, Laurence. *Rattlesnakes: Their Habits, Life Histories, and Influence on Mankind.* 2 vols. Berkeley: University of California Press, 1956.

Krasner, James. "Doubtful Arms and Phantom Limbs: Literary Portrayals of Embodied Grief." *Publication of the Modern Language Association* 119, no. 2 (2004): 218–32.

Lakoff, George, and Mark Johnson. *Metaphors We Live By.* Chicago: University of Chicago Press, 1980.

Lancaster, Jane. "'I Could Easily Have Been an Acrobat': Charlotte Perkins Gilman and the Providence Ladies' Sanitary Gymnasium, 1881–1884." *American Transcendental Quarterly* 8, no. 1 (1994): 33–52.

Lane, Ann J. *To "Herland" and Beyond: The Life and Work of Charlotte Perkins Gilman.* New York: Penguin, 1990.

Lazarus, Josephine. "Higher Education: A Word to Women." *The Century Magazine* 41, no. 2 (1890): 315–16.

Lederer, Susan E. *Subjected to Science: Human Experimentation in America Before the Second World War.* Baltimore: Johns Hopkins University Press, 1995.

Lee, Hermione. *Edith Wharton.* New York: Alfred A. Knopf, 2007.

———. *Virginia Woolf.* New York: Alfred A. Knopf, 1997.

Leon, Philip W. *Walt Whitman and Sir William Osler: A Poet and His Physician.* Toronto: ECW Press, 1995.

Long, Lisa A. "'The Corporeity of Heaven': Rehabilitating the Civil War Body in *The Gates Ajar.*" *American Literature* 69, no. 4 (1997): 781–811.

———. *Rehabilitating Bodies: Health, History, and the American Civil War.* Philadelphia: University of Pennsylvania Press, 2004.

Louis, Elan D. "Silas Weir Mitchell's Essential Tremor." *Movement Disorders* 22, no. 9 (2007): 1217–22.

Louis, Elan D., Stacy Horn, and Lisa Anne Roth. "The Neurologic Content of S. Weir Mitchell's Fiction." *Neurology* 66, no. 3 (2006): 403–7.

Lozynsky, Artem, "S. Weir Mitchell on Whitman: An Unpublished Letter." *American Notes and Queries* 13 (April 1975): 120–21.

Lutz, Tom. *American Nervousness, 1903: An Anecdotal History.* Ithaca: Cornell University Press, 1991.

Lynn, Kenneth S. *William Dean Howells: An American Life.* New York: Harcourt Brace Jovanovich, 1971.

Malamud, William. "The History of Psychiatric Therapies." In *One Hundred Years of American Psychiatry,* edited by J. K. Hall, 273–323. New York: Columbia University Press, 1944.

McHenry, Lawrence C., Jr. "Introduction." in Silas Weir Mitchell, *Injuries of Nerves and Their Consequences.* 1872. Reprint, New York: Dover, 1965.

McPherson, James M. *Battle Cry of Freedom: The Civil War Era.* New York: Harcourt Brace Jovanovich, 1970.

Meigs, Charles D. *Females and Their Diseases: A Series of Letters to His Class.* Philadelphia: Lea and Blanchard, 1848.

Metzer, W. S. "The Experimentation of S. Weir Mitchell with Mescal." *Neurology* 39 (February 1989): 303–4.

Michaels, Walter Benn. *The Gold Standard and the Logic of Naturalism.* Berkeley: University of California Press, 1988.

Mills, Charles K. "Silas Weir Mitchell, M.D., LL.D.: His Place in Neurology." *Journal of Nervous and Mental Disease* 41, no. 2 (1914): 65–74.

Mitchell, John Kearsley. *Impediments to the Study of Medicine: A Lecture, Introductory to the Course of Practice of Medicine.* Philadelphia: T. K. and P. G. Collins, 1850.

———. *Introductory Lecture to the Course of the Practice of Medicine.* Philadelphia: C. Sherman, 1849.

———. *A Lecture on Some of the Means of Elevating the Character of the Working Classes.* Reprinted from the *Journal of the Franklin Institute.* Philadelphia: Jesper Harding, 1834.

———. *An Oration Delivered Before the Philadelphia Medical Society, Pursuant to Appointment.* Philadelphia: I. Ashmead, 1825.

Mitchell, Silas Weir. "Address Before the Fiftieth Annual Meeting of the American Medico-psychological Association, Held in Philadelphia, May 16, 1894." *Journal of Nervous and Mental Disease* 21 (July 1894): 413–37. Reprinted in the *American Journal of Psychiatry* 151, no. 6 (1994): 29–36.

———. "Address Delivered on the Opening of the New Hall of the College of Physicians of Philadelphia." November 11, 1909. Harvard Medical Library in the Francis A. Countway Library of Medicine.

———. "Address of Dr. S. Weir Mitchell to the Nurse–Graduates of the Philadelphia Orthopedic Hospital and Infirmary for Nervous Diseases." November 16, 1906. New York Public Library.

———. "Address to the Graduating Class of the New York Hospital Training School for Nurses." February 28, 1908. New York Public Library.

———. "Address to the Students of Radcliffe College." January 17, 1895. Schlesinger Library, Radcliffe Institute for Advanced Study, Harvard University.

———. "The Annual Oration Before the Medical and Chirurgical Faculty of Maryland, 1877." Reprinted from *Transactions of the Medical and Chirurgical Faculty of Maryland.* Baltimore: Innes, 1877.

———. "An Appreciation of Phillips Brooks." In *Life and Letters of Phillips Brooks,* edited by Alexander V. G. Allen, 1:631–35. New York: E. P. Dutton, 1900.

———. "Autobiography." Unpublished manuscript. S. Weir Mitchell Papers. College of Physicians of Philadelphia Historical Medical Library.

———. "The Autobiography of a Quack." In *The Autobiography of a Quack and The Case of George Dedlow,* 1–112. New York: The Century Company, 1900.

———. "The Autobiography of a Quack: In Two Parts." *Atlantic Monthly* 20 (1867): 466–75, 586–98.

———. *A Brief History of the Two Families: The Mitchells of Ayrshire and the Symons of Cornwall.* Philadelphia: Privately printed by Dornan, 1912.

————. "The Case of George Dedlow." In *The Autobiography of a Quack and The Case of George Dedlow*, 115–49. New York: The Century Company, 1900.

————. *Characteristics*. New York: The Century Company, 1900.

————. *Circumstance*. New York: The Century Company, 1901.

————. *Clinical Lessons on Nervous Diseases*. Philadelphia: Lea Brothers, 1897.

————. "Co-education and the Higher Education of Women: A Symposium by Professors William Goodell, M.D., T. Gaillard Thomas, M.D., James R. Chadwick, M.D., S. Weir Mitchell, M.D., M. Allen Starr, M.D., and J. J. Putnam, M.D." *Medical News: A Weekly Journal of Medical Science* 55 (1889): 667–73.

————. *The Complete Poems*. New York: The Century Company, 1914.

————. *Constance Trescot*. New York: The Century Company, 1905.

————. *Doctor and Patient*. Philadelphia: Arno Press, 1887.

————. *Dr. North and His Friends*. New York: The Century Company, 1900.

————. "The Evolution of the Rest Treatment." *Journal of Nervous and Mental Disease* 31 (June 1904): 368–73.

————. "Experimental Contributions to the Toxicology of Rattle-Snake Venom." *New York Medical Journal* 6, no. 4 (1868): 289–322.

————. *Fat and Blood: And How to Make Them*. Philadelphia: J. B. Lippincott, 1877.

————. *Hugh Wynne, Free Quaker: Sometime Brevet Lieutenant-Colonel on the Staff of His Excellency General Washington*. New York: The Century Company, 1922.

————. *Injuries of Nerves and Their Consequences*. Philadelphia: J. B. Lippincott, 1872.

————. *Injuries of Nerves and Their Consequences*. 1872. Reprint, with an introduction by Lawrence C. McHenry, Jr., New York: Dover, 1965.

————. *In War Time*. New York: The Century Company, 1915.

————. *Lectures on Diseases of the Nervous System, Especially in Women*. Philadelphia: Henry C. Lea's Son, 1881.

————. "The Literary Side of a Physician's Life: Ronald Ross as a Poet." *Journal of the American Medical Association* 49, no. 10 (1907): 852–53.

————. "The Medical Department in the Civil War." *Journal of the American Medical Association* 62, no. 19 (1914): 1445–50.

————. "Memoir of John Call Dalton, 1825–1889." In *Biographical Memoirs* 3, 177–85. Washington, D.C.: National Academy of Sciences, 1890.

————. *Nurse and Patient, and Camp Cure*. Philadelphia: J. B. Lippincott, 1877.

————. "On the Diseases of Nerves, Resulting from Injuries." In *Contributions Relating to the Causation and Prevention of Disease, and to Camp Diseases; Together with a Report of the Diseases, Etc., Among the Prisoners at Andersonville, GA*, edited by Austin Flint, 412–68. New York: Hurd and Houghton, 1867.

————. "On the Treatment of Rattlesnake Bites." *North American Medico-chirurgical Review* 5 (1861): 269–311.

————. "Phantom Limbs." *Lippincott's Magazine of Popular Literature and Science* 8 (December 1871): 563–69.

————. "The Poison of Serpents." *The Century Magazine* 38, no. 4 (1889): 503–14.

————. "The Poison of the Rattlesnake." *Atlantic Monthly* 21 (April 1868): 452–61.

————. *The Red City: A Novel of the Second Administration of President Washington*. New York: The Century Company, 1908.

————. "The Relations of Nervous Disorders in Women to Pelvic Disease." *University Medical Magazine*, March 1897.

————. "Remarks on the Effects of *Anhelonium lewinii* (the Mescal Button)." *British Medical Journal* 2 (1896): 1625–28.

————. *Researches upon the Venom of the Rattlesnake: With an Investigation of the Anatomy and Physiology of the Organs Concerned*. Washington, D.C.: Smithsonian Institution, 1860.

————. "Rest in the Treatment of Nervous Disease." In *A Series of American Clinical Lectures*, edited by E. C. Sequin, vol. 1, no. 4, 83–102. New York: G. P. Putnam's Sons, 1875.

————. "Review of *Leçons de physiologie expérimentale appliquée à la médecine, faites au Collège de France*, by M. Claude Bernard." *North American Medico-chirurgical Review* 1 (1857): 529–47, 699–701.

————. "Some Personal Recollections of the Civil War." *Transactions of the College of Physicians of Philadelphia* 27 (1905): 85–94.

————. "The Treatment by Rest, Seclusion, Etc., in Relation to Psychotherapy." *Journal of the American Medical Association* 50, no. 25 (1908): 2033–37.

————. *Two Lectures on the Conduct of the Medical Life*. Philadelphia: University of Pennsylvania Press, 1893.

————. *Wear and Tear; or, Hints for the Overworked*. 1871. Reprint, New York: AltaMira Press, 2004.

————. *When All the Woods Are Green*. New York: The Century Company, 1915.

Mitchell, S. Weir, and William A. Hammond. "An Experimental Examination of the Physiological Effect of Sassy-Bark, the Ordeal Poison of the Western Coast of Africa." *Proceedings of the Academy of Natural Science* 13 (1859).

————. "An Experimental Examination of Toxicological Effects of Sassy-Bark, the Ordeal Poison of the West Coast of Africa." *Charleston Medical Journal* 14 (November 1859).

Mitchell, S. Weir, George Morehouse, and William Williams Keen. *Gunshot Wounds and Other Injuries of Nerves*. 1864. Reprint, San Francisco: Norman Publishing, 1989.

————. "On Malingering, Especially in Regard to Simulation of Diseases of the Nervous System." *American Journal of the Medical Sciences* 48 (1864): 367–94.

————. "On the Antagonism of Atropia and Morphia, Founded upon Observations and Experiments Made at the USA Hospital for Injuries and Diseases of the Nervous System." *American Journal of the Medical Sciences* 50 (1865): 67–76.

————. *Reflex Paralysis*. Circular No. 6. Surgeon General's Office. March 10, 1864. Reprint, Yale University School of Medicine, 1941.

Mitchell, S. Weir, and Edward T. Reichert. *Researches upon the Venoms of Poisonous Serpents*. Washington, D.C.: Smithsonian Institution, 1886.

Moore, Withers. "The Higher Education of Women." *British Medical Journal*, August 14, 1886.

Morantz, Regina Markell. "Feminism, Professionalism, and Germs: The Thought of Mary Putnam Jacobi and Elizabeth Blackwell." *American Quarterly* 34, no. 5 (1982): 459–78.

Morantz-Sanchez, Regina. *Sympathy and Science: Women Physicians in American Medicine*. Chapel Hill: University of North Carolina Press, 1985.

Morris, Edmund. *The Rise of Theodore Roosevelt*. New York: Coward, McCann, and Geoghegan, 1979.

Morse, John T. *Life and Letters of Oliver Wendell Holmes*. Vol. 1. New York: Chelsea House, 1980.

Moscucci, Ornella. *The Science of Woman: Gynaecology and Gender in England, 1800–1929*. Cambridge: Cambridge University Press, 1990.

Mosedale, Susan Sleeth. "Science Corrupted: Victorian Biologists Consider 'The Woman Question.'" *Journal of the History of Biology* 11, no. 1 (1978): 1–55.

Neilson, Sarah Mitchell. "Recollections of Mrs. Neilson." In Silas Weir Mitchell, "Autobiography," 296–310. S. Weir Mitchell Papers. College of Physicians of Philadelphia Historical Medical Library.

Norwood, William Frederick. "Medical Education in the United States Before 1900." In *The History of Medical Education*, UCLA Forum in Medical Sciences 12, edited by C. D. O'Malley, 463–99. Berkeley: University of California Press, 1970.

Oberholtzer, Ellis P. "Personal Memories of Weir Mitchell." *Bookman* 39 (April 1914): 132–38.

O'Connor, Erin. *Raw Material: Producing Pathology in Victorian Culture*. Durham: Duke University Press, 2000.

Osler, William. *"Aequanimitas," with Other Addresses to Medical Students, Nurses, and Practitioners of Medicine*. New York: Blakiston Company, 1932.

————. "Obituary." *British Medical Journal* 18 (January 1914): 119–21.

————. *Science and Immortality.* Boston: Houghton, Mifflin, and Company, 1904.

Otis, Laura, ed. *Literature and Science in the Nineteenth Century: An Anthology.* Oxford: Oxford University Press, 2002.

Pappert, E. J. "Philadelphia Infirmary for Nervous Diseases: America's Original Model of Institutional Neurology." *Neurology* 50, no. 6 (1998): 1847–53.

Playfair, William S. "Notes on the Systematic Treatment of Nerve Prostration and Hysteria Connected with Uterine Disease." *Lancet* 117 (1881): 131–36.

Porter, Roy. "The Body and the Mind, the Doctor and the Patient: Negotiating Hysteria." In *Hysteria Beyond Freud,* edited by Sander L. Gilman, Helen King, Roy Porter, G. S. Rousseau and Elaine Showalter, 225–85. Berkeley: University of California Press, 1993.

Ramachandran, V. S., and Sandra Blakeslee. *Phantoms in the Brain: Probing the Mysteries of the Human Mind.* New York: Harper, 1998.

Reynolds, David. S. *Walt Whitman's America.* New York: Vintage, 1995.

Richards, R. L. "Causalgia: A Centennial Review." *Archives of Neurology* 16, no. 4 (1967): 339–50.

Rylance, Rick. "The Theatre and the Granary: Observations on Nineteenth-Century Medical Narratives." *Literature and Medicine* 25, no. 2 (2006): 255–76.

Scarry, Elaine. *The Body in Pain: The Making and Unmaking of the World.* New York: Oxford University Press, 1985.

Schneck, Jerome. "S. Weir Mitchell, M.D. (1829–1914): Neurologic and Psychiatric Observations in 'The Case of George Dedlow.'" *New York State Journal of Medicine* 79, no. 11 (1979): 1777–82.

Schuster, David. "Personalizing Illness and Modernity: S. Weir Mitchell, Literary Women, and Neurasthenia, 1870–1914." *Bulletin of the History of Medicine* 79, no. 4 (2005): 695–722.

Shine, Richard. *Australian Snakes: A Natural History.* Ithaca: Cornell University Press, 1991.

Sicherman, Barbara. "The Uses of Diagnosis: Doctors, Patients, and Neurasthenia." *Journal of the History of Medicine and Allied Sciences* 32, no. 1 (1977): 33–54.

Sigerman, Harriet. "Laborers for Liberty: 1865–1890." In *No Small Courage: A History of Women in the United States,* edited by Nancy F. Cott, 289–352. Oxford: Oxford University Press, 2000.

————. "An Unfinished Battle: 1848–1865." In *No Small Courage: A History of Women in the United States,* edited by Nancy F. Cott, 237–88. Oxford: Oxford University Press, 2000.

Small, Miriam R. "Afterword." In *Elsie Venner: A Romance of Destiny,* by Oliver Wendell Holmes, 359–66. New York: New American Library, 1961.

Strouse, Jean. *Alice James: A Biography.* Boston: Houghton Mifflin, 1980.

Thomas, M. Carey. *Education of Women.* Monographs on Education in the United States, edited by Nicholas Murray Butler. Albany, N.Y.: J. B. Lyon, 1899.

————. "Open Letter." *The Century Magazine* 41, no. 4 (1891): 636–37.

Traubel, Horace. *January 21, 1889–April 7, 1889.* Edited by Sculley Bradley. Vol. 4 of *With Walt Whitman in Camden.* Philadelphia: University of Pennsylvania Press, 1953.

————. *July 16, 1888–October 31, 1888.* Vol. 1 of *With Walt Whitman in Camden.* New York: Appleton, 1908.

————. *October 1, 1891–April 3, 1892.* Edited by Jeanne Chapman and Robert MacIsaac. Vol. 9 of *With Walt Whitman in Camden.* Oregon House, Calif.: W. L. Bentley, 1996.

————. *September 15, 1889–July 6, 1890.* Edited by Gertrude Traubel and William White. Vol. 6 of *With Walt Whitman in Camden.* Carbondale: Southern Illinois University Press, 1982.

Tucker, Beverley R. "Speaking of Weir Mitchell." *American Journal of Psychiatry* 93, no. 2 (1936): 341–46.

————. *S. Weir Mitchell: A Brief Sketch of His Life with Personal Recollections.* Boston: Richard G. Badger, 1914.

Veith, Ilza. *Hysteria: The History of a Disease.* Chicago: University of Chicago Press, 1965.

Walter, Richard D. *S. Weir Mitchell, M.D.—Neurologist: A Medical Biography.* Springfield, Ill.: Charles C. Thomas, 1970.

Wharton, Edith. *The Age of Innocence.* 1920. Reprint, New York: Barnes and Noble, 2004.

Whitehorn, John C. "A Century of Psychiatric Research in America." In *One Hundred Years of American Psychiatry,* edited by J. K. Hall, 167–93. New York: Columbia University Press, 1944.

Whitman, Walt. *1876–1885.* Edited by Edwin Haviland Miller. Vol. 3 of *The Correspondence.* New York: New York University Press, 1964.

Will, Barbara. "The Nervous Origins of the American Western." *American Literature* 70, no. 2 (1998): 293–316.

Wood, Ann Douglas. "'The Fashionable Diseases': Women's Complaints and Their Treatment in Nineteenth-Century America." *Journal of Interdisciplinary History* 4, no. 1 (1973): 25–52.

Wood, W. Barry. *From Miasmas to Molecules.* New York: Columbia University Press, 1961.

Woolf, Virginia. *The Letters of Virginia Woolf.* Edited by Nigel Nicolson and Joanne Trautmann. 6 vols. New York: Harcourt Brace Jovanovich, 1975.

Woolverton, John F. *The Education of Phillips Brooks.* Urbana: University of Illinois Press, 1995.

Wordsworth, William. "Lines Composed a Few Miles Above Tintern Abbey, on Revisiting the Banks of the Wye During a Tour. July 13, 1798." In *The English Romantics: Major Poetry and Critical Theory,* edited by John L. Mahoney, 123–24. Prospect Heights, Ill.: Waveland Press, 1978.

———. "Ode: Intimations of Immortality." In *The English Romantics: Major Poetry and Critical Theory,* edited by John L. Mahoney, 170–73. Prospect Heights, Ill.: Waveland Press, 1978.

Ziporyn, Terra. *Disease in the Popular American Press: The Case of Diphtheria, Typhoid Fever, and Syphilis, 1870–1920.* New York: Greenwood Press, 1988.

INDEX

Page numbers in *italics* indicate photographs.